DATE DUE

JUN 12	

We Are Anonymous

We Are Anonymous

Inside the Hacker World of LulzSec, Anonymous, and the Global Cyber Insurgency

Parmy Olson

LITTLE, BROWN AND COMPANY
New York Boston London

Little, Brown and Company
Hachette Book Group
237 Park Avenue, New York, NY 10017
www.littlebrown.com

First Edition: June 2012

Little, Brown and Company is a division of Hachette Book Group, Inc., and is celebrating its 175th anniversary in 2012. The Little, Brown name and logo are trademarks of Hachette Book Group, Inc.

The publisher is not responsible for websites (or their content) that are not owned by the publisher.

The Hachette Speakers Bureau provides a wide range of authors for speaking events. To find out more, go to www.hachettespeakersbureau.com or call (866) 376-6591.

ISBN 978-0-316-21354-7 (hc) / 978-0-316-22765-0 (int'l pb)
LCCN 2012936919

10 9 8 7 6 5 4 3 2 1

RRD-C

Printed in the United States of America

For Avó

Contents

Contents

Before you read this book

Names

Most of the real names and online nicknames used in this book are real, but a few are not. All fabricated names in this book relate to "William," a young man living in the UK whose nightly attempts to prank and harass people give us a peek into the world of 4chan's most popular discussion board, /b/. His name and the names of his victims have been changed.

Sourcing

Most of the information and anecdotes in this book are sourced directly from interviews with those who played key roles in the story, such as Hector "Sabu" Monsegur and Jake "Topiary" Davis. However, hackers are known to occasionally share nicknames to help obfuscate their identities or even flat-out lie. As such I have attempted to corroborate people's stories as much as time has allowed. When it comes to personal anecdotes—Sabu's stop-and-search experience with the NYPD, for example—I have indicated that this is the hacker's own testimony. In my year of gathering research for this book, certain hackers have proved themselves more trustworthy than others, and I have also leaned toward the testimony of sources I deem most reliable. Notes on the sourcing of key pieces of information, media reports, and statistics are found at the back of this book.

Spelling

To help maintain story momentum, I have cleaned up spelling and some grammar for quotes that were sourced from chat logs and have been used for dialogue between characters. In cases where I have interviewed people on Internet Relay Chat, I have also cleaned up spelling; however, if a source skipped a word or two, I have framed brackets [ ] around the implied words.

People

A few of the people featured in this book are figureheads in Anonymous, but they are not representative of Anonymous as a whole. It is worth saying that again: they are not representative of Anonymous as a whole. Some key characters, like William or Sabu, have volatile personalities, and in hearing their extraordinary stories, you, the reader, will come to learn about social engineering, hacking, account cracking, and the rise of the online disruptor perhaps more engagingly than if you read about these techniques alone. There are many people in Anonymous who are not the subject of police investigations like the ones featured in this book, and they also seek to uphold genuine standards of legality and political activism. For other perspectives on Anonymous, keep an eye out for work by Gabriella Coleman, an academic who has been following Anonymous for several years, and a book on Anonymous by Gregg Housh and Barrett Brown, due out in 2012. The documentary *We Are Legion* by Brian Knappenberger also gives more focus to the political activism of Anonymous.

PART 1

We Are Anonymous

CHAPTER 1

The Raid

Across America on February 6, 2011, millions of people were settling into their couches, splitting open bags of nachos, and spilling beer into plastic cups in preparation for the year's biggest sporting event. On that Super Bowl Sunday, during which the Green Bay Packers conquered the Pittsburgh Steelers, a digital security executive named Aaron Barr watched helplessly as seven people whom he'd never met turned his world upside down. Super Bowl Sunday was the day he came face-to-face with Anonymous.

By the end of that weekend, the word *Anonymous* had new ownership. Augmenting the dictionary definition of being something with no identifiable name, it seemed to be a nebulous, sinister group of hackers hell-bent on attacking enemies of free information, including individuals like Barr, a husband and a father of twins who had made the mistake of trying to figure out who Anonymous really was.

The real turning point was lunchtime, with six hours to go until the Super Bowl kickoff. As Barr sat on the living room couch in his home in the suburbs of Washington, D.C., dressed comfortably for the day in a t-shirt and jeans, he noticed that his iPhone hadn't buzzed in his pocket for the last half hour. Normally it alerted him to an e-mail every fifteen minutes. When he fished the phone out of his pocket and pressed a button to refresh his mail, a dark blue window popped up. It showed three words that would change his life: Cannot Get Mail. The e-mail client then asked him to verify the right password for his e-mail. Barr went into the phone's account settings and carefully typed it in: "kibafo33." It didn't work. His e-mails weren't coming through.

He looked down at the small screen blankly. Slowly, a tickling anxiety crawled up his back as he realized what this meant. Since chatting with a hacker from Anonymous called Topiary a few hours ago, he had thought he was in the clear. Now he knew that someone had hacked his HBGary Federal account, possibly accessing tens of thousands of internal e-mails, then locked him out. This meant that someone, somewhere, had seen nondisclosure agreements and sensitive documents that could implicate a multinational bank, a respected U.S. government agency, and his own company.

One by one, memories of specific classified documents and messages surfaced in his mind, each heralding a new wave of sickening dread. Barr dashed up the stairs to his home office and sat down in front of his laptop. He tried logging on to his Facebook account to speak to a hacker he knew, someone who might be able to help him. But that network, with his few hundred friends, was blocked. He tried his Twitter account, which had a few hundred followers. Nothing. Then Yahoo. The same. He'd been locked out of almost every one of his Web accounts, even the online role-playing game World of Warcraft. Barr silently kicked himself for using the same password on every account. He glanced over at his WiFi router and saw frantic flashing lights. Now people were trying to overload it with traffic, trying to jam their way further into his home network.

He reached over and unplugged it. The flashing lights went dead.

Aaron Barr was a military man. Broad shouldered, with jet-black hair and heavy eyebrows that suggested distant Mediterranean ancestors, he had signed up for the U.S. Navy after taking two semesters of college and realizing it wasn't for him. He soon became a SIGINT, or signals intelligence, officer, specializing in a rare assignment, analytics. Barr was sent abroad as needed: four years in Japan, three in Spain, and secondments all over Europe, from Ukraine to Portugal to Italy. He was stationed on amphibious warships and got shot at on land in Kosovo. The experience made him resent the way war desensitized soldiers to human life.

After twelve years in the navy he picked up a job at defense contractor Northrop Grumann and settled down to start a family, covering over his navy tattoos and becoming a company man. He got a break in November 2009 when a security consultant named Greg Hoglund asked Barr if he wanted to help him start a new company. Hoglund was already running a digital security company called HBGary Inc., and, knowing Barr's military background and expertise in cryptography, he wanted him to start a sister company that would specialize in selling services to the United States government. It would be called HBGary Federal, and HBGary Inc. would own 10 percent. Barr jumped at the chance to be his own boss and see more of his wife and two young children by working from home.

He relished the job at first. In December 2009, he couldn't sleep for three nights in a row because his mind was racing with ideas about new contracts. He'd get on his computer at 1:30 a.m. and e-mail Hoglund with some of his thoughts. Less than a year later, though, none of Barr's ideas was bringing in any money. Barr was desperate for contracts, and he was keeping the tiny company of three employees afloat by running "social media training" for executives, bringing in twenty-five thousand dollars at a time. These were not lessons in how to maintain friendships on Facebook but in how to use social networking sites like Facebook, LinkedIn, and Twitter to gather information on people—as spying tools.

In October 2010, salvation finally came. Barr started talking to Hunton & Williams, a law firm whose clients—among them the U.S. Chamber of Commerce and Bank of America—needed help dealing with opponents. WikiLeaks, for example, had recently hinted at a trove of confidential data it was holding from Bank of America. Barr and two other security firms made PowerPoint presentations that proposed, among other things, disinformation campaigns to discredit WikiLeaks-supporting journalists and cyber attacks on the WikiLeaks website. He dug out his fake Facebook profiles and showed how he might spy on the opponents, "friending" Hunton & Williams's own staff and gathering intelligence on their personal lives. The law firm appeared interested, but there were still no contracts come January 2011, and HBGary Federal needed money.

Then Barr had an idea. A conference in San Francisco for security professionals called B-Sides was coming up. If he gave a speech revealing how his social media snooping had uncovered information on a mysterious subject, he'd get newfound credibility and maybe even those contracts.

Barr decided that there was no better target than Anonymous. About a month prior, in December 2010, the news media exploded with reports that a large and mysterious group of hackers had started attacking the websites of MasterCard, PayPal, and Visa in retaliation for their having cut funding to WikiLeaks. WikiLeaks had just released a cache of thousands of secret diplomatic cables, and its founder and editor in chief, Julian Assange, had been arrested in the U.K., ostensibly for sexual misconduct.

Hackers was a famously imprecise word. It could mean enthusiastic programmer, it could mean cyber criminal. But people in Anonymous, or Anons, were often dubbed hacktivists—hackers with an activist message. From what anyone could tell, they believed all information should be free, and they might just hit your website if you disagreed. They claimed to have no structure or leaders. They claimed they weren't a group but "everything and nothing." The closest description seemed to be "brand" or "collective." Their few rules were reminiscent of the movie *Fight Club*: don't talk about Anonymous, never reveal your true identity, and don't attack the media, since they could be purveyors of a message. Naturally, anonymity made it easier to do the odd illegal thing, break into servers, steal a company's customer data, or take a website offline and then deface it. Stuff that could saddle you with a ten-year prison term. But the Anons didn't seem to care. There was strength and protection in numbers after all, and they posted their ominous tagline on blogs, hacked websites, or wherever they could:

> We are Anonymous
> We are Legion
> We do not forgive
> We do not forget
> Expect us.

Their digital flyers and messages featured a logo of a headless, suited man surrounded by U.N.-style peace branches, supposedly based on the surrealist painting of a man with a bowler hat and apple by René Magritte. Often it included the leering mask of Guy Fawkes, the London revolutionary embellished in the movie *V for Vendetta* and now the symbol of a faceless rebel horde. Anonymous was impossible to quantify, but this wasn't just dozens or even hundreds of people. Thousands from all over the world had visited its main chat rooms in December 2010 to take part in its attacks on PayPal, and thousands regularly visited Anonymous-related blogs and new sites like AnonNews.org. Everyone in the cyber security field was talking about Anonymous, but no one seemed to know who these people were.

Barr was intrigued. He had watched the world's attention to this mysterious group grow and seen reports of dozens of raids and arrests in the United States and Europe. Yet no one had been convicted, and the group's leaders had not been tracked down. Barr believed he could do better than the Federal Bureau of Investigation—maybe help the FBI, too—with his social media snooping expertise. Going after Anonymous was risky, but he figured if the collective turned on him, the worst they could do was take down the website of HBGary Federal for a few hours—a couple of days, tops.

He had started by lurking in the online chat rooms where Anonymous supporters congregated and creating a nickname for himself, first AnonCog, then CogAnon. He blended in, using the group's lingo and pretending to be a young new recruit eager to bring down a company or two. On the side, he'd quietly note the nicknames of others in the chat room. There were hundreds, but he paid attention to the frequent visitors and those who got the most attention. When these people left the chat room, he'd note the time, too. Then he'd switch to Facebook. Barr had created several fake Facebook personas by now and had "friended" dozens of real-world people who openly claimed to support Anonymous. If one of those friends suddenly became active on Facebook soon after a nickname had exited the Anonymous chat room, Barr figured he had a match.

By late January, he was putting the finishing touches on a twenty-page document of names, descriptions, and contact information for suspected Anonymous supporters and leaders. On January 22, 2011, Barr sent an e-mail to Hoglund and HBGary Inc. co-president Penny Leavy (who was also Hoglund's wife) and Barr's second in command, Ted Vera, about his now forthcoming talk at B-Sides on Anonymous. The big benefit of the talk would be the press attention. He would also tell a few people in Anonymous, under a false persona, about the research of a "so-called cyber security expert" named Aaron Barr..

"This will generate a big discussion in Anonymous chat channels, which are attended by the press," Barr told Hoglund and Leavy. Ergo, more press about the talk. "But," he added, "it will also make us a target. Thoughts?"

Hoglund's reply was brief: "Well, I don't really want to get DDoS'd, so assuming we do get DDoS'd then what? How do we make lemonade from that?" Hoglund was refering to a distributed denial of service attack, which described what happened when a multitude of computers were coordinated to overwhelm a site with so much data that it was temporarily knocked offline. It was Anonymous's most popular form of attack. It was like punching someone in the eye. It looked bad and it hurt, but it didn't kill you.

Barr decided the best thing to do was reach out directly to the press before his talk. He contacted Joseph Menn, a San Francisco–based reporter for the *Financial Times,* offering an interview about how his data could lead to more arrests of "major players" in Anonymous. He gave Menn a taste of his findings: of the several hundred participants in Anonymous cyber attacks, only about thirty were steadily active, and just ten senior people managed most of the decisions. Barr's comments and the story of his investigation suggested for the first time that Anonymous was a hierarchy and not as "anonymous" as it thought. The paper ran the story on Friday, February 4, with the headline "Cyberactivists Warned of Arrest," and quoted Barr.

Barr got a small thrill from seeing the published article and e-mailed Hoglund and Leavy with the subject line, "Story is really taking shape."

"We should post this on the front page, throw out some

tweets," Hoglund replied. "'HBGary Federal sets a new bar as private intelligence agency.' The pun on bar is intended lol."

By the end of Friday, detectives from the FBI's e-crime division had read the article and contacted Barr asking if he wouldn't mind sharing his information. He agreed to meet them Monday, the day after the Super Bowl. At around the same time, a small group of hackers with Anonymous had read the story, too.

They were three people, in three different parts of the world, and they had been invited into an online chat room. Their online nicknames were Topiary, Sabu, and Kayla, and at least two of them, Sabu and Topiary, were meeting for the first time. The person who had invited them went by the nickname Tflow, and he was also in the room. No one here knew anyone else's real name, age, sex, or location. Two of them, Topiary and Sabu, had only been using their nicknames on public chat rooms for the last month or two. They knew snippets of gossip about one another, and that each believed in Anonymous. That was the gist of it.

The chat room was locked, meaning no one could enter unless invited. Conversation was stilted at first, but within a few minutes everyone was talking. Personalities started to emerge. Sabu was assertive and brash, and he used slang like *yo* and *my brother*. None of the others in the room knew this, but he was a born-and-bred New Yorker of Puerto Rican descent. He had learned to hack computers as a teenager, subverting his family's dial-up connection so they could get Internet access for free, then learning more tricks on hacker forums in the late 1990s. Around 2001, the nickname Sabu had gone underground; now, almost a decade later, it was back. Sabu was the heavyweight veteran of the group.

Kayla was childlike and friendly but fiercely smart. She claimed to be female and, if asked, sixteen years old. Many assumed this was a lie. While there were plenty of young hackers in Anonymous, and plenty of female supporters of Anonymous, there were very few young hackers who were female. Still, if it was a lie, it was elaborate. She was chatty and gave away plenty of colorful information about her personal life: she had a job in her salon, babysat for extra money, and took vacations in Spain. She even claimed Kayla was her real name, kept as a "fuck you" to anyone who dared try to identify her. Paradoxically, she was obsessive about her computer's privacy. She never typed her real name into her netbook in case it got key-logged, had no physical hard drive, and would boot up from a tiny microSD card that she could quickly swallow if the police ever came to her door. Rumor even had it that she'd stabbed her webcam with a knife one day, just in case someone took over her PC and filmed her unaware.

Topiary was the least skilled of the group when it came to hacking, but he had another talent to make up for it: his wit. Cocksure and often brimming with ideas, Topiary used his silver tongue and an unusual knack for public promotion to slowly make his way up the ladder of secret planning rooms in the Anonymous chat networks. While others strained to listen at the door, Topiary got invited right in. He had become so trusted that the network operators asked him to write the official Anonymous statements for each attack on PayPal and MasterCard. He had picked his nickname on a whim. The low-budget time travel film *Primer* had been a favorite, and when he found out its director was working on a new film called *A Topiary,* he decided he liked the word, oblivious to its definition of clipped ornamental shrubs.

Tflow, the guy who'd brought everyone here, was a skilled programmer and mostly quiet, a person who strictly followed the Anonymous custom of never talking about himself. He had been with Anonymous for at least four months, a good amount of time to understand its culture and key figures within it. He knew the communications channels and supporting cast of hackers better than most. Fittingly, he got down to business. Someone had to do something about this Aaron Barr and his "research." Barr had claimed there were leaders in Anonymous, which wasn't true. That meant his research was probably wrong. Then there was that quote from the *Financial Times* story saying Barr had "collected information on the core leaders, including many of their real names, and that they could be arrested if law enforcement had the same data."

This now posed another problem: if Barr's data was actually right, Anons could be in trouble. The group started making plans. First, they had to scan the server that ran the HBGary Federal website for any source code vulnerabilities. If they got lucky, they might find a hole they could enter, then take control and replace Barr's home page with a giant logo of Anonymous and a written warning not to mess with their collective.

That afternoon, someone looked up "Aaron Barr" on Google and came up with his official company portrait: swept-back hair, suit, and a keen stare at the camera. The group laughed when they saw the photo. He looked so…earnest, and increasingly like fresh meat. Then Sabu started scanning HBGaryFederal.com for a hole. It turned out Barr's site ran on a publishing system created by a third-party developer, which had a major bug. Jackpot.

Though its job was to help other companies protect themselves from cyber attacks, HBGary Federal itself was vulnerable to a simple attack method called SQL injection, which targeted databases. Databases were one of the many key technologies powering the Internet. They stored passwords, corporate e-mails, and a wide variety of other types of data. The use of Structured Query Language (SQL, commonly mispronounced "sequel") was a popular way to retrieve and manipulate the information in databases. SQL injection worked by "injecting" SQL commands into the server that hosted the site to retrieve information that should be hidden, essentially using the language against itself. As a result, the server would not recognize the typed characters as text, but as commands that should be executed. Sometimes this could be carried out by simply typing out commands in the search bar of a home page. The key was to find the search bar or text box that represented a weak entry point.

This could be devastating to a company. If DDoSing meant a sucker punch, SQL injection was secretly removing someone's vital organs while they slept. The language it required, a series of symbols and key words like "SELECT," "NULL," and "UNION," were gibberish to people like Topiary, but for Sabu and Kayla they rolled off the tongue.

Now that they were in, the hackers had to root around for the names and passwords of people like Barr and Hoglund, who had control of the site's servers. Jackpot again. They found a list of usernames and passwords for HBGary employees. But here was a stumbling block. The passwords were encrypted, or "hashed," using a standard technique called MD5. If all the administrative passwords were lengthy and complicated, it might be impossible to crack them, and the hackers' fun would have come to an end.

Sabu picked out three hashes, long strings of random numbers corresponding to the passwords of Aaron Barr, Ted Vera, and another executive named Phil Wallisch. He expected them to be exceptionally tough to unlock, and when he passed them to the others on the team, he wasn't surprised to find that no one could crack them. In a last-ditch attempt, he uploaded them to a Web forum for password cracking that was popular among hackers—Hashkiller.com. Within a couple of hours all three hashes had been cracked by random anonymous volunteers. The result for one of them looked exactly like this:

4036d5fe575fb46f48ffcd5d7aeeb5af:kibafo33

Right there at the end of the string of letters and numbers was Aaron Barr's password. When they tried using kibafo33 to access his HBGary Federal e-mails hosted by Google Apps, they got in.

The group couldn't believe their luck. By Friday night they were watching an oblivious Barr exchange happy e-mails with his colleagues about the *Financial Times* article.

On a whim, one of them decided to check to see if kibafo33 worked anywhere else besides Barr's e-mail account. It was worth a try. Unbelievably for a cyber security specialist investigating the highly volatile Anonymous, Barr had used the same easy-to-crack password on almost all his Web accounts, including Twitter, Yahoo!, Flickr, Facebook, even World of Warcraft. This meant there was now the opportunity for pure, unadulterated "lulz."

Lulz was a variation of the term *lol*—"laugh out loud"—which had for years been tagged onto the end of lighthearted statements such as "The pun on bar is intended lol." A more recent addition to Web parlance, lulz took that sentiment further and essentially meant entertainment at someone else's expense. Prank-calling the FBI was lol. Prank-calling the FBI and successfully sending a SWAT team to Aaron Barr's house was lulz.

The group decided that they would not swoop on Barr that day or even the next. They would take the weekend to spy on him and download every e-mail he'd ever sent or received during his time with HBGary Federal. But there was a sense of urgency. As they started browsing, the team realized Barr was planning to meet with the FBI the following Monday. Once they had taken what they could, it was decided all hell would break loose at kickoff on Super Bowl Sunday. There were sixty hours to go.

Saturday started off as any other for Barr. Relaxing and spending time with his family, sending and receiving a few e-mails from his iPhone over breakfast, he had no idea that an Anonymous team of seven was busy delving into his e-mails, or how excited they were with what they had stumbled upon. Their latest find: Barr's own research on Anonymous. It was a PDF document that started with a decent, short explanation of what Anonymous was. It listed websites, a timeline of recent cyber attacks, and lots of nicknames next to real-life names and addresses. The names Sabu, Topiary, and Kayla were nowhere to be seen. At the end were hasty notes like "Mmxanon—states…ghetto." It looked unfinished. As they gradually realized how Barr had been using Facebook to try to identify real people, it looked like he had no idea what he was doing. It looked like Barr might actually point the finger at some innocent people.

In the meantime, Tflow had downloaded Barr's e-mails onto his server, then waited about fifteen hours for them to compile into a torrent, a tiny file that linked to a larger file on a host computer somewhere else, in this case HBGary's. It was a process that millions of people across the world used every day to download pirated software, music, or movies, and Tflow planned to put his torrent file on the most popular torrenting site around: The Pirate Bay. This meant that soon, anyone could download and read more than forty thousand of Aaron Barr's e-mails.

That morning, with about thirty hours until kickoff, Barr ran some checks on HBGaryFederal.com and, just as he had expected, saw it was getting more traffic than usual. That didn't mean more legitimate visitors, but the beginnings of a DDoS attack from Anonymous. It wasn't the end of the world, but he logged into Facebook under the fake profile Julian Goodspeak to talk to one of his Anon contacts, an apparently senior figure who went by the nickname CommanderX. Barr's research and discussions with CommanderX had led him to believe his real name was "Benjamin Spock de Vries," though this was not accurate. CommanderX, who had no idea that a small group of hackers was already in Barr's e-mails, responded to Barr's instant message. Barr was asking politely if CommanderX could do something about the extra traffic he was getting.

"I am done with my research. I am not out to get you guys," Barr explained. "My focus is on social media vulnerabilities." Barr meant that his research was merely trying to show how organizations could be infiltrated by snooping on the Facebook, Twitter, and LinkedIn profiles of their members.

"Not my doing," CommanderX said honestly. He had taken a look at the HBGary Federal website and pointed out to Barr that, in any case, it looked vulnerable. "I hope you are being paid well."

Sunday morning, with eleven hours till kickoff, Tflow was done collating all of Barr's e-mails and those of the two other executives, Vera and Wallisch. The torrent file was ready to publish. Now came the pleasure of telling Barr what they had just done. Of course, to play this right, the hackers wouldn't tell him everything immediately. Better lulz would come from toying with him first. By now they had figured out that Barr was using the nickname CogAnon to talk to people in Anonymous chat rooms, and that he lived in Washington, D.C.

"We have everything from his Social Security number, to his career in the military, to his clearances," Sabu told the others, "to how many shits a day he takes."

At around 8:00 a.m. eastern standard time on Sunday morning, they decided to make him a little paranoid before the strike. When Barr entered the AnonOps chat network as CogAnon, Topiary sent him a private message.

"Hello," said Topiary.

"Hi," CogAnon replied.

In another chat window Topiary was giving a running commentary to other Anons who were laughing at his exploits. "Tell him you're recruiting for a new mission," Sabu said.

"Be careful," said another. "He may get suspicious quickly."

Topiary went back into his conversation with the security specialist, still pretending to believe CogAnon was a real Anonymous supporter. "We're recruiting for a new operation in the Washington area. Interested?"

Barr paused for twenty seconds. "Potentially. Depends on what it is," he said.

Topiary pasted the response in the other chat room.

"Hahahahhaa," said Sabu.

"Look at that faggot trying to psyops me out of info," Topiary said, referring to the tactics of psychological warfare. The word *faggot* was a word so liberally used in Anonymous that it wasn't even considered a real insult.

"I take it from your host that you're near where our target is," Topiary told Barr.

Back in Washington, D.C., Barr held his breath. "Is it physical or virtual?" he typed back, knowing full well it was virtual but at a loss for what else to say. "Ah yeah...I am close..." How exactly could they have figured out he lived in D.C.?

"Virtual," Topiary replied. "Everything is in place."

Topiary relayed this again to the Anons. "I'd laugh so hard if he sends an e-mail about this," he told them.

They couldn't believe what they were reading. "THIS GUY IS A FUCKING DICK," Sabu exclaimed.

"I want to rape his anus," Topiary replied. "Raping" servers was typically a way to describe a hack into its network. Tflow made a new chat room in the Anonymous chat network called #ophbgary and invited Topiary to join it.

"Guys," a hacker named Avunit piped up. "Is this really happening? Because this shit is awesome."

Back in the conversation, Barr tried to sound helpful. "I can be in the city within a few hours...depending on traffic lol."

Topiary decided to give him another fright: "Our target is a security company," he said. Barr's stomach turned. Okay, so this meant Anonymous was definitely targeting HBGary Federal. He opened up his e-mail client and quickly typed out an e-mail to other HBGary managers, including Hoglund and Penny Leavy.

"Now we are being directly threatened," he wrote. "I will bring this up with the FBI when I meet them tomorrow." Sabu and the others quietly watched him send it.

He clicked back into the chat with Topiary. "Ok well just let me know," he wrote. "Not sure how I can still help though?"

"That depends," Topiary said. "What skills do you have? We need help gathering info on Ligatt.com security company."

Barr let out a long breath of relief. Ligatt was in the same line of work as HBGary Federal, so it looked (for now at least) like his company was not the target after all.

"Ahhhh ok let me check them out," Barr replied almost gratefully. "It's been a while since I have looked at them. Anything specific?" At this point he seemed happy to do anything that would keep HBGary from being a target, even if he was just playing along.

There was no reply.

He typed, "I didn't realize they were local to D.C."

A minute later he added, "Man I am racking my brain and I can't remember why they were so popular a while back. I remember their [sic] being a lot of aggression towards them."

Nothing.

"You still there?" Barr asked.

Topiary had gone back to planning with the others. There wasn't much time left and he had to write the official Anonymous message that would replace the home page of HBGaryFederal.com.

About forty-five minutes later, Topiary finally replied. "Sorry about that—stay tuned."

"Ok," Barr wrote.

A few hours later and it was lunchtime, about six hours until the Super Bowl kickoff, with Barr sitting in his living room and staring in dreadful fascination at his phone after realizing he'd just been locked out of his e-mails. When he ran upstairs to try talking to CommanderX again on Facebook, he'd been locked out of that, too. When he saw that his Twitter account was under someone else's control, it hit him how serious this was, and how potentially very embarrassing.

He picked up the phone and called Greg Hoglund and Penny Leavy to let them know what was going on. Then he called his IT administrators, who said they would contact Google to try to regain control of HBGaryFederal.com. But there was nothing they could do about the stolen e-mails.

At 2.45 p.m., Barr got another message from Topiary: "Right, something will be happening tonight. How available are you throughout the evening?" There were just a few more hours to go, and he wanted Barr to have a front-row seat to the end of his career.

As Sunday evening drew near on the eastern seaboard, the Anons, in their own homes and time zones around the world, got ready to pounce. Cowboys Stadium in Arlington, Texas, started filling up. There were a few songs from the Black Eyed Peas, and Christina Aguilera muddling the words to the national anthem. Finally, the coin toss. A player from the Green Bay Packers drew back his foot and kicked the pigskin across the field.

On the other side of the Atlantic, Topiary watched on his laptop as the football flew through the sky. Sitting in his black leather gaming chair, a giant pair of headphones resting on his hair, he swiftly opened up another window and logged into Barr's Twitter account. He had locked Barr out six hours ago with the kibafo33 password and with the Super Bowl finally underway he started posting from it. He felt no inhibition, no sense of holding back from this man. He would let Barr have it: "Okay my fellow Anonymous faggots," he wrote from Barr's Twitter account, "we're working on bringing you the finest lulz as we speak. Stay tuned!"

Then: "Sup motherfuckers, I'm CEO of a shitty company and

I'm a giant media-whoring cunt. LOL check out my nigga Greg's site: rootkit.com." These were statements that Topiary would never have said out loud, or face-to-face with Barr. In real life he was quiet, polite, and rarely swore.

Rootkit.com was Hoglund's website specializing in the latest research on programming tools that gave root access to a computer network. Ironically, Sabu and Kayla now had system administrator access, or "root" on rootkit.com, too. This was because Barr had been an administrator of the company's e-mail system, meaning "kibafo33" let them reset the passwords of other in-boxes, including Hoglund's.

Once he got into Hoglund's in-box, Sabu had sent out an e-mail as Hoglund to one of HBGary's IT administrators, a Finnish security specialist named Jussi Jaakonaho. Sabu was looking for root access to rootkit.com.

"im in europe and need to ssh into the server," Sabu wrote in the e-mail to Jaakonaho, using lowercase letters to suggest he was in a rush. SSH stood for "secure shell" and referred to a way of logging into a server from a remote location. When Jaakonaho asked if Hoglund (Sabu) was on a public computer, Hoglund (Sabu) said, "no I dont have the public ip with me at the moment because im ready for a small meeting and im in a rush. if anything just reset my password to changeme123 and give me public IP and ill ssh in and reset my pw [password]."

"Ok," Jaakonaho replied. "Your password is changeme123." He added, with a smiley face, "In Europe but not in Finland?"

Sabu played along. "if I can squeeze out the time maybe we can catch up...ill be in germany for a little bit. thanks." The password didn't even work right away, and Sabu had to e-mail Jaakonaho a few more times with questions, including whether his own username was "greg or?" before Jaakonaho explained it was "hoglund." Sabu got in. This was a prime example of social engineering, the art of manipulating someone into divulging secret information or doing something they normally wouldn't.

Now Sabu and Kayla had complete control of rootkit.com. First they took the usernames and passwords of anyone who had ever registered on the site, then deleted its entire contents. Now it was just a blank page reading "Greg Hoglund = Owned." Sabu found he enjoyed working with Kayla. She was friendly, and she had extraordinary technical skills. Sabu later told others that *she* had socially engineered Jussi Jaakonaho, partly because the idea of being "owned" by a sixteen-year-old girl would only embarrass HBGary further.

Sabu and Kayla then got busy on HBGaryFederal.com, removing the home page and replacing it with the Anonymous logo of the headless suited man. In place of its head was a question mark. At the bottom was a link that said "Download HBGary e-mails"—Tflow's torrent file. Now anyone could read all of Barr's confidential e-mails to his clients as easily as they might grab a song on iTunes, but for free. The new home page also had a message written by Topiary:

> This domain has been seized by Anonymous under section #14 of the Rules of the Internet. Greetings HBGary (a computer "security" company). Your recent claims of "infiltrating" Anonymous amuse us, and so do your attempts at using Anonymous as a means to garner press attention for yourself. How's this for attention? You've tried to bite at the Anonymous hand, and now the Anonymous hand is bitch-slapping you in the face.

By 6:45 eastern standard time, twenty-four minutes into the Super Bowl, most of the "hacking" was over. There were no distant cheers and whoops for the football game from Barr's neighbors, who were mostly young families. The world around him seemed strangely quiet. With some trepidation, he logged back into the Anonymous chat rooms to confront his attackers. They were ready and waiting. Barr saw a message flash up, an invite to a new chat room called #ophbgary. He immediately saw a group of several nicknames. Some he recognized from his research and others he didn't: along with Topiary, Sabu, Kayla, there were others: Q, Heyguise, BarrettBrown, and c0s. The last nickname was Gregg Housh, a longtime Anon in his midthirties who had helped coordinate the first wave of major DDoS attacks by Anonymous in 2008, against the Church of Scientology (COS).

Topiary got things going. "Now they're threatening us directly," he told Barr, quoting the earlier e-mail. "Amirite?"

Barr said nothing.

"Enjoying the Super Bowl, I hope?" Q said.

"Hello Mr. Barr," Tflow said. "I apologize for what's about to happen to you and your company."

Finally, Barr spoke up. "I figured something like this would happen," he typed.

"Nah, you won't like what's coming next," Topiary said.

Barr tried persuading the group that he'd had their best interests at heart. "Dude...you just don't get it," he protested. "It was research on social media vulnerabilities. I was never going to release the names."

"LIAR." This was Sabu. "Don't you have a meeting with the FBI Monday morning?"

"Sabu, he totally does," said Topiary.

"Ok...Yep," Barr conceded. "They called me."

"Oh guys. What's coming next is the delicious cake," Topiary said.

It was up to Tflow to finally drop the bombshell. "I have Barr's, Ted's and Phil's e-mails," he said. All 68,000.

"Those e-mails are going to be pretty," said Housh.

"Lol," Barr replied inexplicably. He seemed to want to keep

proceedings light, or to convince himself this wasn't as bad as he thought. "Ok guys," he added, "well you got me right :)."

Indeed they had. Topiary made his parting shot. "Well Aaron, thanks for taking part in this little mini social test to see if you'd run to your company with 'news' about Anon. You did, we leeched it, we laughed." He paused. "Die in a fire. You're done."

It was now well into the early hours of Monday morning. Barr was sitting in his home office in front of the laptop, his hopes of a turnaround having dwindled to nothing. On the wall in front of him was a photo he'd bought in New York in October 2011. The 9/11 attacks were still raw, and after visiting Ground Zero he'd popped into a small gallery selling amateur photographs taken during the attacks. One stood out. In the background was the chaos of the fallen towers: papers and bricks strewn everywhere, dazed commuters covered in dust, while in the foreground was John Seward Johnson's *Double Check,* the famous bronze statue of a suited businessman on a park bench, looking into his open briefcase. Something about its incongruence made him like it instantly. Now Barr was that man, so caught up in his ambitions that he'd become oblivious to the chaos going on around him.

His public Twitter feed, an important reputational tool with the public, his clients, and the press, was now an obscene mess. Topiary had posted dozens of tweets filled with swear words and racist commentary. His bio now read, "CEO HBGary Federal. Cybersecurity and Information Operations specialist and RAGING HOMOGAY." His photo had the word *NIGGER* defaced across it in bold red lettering. Topiary did not consider himself racist—no one in his group did. But the graffiti was perfectly in tune with the underground culture of crude humor and cyber bullying that ran through Anonymous.

Topiary felt a thrill as he then posted Barr's home address. Then he tweeted Barr's social security number, then his cell phone number. Anyone with an Internet connection could read this. "Hi guys, leave me voice mails!" Then the number. Then "#callme."

Soon, hundreds and then thousands of people who perused Anonymous chat rooms, blogs, and Twitter feeds had heard about what was happening to Aaron Barr. They clicked on links to Barr's website, now a white screen with the Anonymous logo and message. They watched the Twitter feed and called his number. Quite a few started taking his earnest corporate photo and defacing it, cutting out his head and sticking it on a movie poster for James Bond to mock his spying methods. Another bloated his chin to make him look like the grotesque cartoon from a well-known Internet comic, or "rage comic," called Forever Alone.

Barr had been unable to tear himself away from the Anonymous chat rooms, mesmerized as people joked about the "faggot" Barr and egged each other on to call his cell phone. His phone rang through the night. He answered it once to hear a woman's voice say something inaudible and then hang up. There were a few silent voice mails and one person singing what sounded like "Never Gonna Give You Up," the 1987 song by Rick Astley, homage to a popular prank in Anonymous to "rickroll" someone.

Barr had called in reinforcements. Penny Leavy went online to try her luck at sweet-talking the attackers. They were friendly and polite to her at first, but her requests were met with cold answers.

"Please do not release the HBGary e-mails," she had pleaded. "There is private information there of clients."

"Shouldn't be sending e-mails you don't want your mother reading," Heyguise had said. And the e-mails, in any case, had already been published as a torrent on The Pirate Bay.

"Dozens of innocent people could have gone to jail," Sabu said angrily. Before their attack, his newly formed small clique of Anons, who'd found each other amid hundreds of others in the Anonymous chat networks, had no idea that Barr's research had been so flawed, or that his e-mails would be so easy to hack into. In fact, they still didn't know that Barr had been proposing a dirty-tricks campaign against trade unions and WikiLeaks to a government agency and a major bank. They had been motivated by revenge and a desire, intensified by group psychology, to bully someone who seemed to deserve it. Once enough people trawled through Barr's e-mails and found out what he had done to Hunton & Williams, the attack would suddenly look more than justified, to them almost necessary. Within the Anonymous community, Sabu, Kayla, Topiary, and the others would become heroic purveyors of vigilante justice. Barr had been fair game. He'd provoked a world where taunting, lying, and stealing was how everybody got by. A world that brought euphoric highs, fun, and fulfillment, with hardly any real-world consequences.

As Barr spent the next day fielding phone calls from journalists and trying, desperately, to pick up the pieces, Topiary, Sabu, Kayla, and Tflow met up again in their secret chat room. They celebrated their accomplishments, relived what had happened, laughed, and felt invincible. They had "owned" a security company. In the back of their minds they knew that agents from the Federal Bureau of Investigation would start trying to find them. But over time, members of the small team would conclude that they had worked together so well on Barr, they had to do it all over again on other targets, for lulz, for Anonymous, and for any other cause that came up along the way. No quarry would be too big: a storied media institution, an entertainment giant, even the FBI itself.

CHAPTER 2

William and the Roots of Anonymous

Aaron Barr would never have come face-to-virtual-face with Anonymous if it hadn't been for a skinny blond kid from New York City named Christopher Poole and the extraordinary contribution he made to the Internet. Seven years earlier, in the summer of 2003, fourteen-year-old Poole was surfing the Web in his bedroom, looking for information on Japanese anime. Like thousands of other American teens, he was a big fan. Eventually, he found a peach-colored Japanese image board dedicated to anime called 2channel, or 2chan. Poole had never seen anything like it. Founded in 1999 by a college student named Hiroyuki Nishimura (age thirty-five in 2012), it featured anime discussion threads that moved at lightning speed. Poole would wait thirty seconds, hit F5 to refresh the page, and it would suddenly refill with a stream of new posts, numbering up to a thousand. Almost every poster was anonymous. Unlike English-language Web forums, 2chan didn't require you to register in a name field, and hardly anyone did.

In Japan that same summer, the news media had noticed that 2chan was becoming a rather embarrassing window to the country's underbelly. Discussions of anime had spilled over into talk of kids murdering their teachers, attacking their bosses, or blowing up a local kindergarten. And it was becoming one of the country's most popular websites.

Poole wanted a place to talk to people in English about anime, and 2chan had started blocking English posters. So he decided to clone 2chan by copying its publicly available HTML code, translating it to English, and building from there. He put the whole thing together on his bedroom computer and called it 4chan. When an online friend asked Poole, who went by the nickname moot, what the difference between 4chan and 2chan would be, he replied with some chutzpah, "It's TWO TIMES THE CHAN MOTHERFUCK." On September 29, 2003, Poole registered the domain 4chan.net and announced it on Something Awful, a Web forum where he was already a regular. He entitled the thread: "4chan.net—English 2chan.net!"

4chan had almost the exact same layout as 2chan: the simple peach background, the dark red text, the shaded boxes for discussion threads. Both 4chan and 2chan have barely changed their designs to this day, apart from adding a few color schemes. After opening 4chan to the public, an English-speaking anime hub called Raspberry Heaven started linking to it, as did Something Awful. The first few hundred visitors took to it right away. Discussion boards were listed alphabetically across the top of the site: /a/ was for anime, /p/ was for photography, and so on. Poole had set ups /b/, the "random" board that would become 4chan's most important feature, within the first two months. In one discussion with early users, moot said that /b/ was "the beating heart of this site," but he added that it was "a retard bin." The random board was a free-for-all.

Poole at first configured 4chan so that anyone who posted a comment could do so under a nickname. This continued until early 2004, when a 4chan user and PHP programmer who went by the nickname Shii became irritated with the enforced nicknames. That year, Shii published an essay about the value of anonymity on image boards, pointing to Japan's 2chan as a place where anonymity could counter vanity and stop users from developing cliques and elite status. When a site forced people to register with a nickname, that also kept out interesting people with busy lives, instead attracting those who had too much time on their hands and who tended to make nasty or senseless comments. "On an anonymous forum," he wrote, logic will overrule vanity.

Poole saw the post, liked it, and appointed Shii as a moderator and administrator on 4chan's boards. He asked another admin to implement a new feature called "Forced_Anon" on different parts of the site. Many users were deeply upset when Forced_Anon was implemented on a few of these boards, and some typed in "tripcodes" so they could override the forced anonymity and use a nickname. Others, who embraced the anonymity feature, mocked the signers and christened them "tripfags."

Perhaps as an omen of what was to come, conflict ensued. Supporters of anonymity and tripcodes started creating separate threads, calling on anyone who supported their own view to post a message and demonstrate support, or starting "tripcode vs. anon" threads. The tripfags began mocking the anonymous users as a single person named "Anonymous," or jokingly referring to them as a hive mind. Over the next few years, however, the joke would wear thin and the idea of Anonymous as a single entity would grow beyond a few discussion threads. Poole would fade into the background as Anonymous took on a life of its own. Over the years, /b/ in particular would take on a dedicated base of users whose lives revolved around the opportunities the board afforded them for fun and learning. These users were mostly in the English-speaking world, aged between eighteen and thirty-five, and male. One of them was named William.

*   *   *

William cracked open an eye and stared ahead. It was a cold afternoon in February 2011, and the hard-core user of 4chan considered getting out of bed. In another part of the world, Aaron Barr was trying to repair the damage caused by a group of hackers with Anonymous. William was part of Anonymous, too, and sometimes he liked to attack people. He didn't have the technical skills of Sabu and Kayla, but his methods could still have an impact.

A sheet hung from the wall of his bedroom, draped from the ceiling to the floor, tacked up with nails. More had been suspended around the room. At the end of his bed was a set of low shelves, with a pile of clutter to the left and a window on the right, hidden behind a blackout blind. The room was his cocoon in the winter, his bed a safety net. At twenty-one, he had been on 4chan most days since leaving school six years earlier, sometimes for many hours at a stretch. For various reasons, he had never held a full-time job for longer than a few months. He wanted to. But William was deeply conflicted. In the real world he was kind to his family and loyal to his friends. As an anonymous user on 4chan's /b/, he became something more dark, even venomous.

4chan was more than just a drop-in site for random kicks that millions of people visited every day. For William and a dedicated core, it was a life choice. Beyond the porn, jokes, and shocking images, it offered targets to toy with. On 4chan, toying with or seriously harassing someone was called a "life ruin." Using many of the same Internet sleuthing tactics as Aaron Barr, William would find people on 4chan discussion forums who were being ridiculed or deserved ridicule. Then he would "dox" them, or find their true identities, send them threats on Facebook, or find their family members and harass them, too. The jackpot was nude photos, which could be sent to family, friends, and co-workers for pure embarrassment or even extortion.

Ruining people's lives gave William a thrill, and a sense of power unlike anything he had felt in the outside world. The only other time he felt anything similar was when he would quietly slip outside his house in the dead of night, meet up with a few old friends, and spray colorful graffiti on the local walls or trains. Graffiti was his mistress on summer nights. In the winter, it was 4chan and now, sometimes, the wider activities of Anonymous.

4chan offered some tame content and mature discussion, and plenty more porn, gore, and constant insults between users that created a throbbing mass of negativity. It sometimes got William thinking scary thoughts about suicide. But 4chan also kept him alive. Sometimes he felt depression coming on and would stay up all night on the site, then remain awake for the rest of the next day. When thoughts of killing himself came, he could hide in sleep, tucked safely under his blanket, against the wall that he'd covered with a sheet.

William was brought up in low-income British housing. His parents had met at the YMCA after his mother, an immigrant from Southeast Asia, escaped an unhappy marriage and became temporarily homeless. The couple split when William was seven and he chose to live with his father. He went on to misbehave at school, statistically one of the worst in his country. He would swear at teachers or just walk out of class. It became an endless stream of detentions. He wasn't a social outcast; William just couldn't see the point of his education. After getting expelled at fourteen he was allowed to return, but by the following year, in October 2004, he decided to leave entirely.

By this time, William had already created a new life online. It started when he and some friends began visiting websites frequented by pedophiles, and signing up with usernames like "sexy_baby_girl" to get attention. They'd ask the men to go on webcam, and if they came on naked, as they often did, the boys would burst out laughing. To raise the stakes, they'd paste an official warning from Child Protective Services in MSN Messenger, Microsoft's popular chat client, adding that they had the man's IP address, a series of numbers that corresponded to his computer, which they'd make up. The man would usually just sign off, but they got a buzz knowing he was probably terrified, and that he probably deserved it.

William was always the one who would push his friends to take the joke further or get the male target more sexually excited. Eventually, he started continuing the pranks at home on iSketch.com, TeenChat.net, and other hotbeds of sexual deviants at that time. None of the images shocked William any more. He had first seen porn when he was eleven.

He was soon spending many hours every day immersed in the so-called Deep Web, the more than one trillion pages of the Internet that cannot be indexed by search engines like Google. As well as dynamic Web forums, much of it is illegal content. William trapped himself in a daily digest of images of gore, horrific traffic accidents, and homemade porn, all on the family computer. When some of the more depraved images would flash up on the screen, William would panic and quickly close the browser window. Somehow, though, he'd stumble upon them again that night. And then again the following night. At around fifteen, he finally found 4chan, the website that would become his world for the next few years.

Many people who involve themselves in Anonymous claim to have first found it through 4chan. This was the case for William and Topiary, who both discovered the site at the same time, in 2005. Already that year, the tagline "We are Legion" was appearing around the Internet. Tripcode users on 4chan were rare. A year after Shii wrote his essay, forced anonymity had become widely accepted on the image board. Anyone deemed a tripfag was quickly shot down and mocked.

4chan was booming, a teeming pit of depraved images and nasty jokes, yet at the same time a source of extraordinary, unhindered creativity. People began creating Internet memes—images, videos, or phrases that became inside jokes to thousands of online users after they got passed around to enough friends and image boards. Often they were hilarious.

Alongside gore and videos of abuse, pictures of naked women and men, and anime characters, there were endless photos of people's cats. In 2005, users on /b/ had started encouraging each other to put funny captions under cute cat photos on Saturdays (or what became known as Caturday). These so-called image macros, photographs with bold white lettering at the top and a punch line at the bottom, eventually led to the LOLcats meme. It was the first of many memes to find mainstream popularity outside of 4chan, ultimately spawning other websites and even books.

Thousands of image macros were made and then posted to 4chan and other image boards every day. A few went viral, turning into phrases repeated by millions of others for years afterward. One person who made an image macro that turned into a well-known meme was Andrew "weev" Auernheimer. A former hacker and Internet troll, he had found a stock photo of a man raising his fist in victory in front of a computer. He typed the words "Internet is serious business" over the photo. The meme is now even past the point of cliché as an online catchphrase.

Weev claims to have been in the same online discussion in which the word *lulz* was born. In 2003, a forum moderator on another site was commenting on something funny when he suddenly typed "lulz!" Others in the chat room started repeating it, and it spread from there. "It was far superior to lol," Weev later remembered. Eventually, "I did it for the lulz" or just "for the lulz" would become a symbol of Internet culture and Anonymous itself, as well as an ever-popular catchphrase on 4chan.

Though the site often seemed superficial and crass, 4chan

started developing a dedicated following of passionate users. It became the biggest of the Web's English-speaking image boards, and its users accepted one another not despite their offensive desires and humor but because of them. One attraction of /b/ was that, like some secret club, it wasn't advertised anywhere. People came via word of mouth or links from similar sites, and they were urged not to invite those who wouldn't fit in with the culture. These people were called "newfag cancer." This was why numbers 1 and 2 of the so-called 47 Rules of the Internet, thought to have originated from discussions in 2006 on /b/ and real-time chat networks, were "Don't talk about /b/," and "Don't talk about /b/."

4chan's constituents soon developed their own language, with phrases like "an hero," which meant to commit suicide. This phrase came into use when some MySpace users set up a tribute page for a friend who had committed suicide. One of them, probably meaning to type the phrase "he was truly a hero," instead wrote, "he was truly an hero." It soon became a trend on 4chan to describe someone as "an hero"—before it morphed into the verb form: "I'm going to an hero." There was also "u jelly?," a way of asking if someone was jealous, and "cheese pizza," or "CP," slang for child porn. More shrewd 4chan users would start discussion threads about literal cheese pizza, including photos of pizzas, and add hidden links to a child porn archive within the image code—accessed by opening the pizza images in a text program instead of an image viewer.

The /r/ board stood for requests, for anything from pictures to advice on what to do about being dumped. Pr0nz, n00dz, and rule 34 meant porn. Rule 34 was another one of the 47 Rules of the Internet, which simply stated: "If it exists, there is porn of it." So /r/ing rule 34 on a female celebrity meant requesting porn, perhaps digitally altered, of a singer or actress. "Moar!" meant more, and "lulz" of course meant fun at someone else's expense, typically through embarrassment.

The original posters, or OPs, to each thread were the sole semblance of hierarchy in an otherwise anarchic community. Still, they could only ever expect irreverent responses to their posts and, more often than not, insults. "OP is a faggot" was a generic response, and there were no exceptions. Racist comments, homophobia, and jokes about disabled people were the norm. It was customary for users to call one another "nigger," "faggot," or just "fag." New 4chan users were newfags, old ones oldfags, and Brits were britfags, homosexuals were fagfags or gayfags. It was a gritty world yet strangely accepting. It became taboo to identify one's sex, race, or age. Stripping 4chan users of their identifying features made everyone feel more like part of a collective, and this is what kept many coming back.

A source of the most unpalatable stories and images users could find, /b/ was called "the asshole of the internet" by Encyclopedia Dramatica (ED), a satirical online repository of Internet memes that had the look and feel of Wikipedia, but was far ruder. Like the users' anonymity, /b/ was a blank slate with no label—the users had complete freedom to decide the content and direction it took. Over time, regulars, who called themselves /b/rothers or /b/tards, created their own world. One of the more common threads people started posting on /b/ (besides pr0nz) was titled "bawww." Here users appealed to the sympathetic side of 4chan, with titles such as "gf just dumped me, bawww thread please?" posted with the photo of a sad face. This was the rare instance where /b/ users would offer sincere advice, comfort, or funny pictures to cheer up the OP. There was no way to tell for sure, but the types of people who were hanging out on 4chan appeared to be tech-savvy, bored, and often emotionally awkward. By the time Anonymous started grabbing the world's attention in 2008, most people who supported Anonymous had spent some time on 4chan, and it is said that around 30 percent of 4chan users were regularly visiting /b/.

When William first came across 4chan, he had already seen much worse at sites like myg0t, Rotten, and the YNC. But he lingered on /b/ because it was so unpredictable, so dynamic. Years later, he would marvel at how he could still be surprised each day when he opened up /b/, now his home page. Browsing was like a lottery—you never knew when something salacious, seedy, or funny would pop up. There was something unifying about its utter nihilism. As the media and other outsiders started criticizing what /b/ users got up to, many felt a sense of righteousness too.

There were still two big no-no's on /b/. One was child porn (though this is disputed by some hardcore users who like the way it puts off the newfags) and the other was moralfags. Calling someone a "moralfag" on 4chan was the worst possible insult. These were visitors to /b/ who took issue with its depravity and tried to change it or, worse, tried to get /b/ to act on some other kind of wrongdoing. They knew that hundreds of users on /b/ would often agree en masse about an issue on a discussion thread. And sometimes they would not just agree on an idea, they would agree on an action. Though /b/ was completely unpredictable, sometimes its users seemed to be contributing to a kind of collective consciousness. They created jokes together, hit out at OPs they didn't like together. Like it or not, moralfags would eventually take advantage of this ability to act in sync by persuading /b/ to join protests.

What /b/ eventually became most famous for was how a poster could inspire others on the board to gather together for a mass prank or "raid." Someone would typically start a thread suggesting an issue that /b/ should do something about. The refined way to coordinate a raid was never to suggest one directly but rather to imply that a raid was already about to happen. "Hey guys should we do this?" was almost always met with "GTFO" [get the fuck out]. Whereas "This is happening now. Join in" would appeal to the crowd. If a poster had prepared an image with instructions, like a digital image with instructions on how to join in, it was more likely to have staying power because it could be posted over and over.

There was no exaggerating the speed of /b/. The best time of day to get attention, when the United States was waking up, was also the worst, since this was when your post could get lost in the deluge of other popular posts. You would start a thread with one post at the top, then refresh the page after ten seconds to find it had been pushed from the home page to page 2. The threads were constantly swapping places—once someone contributed a comment to a thread, it would come back to the home page. The more comments, the more likely it would stay on the home page and attract more comments, and so on. A raid was more likely to happen if lots of people agreed to take part. But it could be manipulated if a small group of four or five people suggested a raid and repeatedly commented on it to make it look like the hive mind was latching on. Sometimes this worked, sometimes it didn't. It was a game where seconds counted—if the original poster couldn't post for two minutes, the chance could be lost and the hive mind would lose interest.

Another reason to stick around: /b/ was an endless source of learning, whether it was how to prank pedos or unearth someone's private data. Soon enough, the /r/ requests for porn weren't just for celebrities but for the n00dz of real-life girls, exes, or enemies of /b/tards. As they took up the challenge to sniff out homemade porn, /b/ users taught one another best practices—for instance, how to find a unique string of numbers from each Facebook photo URL, or website address, and use that to access someone's profile and their information. The methods were simple and crude. The kind of skilled hacking used by cyber criminals or the folks who attacked HBGary Federal was often not needed.

From age eighteen onward, William began filling a collection of secret folders on his family computer with homemade porn and information about people, including suspected pedophiles and women he'd met online. Soon he was encouraging other newfags to "lurk moar," or learn more on 4chan. He created another hidden folder called "info," where he would save any new techniques or methods for his snooping, often as screencaps, for anything from hacking vending machines and getting free Coke—posted in "Real Life Hacking" threads—to bringing down a website. The /rs/ (rapid share) board, which compiled links to popular file-sharing sites, became a source of helpful, free programs like Auto-Clicker, which could help swing an online poll or spam a site. Lurk long enough, he figured, and you could get access to almost anything you wanted.

William was primarily attracted to women. But lurking on 4chan he noticed other users saying they were swaying into bisexuality or even homosexuality. A recurring thread ran along the lines of "How gay have you become since browsing /b/?" Many male heterosexuals who visited /b/ found their reaction to gay porn went from negative to indifferent to positive. William didn't feel himself becoming gay or even bi, but he'd come across so much male porn over the years that it was no longer a turnoff. You could almost call it penis fatigue.

William's morals were also becoming increasingly ambiguous as he constantly watched and laughed at gore, rape, racism, and abuse. Everything was "cash" or "win" (good and acceptable). /b/tards knew the difference between right and wrong—they just chose not to recognize either designation on 4chan. Everyone accepted they were there for lulz, and that the act of attaining lulz often meant hurting someone. It was no wonder that a future tagline for Anonymous would be, "None of us are as cruel as all of us." William's increasing ambivalence over sex and morality was being multiplied on a mass scale for others on 4chan and would become a basis for the cultlike identity of Anonymous.

William's online vigilantism meanwhile became his full-time

job. It was fulfilling and effective. He didn't need to hack people's computers to get their private data—he just needed to talk to them, then employ the subtle art of "social engineering," that fancy way to describe lying.

Once William had peeled himself out of bed on that chilly February afternoon, he had something to eat and found his way back to the family computer. As usual, he opened up his Internet browser, and 4chan's /b/ popped up as the home page. He clicked through a few threads and after a few hours stumbled upon the photo of a girl. Black hair partly hid her green eyes and a bewitching half smile. The photo had been taken from above, the customary self-portrait for teenage girls. The original poster wanted /b/ to embarrass the girl by cracking into her Photobucket account, finding several nude photos, and sending them to her friends and family. Clearly there was some sort of grudge. "She's a bitch, anyway," he said, adding a link to her Facebook profile. This was the sort of thing William would do to someone all the time, but the OP had vastly misunderstood /b/.

/b/ users, for a start, wanted more for their time than just n00dz, which were already the biggest commodity on 4chan. More importantly, an OP must never believe he had /b/ at his mercy. Within minutes, his post had accumulated more than a hundred comments—almost all saying "NYPA" (not your personal army)—along with a few other insults.

William said the same, but he was also intrigued. He clicked on the girl's photo again and decided he had nothing to lose by pursuing a night of fun and justice. It was now 1:00 a.m. on a Saturday. Neighbors strolled home from local bars outside as William sat, legs splayed in front of the old computer in his family's kitchen, occasionally running a hand through his ragged hair.

He clicked on the Facebook link and saw another photo of the girl; in this one she was sitting on a brick wall in colorful dancer's leg warmers, scowling at the camera. Her name was Jen, and she lived in Tennessee.

William signed into Facebook with one of his stock of twenty fake profiles. Almost all were fake women. It was much easier to collect friends on Facebook if you were female, and having friends was crucial for a profile to look real. His main fake Facebook account had around 130 friends who were real people. To collect them, he would pick a location like Chicago, then add local guys. If they asked who "she" was, William would claim to have just moved there. Most of the other fake accounts were throwaways, in the sense that most of the friends were other fake profiles of /b/ users. He would collect the friends on /b/ itself, via the occasional thread titled "Add each others' troll accounts here!" The fake users would connect on Facebook and write on each others' walls to make their profiles look more realistic. William would add profile pictures and faked "vacation photos" by downloading whole folders of photos of a single female from online photo repositories or 4chan itself, or by coercing a girl into giving him her photos. Facebook would sometimes delete "troll" accounts like these, especially if they had inane names like I. P. Daily. (William lost about two accounts a month this way.) But real-looking accounts could last for years. This time around, to speak to Jen, he was using a key account populated by real people, under the name Kaylie Harmon.

He took a screenshot of the 4chan post with the girl's photo. Then under the guise of Kaylie, he typed out a private message on Facebook to Jen. Anyone on Facebook can send a private message to another user, even if they aren't connected as friends. "Look what someone's trying to do to you," he said, attaching the screenshot from 4chan. He signed it "Anonymous," as he often did to frighten his targets.

Jen's reply was almost instant. "OMG. Who is this? How did you get my Facebook??" she wrote back.

"I'm a hacker," William replied, lying. "I'm going to hack your Facebook and pictures on Photobucket. No matter how many pictures you've got online I'll make them all public." He kept his answers short and ominous.

"What do I have to do to stop this?" she asked, apparently desperate not to have her photos published. William smiled to himself. Years of raiding girls' Web accounts had taught him this meant she definitely had nude photos she was willing to bargain with.

"Give me the nude photos of yourself and I'll stop everyone else hacking you," he said. "There's dozens of other people trying to hack you as we speak."

Having no reason to believe he was lying, Jen consented and sent him the relevant login details. "Take what you want," she said.

There were maybe three hundred photos in Jen's Photobucket account, mostly of her with friends and family, holiday snapshots on the beach, a group of family members giving the thumbs-up at a Ruby Tuesday restaurant. And about seventy nude photos. One by one, William started downloading each one to his personal collection of homemade porn.

"Done," William told Jen on Facebook's chat feature. "Glad you went along with this. It could have been a lot worse." He advised her to tighten her privacy settings on Facebook and get rid of her security question. The security question, which websites will use to help you recall a lost password, will be along the lines of "What was your first pet's name?" William would have only needed to engage her in small talk to find out the answer, then retrieve her password if he wanted—but this time he was warning her of the ruse.

Within an hour, Jen had forgiven William for his strange actions. She was more intrigued with getting to know the "hacker" who had saved her from an embarrassing fate. The two began chatting about small things like Facebook and friends. Then William proposed an idea. "If you want, I could find out the name of the guy that posted your photo on 4chan," he said.

Jen agreed. "Find the guy, and I can send you over some more pics, especially for you."

"Who's on your blocked list, on Facebook?" William asked.

"Six people, I think."

William studied each of their profiles. By now, it was 6:00 a.m. Eventually, his eyes fell on the Facebook profile photo of Joshua Dean Scott, a sneering, unshaven man in a ripped denim shirt and with piercings in his eyebrow. He instantly knew this had to be the OP from 4chan.. He looked like someone thoroughly distasteful. A smiling woman with punk-shaved hair in several photos appeared to be Josh's fiancée.

Still in his fake Kaylie account, complete with a smiling profile photo of a woman and 130 real friends, William typed Josh a message. "Hello, OP." He clicked send.

William then sent messages to six of Josh's Facebook friends, chosen at random, asking if anyone with an axe to grind would help him punish Josh. A close friend of Josh's named Anthony replied. William explained what had happened on 4chan—that Josh had tried to take revenge on a girl by turning /b/ into his personal army. It turned out Anthony was a longtime 4chan user himself and was instantly appalled at Josh's lack of etiquette on the image board.

"I'll help you out," Anthony said. "He shouldn't have done that." Anthony gave William Josh's full name, cell phone number, and area of residence. Sometimes in social engineering, all you needed was to ask for something nicely.

William sent a few more messages to Josh, the first one posting his home address, the next his cell phone. He was signing the messages "Anon" so that Josh would think there was a group of people behind this. Soon Josh wrote back, begging for mercy.

"Please don't hack me," he wrote. William replied with instructions. Josh was to send a photo of himself holding a paper sign saying, "Jen owns my ass." With his other hand, he was to hold a shoe over his head. The shoe-on-head pose was hugely symbolic on 4chan and was the ultimate admission of defeat in any kind of online argument or attack. (Do a Google Image search on "shoe on head" and see for yourself. Oddly, many people smile for the camera.) For good measure, William told Josh to send a photo of his fiancée, without clothes, holding up a sign that simply said /b/. In full belief that William, a young unemployed guy in his family home who'd been up all night, was actually a group of skilled hackers, Josh did just as he was asked. William forwarded both photos to Jen. By now it was 7:00 a.m. and the rest of his neighborhood was getting ready to go to work. William headed back up to bed.

Not everybody on /b/ did what William did, but he and plenty of others on 4chan lived for this sort of nightly experience. Despite being a young man who struggled to hold down jobs for more than a few months at a time, William, sometimes within the space of an hour, could frighten and coerce someone on the other side of the world into doing something most of us would never dream of: take off their clothes, snap a photo, and send it to a complete stranger. /b/ offered a unique sense of power and unpredictability that drew many more like him into Anonymous, and it kept them hooked. Over time, people found their own roles in the ever-shifting crowd. For the smart-mouthed Anon known as Topiary, that role was to perform.

CHAPTER 3

Everybody Get In Here

The raid on Aaron Barr in February 2011 would be a landmark attack for Anonymous for several reasons: It showed the collective could make a bigger impact by stealing data, not just by knocking a website offline. Once Barr's e-mails were put online, they would have major repercussions for his reputation and that of his associates. It also showed how much more powerful an attack could be with Twitter. The process of signing into Barr's Twitter account had been easy.

Topiary had simply tested the "kibafo33" password he'd been shown and it logged him right in. But hijacking the account and tweeting a stream of ribald humor would end up becoming a highlight of the raid for other Anons and for the press. These tweets were suddenly giving a new voice to Anonymous, showing this was not just a sinister network of hackers who wanted to attack things. They wanted to have fun, too.

Topiary had always enjoyed immersing himself in thrilling new experiences like the HBGary raid. His closely guarded real name was Jake Davis. From a young age, he had regarded the world with intense curiosity, preferring the British TV math·

game *Countdown* to cartoons. He liked numbers so much that when he turned two his mother got him a calculator, letting him gleefully punch the keys with his small fingers while she wheeled him around the grocery store. The boy developed into one of those rare individuals who was both creative and analytical, right-brained and left-brained. He loved numbers but adored music and would later be drawn to avant-garde bands and musicians, listening to them at precisely the same time as other online friends for something akin to a religious experience. Jake assigned colors to numbers: seven was orange, and six was yellow, for instance. It wasn't a vision of color, just the sense of it, and the condition helped him plow through math as a child—remembering the color yellow as 42 made it easier to answer the multiplication sum of 6 x 7; 81 was a blue number because 9 was blue, and so on. He was certain everyone else thought this way until he realized he had a "condition" called sound-to-color synesthesia.

Born in Canterbury, England, at six he moved, with his mother, to a remote group of islands above Scotland known as the Shetlands. The move was occasioned by his grandfather Sam Davis's impulsive purchase of a dilapidated hotel for sale on one of the islands. Someone had told the older man about the building, and he had jumped on a plane to take a look, moving with his wife, Dot, just one week later. Sam Davis was a tough, spontaneous man and a risk taker. Jake's mother, Jennifer Davis, had lost contact with her parents for years, but when she found out by chance where they were, she decided to follow. Till then she had been shuttling her two sons between boarding houses and looking for a permanent home in southern England. Jennifer and her partner, Jake's father, had been on and off for around six years. He was increasingly feckless and had lost himself in alcohol, rambling about finding religion and chasing other women. One day she gave both her small sons a backpack, stuffed what she could into a couple of suitcases, and took them on an eighteen-hour bus journey to Aberdeen, Scotland (the train was too expensive), before getting on a ferry to the Shetland Islands.

They lived on an island called Yell. It was the second largest of the Shetlands but still tiny, with a population of about nine hundred. It was bleak and, by some accounts, about twenty years behind the rest of the country. There was electricity, but there were no chain stores, fast-food joints, or nice restaurants. Local teenagers dabbled in drugs as a recreation of last resort. It was cold, gray, and windswept, with hardly a tree in sight. Narrow, single-lane roads sprawled across the land and tiny stone houses were sprinkled between acres of farmland.

People here were isolated. Their thick dialect was hard for newcomers to understand. Most had lived here all their lives, never venturing off the island or reading anything besides the local newspaper. Despite the farms, the island relied on crates of food and fuel ferried in once a day. When storms brewed over the horizon, residents raided the local grocery store in fear they might go hungry. Islanders didn't associate themselves with the two countries on either side of them, Norway and the United Kingdom. Being close-knit had its advantages: people looked out for each other. The local farmers and fishermen often gave away their oversupply of meat and fish to neighbors. After a few years, Jake's family had three refrigerators bursting with fresh lamb and huge chunks of fresh salmon so thick your fork, when poked in, wouldn't reach the plate. But locals were mistrustful of outsiders, and school would become unbearable for Jake.

While Jake's grandparents looked after him and his brother after school, his mother worked several jobs to help pay the bills. Eventually she found a new partner, Alexander "Allie" Spence. She and her boys moved into Spence's house, and Jake started referring to Allie as his stepfather. At school, Jake was getting bullied. Although he was fiercely witty, he also had amblyopia, a condition known as lazy eye that affected his left pupil. Socializing at school was a struggle, and he decided early on that it was just easier to not try to make friends. He was quiet and kept a distance from most other kids. If anyone taunted him, he'd respond with a withering putdown, and if other kids laughed, he joined in the banter. For the most part, the resulting lack of school friends did not bother him.

More frustrating was the shortfall in learning. Jake sensed his tiny school of a hundred students was teaching little about the world outside their island, with classes instead focusing on the particulars of sheep farming: how to tag them and how to dip them in liquid insecticide. There were compulsory knitting classes twice a week, where Jake was made to churn out colorful toys in the shapes of ghosts and dinosaurs, or hats. One of his dinosaurs won a prize at a local knitting competition, judged by the "world's fastest knitter" who was a local hero. The feeling was bittersweet; he didn't want to know how to knit, he wanted to learn something that could challenge him.

School and the regimen of classes started to seem increasingly pointless. When he started going to Mid Yell Junior High School, he became insolent, openly questioning the logic of teachers, only trying in classes when a teacher said he couldn't do the work properly. He made things tolerable by doing pranks. One day he set off the school fire alarm, then heaved large pieces of furniture with a few classmates to block the entranceway for students and teachers into the main assembly hall. He didn't want to impress the other kids. He just liked causing a stir and longed to do things no one else had done before. By the time he entered his teenage years, teachers were telling his mother that he needed to interact with a wider circle of friends. Jake to them was emotionless, cold, and sassy.

In February 2004, tragedy struck when his stepfather, Allie, was driving down one of the island's narrow lanes, got into a car accident, and died. Jake was thirteen. To make matters worse, he and his family were told that they could not continue living in his stepfather's home. Spence's ex-wife still had the rights to the house and asked them to leave. Jennifer Davis and her two sons eventually were able to find government-assisted living—a small brown house with vertical wooden slats in the middle of Yell.

The experience was too much for Jake, who decided he did not want to go back to school. The best place to be was at home, by himself. He became a recluse. Amid her own grief, his mother was livid, telling her son that he couldn't throw his education away. But he didn't want to be restricted by schedules, a curriculum, or his own mother.

After leaving school, Jake was mostly playing video games or learning with a part-time tutor. By now, his mother had set up a dial-up Internet connection for the home so she could send and receive e-mails. Jake had convinced her to upgrade that to faster broadband, and since the age of eleven he had been going online almost every day, exploring an entirely new world of learning, socializing, then learning by socializing. When he started playing online role-playing games like RuneScape, other players would teach him tricks for getting around the Web, hiding his computer's IP address by chatting through instant messages, and basic programming. Making online friends was easy. No one could see his amblyopia, and people valued his wit and creativity far more. He became bolder and funnier. There was an equality he had never experienced before, an ease of conversation and a sense of shared identity. When the Internet telephone service Skype came along, he used it to talk to his new friends by voice for the first time.

One day on Skype, someone suggested doing a prank call and letting everyone else listen in. Jake jumped at the opportunity. He found the number for a random Walmart outlet in the United States, then told the woman who answered that he was looking for a "fish-shaped RC helicopter." As he begged the woman to help him find one, Jake was keenly aware that his friends (on mute) were dying of laughter. The next day he prank-called an Applebee's restaurant in San Antonio, Texas. The manager became so incensed that he decided to prank them again, calling for an ambulance in a falsetto voice and claiming to be giving birth in the restaurant's basement. When the restaurant threatened to called a local detective of the San Antonio Police Department, Jake and his friend called the same detective and claimed the Applebee's manager was a terrorist. Jake's friends couldn't get enough of his prank calls. They were entranced by the unpredictability and the cockiness coming from his now-baritone voice. They would never have known that just a year before he was the quiet, scrawny kid getting bullied in a village school.

Soon he was doing prank calls for his friends almost every day. He found one or two other good prank callers to collaborate with, including a guy in London with whom he'd pretend to be a father and daughter arguing on an advice line. Everything was improvised, and sometimes he would think up an idea just as the phone was ringing. He pushed for ever more daring ways to upset, scare, or confuse his targets. It was like producing a television show, keeping his audience happy with new ideas and gimmicks. Eventually they moved to a website called Tiny Chat, where dozens of users could listen in on Jake's Skype pranks.

By this time he was an occasional visitor to 4chan and /b/, attracted mainly by the pranks and raids. He noticed he could grab more listeners if he advertised through 4chan. He would start a thread on /b/ and paste in links to the chat room where he was broadcasting his prank call, encouraging more people to join in and listen to something funny. Soon enough he was carrying out live prank calls to 250 listeners at a time. The San Antonio Applebee's became his favorite victim. Throughout the course of a year he ordered them rounds of twenty pizzas at a time and thousands of free boxes from UPS. On another occasion he got a tip-off (through 4chan) from a disgruntled employee at a home furnishings store in the United States. The employee had slipped him the phone-in code to access the store's speaker system. When he called it, he put on an authoritative American accent and told the customers that all items were free for the next twenty minutes. When he called back a few minutes later, the sound coming from the background could only be described as chaos.

Two years in and fourteen-year-old Jake was flitting between his broadcasted prank calls and raids by 4chan's /b/tards. Successful raids could target just about anything online, but they tended to have one thing in common, something that has barely changed to this day: a surge. Whether it was the mass spamming of shock-photos on someone's forum, or overwhelming a website with traffic, or warping the votes for *Time* magazine's Person of the Year or a website's favorite video game character, raids by /b/ involved pooling together and flooding something else to the point of embarrassment. It was strength in numbers. The more people there were, the bigger the deluge.

4chan's first landmark raid is widely considered to have been against Habbo Hotel on July 12, 2006. Habbo was a popular game and real-time chatting site designed as a virtual hangout for teens. Once logged into the site, you could get a bird's-eye view of various rooms in the hotel, and in the form of a character you had created, you could explore and chat with other people's avatars.

One day, someone on 4chan suggested disrupting the virtual environment by joining en masse and flooding it with the same character, a black man in a gray suit and Afro hairstyle. The men with the Afro then had to block the entrance to the pool and tell other avatars it was "closed due to fail and AIDS." When regular Habbo users logged in, they suddenly found the area heaving with what looked like sharply dressed disco dancers. /b/ reveled in the Great Habbo Raid of '06, and the "pool's closed" meme was born. For the next few years on July 12, groups of 4chan users returned to the Habbo Hotel with their Afro-wearing avatars, sometimes moving their characters to create swastikalike formations in the hotel.

By the time he was sixteen and had been out of school for three years, Jake wasn't just taking part in 4chan raids, he was organizing them. In 2008 he helped instigate Operation Basement Dad. News had broken that spring that Austrian engineer Josef Fritzl had raped and imprisoned his forty-five-year-old daughter for the last twenty-four years, fathering seven of her children. Details of Fritzl's monstrous crimes shocked the world, and his trial was in the news for weeks. Naturally, 4chan saw the funny side. Jake and several other 4chan users met in a separate chat room and decided to create a fake Twitter feed for Fritzl. Their goal was for @basementdad to become the first Twitter account to reach one million followers, a race then being fought between actor Ashton Kutcher and CNN. Less than twenty-four hours after they had set up the account and announced it on 4chan, media-sharing site eBaum's World, and other sites, the account had nearly three hundred thousand followers. Nearly half a million ended up following @basementdad before Twitter shut it down; according to Jake's calculations, it was on track to win the race.

Pranks like this couldn't be organized easily on 4chan. There were now millions of people using its forums, and up to two hundred thousand posts going up each day on /b/. The discussion threads changed so quickly it was impossible to have a cogent discussion. Eventually, people realized that to organize a good raid they needed Internet Relay Chat (IRC).

IRC was a simple, real-time chat system created in 1988 by a programmer named Jarkko "WiZ" Oikarinen. (He now works for Google in Sweden.) By 2008, a few million people were using it—you didn't need an account, as you might with MSN or AOL Instant Messenger. You just needed a program, or IRC "client," that could point you to the wide variety of networks on offer. There are hundreds of IRC networks out there today, some aligned with various organizations like WikiLeaks. EFnet is one of the oldest, and beloved by veteran hackers like Sabu. Once you were on a network there could be dozens, even hundreds of chat rooms or more to visit, known as "channels." Some channels had one person, some had thousands. Most had between five and twenty-five people. You would simply enter and start meeting people.

When someone like Jake first started using IRC, it was more than just a casual chat room. IRC was geared toward technically minded people, thanks to its long list of special commands that let you navigate channels, even manipulate the network. The command /whois, for instance, showed you what channels another person was in and an IP address. Starting a private chat would look like this: "msg topiary Hey, how are you?" Depending upon which client you were using, each channel would have a list on one side showing the room's participants, ranked by those who had "operator" status, or the power to kick people out if they were talking IN ALL CAPS or generally being annoying. IRC lingo was littered with abbreviations like rofl (rolling on the floor laughing), lol (laugh out loud), and ttyl (talk to you later). Like 4chan, it gradually developed its own culture and language.

Once you were on a network, anyone could create a new IRC channel. You simply typed /join #channelname, and it would appear. If Jake wanted to organize a new raid like Operation Basement Dad, he would create a room—for example, #opbasementdad—and invite a chosen few to enter. That way, anyone interested could contribute ideas and help plan the raid or stunt.

Once the planners had figured out what to do, they would go back to 4chan. This time, though, they would use /b/ as a recruiting tool, creating a new thread and spamming it with this message: "EVERYONE GET IN HERE." They'd also paste a link next to the message that took other /b/ users into their new IRC channel. Soon there could be scores, even a few hundred people joining the chat room and listening to instructions or throwing out ideas. Anonymous had first emerged on image boards like 4chan, but it was evolving through Internet Relay Chat networks. It was becoming more organized. Although people could use nicknames on IRC, by and large they were maintaining the anonymity encouraged on the image boards. Individual personalities could emerge, but people still had no real-world identities.

IRC networks were helping Anonymous turn from an unpredictable, volatile mass of image board users into well-organized, sometimes-threatening groups. If the raid was interesting enough, or well-publicized enough, more people would join. Things went up another notch once hackers started to jump in. The more people joined an IRC channel, the higher the likelihood that among them would be individuals with particularly strong technical talents: programmers and hackers who could breach a network or write a script to help automate an attack. One of those hackers was Kayla.

CHAPTER 4

Kayla and the Rise of Anonymous

While Topiary was making the /b/tards laugh on 4chan, the Internet entity known as Kayla was teaching herself to rip holes in cyberspace. Her journey into the world of Anonymous, as she told it, had started off with isolation, the discovery of hackers on the Internet, and then finding her place in the rise of hacktivism. But there was one thing many people came to learn about Kayla. She lied.

It was not done in a malicious way. Kayla lied partly to protect herself, partly to stay friendly. Being evasive about information, like the hacker known as Tflow, could be off-putting even when people knew that this was Anonymous etiquette. Instead of refusing to answer a personal question or join in conversations, Kayla freely provided personal details about her life to her online friends, humdrum accounts of stubbing her toe on the door on the way downstairs to get some food or going to the beach with her real-life friends. She shared unusually stark details about her childhood and parents and about other hacks that she had carried out in the past. Whether she was lying about some, none, or all of it, the person behind Kayla seemed to have a deep need to tell stories to prove her value to others.

After the February 2011 attack on HBGary Federal, for instance, Kayla corroborated the story Sabu had told, that a sixteen-year-old girl had hacked into Greg Hoglund's website, rootkit.com. "After resetting Greg's account, I used it to social-engineer Jussi for access to rootkit.com," Kayla said in an interview in March 2011. "It was the icing on the cake." In truth, Sabu had been the hacker to social-engineer the admin and hack the site.

When she was asked to recount the story a few months later, her version changed: "The thing is, the way it all happened... Sabu set the ball rolling with the social engineering, then I finished it off by nuking rootkit.com's server." Kayla did not have to lie about her exploits. She was a skilled hacker and most people who knew her accepted that. But she also didn't want to corrupt Sabu's lie and make things difficult for her friend. That was Kayla—lying so that she didn't have to upset people.

Kayla claimed that, along with being a sixteen-year-old girl, her parents had split when she was eleven. The story went that her father had been the more stable parent and taken custody, then moved with her to a remote town where there were few kids Kayla's age nearby. With little else to do, she started chatting with her old friends on MSN Messenger, logging in with her real name (which she said was also "Kayla") and other credentials. Her father, she said, was a software engineer who worked from home, and the house was littered with books on computer programming, Linux Kernel, Intel, and networking. She started reading his books and asking him questions about what he did. Encouraged by her enthusiasm, he sat with her in front of a computer and showed her how to find bugs in C source code and exploit them, then how to bypass them. Soon she was immersing herself in scripting languages like Perl, Python, and PHP, learning how to attack Web databases with the SQL injection method. It was mostly harmless, but by the time she was fourteen, Kayla claimed she was writing scripts that could automate cyber attacks.

It had all been harmless, "until I went looking for so-called hacking forums," Kayla said. "I registered at some of them and they were all, 'Go away little girl this isn't for you.' Fair enough I was only 14 but it made me so angry!"

Using some of the skills she had picked up from her dad and online research, she claimed she hacked into one forum site and deleted much of its contents using SQL injection. It was an attack unlike any the regulars had seen before.

"Wow you're only 14 and you can do this?" Kayla recalled one of the hackers there saying. He invited Kayla into the more exclusive chat channels on EFnet, one of the oldest Internet Relay Chat networks. The forum user saw potential in Kayla, gave her tips, and pushed her to read more books on programming so she could learn more.

"It got kinda weird because I started meeting some shady people," she said, referring to purely online meetings. "One guy was much older than me, like a lot older and had a weird crush on me. I guess a girl hacker is every guy hacker's dream? Maybe? The only thing was he was 27 and I was only 14, so yeah, weird! I'm so sick of people thinking only old people are smart, and just because I'm young anything I say doesn't count?"

Though Kayla insisted that online life was hard because she was female, the opposite was more likely true. The real person behind her nickname was guaranteed to get more attention and more opportunities to hack others by being a friendly and mysterious girl. Females were a rare sight on image boards and hacking forums; hence the online catchphrase "There are no girls on the Internet," and why posing as a girl has been a popular tactic for Internet trolls for years. But this didn't spell an upper hand for genuine females. If they revealed their sex on an image board like /b/ they were often met with misogynistic comments like "Tits or GTFO"—that is, "Show your tits or get the fuck out." Many girls on image boards would often appease these calls by going down the route of becoming "camwhores," stripping or performing sexual acts on webcam for attention and acceptance. The other option was to simply hide their sex and be male online. With so much ego and reputation at stake, identifying someone's gender on a board like /b/ could be almost impossible, but it made sense to be suspicious of those claiming outright to be young women. This was why number 29 of the Rules of the Internet said that on the Internet "all girls are men and all kids are undercover FBI agents." Kayla probably wasn't an FBI agent, but certainly someone with an elaborate backstory, and one that perhaps hinted at who she really was in real life.

Kayla claimed that, growing up, other kids her age would hang out on street corners while she stayed at home memorizing Windows opcodes, auditing source code, and accepting invitations into private IRC channels where she could learn more from other hackers. She liked using her skills to play tricks on others. A common prank was to "dump" or publish a person's MySQL database, essentially a map for other hackers to try to steal their e-mails or documents. The ultimate goal was to dox someone, discovering and then posting his or her real-life personal details online.

Trolling and Internet vigilantism had been around for some time already, but they were becoming increasingly popular in 2008, and it's no coincidence that at around the same time, anonymizing technologies like Virtual Private Networks (VPNs) and Tor were also becoming popular. These allowed hackers and regular 4chan users like William to hide their IP addresses, the unique number, typically long with several decimals, assigned to every computer connected to the Internet. Part of the address could correspond to the network the device was part of, and the rest to the individual. If you could figure out someone's real IP address, you could usually get his or her real name and real address. But if that person was using a VPN, then people (like the police, or rival hackers) trying to "get their dox" would find a fake IP address, sometimes pointing to another computer in another country.

Trolling was like pranking, but ultimately it meant causing some sort of emotional distress to someone else, often through embarrassment or fear. For some people who couldn't be accepted in the real world, trolling was an easy route to power and one-upmanship. After displaying her skills to the hacker forum she disrupted, Kayla started regularly trolling people for kicks. She angered at the smallest hint of doubt at her skills and was obsessed with proving herself. She took her aggression out on other hackers, "furfags" (people with a penchant for bestiality), and online pedophiles. Each time she and other hackers would find their personal details, she'd aim to scare them with their information, then post it online or threaten to send it to the police. Around 2008, someone invited Kayla to Partyvan, a sprawling network of chat rooms created by a few people who wanted to unite other IRC networks that were linked to image boards like 4chan. The idea was to better collaborate on raids and create a home for the online phenomenon that people were increasingly referring to as Anonymous.

Raids, like that on Habbo Hotel, were a step up from trolling because they involved multiple people working together to cause mischief. Eventually, it was the raids that got Anonymous its first real airing in the mainstream press as a single entity—perhaps not surprisingly by a Fox TV News affiliate in Los Angeles. The segment, aired in July 2007, was given the usual sensationalist treatment: whooshing sound effects and flashes of white light. "They call themselves Anonymous they are hackers on steroids," the anchor said without pausing, "treating the web like a real-life video game."

The camera cut to silhouetted hands typing on a keyboard.

"Destroy. Die. Attack," another disembodied voice intoned. "Threats from a gang of computer hackers calling themselves Anonymous." The segment featured an interview with a MySpace user named "David," who said tormentors from Anonymous had cracked seven of his passwords.

"They plastered his profile with gay sex pictures," the narrator remarked. "His girlfriend left him…. They attack innocent people, like an Internet hate machine." The words "Internet hate machine" zoomed up onto the screen as the narrator added that Anonymous had issued death threats and threatened to bomb sports stadiums, actual pranks that had indeed been carried out by visitors to /b/.

"I believe they're domestic terrorists," a silhouetted woman said before cutting to a clip of an exploding yellow van. "Their name comes from their secret website," the reporter continued, as foreboding music began playing in the background. "It requires everyone posting on the site to remain anonymous."

"They enjoy doing this," a silhouetted man said in a deep, distorted voice. Fox described him as a former hacker who had fallen out with Anonymous. "They get what they call 'lulz.'"

"Lulz," the reporter explained, as the word appeared in a large font on the screen and horns played in the background, "Is a corruption of L.O.L., which stands for laugh out loud…. Their pranks are often anti-Semitic or racist."

The report foreshadowed how the media would continue to overdramatize the exploits of bored and mischievous teenagers, a nebulous crowd of mostly young males who could spontaneously pool together against a target. If there was a "hate machine" as Fox described it, its cogs and wheels were IRC networks and image boards. And while it was nowhere near as organized as Fox (and future news reports) suggested, the Anons were happy to play up to that portrayal.

There was no single leader pulling the levers, but a few organizational minds that sometimes pooled together to start planning a stunt. This was what would happen next for Anonymous, on a grander scale. 4chan had spawned lots of raids on small websites and individual people. Soon the mob would pick a target so controversial that its attacks would gain a measure of popular support and require an impressive act of planning. The following year, 2008, was when one of /b/'s raids turned into a full-blown insurgency against the Church of Scientology.

CHAPTER 5

Chanology

Before Topiary, Sabu, and Kayla could find each other, attack HBGary, and have the conviction to hit a stream of other targets as LulzSec, Anonymous had to grow into something larger than just a mass of young people on image boards or individuals like Topiary making prank calls. In other words, more than just a nuisance. That changed because of the actor Tom Cruise and a video that the Church of Scientology didn't want anyone to see.

Cruise had been involved with Scientology since 1990, quickly becoming its most famous celebrity advocate. In 2004 he sat down for an interview with Scientology filmmakers that would be included in a video shown exclusively to church members. The video had all the trimmings of propaganda: an image of Earth in space, flashes of light and the sound of slicing blades as the symbol of Scientology zoomed into view. Then, as an electric guitar urgently began plucking the theme tune to *Mission: Impossible,* Cruise appeared, dressed in a black turtleneck and wearing a stern expression.

"I think it's a privilege to call yourself a Scientologist," he said. As the *Mission: Impossible* theme continued playing in the background, the video showed segments of Cruise's strange mono-logue, which became increasingly incoherent.

"Now is the time, okay?" Cruise continued. "People are turn-ing to you so you better know it. You better know it. And if you don't?" He smiled. "Go and learn it, you know? But don't pre-tend you know it or whatever, you know we're here to help." Another segment started by showing Cruise, grinning, with his eyes closed, before suddenly convulsing with laughter. "And they said, so, so you have you met an SP [Scientology acronym for Suppressive Person]? Ha ha ha ha! And I looked at them. Ha ha! You know, and what a beautiful thing because maybe one day it'll be like that. Wow." Though some of what Cruise was saying made sense, most did not. The church was not exactly keen for the video to get out. In 2007, an unnamed church mem-ber decided to leak the video, mailing it on a DVD to an anti-Scientology campaigner named Patty Pieniadz.

A former high-ranking Scientolgist, Pieniadz held on to the video for about a year, waiting for the right moment to release it. When she heard that a new biography of Cruise would be re-leased on January 15, 2008, she decided that was her moment. She offered the video to TV network NBC to show exclusively, but to her surprise, it balked at the last minute on copyright con-cerns. With only a few days to go, Pieniadz had just one other option: the Internet. She had no idea how to upload the video to the Web, so she mailed the DVD to several other people in the hope it would eventually wind up on YouTube. One of those peo-ple was Mark Ebner, an investigative journalist in Los Angeles. At 2:00 a.m. West Coast time on January 15, Ebner sent a message to the founder of the media news website Gawker, Nick Denton, asking if Gawker wanted to host what would later be called "the crazy Tom Cruise video." Denton was "giddy" with excitement, according to Ebner.

At around the same time, other copies of the video were being uploaded onto YouTube and promptly being taken down on apparent copyright violations. The Church of Scientology was notoriously litigious, and it is likely that YouTube's parent company, Google, which had been sued for $1 billion in damages by Viacom in a copyright lawsuit the previous year, did not want to take any chances.

This did not put off Gawker. On the fifteenth, founder and editor Denton published the video in a blog post titled "The Cruise Indoctrination Video Scientology Tried to Suppress." In the accompanying article, he wrote, "Gawker is now hosting a copy of the video; it's newsworthy; and we will not be removing it." The video went viral almost instantly. To date, Denton's blog post has received more than 3.2 million views, while a copy of the video that eventually stayed up on YouTube has received more than 7.5 million.

But things were about to get even more embarrassing for the Church of Scientology, thanks to 4chan and /b/.

Later that day, at 7:37 p.m. eastern standard time, a /b/ user who had seen Gawker's story and who, it is claimed, was female, started a discussion thread on the board. The title was simply, "Scientology raid?" Every Original Post on /b/ had to include an image, and she had picked the church's gold-and-white logo. Her accompanying text was heavy with platitudes and appealed to the regular users of /b/ to galvanize themselves:

> I think it's time for /b/ to do something big. People need to understand not to fuck with /b/...
> I'm talking about "hacking" or "taking down" the official Scientology website.
> It's time to use our resources to do something we believe is right.
> It's time to do something big again, /b/.
> Talk amongst one another, find a better place to plan it, and then carry out what can and must be done.
> It's time, /b/.

Fellow /b/ posters were immediately dubious. "Yeah, good luck with this fail," said one of the first to reply.

"A random image board cannot take down a pseudo-religion with the backing of wealthy people and an army of lawyers," said another. "Even if every person who has ever browsed /b/ ONCE joined in on a mass invasion it would still amount to nothing. Plus...they would have 500 lawyers up their ass before they could say 'litigation.'"

"4chan vs. scientology = M-M-MONSTER FAIL."

"Can we take Mormonism next? Then Christianity?" another Anonymous poster asked sarcastically. "Then, if we really got balls, Islam?" A few /b/ users who had a background in Scientology also defended the religious group: "Scientology isn't fundamentally wrong or harmful as a belief system," one said.

The discussion continued, but soon the original, skeptical comments were drowned out by the comments of people who supported the OP. It was as if the more /b/ thought about hitting Scientology in a big way, the more its users liked the idea. "You don't get it do you," said one. "We are the anti-hero, we will do good, and fuck anyone, good or bad, who happens to be in the way."

"This is the first step in something larger, something epic," another agreed.

"We can do this," said another. "We are Anon, and we are interwebs superheroes."

Suddenly, the thread's opinion was rushing toward all-out agreement on a raid. The initial skepticism and objections that /b/ was "not your personal army" were forgotten by the now-zealous throng:

"We are thousands strong, they can't sue all of us!"

"I say it's time to stop talking about shitting dick nipples and do something even half-worth while, even if it IS just pissing off a bunch of scam artists."

"Future generations of /b/tards will look back to this as the day we fucked with batshit insane scientologists."

"Let's do it, /b/."

"I have three computers. How can I help?" someone asked.

"Jesus will someone write the newfags some explanations on how to do a DDoS? And then we can get this shit underway."

Before Anonymous emerged, DDoS attacks had been mostly confined to use by cyber criminals against financial websites or companies from which they could extort money. But by 2008, it was already becoming one of the most popular forms of Anonymous attacks. Two years earlier, /b/ users had been DDoSing the site of white nationalist radio host Hal Turner, temporarily knocking it offline. He later tried suing 4chan, another image board called 7chan, and eBaum's World, claiming thousands of dollars in bandwidth costs, with no success.

You could take part in a DDoS attack simply by downloading one of at least a dozen free software tools available on 4chan's /rs/ board. When enough people did so and flooded a target with junk traffic, the effect was like fifteen fat men trying to get through a revolving door at the same time, according to an analogy by security writer Graham Cluley. Nothing could move. The result: legitimate visitors got an error page when they visited the site, or their browser just kept loading. The downtime was always temporary—similar to when an online retailer holds a 75 percent off sale and can't handle the flood of visitors. This may seem trivial, since anyone who surfs the net has experienced a bad connection and error pages. But downtime that lasts for hours or days can cost companies thousands in lost revenue or extra bandwidth cost. Participating in a DDoS attack is also illegal, breaking the Computer Fraud and Abuse Act in the United States as well as the 2006 Police and Justice Act in the United Kingdom; in both countries, perpetrators face a maximum penalty of ten years in prison.

This, of course, rarely deterred /b/ and made raids seem more like a high-stakes game. With Scientology, participants agreed it was worth getting the newfags on board to create an army and spread the word to the other Internet image boards, also known as "chans." These included 7chan, a popular image board for ex-/b/ users; GUROchan, an image board whose posts mainly consisted of gore; and Renchan, a now-defunct site whose content bordered on pedophilia. 4chan needed to gather at least a thousand people, said one /b/ user on the still-developing Scientology thread that day, and who knew, they could probably find at least five thousand willing to fight for the cause.

People quickly got down to business. One /b/tard suggested "Phase one": prank-calling the Dianetics hotline and rickrolling them, or asking the call center "why there's a volcano on the cover of Dianetics...generally bug the hell out of them."

Another /b/tard instructed everyone to DDoS a list of Scientology sites. You could do this by simply visiting Gigaloader.com and inputting a list of URLs that pointed to eight images on Scientology.org. The Gigaloader site (now defunct) was originally meant to stress-test a server, but from as early as 2007 people figured out they could exploit it for DDoS-style attacks. You could enter several Web addresses for images on a website, and Gigaloader would constantly reload the images in your browser — that would burden the image server and eat up the site's bandwidth, an effect multiplied by the number of people participating.

The best part was /b/ could include a message in the traffic that was being sent. In a separate incident, a webmaster whose website was being hit by Gigaloader in 2007 said the traffic he was getting looked like this:

```
75.185.163.131 - - [27/Sep/2007:05:10:16 -0400] "GET /styles/
xanime/top.jpg?23461411190864713656_ANON_DOES_NOT_FORGIVE
```

HTTP/1.1" 200 95852 "http://www.gigaloader.com/user-message/
ANON_DOES_NOT_FORGIVE" "Mozilla/5.0 (Windows; U; Windows NT 5.1;
en-US; rv:1.8.1.7) Gecko/20070914 Firefox/2.0.0.7"

In the case of Scientology.org, 4chan was sending the message "DDOS BY EBAUMSWORLD" to the church's servers, part of a running gag to blame 4chan's antics on the rival, slightly tamer site. Once the thread's participants started hitting Scientology.org with Gigaloader, another poster described "Phase 2": /b/ would create a shell site and upload to it a video that repeatedly flashed "facts of Scientology and its inner workings." /b/ users would then suggest links to content-sharing site Digg and upload the video to YouTube and YouPorn. Phase 3 would be when mainstream news outlets like Fox and CNN picked up on the video, and an e-mail address on the shell site got a cease and desist order from the Scientology lawyers, which would include the lawyers' names, phone numbers, office addresses, and fax numbers. /b/ should then harass the lawyers, prank-call them, fax them pictures of shock site Goatse, and "complain to her/his boss that she/he is a crack whore/rapist/nigger whatever."

As the /b/ thread on Scientology continued, its contributors became philosophical. This raid was about self-preservation, said one. /b/ was dying. The board had become elitist, sniping at participants who appeared too nerdy and discussing increasingly tame subjects. "The gaiafags, furfags, all the fags that you pushed out, we need to amass a number in the thousands and then strike," they said. "The 3-phase program that anon posted a bit up [*sic*] is foolproof, as long as we work together." Longtime users who had become disenchanted with the site knew it had potential to be more than just an image board, and to live up to the immortal Fox11 line "Internet hate machine."

"We used to be something powerful," another old hand said wistfully. /b/ was now filled with "newfags" who would "bitch and moan" whenever a new raid was proposed. "Long ago, people would jump on the chance to cause massive lulz, annoy the hell out of people, and possibly do some good for the world. I found an army that did not belong to one person, but belonged to each other."

Now an Anon had posted Phase 4, which was getting into Scientology's computer network. "This is the climax of everything," the person said. "Whoever will complete this will be a god in the eyes of Anonymous." Someone had to get into an actual Scientology church, preferably a small one in a small town somewhere. They had to bring a USB drive with a keylogger program, software that could log everything typed into a computer. "You must do whatever is possible to get behind the front desk," they explained. "While they are busy, sneak to the tower of the computer under the desk, load the keylogger, and let it sit. Walk out, and come back in a day or two."

About an hour and ten minutes after that first call-to-arms post, someone noticed the spontaneous DDoS attack they'd been hoping for was working. Gigaloader.com was working. "The scientology site's running slow as shit," they said. It was taking two minutes to load a page that had previously been instantaneous.

"COME ON GUYS," shouted one Anon. "KEEP GIGALOADING!" So frenzied was the atmosphere that only four posts out of hundreds mentioned using a VPN or other anonymizing tools so that people taking part could hide their IP addresses.

By 9:30 p.m., the raid had moved into everyone-get-in-here mode. Someone had posted an IRC network and channel for people to hop in and discuss what would happen next in more detail. The channel was called #raids, and eventually the original poster who had started the thread created a new IRC channel called #xenu. In the Scientology belief system, Xenu was the dictator of the Galactic Confederacy who first brought humans to Earth around seventy-five million years ago, then placed them around various volcanoes and killed them with hydrogen bombs.

By now, hundreds of people were piling into #xenu, and then #target, where self-appointed planners could specify targets with a topic title at the top. Everyone was talking at once in the #xenu channel about what to do next.

"HEY /B/," someone wrote at 9:45 p.m. back on 4chan. The Anon claimed to have found "a bunch of" XSS vulnerabilities on Scientology.org. XSS, or cross-site scripting, was said to be the second most common hacking technique after SQL injection. "I'LL TRY TO MAKE AN EXPLOIT OUT OF IT." The address of the IRC channel kept being spammed. There was a sense the thread was coming to an end, so a few people posted one key takeaway from the discussions on IRC: remember the date January 20. "Shit will go down."

The entire thread had amassed 514 posts in about three hours. Spirits were high. The third to last poster estimated that around two hundred people had been involved in the discussion. By now, Scientology centers around the world were already getting a trickle of prank calls playing the music of Rick Astley, faxes of black paper that would drain their printer cartridges, unwanted pizza deliveries, and unwanted taxis. Their main website was also loading slowly.

The following day, January 16, someone using the nickname Weatherman started a page on Encyclopedia Dramatica, the online repository whose slogan was "In lulz we trust." That page included a declaration of war on Scientology. Then, at 5:47 p.m. eastern standard time, the original poster who had first suggested a chan raid on Scientology congratulated the galvanized troops on /b/ and geared them up for more dramatic action.

"On 15/1/08 [*sic*] war was beginning. Scientology's site is already under heavy bombardment," the OP said. "This is just the tip of the iceberg, the first assault in many to follow. But without the support of the chans, Scientology will brush off this attack. 4chan, answer the call! ... We must destroy this evil and replace it with a greater one—Chanology!"

The portmanteau of "chan" and "Scientology" signified an event that would unite the different image boards, turning their individual battles against pedophiles, MySpace users, and each other into a larger battle against a larger organization. Scientology may have seemed like an odd choice for a target—until then, most visitors to chans probably only knew it as a kooky religion with a few celebrity followers. Suddenly it was becoming the biggest target Anonymous had ever attacked (there were thought to be around twenty-five thousand Scientologists in the United States in 2008) with what seemed like the biggest wave of interest. No one, not even the original poster, knew where this was going, if this would be a single incident or a step forward from the creative anarchy of the Internet.

But why Scientology? A bizarre performance by a celebrity and the unusual belief system of Scientology initially appealed to people who browsed image boards and eBaum's World looking for the strange, new, and titillating. Then Scientology's attempts to suppress the Cruise video invited a vigilante-style attack to right their wrong. Another factor was Scientology's almost neurotic defensiveness. The church was well known by this time to have used intimidation tactics against its critics both in real life and on the Web, which made it perfect "troll bait" for the likes of 4chan and the increasingly organized Anons on Partyvan. Scientology's previous scuffles with online dissenters were already so well known that Canada's *Globe and Mail* dubbed its attempts to remove the Cruise video from YouTube "Scientology vs. The Internet, part XVII." The church had been fighting a war with online dissenters for fifteen years, all the way back to the old days of Usenet newsgroups like alt.religion.scientology in 1994, when ex-members infuriated the church by leaking secret documents.

One other reason, which often applied to the seemingly random things Anonymous did, was because they could. Technology was developing to the point where anyone with an Internet connection could access free web tools like Gigaloader and help take down a website. The Tom Cruise video and the original poster on /b/ had come in at just the right moment. As the attack developed, so did the opportunity to take part. The "firing" on Scientology.org didn't let up; if one person stopped using Gigaloader, two or three others were getting involved.

This was the beginning of a new chapter of Anonymous. The OP had continued on her second post: "If we can destroy Scientology, we can destroy whatever we like!" She reminded 4chan that its users had to "do the right thing" as the largest of the chans, holding the manpower that the "legion" needed. The new thread was as popular as the previous day's, getting 587 responses, including the repeated instructions for using Gigaloader and comments like "I'M IN."

Soon the Anons were DDoSing other websites affiliated with Scientology: rtc.org, img2.scientology.org, and volunteerministers.org. As a result, Scientology.org shut down for twenty-four hours before the church moved its servers to an outside company called 800hosting. There were about ten different software tools that Anons could choose from to help take down the Scientology sites, but the most popular was Gigaloader.

By now, #xenu was teeming with so many people it was becoming impossible to organize anything. Then almost out of nowhere on the second day, a male Anon who was also an administrator on Encyclopedia Dramatica yelled, ALL CAPS: "YOU GUYS NEED TO TALK TO THE PRESS. PUT A PRESS RELEASE TOGETHER. THIS IS BIG." No one so far had organized a group of people to deal with publicity, and hardly anyone in the channel wanted to step up. But a few did. With a few clicks, one person created a channel called #press, announced to the #xenu channel that it was there, and five people joined it. At the top of the channel they had set a topic: "Here's where we're going to talk to the press."

One of the people joining the #press channel was a round-faced man in glasses sitting in his bedroom in Boston. The room doubled as a home office for his freelance software work. Gregg Housh would become instrumental in helping organize the Anons over the next few months, though like others in Anonymous, he would eventually fade into the background as a new generation of figureheads like Sabu and Topiary later emerged. Originally from Dallas, Texas, Housh loved trolling and organizing pranks and was a regular on the Partyvan IRC network. He had a commanding, talkative personality that belied any outward appearance of being a computer geek. He'd done some jail time for his part in coordinating illegal file sharing in his late teens, his term helpfully cut short after he agreed to cooperate with the FBI, according to court documents, and the judge considered his tough upbringing. Housh's father had left when he was four, and his mother was a housecleaner who also cared for a grown daughter with cerebral palsy. Having now been out of jail for a while, Housh was looking to stay out of trouble, since he also had a young daughter. But he couldn't help feeling intrigued by what was happening to Scientology. He jumped into #press and, together with a few others in the chat room, wrote a press release called the "Internet Group Anonymous Declares War On Scientology," listing the tongue-in-cheek source as "ChanEnterprises." They published it.

When the #press channel's participants read over the press release, it sounded so dramatic and ominous that they decided something similar should be narrated in a video, too. A member of the group, whose nickname was VSR, created a YouTube account called Church0fScientology, and the group spent the next several hours finding uncopyrighted footage and music, then writing a video script that could be narrated by an automated voice. The speech recognition technology was so bad they had to go back and misspell most of the words—destroyed became "dee stroid," for instance—to make it sound natural. The final script ended up looking like nonsense but sounding like normal prose.

When they finally put it together, a Stephen Hawking–style robotic voice said over an image of dark clouds, "Hello, leaders of Scientology, we are Anonymous." It climbed to new heights of hyperbole, vowing to "systematically dismantle the Church of Scientology in its current form....For the good of your followers, for the good of mankind—for the laughs—we shall expel you from the Internet." Housh and the group of publicity reps weren't taking any of this seriously. But as they were putting finishing touches on the video and joking about how this "war" would be one of the funniest trolling events of all time, lasting a few days at most, a French PhD student in the group suddenly got serious with them.

"Guys, what we are doing today is going to change the world," he said.

The others in the group stopped for a moment and then laughed, Housh later recalled.

"Gtfo," wrote one. "Quit your jibber jabber." But the French Anon was unrelenting. Tens of thousands of people were going to watch the video they were making. This was the start of something major, "and we just don't know what it is yet."

Housh and the others shrugged and carried on, according to Housh. They called the video *Message to Scientology,* published it on January 21, and posted links all over the chans and Digg. Having worked on the video through the night, most of them went to sleep.

The next morning, Housh's girlfriend at the time nudged him awake. "You need to get back onto your computer," she said. "Stuff is blowing up."

Housh fell out of bed, fumbled for his glasses, and stared at his screen. The Partyvan IRC network was crashing as thousands of new people tried piling into #xenu.

"We had DDoS'd ourselves," he later recalled in an interview. The video had been picked up by Gawker and another tech site called The Register, and thousands had seen it. Later that day, around ten thousand people were trying to get into #xenu, and the IRC network hosts on Partyvan kicked everyone off the network. Housh and the others tried to get everyone to move to another IRC network, which immediately went down. Fortunately, the Partyvan admins came back, saying they had added five more servers so that the horde could return. Most communication for Anonymous was now taking place on Partyvan IRC servers.

It was a whirlwind for Housh and the others. Waking up and realizing that thousands of people wanted to take part in this prank, they suddenly had it dawn on them that people were paying attention and they couldn't just do something silly.

Over the next forty-eight hours, #press began filling up with a few more people who liked setting agendas. Realizing that the chat room was starting to turn into an organizational hub, the group, who hadn't known one another before these last few days, changed the channel's name to #marblecake. By picking a random name, their room was more likely to remain private, allowing them to avoid the distraction of visitors and focus on organizing. For the first couple of days they were stumped on what to do next and argued about how the masses should proceed.

"We had no clue what we were doing," Housh remembered. Should they hit Scientology with more DDoS attacks? Prank them in some other way? They decided the first port of call was to stop #xenu from collapsing. They asked the IRC operators to limit the channel to a hundred people so that any more than that would be automatically kicked out. They then directed people to join channels based on the city nearest to them, such as #London, #LA, #Paris, or #NY. Over the next six hours, the legion self-segregated.

The first DDoS attacks on Scientology had been carried out using simple Web tools like Gigaloader and JMeter. Within a few days, though, they were usurped by what would become the two most popular weapons in the Anonymous arsenal: botnets and the Low-Orbit Ion Cannon (LOIC).

Botnets would not be used significantly by Anonymous for a few more years, but they were easily the more powerful of two key weapons. These were large networks of "zombie" computers usually controlled by a single person who gave them commands from a private IRC channel. It's rumored that botnets were used just once or twice during the first Anonymous attacks on Chanology, though few details are known. Often botnets are made up of between ten thousand and one hundred thousand computers around the world. The biggest botnets, ones that have the power to take out the servers of small governments, have upward of a million computers. The computers belong to average people like you and me, oblivious to what is going on—often we'll have joined a botnet by accidentally downloading infected software or visiting a compromised website. Perhaps someone sent us a spam e-mail with a link promising free photo prints or a cash prize, or we clicked on an interesting video that disguised malicious code.

Nothing appears to be amiss after such software downloads. It installs itself quickly and quietly and for the most part remains dormant. When the botnet controller issues commands to a network of "bots," a signal is sent to the infected computer, and the small program that was downloaded starts up in the background without the owner's realizing it. (Who knows—your computer could be taking part in a DDoS attack right now.) The network of thousands of computers will act together, as if they were one single computer. Typically, botnets will use their bots to send spam, find security vulnerabilities in other websites, or launch a DDoS attack on a corporate website while the controller demands a ransom to stop. In underground hacker culture, larger botnets translate to greater street cred for the controllers, or botmasters.

It's unclear how many computers in the world have been assimilated into botnets, but the number is at least in the tens of millions, with the greatest number of bot-infested computers in the United States and China. In 2009 the Shadowserver Foundation reported that there were thirty-five hundred identified botnets in the world, more than double the number in 2007. In March 2010 Spanish police arrested three men behind a botnet called Mariposa, Spanish for "butterfly." Discovered by white-hat hackers (cyber security specialists) and law enforcement agents in 2008, the monster botnet was made up of as many as twelve million zombie computers and had been used to launch DDoS attacks, send out e-mail spam, and steal personal details. The ringleaders made money on the side by renting it out.

Renting a botnet was far less risky than making one yourself, and with the right skill set and contacts, they were surprisingly easy to come by. A 2010 study by Web infrastructure company VeriSign showed the average rate for renting a botnet from an underground marketplace was $67 for twenty-four hours and just $9 for one hour. Renting a botnet that could take out the servers of a small government might cost around $200 an hour. Botnets used by Anonymous in both the Chanology attacks of 2008 and Op Payback in 2010–11 were both rented and self-created, and sources say there was also a range of botnet sizes. But it was the super botnets, controlled by a small handful of people, that could do the most damage.

The second weapon in the Anonymous arsenal was the Low Orbit Ion Cannon, whose acronym is pronounced "lo-ick." In terms of power, it was piddling against a botnet—like the difference between a long-range missile and a handgun—but the software was free and easy for anyone with a computer to access. From the start of Chanology onward, LOIC started replacing Gigaloader in popularity. The origins of the software program are a little unclear, but it is widely thought to have first been developed by a programmer nicknamed Praetox, who was eighteen at the time, lived in Oslo, Norway, and enjoyed programming and "running in the woods," according to his website.

Praetox made all sorts of things on his computer, including cheats for the online role-playing game Tibia and a program that would make windows on a computer desktop look transparent. He was also versed in chan culture and used the cartoon image of a "Pool's closed" sign for his YouTube account. The name LOIC itself comes from a weapon in the Command & Conquer video game series, and of all his creations it would be Praetox's legacy.

Praetox appears to have originally created LOIC as an open source project, which meant anyone could improve it. Eventually, a programmer nicknamed NewEraCracker made some tweaks that allowed LOIC to send out useless requests or "packets" to a server, making it what it is today. At the time, packets were part of everything one did on the Internet. Visiting a web page involved receiving a series of packets, as did sending an e-mail, with a typical packet containing 1–1,500 bytes. They can be compared to addressed envelopes in the postal service. "Packet sniffing" meant trying to figure out what was inside a piece of mail by looking at what was on the envelope. The data inside a file could be encrypted, but the packet itself would always identify the sender and receiver.

A DDoS attack was, in one way, like overwhelming someone with thousands of pieces of junk mail that they had no choice but to open. One defense was to "filter the packets," which would be like asking a doorman to not allow any mail from a certain sender. But DDoS protection costs money, and it was difficult to filter the junk packets from LOIC, since they were coming from many different users. Ultimately, if enough people used the program and "aimed" it at the same site at the same time, they could overload it with enough junk traffic to take it offline. The effect was similar to a botnet's, except instead of having infected computers, the participants were voluntarily joining the network. A key difference was effectiveness. The effect of LOIC was far more unpredictable than that of traditional botnets, since popularity and human error came into play. You might need four thousand people to take the website of a major corporation down, in the same way you'd need four thousand people wielding handguns to destroy a small building. You'd need just a few hundred people to take down a tiny homemade website belonging to an individual. The upside was that downloading LOIC was free and easy—you could get it from a torrent site or 4chan's /rs/ board.

One of the hundreds of people who downloaded LOIC and took part in some of the first impromptu Scientology attacks was a college student named Brian Mettenbrink. An Iowa State University student with a mop of brown hair and a beard, Mettenbrink, eighteen, was sitting in front of his desktop computer in a dorm room, browsing through his favorite website, 7chan, when he first saw posts about a Scientology raid in January 2008. He did not care about Scientology, but he was interested in exploring the world of IT security and reasoned that taking part in an attack like this was a good way to learn about the other side of the industry. Besides, with so many other people contributing to the attack, he wouldn't get caught.

Mettenbrink, who had been regularly visiting 4chan since he was fifteen, went to the site's /rs/ board and downloaded LOIC. The download took a few seconds, and it included a "readme" file to explain how to use it. The program gave the impression that it was connecting users to an army of rebel fighters. When Mettenbrink first opened LOIC, the main window that popped up had a *Star Wars*–themed design: dark and light green text boxes, and a Photoshopped mock-up of the Anti-Orbital Ion Cannon used in *Star Wars: The Clone Wars,* blasting a thick green laser beam toward a planet.

There were options to "Select a target," by adding in a URL, and a button saying "Lock on." Once you had a locked target, a large box in the middle would show its server's IP address as the program geared up for an attack. Next came another big button labeled "IMMA CHARGIN MAH LAZER," followed by options to configure the attack. During the first DDoS attacks on Scientology, the LOIC was always in "manual mode," which meant users would decide where and when to fire and what type of junk packets to send out.

Once an attack was under way, a status bar at the very bottom would show the program as being Idle, Connecting, Requesting, Downloading, or Failed. If "Requesting," a number would start rising rapidly. Once it froze, that meant the LOIC was stuck or the target was down. You could check by visiting the target website—if you got a "Network Timeout" error message, it meant mission accomplished.

There was no buzz or rush of feeling when Mettenbrink first fired LOIC at Scientology.org, especially since the program froze as soon as it started. He checked his configurations, and when the program got going again, he minimized the window and went back to wasting time on 7chan. Unlike Gregg Housh, Mettenbrink was a casual participant in Chanology. He did not bother joining an IRC channel like #xenu or finding out what Anonymous might do next. Instead, he kept LOIC running for several days and nights in the background of his computer, eventually forgetting he was running it at all. Only when he noticed that the program was starting to slow down his Internet connection did he switch it off—about three days after starting it.

"I am not responsible for how you use this tool," LOIC programmer NewEraCracker had written as a disclaimer for the program when he uploaded his tweaked version to the Web. "You cannot blame me if you get caught for attacking servers you don't own." It was crucial for people who were using LOIC to run it through an anonymizing network like Tor to hide their IP addresses from the target or police. But there were plenty of oblivious supporters, like Mettenbrink, who ran LOIC straight off their own computer with no special software. This was often because they did not know how, or they didn't realize that using LOIC was illegal.

On top of that, more Anons were communicating on IRC networks, which meant they had nicknames and reputations to uphold. Now there wasn't just the attraction of being part of a mob—there was a sense of obligation to return and join in with future attacks. Some participants in a Chanology IRC channel knew, for instance, that returning to an IRC channel the following day also meant reacquainting themselves with a new stable of online friends, who might think less of them if they didn't turn up. This wasn't like /b/, where you could suddenly disappear and no one would notice.

Chanology was turning into a new community of hundreds of people, and it brought the collective to a point where communication was gradually splitting between image boards and IRC networks. Image boards like 4chan had been using LOIC for a couple of years; the /b/tards were forever declaring war on other sites that they claimed were stealing credit for their memes and content, such as eBaum's World or the blogging site Tumblr. But now more Anons were starting to use IRC networks to coordinate and follow instructions for DDoS attacks. Beginning in January 2008, organizers had also started publishing announcements on Chanology and how-to guides on the Partyvan network so that the sudden influx of thousands of "newfags" from all over the world to these new online protests could learn about LOIC and IRC channels without having to ask.

The DDoS attacks on Scientology reached a pinnacle on January 19, when the church's main website was hit by 488 attacks from different computers. Several media outlets, among them Fox and Sky News, reported that the online disruptions were being caused by a "small clique of super hackers." This was a terrible misconception. Only a few Anonymous supporters were skilled hackers. Many more were simply young Internet users who felt like doing something other than wasting time on 4chan or 7chan.

When someone posted an announcement on Partyvan that there would be a third, bigger DDoS attack on January 24, about five hundred people are rumored to have taken part. But by then, Scientology had called in Prolexic Technologies, a specialist in DDoS protection based in Hollywood, Florida, to help shield their servers. Soon the LOIC-based attacks stopped having an effect and the Scientology sites were up and running as normal.

Scientology then hit back through the media, telling *Newsweek* in early February that Anonymous was "a group of cyber-terrorists...perpetrating religious hate crimes against Churches of Scientology." The strong wording didn't help Scientology's cause, bearing in mind a famous phrase on the Internet: "Don't feed the troll." By appearing defensive, Scientology was inadvertently provoking more Anons to take part in the attacks. And because joining Anonymous was so easy—at minimum you had to enter an IRC channel, or /b/, and join in the conversation— hundreds of new people started looking in.

Then Anonymous found another way to cause a stir. Back in #marblecake, Housh had noticed one team member who had been quiet for the past four days. He asked him to figure out how many cities and countries were being represented on the chat network. When the scout came back, he reported that there were 140 to 145 different Chanology channels and participants in forty-two countries in total.

"What do we do with all these people?" one of the team asked. They started searching the Internet to see what opponents of Scientology had done in the past and stumbled across a video of anti-Scientology campaigner Tory "Magoo" Christmam, who was dancing and shouting in front of a Scientology center.

"This is hilarious," a team member said. "We should totally make the Internet go outside."

"We have to put them in the streets," the French member who'd been studying for a PhD said. Housh didn't agree, and he argued with the Frenchman for the next three hours. Eventually, Housh relented, deciding that a real-world confrontation between Anons and the public could be rather amusing.

"We honestly thought the funniest thing we could do to Scientology was get in front of their buildings," Housh later said.

The group started working on their next video, their "call to arms," and then a code of conduct after a Greenpeace activist came on IRC and said they needed to make sure protesters didn't throw things at buildings or punch cops. Housh started taking an increasingly organizational role, dishing out responsibilities and bringing discussions back on topic when they veered off into jokes of firebombing or Xbox games.

On January 26, someone calling himself "Anon Ymous" sent an e-mail to Gawker's "tips" address, about a forthcoming protest outside the Church of Scientology in Harlem. "Wear a mask of your choosing," it said. "Bring a boombox. Rickroll them into submission. We will make headlinez LOL." There was also a tagline at the bottom, which was appearing on YouTube, blogs, and forum posts:

We are Anonymous
We are Legion

We do not forgive
We do not forget
Expect us.

This now infamous closing signature, reminiscent of *Star Trek* bad guys the Borg, comes from the 47 Rules of the Internet. After rules 1 and 2, which were to never talk about /b/, came:

Rule 3. We are Anonymous.
Rule 4. Anonymous is legion.
Rule 5. Anonymous never forgives.

Some say the twisting of rule 4 into "we" are legion comes from the Bible passage of Mark 5:9, wherein Jesus approaches a man possessed by demons. "And He [Jesus] asked the man, 'What is thy name?' And he answered saying, 'My name is Legion: for we are many.'" The *Message to Scientology* YouTube video said: "If you want another name for your opponent, then call us Legion, for we are many."

Over the next few months, more people from 4chan, 711chan, and IRC were taking part in real-world protests. On February 2, 2008, about 150 people gathered for the first time outside a Church of Scientology center in Orlando, Florida. A week later, the *Tampa Bay Tribune* reported that seven thousand people had protested against church centers in seventy-three cities world-wide. Often the protesters were people in their teens and early twenties, standing in groups or sitting around in lawn chairs, holding signs with Internet memes and yelling at passersby. Some of the participants saw the demonstrations as being tongue-in-cheek, an elaborate prank by the Internet itself on an established organization. Many others took the protests seriously and held up signs with messages like "$cientology Kills." One YouTube account associating itself with Anonymous ran a regular news program on YouTube called AnonyNews. It featured an anchor reporting on the real-life protests around the world. He wore a dark suit and a red tie, slicked-back hair, and the same grinning white mask worn by the protagonist V in the 2006 dystopian movie *V for Vendetta* that was fast becoming a symbol for Anonymous. This was thanks to a key scene in the film, which showed thousands of people wearing V's mask in solidarity with the main character, loosely based on British revolutionary Guy Fawkes.

That V mask was everywhere at Anonymous's demonstrations, hiding protesters' faces so that in at least some form they could still be anonymous in the real world. Over time, the mask would come to represent the one-half of Anonymous who took the idea of revolution and protest seriously. People like William, who thought Anonymous should be about fun and pranks, abhorred it. (Time Warner profited from the sale of more than one hundred thousand V masks every year by 2011, while other masks associated with its films sold barely half that figure.)

When passersby approached the demonstrators to ask who had organized the protests, DDoS attacks, pranks, and cyber attacks, no one knew an official answer. Most regular volunteers did not see the small groups of self-appointed organizers in the background who were pulling various strings.

But the physical protests were working, and when they first got under way, Housh remembered the scout who had counted all the different country and city chans and, assuming that he liked grunt work, asked him to go into the channels for each major city and look for one person who appeared to be giving orders and generally taking responsibility. "Look for them in Paris, London, New York," Housh said.

The scout spent the next three days dropping in on an array of city-based chat rooms and looking out for the organizational minds, anyone who seemed especially keen on the cause. He then started a private chat with each, asking if they had seen the first

Message to Scientology video. "One of the guys who made that wants to talk to you," he would tell them. Intrigued, and probably a little nervous, they would then be led into #marblecake and told not to tell anyone about the channel.

"We're not trying to control everyone," Housh would explain to them. "But bringing lists of suggestions and hoping people go with it." Over the next two weeks #marblecake grew to about twenty-five talented members, including Web designers who could throw together a website in a day and organizational types who knew to call the police about obtaining protest permits.

By the end of March, a few people had also set up new websites for Chanology, which included discussion forums. These were places for the new Chanology community to hang out, and two popular sites were Enturbulation.org and WhyWeProtest.net. Chanology was now no longer being discussed on 4chan—it had permanently moved to these sites and IRC channels. For the next few months, Anonymous continued holding mostly small, physical protests around the world, while Housh was helping maintain regular meetings every three days in #marblecake to discuss attack strategies against Scientology.

The meetings would last anywhere from three to six hours, Housh remembered. He would post an agenda of points, hear reports of what people had done, and delegate responsibilities, from making a website, to designing a flyer that advertised the next raid, to finding background music for the next YouTube video. The group tried to plan Anonymous events over the following month. Before then, no one had actually been scheduling Anonymous raids or pranks in advance.

Here's an example of what the #marblecake channel had as a "topic," based on a chat log from Friday, June 6:

03[19:44] * Topic is 'press releases, videos, ideas, collaboration, basically things we need done. || Meeting thursday nights at 9pm EST ||

/msg srsbsns for cosnews.net writefagaccounts || you should think of things you hate about the present state of chanology and want changed.'
03[19:44] * Set by gregg on Fri Jun 06 19:27:08

"I started running it with an iron fist," he said. "Very few [meetings] were missed." If someone couldn't make it to a meeting, there was a Google doc they could read to catch up.

By June, motivations were fizzling out and people in #marblecake were reminiscing about when Chanology first kicked off in January.

"I loved the old days," said one user called 007, in a June meeting. "No one knew what was gonna happen IRL [in real life]. Everyone was totally into it. I wish we could get the same amount of participation as before."

By the summer of 2008, Project Chanology was also suffering from infighting among organizers, and the number of participants in physical demonstrations, which had been occurring monthly in major cities, was tapering off. Housh claimed that a blow to the fledgling movement came that summer when a couple of Anons nicknamed King Nerd and Megaphonebitch outed #marblecake and the people in it, labeling them "leaderfags" and prompting most of the people who started the organizational hub to leave. In the coming months, Chanology wouldn't so much wrap up as unceremoniously fade away. Many Anons were simply bored with Project Chanology, by any measurement the longest and biggest series of attacks that Anonymous had ever initiated against a single target.

The Federal Bureau of Investigation, meanwhile, was just getting started. Also by the summer of 2008, the FBI, or "feds" as Anons referred to them, had managed to track down and apprehend two out of the hundreds of people who participated in the

DDoS attacks on Scientology. They would be the unlucky sacrificial lambs and the first of scores more arrests over the next few years. Anons had always thought till now that they were immune to arrest, or well hidden from the authorities. One of the first to learn the hard truth was Brian Mettenbrink, the bored college student who in January 2008 had left LOIC running in the background of his computer for a little too long.

"Brian."

"Yeah?" Brian Mettenbrink was asleep on his couch in the basement when he heard the voice of his housemate calling his name. It was a cool morning in mid-July 2008, six months since he had downloaded LOIC and taken part in the very first DDoS attacks by Anonymous against Scientology. He barely remembered that weekend spent mostly in his dorm room. Since then, he had dropped out of his aerospace engineering classes at Iowa State, moved into a large, pea-green house with a few friends in Omaha, Nebraska, and started looking for a job to help pay the rent.

"There's some men here to see you."

He sat up. Bleary-eyed, Mettenbrink padded up the stairs and went to the door, wearing the plain t-shirt and shorts he'd been sleeping in. Two men in suits were standing on the doorstep. They each took out a badge and identified themselves as FBI agents. They asked Mettenbrink if he had time for "a friendly conversation." Mettenbrink answered yes and invited them in. He still had no idea that this had anything to do with DDoS attacks.

The agents walked through the arched entranceway of Mettenbrink's house, their shoes clicking on the ceramic tile floor as they entered the dining room, and sat at a wooden table. Mettenbrink adjusted the wire-rim glasses on his nose. He was more oblivious than nervous at this point. The agents began asking him questions about the attacks last January and about Anonymous itself.

"What does Anonymous think of Scientology?" one of them asked. "What's its stance?"

"I know Anonymous doesn't like Scientology," Mettenbrink said, telling them about the flurry of excited posts about a Scientology raid on 4chan and 7chan. "They were saying we should attack their websites." Mettenbrink had been reading up on Scientology after the attacks and added that the religion's beliefs were "weird," and that it charged people hundreds of dollars to be members.

"Were you involved in the DDoS attacks?" one of the men asked. Mettenbrink shifted in his seat.

"I was involved for a little bit," he said. The computer he had used to run LOIC was now sitting downstairs in the basement.

"Did you…enjoy taking part in the attacks?"

"Yeah," said Mettenbrink, thinking back to how dull he had found college. "It was fun. It was something new and interesting to do."

"Did you know that your actions were a criminal violation?" one of the men asked.

"Sure," Mettenbrink said, "I just didn't think the FBI would be showing up at my door." He stared at the two men. Mettenbrink had known all along that using LOIC was illegal, but he had no idea it was a serious criminal offense. He believed the crime was as bad as running a red light, the punishment akin to a speeding ticket or hundred-dollar fine. Later he would regret being so open with the agents.

The two men then told Mettenbrink that an FBI investigation had shown that an IP address used in the attacks traced back to Mettenbrink's computer. "Do you understand that?" they asked.

"Yes," he said.

"Do you know anyone from the group in real life?" one of the agents asked.

"No," said Mettebrink.

The "friendly conversation" lasted about an hour, giving the FBI and, later, prosecuting attorneys representing the Church of Scientology evidence to use against the hapless Mettenbrink. Later, the FBI would contact his old college to access his Internet records. Mettenbrink didn't hear from the FBI again for months, and it was a year before he truly realized, during a conversation with his lawyer, the seriousness of his offense. "Do you have any idea how much monetary damage the Church of Scientology is saying you caused?" the lawyer had asked during one of his meetings with Mettenbrink.

The young man thought for a moment. "I can't imagine there was any monetary damage," he said. All he'd done was help send a bunch of spoof traffic to a website and slow it down for a couple days.

"They're claiming one hundred thousand dollars," the lawyer replied. Mettenbrink was stunned. He had attacked Scientology.org on a whim, his weapon a tiny, freely available program he'd run in the background for three days while he browsed an image board. How could that have cost someone a hundred thousand dollars?

Eventually, Scientology lowered its estimate for damages to twenty thousand dollars. Mettenbrink would have to pay it all back, but at least it wasn't a hundred thousand. Prosecutors representing the Church of Scientology in Los Angeles also called for a twelve-month jail sentence, adding that a probationary sentence, or one that avoided jail time, "might embolden others to use the Internet to engage in hate crimes."

According to his sentencing memo, Mettenbrink had been given "every advantage in life," coming from a close, "supportive" family in Nebraska and parents who helped pay his way through college. He was also said to have "special skills" with computers and hardware. In court, a lawyer representing Scientology used words like *Nazis* and *terrorism* when he described Anonymous.

On January 25, 2010, almost two years to the day he downloaded the LOIC tool, Mettenbrink pleaded guilty in a federal court to accessing a protected computer, having agreed to serve a year in prison. He would be only the second person to be sent to jail for joining in an Anonymous DDoS attack. In November 2009, nineteen-year-old Dmitriy Guzner of Verona, New Jersey, had been sentenced to a year and a day in federal prison.

In the meantime, IT security experts were scratching their heads about this new breed of hacktivists who seemed to have come out of nowhere. Prolexic, the security company that had gained some experience protecting Scientology from the DDoS attacks, had some advice for future targets of Anonymous.

"Let sleeping dogs lie," the company said, adding that, once a DDoS attack finished, stop talking about it. "Don't issue warnings or threats to the attackers via the media; this will only keep the issue alive, raise tempers and greatly enhance the possibility of another assault. Most DDoS attackers seek publicity, so don't hand it to them on a silver platter." Scientology, of course, had done just that.

What few realized was that as Anonymous had responded to Scientology's provocations, its participants also split into two camps. People had already seen it in the demonstrations, with the differences between the signs scrawled with lighthearted jokes and those with serious remonstrations against Scientology. This was the evolution of a fundamental divide between those who believed in Anonymous's roots in fun and lulz, and the new, activist direction it was taking. In the coming years, this split in motivations would make it harder to define what Anonymous was trying to be. It would even drive a wedge between Topiary and Sabu, and as Chanology started to fizzle out, one of Sabu's biggest future adversaries would take to the stage.

CHAPTER 6

Civil War

While most of the participants in Anonymous were young single men, women joined in, too, some of them married and with children. When news of Chanology reached California, a married mother of four named Jennifer Emick decided to investigate. At thirty-six with black hair and Celtic jewelry, Emick was intrigued by the snippets of information she had heard about Chanology. When she was younger, a member of her family had become involved with Scientology and had had a harrowing experience, convincing Emick that the church was evil. Emick ended up becoming a writer who specialized in new religious movements and religious symbolism. By the time Chanology came along she was writing off and on about religion and esoteric issues for About.com, an informational website affiliated with the *New York Times*.

Armed with a notebook, she went along to the first Anonymous protests in front of a Scientology center in San Francisco on February 10, 2008, to write a report. There were between two hundred and three hundred people at the event, including ex-Scientologist celebrities and the son of founder L. Ron Hubbard.

On the same day, about eight hundred Anonymous supporters attended protests in front of Scientology centers in Australia, and more in London, Paris, Berlin, New York, Los Angeles, Chicago, Toronto, and Dublin. Between seven thousand and eight thousand people took part, in ninety-three cities worldwide, according to local news reports. But Emick saw past the protesters' playful attitude. She was enthralled by how momentous these new demonstrations seemed to be. Emick decided to return for another protest the following month, this time as a participant.

She liked the way demonstrators were well behaved toward police officers. The protesters were equally impressed by Emick's forceful personality and ability to throw watertight arguments at Scientology representatives. They designated her a resident expert on Scientology. Emick explained that the church's intimidation tactics were perfectly normal. Scientology reps had been following demonstrators home, accusing them of "perpetrating religious hate crimes." At the Los Angeles event in March, a man thought by some protesters to be aligned with Scientology flashed a gun to the crowd. A protester began following him around with a placard saying, "This guy has a gun." Emick noticed that the more Scientology overreacted, the more enthusiastic the protesters became. The organization's prickly defensiveness made it the perfect troll bait.

As more Anonymous supporters published research on Scientology online, they discovered new reasons to keep up the fight. "People were thinking, 'Holy cow, they're not just entertainingly crazy, they've hurt people,'" Emick remembered a few years later. When one researcher got hold of what was alleged to be a list of murdered Scientology defectors, the mood toward the church darkened considerably. Scientology had gone from being a kooky plaything to an evil organization that the protesters felt deserved punishment and exposure. Emick threw herself into the cause. This was now full-blown activism.

Of course, not everyone liked where this was going. Activism was not what Anonymous was about, some argued, and betrayed its origins in fun and lulz. Many of the original /b/tards who had pushed for a Scientology raid were now criticizing the continuing campaign as being hijacked by "moralfags."

One of those critics was Wesley Bailey. Tall, thin, with a military buzz cut, Bailey was twenty-seven and a network administrator for the army, working on a Fort Hood military base in dusty Killeen, Texas. He had been a soldier for nine years, enlisting when he was eighteen. In the summer of 2008, he was married and had two small children, a boy and a girl. His was an unconventional family life: Bailey and his wife were swingers, and he loved spending hours surfing the net and chatting with people online. When he first stumbled on 4chan, he was confused by forced anonymity and disturbed by the wild creativity and shocking images. It took him months to get used to the phrases and weird porn, but slowly he got hooked. He realized that this was a unique place in which people could say whatever they wanted, no matter how dark or improper. He also liked the vigilante justice, watching someone on /b/ post the photo of a known pedophile and getting scores of others to help him find out his name and address. He started seeing "Anonymous" referred to as an entity and realized it had power. When he saw a series of 4chan posts on Project Chanology, including long articles about Scientology that were being farmed to other websites like Enturbulation.com, he realized this was a new level of collective pranks and online harassment.

Like Emick, Bailey went to one of the simultaneous worldwide protests on February 10, in Houston, Texas. Like Emick, he was also enthralled by the demonstrators, but not because of the good behavior or collaboration. Messing with Scientologists was entertaining. He saw one woman draw occult symbols on the sidewalk in front of the Scientology center, then sprinkle foot powder around the symbols and add flickering black candles. The idea was to spook Scientologists who were deeply suspicious of black magic and the occult. He joined other Anons in offering Scientologists cake if they would come join the protest. This was a nod to the "delicious cake" meme. They also played an audio version of OT3, confidential documents that are believed by Scientologists to lead them to a spiritual state known as Operating Thetan. Adherents are not supposed to listen to or read them until they are ready. Bailey found it hilarious.

"But then," he remembered a few years later, "they stopped coming out to play." By the end of 2008, Scientology stopped responding, and the demonstrations and cyber attacks stopped altogether. Bailey and Emick wound up in the middle of the infighting that followed.

There were dramatic rows between the IRC network operators and admins on Partyvan, between the people who ran Anonymous forums, and between protest organizers. There was discord among the original anti-Scientologist campaigners who had been there long before the Anonymous flood came along. Emick recalled a spat between two organizers, with one supporter accusing another of cheating with her husband, then "freezing out" mutual acquaintances to create a rift. The war of words escalated to lofty heights of machismo—this was the Internet, after all.

"You have no idea who you're fucking with," Emick remembered one person saying. "Just wait and see what's coming."

If 2008 was the year Anonymous burst into the real world with well-organized demonstrations, 2009 was when it started unraveling into the chaos of e-drama. The biggest rift was over what Anonymous was about. Activism? Or lulz? And it was to be fought between moralfags like Emick and trolls like Bailey.

In late 2008, just before being deployed with the army to South Korea for a year, Bailey had set up a new website called ScientologyExposed.com. The protests were dying down, but Anons were still communicating online, albeit more chaotically. His idea was to create an alternative to Gregg Housh's more popular Enturbulation.com (which turned into the slick-looking WhyWeProtest.net). Housh had by now given many interviews to newspapers and television reporters about Anonymous after being outed by name, and Enturbulation was his baby. He told journalists that he was absolutely not an Anonymous "spokesman," since no one could speak for the collective, but more of an observer. By then, he'd gotten burned in the courts. The Church of Scientology had sued Housh for trespassing, criminal harassment, disturbing an assembly of worship, and disturbing the peace. When the protests were at their peak, a Scientology spokesman told CNN that the church was "dealing with six death threats, bomb threats, acts of violence," and vandalism from Anonymous. Housh didn't exactly fit the stereotype of an activist, but Bailey didn't like him or his site.

Bailey believed the people surrounding Enterbulation were too earnest, too "moralfaggy" to be effective. Housh's site had become the de facto meeting ground, and there needed to be an alternative. Bailey designed his site to encourage pranks and trolling over peaceful activism against the church. The site contained hidden forums, a section of "fun stuff" like WiFi-router passwords used by Scientology organizations, and tips for pranks. One was to send an official-looking letter of warning to each of the highest-ranking leaders of Scientology to freak them out.

Bailey was dedicated to maintaining his site even while stationed in South Korea, working on it for four to six hours in the evening and on weekends. It was a tough schedule. He would work on the site until 1:00 or 2:00 in the morning, then get up at 5:00 a.m. to do an hour of jogging and physical training with the other soldiers while it was still dark outside. Bailey hated all the running and developed shin splints, but he looked forward every evening to getting back on his laptop in his dorm. He had fully embraced the goal of destroying Scientology and made new friends along the way. One of them was Jennifer Emick.

Bailey and Emick first began talking on an online forum. Bailey liked Emick's chutzpah and invited her to be an administrator on his site. Over time, though, he realized the two had starkly different views about Anonymous. Emick didn't understand the darker side of chan culture and seemed to think Anonymous should focus on peaceful protest. The two hard-talking individuals began to have blazing public arguments. The final straw came one day when the pair was fighting on the site's anonymous forum, and Emick suddenly said, "I know it's you, Raziel." By outing Bailey's regular online nickname, Raziel, Emick had betrayed an important custom on forums like this: that hiding your online identity, or nickname, could be just as important as hiding your real-world identity. Enraged, Bailey removed Emick's administrative access and the two stopped talking.

Looking back, Bailey said Emick had realized that Anonymous was not a peaceful protest group but "full of hackers and people on the net who don't do nice things for fun....It broke her," Bailey added. "She had invested so much personal pride in it."

Years later Emick also found it hard to talk about why she broke away from Anonymous. "The group itself was losing sight of...I don't want to pinpoint exactly," she said. "In 2008 and 2009 there was a group ethos. You weren't confrontational with the community, you didn't yell at cops, you were a good example. You fight an evil cult you can't be evil yourself. Then at some point they said, 'Well, why not?'"

Emick seemed to revel in the drama and gossip, but she hated the threats and real-life mischief. What had happened to the well-behaved ethos at those first protests? Anonymous was becoming increasingly vindictive not only toward Scientology but to other Anons who didn't agree with its methods. This nastiness was nothing new for people like Bailey, who had found Anonymous via the netherworld of 4chan, but for Emick it was a crushing betrayal.

"We tried to tell her Anonymous isn't nice and it isn't your friend," Bailey said. "We tried to tell her these aren't good people. They are doing fucked-up things because it's funny." Eventually, Emick became a target herself. The more she tried telling other Anons that they were being irresponsible bullies, the more they threw insults and threats back at her. People found out her real name and address and posted it online, along with her husband's details. People from various schisms in Anonymous began harassing her stepdaughter. There was talk of SWATing her house—calling up the FBI to send a SWAT team, a surprisingly easy prank to carry out. Soon Emick got her family to move to Michigan and started going online from a fake server that hid her true IP address. Though she was breaking away, Emick would come back more than a year later, having honed her skills in social engineering and "doxing," helping to nearly rip Anonymous apart.

Military man Bailey had meanwhile become fascinated by a subset of Anonymous that everyone wanted to join but few could understand: the hackers. He had noticed that a small contingent of skilled hackers had checked out Chanology early on in the project but had left. As Anonymous descended into a chaotic civil war between moralfags and trolls, Bailey set out to find the hackers. He wanted to be able to do what they could do: track down an enemy, steal someone's botnet, or hack their servers. It bothered Bailey that he didn't have these skills already. First, however, he had to make a drastic change to his personal life, after leaving the army in 2009.

Since childhood, Bailey had harbored deep, secret feelings that he was really female. Even as he and his wife pursued a polyamorous relationship and went to swinging parties, he had kept those particular feelings repressed. Soon after leaving the army, though, Bailey became friends online with a transgender woman and felt an instant attraction. She was beautiful and confident, and Bailey started to believe it might be possible for him to look and feel the same. On May 26, 2009, he bought a case of hormone replacement therapy (HRT) pills online and started secretly taking them. He was excited but decided to see how he felt before telling his family about his decision. The pills ended up taking effect more quickly than he had expected; within a month he had developed B-cup breasts.

He asked his mother and brother to come over and sat them down in the living room with his wife and two children, ages three and two at the time. It took him an hour of stalling to finally get to the point, but eventually he told them why they were there. He wanted to undergo a sex change and become a woman. They were stunned into silence. Eventually one of them asked if Bailey was sure he wanted to do it. He told them flat-out that he had already begun taking estrogen supplements. He knew that they would try to talk him out of it, so he had resolved to be firm.

He gave them two choices: accept that he was becoming a woman or stay out of his life. Not long after that meeting, he and his wife filed for divorce, agreeing to share custody of their two children. Bailey's mother and brother were accepting. Bailey went by the name Laurelai, the name his mother had picked in case he'd been born a girl.

Laurelai had an educational mountain ahead of her. Learning how to be female was like going through puberty all over again. It was tough, but she felt that she was becoming the person she was meant to be. Soon her soldier's buzz cut had grown long and she was walking around the house in pink tank tops. In the mornings she would sit down in front of her computer and take a few hormone pills with a swig from a bottle of Coke. As she left her old sexuality behind, she also wanted to change what she was online, from a simple website administrator to a full-fledged hacker. She started exploring the darker arts of the Web while maintaining her website, ScientologyExposed. It was now late 2009, and as the site got fewer visitors, Laurelai realized the goal of "destroying Scientology" was probably too grand.

One day, someone started attacking her site. Laurelai checked the site's configurations and saw it was getting flooded with so much junk traffic that it was now offline—a classic DDoS attack. She hopped onto an IRC network, and, as she was discussing the problem with a few of her site's moderators, a new person came into the chat room to claim responsibility. The moderators suspected that this was just a troll, but when Laurelai exchanged private messages, the person explained that someone was using a botnet to hit her site. To Laurelai's surprise, the stranger invited her into the botnet's command channel to speak to the person causing the damage. Laurelai agreed and went into a new channel on another IRC network. There, controlling the botnet that had shut down her website, was Kayla. Laurelai had never heard of her before.

"Who the fuck is this?" Kayla asked.

A little taken aback, Laurelai explained that she was the owner of the website ScientologyExposed, the one that Kayla happened to be attacking. Kayla seemed surprised. She explained that she hadn't meant to hit ScientologyExposed but rather Enturbulation.org. Laurelai knew it as Gregg Housh's site. Thanks to some technical complications from a previous time when they had briefly worked together, she and Housh shared the same server. By hitting Enturbulation, Kayla had caused collateral damage to Laurelai's site. Laurelai explained that her site was an alternative to Housh's, concentrating more on trolling. Kayla's mood suddenly lightened.

"Oh, sorry," she said. "Why are you on the same server as

those moralfags anyway?" Laurelai realized that Kayla hated moralfags; it was why she was hitting Enturbulation in the first place. Kayla explained that she disliked the way the Chanology organizers had put a stop to black hat hacking. She believed that hitting Scientology with hard and fast attacks was more effective than a long, drawn-out protest. Laurelai felt an instant meeting of minds and was especially intrigued when Kayla mentioned black hat hackers. The adversaries of white hats, black hats were people who used their computer programing skills to break into computer networks for their own, sometimes malicious, means. The two talked for about an hour, after which Kayla said she would put the brakes on for a few hours to give Laurelai some time to move her site to a different server. Kayla then resumed her DDoS attack.

Later Laurelai asked some black hat hackers she had recently met if they'd heard the name Kayla. She learned that her new acquaintance had the reputation of someone not to be crossed. "A lot of people were afraid of her," Laurelai later remembered. Some were surprised that Kayla would even talk to Laurelai— who at the time was just somebody with a website.

Regardless, the two kept in touch. A few days later, Kayla found Laurelai on IRC and invited her to the public chat network where she normally hung out. The two got to know each other a little better. At one point, Laurelai asked Kayla her age. Kayla replied that she was fourteen. When she asked her sex in real life, Kayla said she was female. Kayla asked the same, and when Laurelai replied that she was transgender, Kayla launched into topics like hormone supplements. To Laurelai's surprise, Kayla seemed to know the details about hormone dosages and their side effects better than she did. Kayla even used the nickname for the little blue pills sold as Estrofem: titty skittles.

Laurelai wondered if she was speaking to a transgender hacker.

There was not much research on hackers who were trans but plenty of anecdotal evidence suggesting the number of transgender people regularly visiting 4chan or taking part in hacker communities was disproportionally high. One reason may have been that as people spent more time in these communities and experimented with "gender bending" online, they could more easily consider changing who they were in the real world. Lines between the offline and online selves could become blurred, and some people in these communities were known to talk about gender as just another thing to "hack on," according to Christina Dunbar-Hester, a professor at Rutgers University who studied gender differences in hardware and software hacking. If people were already used to customizing a machine or code, they might have come to see their own bodies as the next appealing challenge, especially if they already felt uncomfortable with the gender they were born with. Still, according to Dunbar-Hester, plenty of people immersed themselves in another gender online, but didn't replicate that in real life. In other words, Kayla could have been a man who enjoyed being female online, and nothing more.

"Are you trans?" Laurelai ventured.

"No," said Kayla. "I just know someone trans. :)" Kayla had answered this quickly, and it strengthened Laurelai's suspicions.

"Well it doesn't matter if you're trans or not," Laurelai replied, adding that if Kayla wanted to be called "she" online, then Laurelai would refer to her as "she" out of respect for her wishes. The two talked more about hacking, trolling, and social engineering, Laurelai as student and Kayla as teacher. In the coming years, Kayla would introduce Laurelai to her secretive world, while Anonymous would fall back into the shadows. All that was needed was for a new cause to come along, and in late 2010 one finally did, pushing Anonymous into the international spotlight.

CHAPTER 7

FIRE FIRE FIRE FIRE

It was September 2010, and for a couple of years now the Anonymous phenomenon had vanished from news headlines. Raids were small, petty assaults on other sites, mostly carried out by chans or /b/ itself. Very little was happening on IRC, either. The thousands who had piled into #xenu had moved on, put off by the internal discord, their interest lost in the novelty.

On September 8, an article about an Indian software company called Aiplex started getting passed around online. Girish Kumar, Aiplex's CEO, had boasted to the press that his company was acting as a hit man for Bollywood, India's booming film industry. Aiplex didn't just sell software. It was working on behalf of movie studios to attack websites that allowed people to download pirated copies of their films.

Recently, for instance, it had launched DDoS attacks against several torrent sites, including the most famous of them all, The Pirate Bay. Founded in 2003, The Pirate Bay was the most popular and storied BitTorrent site on the net, a treasure trove from which anyone could illegally download movies, songs, porn, and computer programs. Aiplex had used a botnet to flood The Pirate

Bay with traffic, overload its servers, and temporarily shut it down. Kumar had explained that when torrent sites didn't respond to a notice from Aiplex, "we flood the website with requests, which results in database error, causing denial of service."

Tech bloggers and journalists already suspected that antipiracy groups were DDoSing torrent sites like The Pirate Bay, but Kumar's admission was the first proof. It was still a shocking admission; DDoS-ing was illegal in the United States, having sent Brian Mettenbrink to jail for a year. Now the Indian company was openly boasting of using the same method.

Soon enough, users on /b/ started discussing the news. It turned out that lots of people wanted to hit back at Aiplex. A few started pasting an everyone-get-in-here link to a channel on IRC for proper planning. This time, there weren't thousands piling in like they had done with #xenu. Fighting copyright wasn't as sexy as hitting a shady religious group that suppressed a video of Tom Cruise. But piracy was popular among /b/ users, and, soon enough, roughly 150 people had entered the new IRC channel, game for Anonymous to give Aiplex a taste of its own medicine.

Coordinating an attack would not be easy. By now, IRC network hosts had become more aware of Anonymous and would quickly shut down a chat room if they thought people were using it to discuss a DDoS attack. To deal with this, the Anons jumped from IRC network to IRC network, pasting links to the new rooms on 4chan and Twitter each time they moved so others could follow. No one was appointed to find the new locations; whenever the group had to move, someone would find a new network and make a channel. The channels were always innocuously named so as not to attract attention, but the regular channel name for attacking Aiplex was called #savethepb, abbreviating Pirate Bay.

After some planning, the group launched its first DDoS attack on Aiplex on September 17 at 9:00 p.m. eastern standard time.

Just as they had hoped, the software company's website went dark—and remained so for twenty-four hours. Feeling confident, the Anons quickly broadened their attack, posting digital flyers on /b/ so others could use LOIC against another organization trying to end piracy: the Recording Industry Association of America, or RIAA. The tech blog TorrentFreak.com posted a news article headlined "4chan to DDoS RIAA Next—Is This the Protest of the Future?" The group then hit another copyright organization, the Motion Picture Association of America (MPAA).

Two days later they began circulating a message to the media, saying that Anonymous was avenging The Pirate Bay by hitting copyright associations and "their hired gun," Aiplex. They called the attacks "Operation: Payback Is A Bitch" and claimed to have taken down Aiplex thanks to a "SINGLE ANON" with a botnet.

"Anonymous is tired of corporate interests controlling the internet and silencing the people's rights to spread information," the letter said, adding, "Rejoice /b/brothers."

In unashamedly romanticizing pirated movies and music, they were also positioning Aiplex's attacks on The Pirate Bay as "censorship," giving their fight-back broader appeal. For the first time in two years, it looked like Anonymous might be onto another major project after Chanology, and the spark had been that all-important provocation in hacker culture: you DDoS me, I DDoS you.

It was around this time that Tflow, the quiet hacker who would later bring together Sabu, Topiary, and Kayla, read the TorrentFreak article and jumped into his first Anonymous operation. It would later emerge that the person behind Tflow lived in London and was just sixteen years old. He never talked about his age or background when he was online.

"I thought it was a good and unique cause," he later remembered. "Of course, DDoS attacks got boring after that." What Tflow meant was that he was more interested in finding ways that Anons could disrupt antipiracy organizations other than knocking their sites offline. He hopped into #savethepb to observe what other supporters were saying and was pleasantly surprised. A few people appeared to have as much technical knowledge as he did. After Tflow approached a few privately and they met in a separate IRC channel, the smaller team started looking for vulnerabilities in antipiracy groups and found one in the website CopyrightAlliance.org.

About a week after the DDoS attack on Aiplex, the hackers in Tflow's group carried out the first SQL injection attack in their campaign, possibly one of the first to be committed under the banner of Anonymous. They hacked into the CopyrightAlliance.org Web server and replaced the site with the same message used on September 19, "Payback Is A Bitch." Defacing a site was harder to do than carrying out a DDoS attack—you had to get root access to a server—but it had a bigger impact. They then turned CopyrightAlliance.org into a repository for pirated movies, games, and songs, including, naturally, "Never Gonna Give You Up" by Rick Astley, and Classic Sudoku. They also stole 500 megabytes of e-mails from London copyright law firm ACS:Law and published them on the same defaced site.

Tflow and the others were all the while herding supporters from place to place. Between September and November 2010, he helped move roughly three hundred regular chat participants between ten different IRC networks so that they could keep collaborating.

"We chose whatever IRC we could go to really," Tflow later recalled. "There weren't that many options. Not many IRCs allow DDoS attacks."

The group of organizers then created what would become a very important private channel, #command. Like #marblecake, it was a place to make plans without distraction. They started making digital flyers and inviting new people to join this new, broader battle against copyright, DDoSing legal firms, trade organizations, even the website of Kiss bassist Gene Simmons. Soon it looked like Anonymous was hitting benign targets—for instance, the U.S. Copyright Office—and the public support they'd been getting on blogs and Twitter was waning. By November 2010, the Anons themselves were losing interest, and only a few dozen were still talking in the Operation Payback chat room. The campaign had gone into hiatus.

With more time to focus, some of Operation Payback's organizers started working on the first-ever communications infrastructure for Anonymous. Scattered between Britain, mainland Europe, and the United States, these mostly young men pooled their access to ten computer servers around the world. Some had rented the servers, some owned them, but with them they could make a chat network that Anonymous could finally call home. No more herding hundreds of people between different places before getting kicked off. That month they established what they called AnonOps, a new IRC network with dozens of chat rooms just for Anons, some public and some private. One of the first people to check it out was Topiary.

By now Topiary was almost eighteen and, in the offline world as Jake, had moved out of his mother's home on the tiny island of Yell. He lived in a small, government-financed house in Lerwick, the capital of Shetland Mainland, and had been out of the education system for four years. Lerwick was more modern than Yell, but not by much. There were still no fast-food restaurants, no big department stores. It was a cold, windswept place with patches of green fields, craggy brown cliffs, and gray stone ruins dotting its rolling hills. Jake knew hardly anyone here, but he preferred to be on his own anyway.

His home was part of an assortment of chalet-style wooden houses on a hillside about a twenty-minute walk from the center of Lerwick, in an area known as Hoofields. Drug raids by the police were common on his street, some of his neighbors being avid heroin users. Jake's house was small, yellow, and comprised one story, with a large living room and kitchen on one side and a bathroom and bedroom on the other. The front yard occasionally saw daisies in the spring, and in the back was a shed where he kept an old fridge—one that still smelled from when he accidentally left it filled with raw salmon, without power, for three weeks. He had bought all his furniture from local people, often benefiting from the good deals that could be found in a tight-knit island community. His cooker, for instance, had originally cost five hundred pounds (about eight hundred dollars), but he bought it off a family friend for twenty-five pounds (roughly forty dollars).

Jake had found a part-time job in an auto store and was just about getting by. He still looked forward to being online where most of his friends were and still got a small thrill from doing prank calls.

One evening while visiting his mother, Jake took a phone call from a man who claimed to be a friend of his father's. This was a shock. Jake hadn't spoken to his father for years. There had been occasional phone calls on his birthday, but even those had petered out after he turned thirteen. It was strange to suddenly be hearing about him. The man asked if he could take down Jake and his brother's cell phone numbers, adding that his father wanted to get in touch with both of them. Apparently, he felt bad about something. His brother didn't want to talk, but Jake gave the man his own number to see what would happen.

For several weeks, Jake kept his phone charged at all times and next to his bed when he slept, but there was no call. Then in mid-October, a week after his eighteenth birthday, a call came from his father's friend again, this time with the weight of bad news in his voice. The man apologized for what he was about to say and then explained: Jake's father was dead. He explained that in the preceding weeks, Jake's father had sat at home for hours trying to make himself pick up the phone.

"But he didn't have the confidence," the man said, adding that, "instead," he had killed himself. Jake wasn't quite sure what to think. He felt numb at first. His father hadn't been a member of the family, so in one way, Jake didn't need to care or feel upset. When he asked how it had happened, the friend explained that his father had gassed himself, opening the double doors of a church garage late one night, driving inside, and turning the car on.

It was a surreal image. For the first two days after the phone call Jake felt angry. It seemed almost selfish of his father to ask for his number and suggest that he would call, almost as if he wanted Jake to pay attention to what was really about to happen. With more consideration, though, he realized he was probably wrong, and that his father may not have meant to hurt him.

Jake continued his online gaming and visits to 4chan, and a month later discovered the new chat network that had been set up for Anonymous: AnonOps IRC. Intrigued, he signed on, picking the name Topiary, and tried to get a better sense of how he could join in. He didn't see himself as an activist, but Operation Payback sounded well organized and potentially influential. He had no idea that, even though the anticopyright battle was dying, Operation Payback was about to explode with support for a little organization called WikiLeaks.

Jake, now as Topiary, explored the AnonOps chat rooms while a former, widely-revered hacker from Australia named Julian Assange was getting ready to drop a bombshell on the American government. Earlier in 2010, a U.S. army private named Bradley Manning had allegedly reached out to Assange and given his whistleblower site, WikiLeaks, 250,000 internal messages, known as cables, that had been sent between American embassies. These diplomatic cables revealed American political maneuverings and confidential diplomatic reports. In exposing the documents, Assange would hugely embarrass American foreign policy makers.

The WikiLeaks founder had struck deals with five major newspapers, including the *New York Times* and the U.K.'s *Guardian,* and on November 28, 2010, they started publishing the cables. Almost immediately, Assange became both a global pariah and a hero. Until then, WikiLeaks had been moderately well known for collecting leaked data pointing to things like government corruption in Kenya or the untimely deaths of Iraqi journalists. But exposing private data from the American government sparked a whole new level of controversy. U.S. news commentators were calling for Assange to be extradited, charged with treason, even assassinated. Former Alaskan governor Sarah Palin said the United States should pursue Assange with the same urgency as it did the Taliban, while Fox News commentator Bob Beckel, live on television, suggested someone "illegally shoot the son of a bitch." Secretary of State Hillary Clinton said the leaks "threatened national security," and U.S. State Department staff were barred from visiting the WikiLeaks website.

WikiLeaks.org quickly came under attack. An ex–military hacker nicknamed The Jester DDoS'd the site, taking it offline for more than twenty-four hours. Jester was a self-styled patriotic hacker who had been known for attacking Islamic jihadist websites; later he would become a sworn enemy of Anonymous. Now he claimed on Twitter that he was hitting WikiLeaks "for attempting to endanger the lives of our troops."

To try to stay on the web, WikiLeaks moved its site to Amazon's servers. It was booted offline again, with Amazon claiming it had violated its terms of service on copyright. The rebuffs kept coming: a hosting firm called EveryDNS yanked out its hosting services for WikiLeaks. On December 3, online payments giant PayPal announced it was cutting off donations to the site, saying on the official PayPal blog that it had "permanently restricted the account used by WikiLeaks due to a violation of the PayPal Acceptable Use Policy." Soon MasterCard and Visa cut funding services.

It is doubtful that anyone from these companies had any idea that a brand of Internet users known for pranking restaurant managers, harassing pedophiles, and protesting the Church of Scientology would suddenly team together to attack their servers.

The people who had set up AnonOps were talking about the WikiLeaks controversy in their private #command channel. They were angry at PayPal, but, more than that, they saw an opportunity. With Anons no longer riled up about copyright, this could be the cause that brought them back in droves. The copyright companies had been bad, but PayPal snubbing WikiLeaks was even worse. That was an unholy infringement on free information in a world where, according to the slogan of technology activists, "information wants to be free" (even if it *was* secret diplomatic cables). The victimization of WikiLeaks, they figured, would strike a chord with Anonymous and brings hordes of users to their new network. It was great publicity.

Who were these people in #command? Known also as "operators" of the new chat network, they weren't hackers per se but computer-savvy individuals who maintained the network and who would play a crucial role in organizing ad hoc groups of people, large and small, over the coming weeks. Many of them got a kick out of hosting hundreds of people on their servers. It was often argued that these operators, who had names like Nerdo, Owen, Token, Fennic, evilworks, and Jeroenz0r, were the true, secret leaders of Anonymous because of the power they could wield over communication. They avoided culpability for what Anonymous did, though, in the same way that Christopher "moot" Poole avoided litigation by claiming he was not responsible for what happened on 4chan.

Now, though, the operators were doing more than just maintaining the chat network. They were organizing an attack on the PayPal blog, where the company had made its announcement about WikiLeaks. On Saturday morning, December 4, the day after PayPal said it would cut funding, the AnonOps organizers DDoS'd thepaypalblog.com. The blog went down at 8:00 a.m. eastern standard time.

Soon after, the Twitter account @AnonyWatcher posted "TANGO DOWN—the paypalblog.com," adding: "Close your #Paypal accounts in light of the blatant misuse of power to partially disable #Wikileaks funding. Join in the #DDoS if you'd like."

PayPal's blog remained offline for the next eight hours. Anyone who visited it saw a white screen and the "error 403" message "Access forbidden!" in large type.

The next day, Sunday, someone posted an announcement on Anonops.net, the official website for AnonOps IRC, saying that Anonymous planned to attack "various targets related to censorship" and that Operation Payback had "come out in support of WikiLeaks."

At around the same time, a digital flyer was being circulated on image boards and IRC networks, with the title Operation Avenge Assange and a long note that stated, "PayPal is the enemy. DDoS'es will be planned." It was signed, "We are Anonymous, We do not forgive, We do not forget, Expect us."

These flyers came from new channels on AnonOps called #opdesign and #philosoraptors, which later combined to make #propaganda. Here, anyone who wanted to help with publicity collaborated on writing press releases and designing digital flyers to advertise future attacks. Others would then post the flyers all over 4chan and Twitter. Another channel, #reporter, was where Anons could answer the questions of any bewildered journalists who had figured out how to access IRC. Topiary was jumping between the publicity channels, more interested in spreading the word than firing weapons.

At around 5:00 p.m. eastern standard time on Monday, December 6, the organizers from AnonOps started DDoSing PostFinance.ch, a Swiss e-payment site that had also blocked donations to WikiLeaks. The site would stay down for more than a day.

The attack was "getting in the way of customers doing business with the company," Sean-Paul Correll, a researcher with Panda Security, said in a blog post that day. Correll, who was on the West Coast of the United States, stayed up into the early hours to monitor the attacks, which seemed to keep coming.

That day, nine hundred people suddenly jumped into #operationpayback, the main public chat room on AnonOps IRC, which had been quiet for months. About five hundred of these people had volunteered their computers to connect to the LOIC "hive." By now LOIC had an automatic function; you only needed to set it to hive mode and someone in #command would set the target and time. They would type simple instructions into their configured IRC channel — "lazor start" and "lazor stop." Normal users didn't have to know who the target was or when you were supposed to fire. They could just run the program in the background.

At 2:00 p.m. eastern standard time on Tuesday, AnonOps started attacking the website of Swedish prosecutors against Assange, who was now looking at extradition to Sweden where he faced questioning for sexual misconduct against two women in that country. Many in Anonymous saw the case as a whitewash. Once again, some five hundred people were using LOIC, and now more than a thousand people were in the main chat channel. At 6:52 p.m., AnonOps announced a new target: EveryDNS.com, the server provider that had yanked the rug from under WikiLeaks.org. One minute later, that site was down. At 8:00 p.m. the target switched to the main site of Senator Joseph Lieberman, the chairman of the U.S. Senate Homeland Security and Governmental Affairs Committee, which had first pushed Amazon to stop hosting WikiLeaks. All of these sites were going down for minutes or sometimes hours at a time, one by one, like dominoes.

By the early hours of December 8 on the West Coast, Correll had tallied ninety-four hours of combined downtime for these sites since December 4. The worst-hit were PostFinance and the PayPal blog. But this was just the beginning.

Word was spreading that if you wanted to help WikiLeaks, all the action was happening on AnonOps IRC. Newcomers could get a quick overview of what was happening from different chat rooms: #target was for talking about future or current attacks and #lounge was a place to just shoot the breeze. In #setup, new recruits could find a link to download LOIC and get help using it from experienced users.

The room contained a link to a digital flyer with step-by-step instructions titled "HOW TO JOIN THE FUCKING HIVE—DDoS LIKE A PRO."

1. Get the latest LOIC from github.com/NewEraCracker
2. FIX YOUR GODDAMN INTERNET. THIS IS VERY FUCKING IMPORTANT

(If your broadband kept cutting out, LOIC wouldn't work properly.)

Things were moving quickly. Topiary had now gained higher "operator" status in the publicity channels, which gave him the ability to kick out participants and a generally louder voice in the room. His enthusiasm, ideas, and witty remarks caught the attention of one of the AnonOps operators in #command, and they sent Topiary a private message inviting him into a secret command channel, which Topiary had never heard of. Intrigued, he went in.

Here the operators were talking excitedly about all the new

volunteers and media attention they were suddenly getting. They decided to pick a bigger target: the main PayPal website. They quickly chose dates and times and pasted the coordinates at the top of the main IRC channels, then tweeted them. Topiary and the others in #command expected that the call to arms would get stronger feedback than usual, but nothing prepared them for what happened next.

On December 8, just four days after AnonOps had first hit the PayPal blog, the number of visitors to AnonOps IRC had soared from three hundred to seventy-eight hundred. So many people were joining at once that Topiary's IRC client kept freezing and had to be restarted. Lines of dialogue between people in the main channel, still named #operationpayback, were racing up the screen so quickly it was almost impossible to hold a conversation. "It was mind-blowing," Topiary later remembered. "Insane."

"Do you think this is the start of something big?" someone called MookyMoo asked amid the flurry in the main channel.

"Yes," replied an operator named shitstorm.

Jokes were often being cracked about how the mainstream press had started reporting the attack. "They're calling us hackers," said one called AmeMira.

"Even though we don't really hack," another, called Lenin, replied.

The IRC network itself was seizing up because of the flood of users. "Are we being attacked or are there just too many people on this server?" one participant asked. Once the LOIC network itself was crashing, newcomers were told to set their "cannons" on manual mode, directly typing the target address and clicking "IMMA CHARGIN MAH LAZAR."

At around the same time, Topiary watched two very important people enter the private #command room. Their nicknames were Civil, written as {Civil} and Switch. These were botmasters. Each had control of his own botnet, Civil with fifty thousand infected bots and Switch with around seventy-five thousand. Anons who owned botnets could expect to be treated with unusual reverence in Anonymous—with only a few clicks they had the power to bring down a website, IRC network, whatever they wanted. Switch had the bigger ego and could be unbearable to talk to at times.

"I have the bots, so I make the shots," he would say.

Everything was controlled on IRC. Civil and Switch even controlled their botnets from private chat rooms with names like #headquarters and #thedock. The latter was fitting, since bots were often referred to as "boats," as in "How many boats are setting sail?" And in the public channel, the thousands of new visitors only had to type "!botnum" and press enter to see how many people were using LOIC. The day before, December 7, the number of people joining the hive option of LOIC had been 420. For the attack on PayPal on December 8, it was averaging about 4,500.

Topiary noticed that Civil and Switch had their botnets prepared to help the attack but that they were waiting for the hordes with LOIC to fire first. Launch time was 2:00 p.m. GMT, when most people in Europe were at their desks and America was just getting into the office. With minutes to go, supporters and IRC operators posted out a flurry of tweets, links to digital posters, and posts on 4chan reminding everyone: "FIRE AT 14:00 GMT." When 2:00 p.m. finally came around, the IRC channels, Twitter, and 4chan exploded with *FIRE FIRE FIRE FIRE* and FIIIIIRE!!! Along with all the junk traffic, the LOIC hive configured a message to PayPal's servers: "Good_night_Paypal_ Sweet_dreams_from_AnonOps."

There was a rush of excitement as thousands of copies of LOIC all over the world started shooting tens of thousands of junk packets at PayPal.com, putting its servers under sudden pressure that seemed to be coming out of nowhere.

"If you are firing manually, keep firing at 'api.paypal.com:443,'" a user called Pedophelia kept saying over and over in the main channel. "Don't switch targets, together we are strong!"

An IRC operator nicknamed BillOReilly was in a chat room called #loic. Here he could steer the hive of LOIC users from all over the world to attack whatever website was next on the hit list. Anyone who looked in the channel saw a long list of each person who was using LOIC in the attack. Each participant was identified by six random letters and the country his or her computer was in (though many had spoofed that with proxy servers to avoid detection). The countries with the greatest number of participating computers were Germany, the United States, and Britain.

A few minutes into the attack, the IRC operators checked PayPal.com and found that the site was now running slowly—but technically it was still up. There followed much confusion in the horde. Was something wrong with LOIC or AnonOps, or did PayPal have DDoS protection that was too strong?

"The attack is NOT working," someone named ASPj wrote to Kayla—a name Topiary didn't recognize yet—in the main chat room. "I repeat, PAYPAL IS NOT DOWN."

No one outside of #command knew this, but they needed Civil and Switch.

"Let's add on a few thousand bots," someone in #command said. Civil knew what he had to do. He typed in commands for all of his bots to join up to his botnet. The operator evilworks messaged Topiary. "Check out these bots," he said, inviting him into Civil's botnet control room, eager to show it off.

In the botnet control room, which was like any other chat channel, Topiary could see a list of Civil's bots suddenly running down the screen in alphabetical order as they started up around the world. There were a few hundred in the United States, a few

hundred more in Germany; all were invisibly connected to this
IRC channel. Each bot had nicknames like:

[USA | XP] 2025
[ITA | WN7] 1438

It was very similar to the list that BillOReilly was seeing in
his room, except these were computers that were infected with a
virus that had linked them to Civil's botnet. These were not vol-
untary participants. None of the computers in this room belonged
to people who wanted to be part of the attack. They were, as the
phrase went, zombie computers.

If one of the bots suddenly turned off, it was probably because a
random person in Nebraska or Berlin had switched off his or her
computer for the day, and the list would go down by one. Civil
thus didn't like using all fifty thousand of his bots at once; instead, he switched between a few thousand every fifteen minutes
to let the other ones "rest." Once the botnet was firing, the people
behind each infected computer would notice that their Internet
connection had become sluggish. Thinking there was a router
problem, they'd usually start fiddling with their connection or
switching off all together. Constantly refreshing the bots ensured
their owners didn't switch off or, worse, call the IT guys. (Incidentally, some believed that the best people to infect with viruses
so they could join into botnets were those on /b/—they left their
computers on all day.)

Civil gave the command to fire. It looked something like this:

!fire 30000 SYN 50 296.2.2.8

A SYN was a type of packet, and this meant flooding
PayPal.com with thirty thousand bots at fifty packets each for
thirty seconds. The type of packet was important because simply

flooding a server with traffic wasn't always enough to take it offline. If you think of a server like a call center manned by hundreds of people, sending "ping" packets was like calling them all and simply saying "Hello" before hanging up. But sending "SYN" packets was like calling all the workers and staying on the line saying nothing, leaving the other end repeatedly saying "Hello?" The process sent thousands of requests, which the server could not ignore, then left it hanging.

Within a few seconds the PalPal site had gone down completely. It would stay down for a full hour. The thousands of Anons in #OpPayBack cheered at having taken down the world's biggest e-payment website. Mainstream news sites, from the BBC to the *New York Times* to the *Guardian,* reported that the "global hacking group" Anonymous had brought down PayPal.

Panda Security's Correll hopped on IRC using the nickname muihtil (lithium spelled backward) and sent a message to Switch himself, asking about the size of his botnet and clarifying that he was a security researcher. Switch was surprisingly happy to answer that his friend (presumed to be Civil) had helped in the attack by offering thirty thousand bots, while there had been five hundred in the LOIC hive, and that Switch himself had attacked with thirteen hundred bots.

What this confirmed was that around 90 percent of all the firepower from the attack on PayPal.com had come not from Anonymous volunteers but from zombie computers.

Topiary quietly started thinking about the true power of the hive. When he had joined the #command channel two days earlier, he had thought that the Anonymous DDoS attacks were primarily caused by thousands of people with LOIC, with backup support from the mysterious botnets. Now he realized it was the other way around. When it came to hitting major websites like PayPal.com, the real damage came from one or two large botnets. Thousands of LOIC users could have taken down a smaller site like Scientology.org, but not the planet's biggest e-payment provider. In practice, finding someone willing to share his botnet was more useful than getting thousands of people to fire LOIC at the same time.

Correll's observations were reported by Computerworld.com but largely ignored by the mainstream media. Someone nicknamed skiz pasted a link to the story in the AnonOps main chat room, saying skeptically, "They claim Anonymous used a 30,000 person botnet. :D." Most of these eager volunteers did not want to believe that botnets had more firepower than their collective efforts.

The operators in #command did not like to advertise it, either. Not only could that information put off others from joining, but it could bring unwanted attention to their channel, both from other hackers and from the police. But Civil and Switch continued bragging about how large and powerful their botnets were. Spurred on by the media reports and their audience in #command, they were eager to show off again. The operators agreed that since they had the power to launch another attack, they should. They duly planned a second attack on PayPal for December 9. Once again they chose the morning—eastern standard time—to get the attention of American Internet users and the media.

This time, though, there was less enthusiasm and coordination. Only a day had passed since seventy-eight hundred people had been in the main AnonOps chat room, but the numbers using LOIC had started tapering off. Then, when it came time to fire on PayPal a second time, volunteers in the chat room, #operationpayback, were told to wait. They were not told why. Topiary was also in #command waiting for the attack to happen so he could write his first press release. The problem was that in some unknown part of the world Civil was still sleeping.

"Do we have anything to write about?" asked Topiary. "Because nothing's happened."

"No, we have to wait for Civil to come online," was the reply.

An hour later, Civil finally signed into #command and made a few grumpy remarks. As the operators told the hive to fire their (largely ineffective) cannons, Civil turned on his botnet and took down PayPal.com. He then signed off and went to have his breakfast.

As Topiary watched, the secret power of botnets was reconfirmed. The botnets had boosted the first PayPal attack, since the hive was so big, but the second time around just one botnet had done all the work. The second attack also wouldn't have happened if Civil had not been bragging. But the operators still wanted Anonymous and the media to think that thousands of people had been responsible. Ignoring these uncomfortable truths, Topiary wrote up a press release about the "hive" striking back.

After the second PayPal attack, there was more bragging from Civil and Switch and the AnonOps operators told them they could hit MasterCard.com on December 12. They broadcast the date and time of the attack across the Internet, knowing that, with the botnets doing most of the work, it would be fun but not crucial to get another horde of people firing. This time around, only about nine hundred people had hooked up their LOICs to the AnonOps chat network and fired on MasterCard.com. It didn't matter. Thanks to Civil and Switch, the website for one of the world's biggest financial companies went down for twelve hours, and right on schedule.

Over time, a handful of other people with botnets would help AnonOps. One of them was a young hacker named Ryan. Aged nineteen and living with his parents in Essex, England, Ryan's real name was Ryan Cleary. In the offline world, Ryan, who would later be diagnosed with Asperger syndrome, rarely left his room, taking dinner from a plate that his mother would leave

outside his bedroom door. But his dedication to becoming powerful online had paid off; over the years he amassed servers and
what he claimed was a 1.3 million-computer monster botnet.
Other online sources put the number at a still-enormous one hundred thousand computers. Though he rented the botnet, he also
sublet it for extra cash.

Like Civil and Switch, Ryan was happy to brag about his botnet to operators and hackers and keep its true power a secret from
new volunteers. Later in February, for instance, when about fifty
people on AnonOps announced they were attacking small government websites in Italy, Ryan quietly used his botnet for them.
As the attacks were happening, whenever anyone typed "!bot-
num" to learn the number of people using LOIC, it would say
550.

"Did you just add 500 computers to your botnet?" Topiary
would privately ask Ryan.

"No," Ryan would reply. "I just changed the LOIC commands
to make it look like 512 people were using it." What this meant
was that Ryan not only wielded the real firepower, he was deliberately manipulating other Anons so that they would think they
were causing the damage instead. It was not hard to do this. If
you were controlling the network of LOIC users, you could spoof
the number of people using the tool by typing +500 or even +1000
into the corresponding IRC channel. This ability to fake numbers
was an open secret in #command, but people brushed the topic
aside whenever it came up. Anonymous was "Legion," after all.

"It didn't seem sketchy at all," said one source who knew about
the botnets being used to support AnonOps in December 2010
and January 2011. "More fun trickery I guess." The upper tier
of operators and botnet masters also did not see themselves as
being manipulative. This is partly because they did not distinguish the hive of real people using LOIC from the hive of infected
computers in a botnet. In the end they were all just numbers to

them, the source added. If there weren't enough computers over-all, the organizers just added more, and it didn't matter if they were zombie computers or real volunteers.

Botnets, not masses of volunteers, were the real reason Anonymous could successfully take down the website of PayPal twice, then MasterCard.com for twelve hours on December 8 and Visa.com for more than twelve hours on the same day. According to one source, there were at most two botnets used to support AnonOps before November 30, rising to a peak of roughly five botnets until February, before the number of botnets went down to one or two again. Only a handful of people could call the shots with bots. For the most part, they were not lending their fire-power for money. "People offered things because they believed in the same idea," claimed the source. More than that, they liked showing off how much power they had.

Naturally, with ego such a big driver of the early December attacks, discussions in #command soon broke down. After Civil, Switch, and the nine hundred people fruitlessly using LOIC hit Mastercard.com, the small group in #command decided, on a hubristic whim, to attack Amazon.com the next day, December 9, at 10:00 a.m. eastern standard time. That's when the operators realized that Civil and Switch had disappeared.

The operators pushed the attack time to December 9 at 2:00 p.m., hoping the botmasters would return. At 1:30 p.m., the entire AnonOps IRC network went down. It turned out that Civil and Switch had been squabbling with some of the operators in #com-mand and were now using their botnets to attack AnonOps in retribution. When the IRC network came back online about an hour later with a few hundred participants, nobody wanted to attack Amazon anymore. There weren't enough bots and there didn't seem to be a point.

Topiary estimated that LOIC users represented on average 5 percent to 10 percent of the damage done against sites like PayPal,

MasterCard, and Visa in early December 2010, and in the months that followed less than 1 percent, as fewer people stayed involved. Another source close to the operators at the time estimated more graciously that the LOIC tool contributed about 20 percent of DDoS power during AnonOps attacks in December and January. The truth became especially hard to accept when, seven months later, the FBI arrested fourteen people who had taken part in the PayPal attacks by downloading and using LOIC. These users included college students and a middle-aged woman.

"People who fought for what they believe in shouldn't be told what they did was in vain," the source close to the operators said. In a small way, LOIC did help. It made people feel they were contributing to something, which encouraged more to join. Plus, Civil, Switch, and other botmasters might not have helped if they hadn't seen the groundswell of support.

Regardless, Topiary decided to stick to the party line on December 10 when he was contacted by a reporter from state-backed TV network Russia Today and invited to give his first ever live television interview, an audio discussion over Skype. He was nervous in the moments leading up to the interview, but when it came to it, he proclaimed as confidently as he could that the hive had hit back at PayPal and others.

"We lied a bit to the press," he said, many months later, "to give it that sense of abundance." The press liked reporting on this new powerful phenomenon of a hive that nobody seemed able to quantify. "They liked the idea and amplified the attention."

"Lying to the press" was common in Anonymous, for understandable reasons. Here was a network of people borne out of a culture of messing with others, a paranoid world whose inhabitants never asked each other personal questions and habitually lied about their real lives to protect themselves. It was also part of Anonymous culture to make up random, outrageous statements. If, for instance, someone was about to leave his or her computer for a few minutes to get coffee, he or she might say, "Brb, FBI at the door." Not only was there a sense of a higher purpose to Anonymous that made it seem okay to inflate figures and lie to the media; Anons were also part of a secret institution that no one in the real world understood anyway.

Anons particularly disliked journalists who would come into the #reporter channel asking, "So who are you attacking next?" or pushing for a quick quote. A few would first exaggerate, saying that there were tens of thousands of people attacking a site. At one point an Anon told a magazine reporter that Anonymous had "colonies" all over the world, a physical headquarters, and that its name was based on a real man named Anonymous.

"So who is Anonymous?" a reporter asked about the supposed man.

"He's this guy," the Anonymous supporter said. "He lives in our headquarters in West Philadelphia." That was actually an Internet meme: tell an elaborate story, then catch the person out by quoting the introductory rap to the sitcom *The Fresh Prince of Bel Air.*

Later in February 2011, Topiary would create an IRC channel called #over9000—in reference to another famous meme, which involved a few core Anons discussing a bogus hacking operation to mess with a journalist from the *Guardian.* The reporter had asked for access to "secret" inner channels.

"We need to troll her hard," Topiary had told the others.

The group went on to spam the room with cryptic messages like: "Charlie is c85 on excess, rootlog the daisy chain and fuzz out dawn mode."

Lying was so common in Anonymous that people were rarely surprised to hear different versions of events, or to find out that the nickname they thought they were talking to was being hijacked by someone else. There was a constant suspension of disbelief and skepticism about almost everything. Even when people professed genuine admiration for someone or for the ops that were taking place on PayPal and MasterCard, their opinions could change just days later. It wasn't that people in Anonymous were shallow or that there was little value to their experiences— it was just that events and relationships on the Internet moved far more quickly and dramatically than in real life. The data input for Anons could be overwhelming, and often the result was detachment—from emotions, from morals, and from awareness of what was really going on. But there was one truth in particular that at least a dozen Anons would later regret ignoring. It was about LOIC. Not only was their all-important weapon useless against big targets like PayPal, it could lead the police straight to their doors.

CHAPTER 8

Weapons that Backfired

When nearly eight thousand people had rushed into the main AnonOps IRC channel on December 8, eager to avenge Wiki-Leaks, the dozen or so operators in #command were stunned and then overwhelmed. Hundreds had been clamoring for direction, and the obvious one was to download and use LOIC. The operators made sure that at the top of the main chat channels there was a link to downloading the program, along with a document explaining how to use it.

But no one knew for sure if LOIC was safe. There were rumors that LOIC was tracking its users, that the feds were monitoring it, or that it carried a virus. More confusingly, the LOIC that Anons were downloading in droves during Operation Chanology three years ago was very different from the LOIC that they were downloading now for Operation Payback. In the fast-moving world of open source software, developers were tweaking things all the time, and there was no one deciding if they should be helping or hindering Anonymous. One person who took a closer look at LOIC realized it was doing the latter.

Around the same time that the PayPal attacks were getting under way, a highly skilled software developer hopped onto AnonOps IRC for the first time. The programmer, who did not want to reveal his nickname or real name, had worked with WikiLeaks in the past and was keen to help attack its detractors. When he downloaded LOIC from the link at the top of the main chat channels, he thought to look at the program's source code.

"I took it apart," he said, "and it looked like shit."

The big problem was that the application was sending junk traffic directly from users' IP addresses. It did nothing to hide their computer in the network. This meant the people who used LOIC without also using anonymizing software or a proxy server were just asking to get arrested.

The programmer quickly sent private messages to a few of the operators and let them know his concerns, asking them to remove the LOIC link at the top of the channel. About half of them agreed—but the other half refused. According to the programmer, the operators who refused didn't understand the technology behind LOIC. Making things more complicated was the range of operators, all offering different interpretations of LOIC on the chat network. AnonOps had different levels of operators—network operators at the top, and channel operators below them. The channel operators were like middle managers, with the ability to kick people out of channels with a few simple commands. One young female student who went by the nickname No managed to work her way up to channel operator by the time of the PayPal attacks, and she became known for banning people from the main #operationpayback channel if they tried to tell others not to use LOIC. (Ironically, police ended up tracking down No and arresting her a few months later because she had used LOIC.)

New volunteers and operators alike also assumed there was

safety in numbers. Anonymous, as the saying went, was everyone and no one.

"Can I get arrested for doing this?" a person called funoob asked in the #setup channel on December 8.

"Nah, they won't arrest you," answered someone called Arayerv. "Too many people. You can say you have spyware. They can't charge you."

Another called whocares concurred: "If you get arrested just say you don't know but it's probably a virus."

"I hope in a way to get arrested," one called isuse joked. "The trial would be hilarious." (Those who did go to trial for using LOIC later on most likely don't agree.)

"They honestly believed that because of the amount of people it would be impossible to prosecute any single individual," the programmer later remembered. "No one talked about prosecutions. They didn't want to hear about your IP being exposed or anything like that." And the overwhelming sense of camaraderie and accomplishment dominated reasonable argument. The world's media were paying attention to Anonymous and its extraordinary hive mind; the last thing they needed was to start fiddling with the technology they were relying on and slowing things down.

Even when Dutch police swiftly arrested sixteen-year-old AnonOps IRC operator Jeroenz0r and nineteen-year-old Martijn "Awinee" Gonlag on December 8 and 11, 2010, people on AnonOps initially didn't believe it.

"BS, no one is getting arrested," said a user called Blue when links to the arrest stories started getting passed around. Then, when more articles about the arrests started appearing online, a flood of new Dutch supporters poured into AnonOps. There were so many that a new channel was started to host them all, called #dutch.

Around December 13, a rare digital flyer was released warning anyone who had recently used LOIC that they were at "high risk" of arrest and needed to delete all chat logs. The organizer shit-storm said: "Ridiculous. This is an obvious ploy to try and scare people away."

"It's a troll," another organizer told Panda Security's Correll.

The operators, including one who went by the name Wolfy, continued to encourage people to use LOIC even as Correll reported on the Panda Security blog around December 9 that LOIC didn't mask a user's IP address.

"People were so excited," the programmer recalled. "They were in the Christmas spirit and were going crazy."

The programmer wasn't giving up. He decided to help build a new tool to replace LOIC. He started asking around on AnonOps for any interested volunteers who could prove they were developers. After gathering a team of eight from all over the world, they met on a separate IRC server and spent the next three weeks doing nothing but rewriting LOIC from scratch. It was the fastest program making he had ever experienced, fueled by a sense of justice against corporations and the governments and the idea of contributing to the wider collective. The programmer was at his computer all day including during work at his day job, skipping meals and drinking alcohol at the same time as his new colleagues in other parts of the world.

The team added new features to the program, which was like LOIC but let users fire junk packets at a target through Tor, the popular anonymizing network. The tool was not only safer than LOIC but more powerful and far-reaching, too. The programmer claimed it got two hundred thousand downloads on AnonOps IRC when it was finally completed on December 23. When it was posted on a popular blog run by an AnonOps IRC operator named Joepie91, it was downloaded another 150,000 times. Still, many newbie Anons continued to download LOIC because it was so well known. The link to LOIC download was still everywhere on AnonOps IRC. And the programmer's new tool was more complicated to set up. LOIC may have even acquired a veneer of legitimacy from frequent mentions in the mainstream press—from the *New York Times* to BBC News.

Later, in March 2011, the programmer and his crew disassembled LOIC again and found it had indeed been trojaned, or infected with a malicious program. "It had a code that would record what you sent and when you sent it, then send it to a server," he said, adding it was possible that users' IP addresses were being sent to the FBI.

As it happened, the FBI had been investigating Anonymous since the attacks on copyright companies in October and November 2011, and had also been working closely with PayPal since early December. Two days after the December 4 DDoS attack on the PayPal blog, FBI agents spoke on the phone to PayPal cyber security manager Dave Weisman. As the attacks intensified, the two parties kept in touch while a security engineer at PayPal's parent company, eBay, took LOIC apart and analyzed its source code.

On December 15, a member of PayPal's cyber security team gave a small USB thumb drive to the FBI. It was the mother lode. The thumb drive contained a thousand IP addresses of people who had used LOIC to attack PayPal, the ones who had sent the largest number of junk packets. Once the Christmas holidays were over, the FBI would start serving subpoenas to broadband providers like AT&T Internet Services to unmask the subscribers behind some of those IP addresses. Then they would start making arrests.

"Switch is basically under a shoot on sight watch list," the operator Owen told other operators on December 20. The botmaster who had helped make the PayPal attacks happen in early December had gone AWOL after making trouble on the network and getting banned from a few of the main chat rooms, including

#command. He had become aggrieved that his contribution to the attacks hadn't led to more power.

Civil was said to be similarly bitter. After the Visa and MasterCard attacks, he told AnonOps operators like Owen that he was being used, and that they were pretending to like him for his bots. Though it wasn't the case for all botnet masters who supported AnonOps, Civil and Switch were largely uninterested in the activism that Anonymous was publicly fronting, according to Topiary, and more keen to parade their power to the Anon operators, getting the wow factor with their ability to take down a major website on a whim.

Meanwhile, as their former allies started attacking the AnonOps network from December 13, its operators found themselves overwhelmed with extra maintenance work. With folks like Civil, Switch, The Jester, and God knows who else attacking the network, there was no time to dictate a central strategy from #command.

The result was that the masses of original participants started splintering off and starting their own operations. Often they were legal and coherent. One former operator called SnowyCloud helped start Operation Leakspin, an investigative op calling on people to trawl through the WikiLeaks cables and then post short summaries of them on YouTube videos that could be searched with misleading tags like Tea Party and Bieber. There was also Operation Leakflood, where Anons posted a digital flyer with the headquarters fax numbers of Amazon, Mastercard, PayPal, and others with directions to fax "random WikiLeaks cables, letters from Anonymous…" People were creating the flyers in #Propaganda, where Topiary was still spending much of his time. From #Propaganda a few spearheaded Operation Paperstorm, calling on Anon to take to the "real life" streets—not in protest this time, but to plaster them with printed logos of Anonymous on Saturday, December 18. Another channel called #BlackFax listed the fax numbers of several corporate headquarters and encouraged Anons to send them ink-draining black faxes.

Soon, AnonOps was splintering into all sorts of side operations, often under agendas completely different from WikiLeaks, but always as "Anonymous." In mid-December, a few Anons hit Sarah Palin's official website and Conservatives4Palin with a DDoS attack, and a group of about twenty-five attacked a Venezuelan government site to protest Internet censorship. Another operation called Operation OverLoad saw Irish hackers team together to map their government's entire network in an effort to deface every .gov and .edu site they could.

Each time someone would produce a press release announcing an attack by Anonymous, the media would suggest it was coming from the same "group of hackers" that hit PayPal and MasterCard. Not only were these people not all from the same group, more often than not they weren't even hackers and didn't know the first thing about SQL injection. They were armed mostly with an ability to coordinate others and with access to free software tools they could get on 4chan's /rs/ board.

Topiary had been dipping into some of the different operations that had briefly taken off after the PayPal and MasterCard attacks. In late December, while he was lurking in #operationpayback, he noticed a number of people talking to a participant called 'k. "So you're THE Kayla?" someone asked. They asked about an incident on 4chan—someone had taken full control of the /b/ board and spammed it with repeated loops of "Kayla <3" in 2008. 'k said yes and added a smiley face. Another name, Sabu, was lurking among the participants, not saying anything, just listening.

Soon Sabu and Kayla had moved into another secret channel that was slowly replacing #command as a tactical hub for Anonymous: #InternetFeds. This channel was so highly classified that it wasn't even on the AnonOps network but allegedly on the server of a hardcore hacktivist with Anonymous. About thirty people had found their way in, mainly via invitation. They included Sabu, Kayla, and Tflow, some of the original AnonOps operators, and a botmaster or two. Most were skilled hackers.

Here they could share flaws they had found in servers hosting everything from the official U.S. Green Party to Harvard University to the CERN laboratory in Switzerland. Sabu even pasted a list of exploits—a series of commands that took advantage of a security glitch—to several iPhones that anyone could snoop on. They threw around ideas for future targets: Adrian Lamo, the hacker that had turned in WikiLeaks's military mole Bradley Manning, or defected botmaster Switch.

"If someone has his dox," said Kayla, "I can pull his social security number and we can make his life hell." To those who didn't know her, Kayla came across as someone who was especially keen to dish out vigilante justice.

As the InternetFeds participants got to know each other more, they also saw that Sabu was the one with the loudest voice, the biggest opinions, and the strongest desire to coordinate others into action. Sabu, who was well connected to the underground hacker scene, wanted to relive the days of the so-called Antisecurity movement and would eventually realize he could do so with an elite group of Anons like Kayla, Topiary, and Tflow. What's extraordinary is that, while his actions gradually betrayed the rhetoric, Sabu was gradually positioning himself as Anonymous's most spectacular revolutionary hero.

CHAPTER 9

The Revolutionary

Sabu's dramatic involvement in Anonymous might never have happened if it weren't for an important introduction: around mid-December 2011, Tflow invited Sabu, who in real life was a twenty-eight-year-old New Yorker with a string of criminal misdemeanors behind him, into the #InternetFeds chat room. It was in this chat room that Sabu first met Kayla and other hackers who would help him attack myriad other targets with the mission of revolution in his mind. Until now, Anonymous raids had reacted to circumstance: Chanology because of Tom Cruise; Operation Payback because a few companies snubbed WikiLeaks. But Sabu wanted Anonymous to be more than just kids playing hacker. He wanted Anonymous to change the world.

Sabu was an old-time cyber punk. He did not use words like *moralfag* and *lulz,* and he did not go on 4chan. He conquered networks, then basked in his achievement. He was more interested in the cachet of taking over entire Internet service providers (ISPs) than pranking Scientologists. While 4chan trolls like William were looking for random fun, Sabu wanted to be a hero by taking figures of authority down a notch or two. He did not shy away from big targets or big talk. In his decade underground he claimed to have taken control of the domain-name systems of the governments of Saudi Arabia, Puerto Rico, the Bahamas, and Indonesia.

Sabu was known to exaggerate, and other hackers who dealt with him listened to his claims with some skepticism. Though he was highly skilled, Sabu would often lie about his life, telling people things he perhaps wished were true—that he came from Puerto Rico; that his real mother had been an upstanding member of the local political community; that in real life, he was married and "highly successful in his field." The truth was that he was jobless, insecure, and struggling to support his family.

Sabu's real name was Hector Xavier Monsegur. He lived in a low-income housing project on New York's Lower East Side, and with help from government welfare, he supported his five brothers, a sister, two female cousins for whom he was legal guardian, and a white pit bull named China. Monsegur would refer to the two girls, who were seven and twelve, respectively, in 2012, as his daughters. He was of Puerto Rican descent and a stickler for left-wing activism. As a child, he listened to tales of the El Grito de Lares revolt and told his family that one day, he would launch his own revolution.

Born in New York City in 1983, Monsegur grew up in relative poverty. His father, also named Hector, and his aunt Iris sold heroin on the streets. When Monsegur was fourteen, they were both arrested for drug dealing and sentenced to seven years in prison. Monsegur went to live with his grandmother Irma in a sixth-floor apartment in the Jacob Riis housing project on New York's Lower East Side.

As he settled into his new home, he discovered *The Anarchist Cookbook,* the notorious book originally published in 1971 that led him to tips for hacking phone lines to make free calls as well as directions for making napalm bombs out of soap. His grandmother could not afford a fast Internet connection, so the young Monsegur followed instructions to get the family computer hooked up to the Internet service EarthLink for free. As he explored the Web, he also found his way onto EFnet, a storied Internet relay chat network popular with hackers that Kayla would join years later. Monsegur eventually came across an online essay from a notorious 1980s hacker nicknamed the Mentor. It was called "The Hacker's Manifesto" and spoke to Monsegur more than anything else he had read online. The Mentor, whose real name was Lloyd Blankenship, had written the short essay on a whim on January 8, 1986, a couple of hours before police arrested him for computer hacking.

"Did you, in your three-piece psychology and 1950's techno-brain, ever take a look behind the eyes of the hacker? I am a hacker, enter my world...."

"Oh man," Monsegur said, recalling the event years later in an interview. "That right there is what made me who I am today." The last line of the manifesto was especially resonant for him: "My crime is that of outsmarting you, something that you will never forgive me for."

The idea that figures of authority, from teachers to the media, misunderstood the true talents of hackers was something Monsegur understood all too well. As a young Latino living in the projects where his own family dealt drugs, he did not fit the description of nerdy computer hacker. More than likely he was confronted by people who doubted his abilities. But he was eager to learn. After successfully hooking his family up with free Internet, Monsegur wanted to find the next challenge to conquer.

He read more online, experimented, and took a few pointers from people on IRC networks like EFnet. Still at just fourteen, Monsegur taught himself software programming in Linux, Unix, and open-source networking.

Outside of school, Monsegur was showing off his talents: he

joined a local training scheme for talented young programmers called the NPowerNY Technology Service Corps, then got work experience researching network security at the Welfare Law Center. At eighteen he had joined mentoring program iMentor as a technology intern.

By now he had grown into a tall, broad-shouldered young man, but he had a tenuous relationship with authority. According to an essay the teenaged Monsegur wrote in August 2001, it boiled down to an incident at his Washington Irving High School in Manhattan. He had been working for the school during class hours, installing Windows on what he called their "obsolete" computers, when one day while Hector was walking through the school's metal detector, its chief of security stopped him to ask about the screwdriver he was carrying.

"I am the geek that fixes your system when you forget not to execute weird .exes," he recalled saying.

"Hey, don't give me an attitude, boy," the head of security replied, staring at him. Monsegur explained it again. He was a student who worked on the "non-functioning computers during my school time." The security head took the screwdriver.

"Thanks," he said. "I'm keeping this." Embarrassed and angry, Monsegur wrote a complaint and gave it the school's authorities, accusing the security head of "corporal punishment" and "disrespect." When the complaint was ignored, he distributed a "controversial piece of writing" to his teachers. During class, the school's principal paid him a visit, asking if he would step aside so they could talk. He and other school officials found Monsegur's writing threatening, he said.

"The guy stares me down," Monsegur wrote in his essay. "Disrespects me physically in front of tens of students. What happened to my complaint? Where is the justice I seek?" Monsegur felt jilted. Weeks later he got a call from his teacher, who he described as saying he was "temporarily expelled from the school."

Monsegur replied, "Very well then, it is such a shame that one such as myself would have to be deprived of my education because of my writing." Just as the teacher was about to reply, Monsegur hung up. New York's Administration for Children's Services then requested he meet with a psychologist for a mental evaluation. Monsegur claimed that he passed. But he also left high school without finishing the ninth grade.

Online, he could live out his ambitions and avoid the "disrespect" he felt from figures of authority. By now he was learning how to break into the web servers of big organizations, from Japanese universities to third-world governments. Monsegur liked the buzz of subjugating a computer system, and soon he was veering from protecting them on his internships, to breaking into them in his spare time.

He had meanwhile discovered hacktivism. When he was sixteen and watching TV one day, Monsegur saw a news broadcast about protests in Vieques, an island off the coast of Puerto Rico. The U.S. Navy had been using the surrounding waters as a test-bombing range, and a year earlier, in 1999, a stray bomb had killed a local civilian guard. The guard's funeral received global press attention and sparked a wave of protests against the bombings. In the TV broadcasts, soldiers pushed against protesters, including the Reverend Al Sharpton, a community leader in New York that Monsegur had become aware of through his growing interest in left-wing activism. Something snapped inside him.

He went to his computer and drew up a network map of the entire IP space for Puerto Rico, and he found that a company called EduPro was running the government sites. He hacked into the servers, discovered the root password, and got administrative access. In the heat of the moment, he also typed up an angry missive in Microsoft Word, ignoring his own typos: "Give us the Respect that we deserve," he wrote. "Or shall we take it by force? Cabron." He brought down the Puerto Rican government's websites and replaced them all with his message, which stayed up for several days. Smiling at his work, Monsegur considered this his first act of hacktivism. When the U.S. military gave control of the Vieques base back to the locals two weeks later, he felt it was partly thanks to him.

Monsegur wanted to keep going. He threw himself into hacking, joining the first stirrings of a cyber war between American and Chinese hackers, which mostly involved young men from each side trash-talking and defacing websites in the other side's country. Operation China took place in 2001, the same year that Monsegur appears to have dropped out of high school. Beijing at that time had refused to give President Clinton access to a U.S. spy plane that had collided with a Chinese fighter jet and crash-landed on Hainan island. The surviving U.S. crew were held for eleven days, and in that time a few gung-ho American computer hackers like Monsegur broke into hundreds of Chinese websites and defaced them with messages like "We will hate China forever." The Chinese hackers hit back with the likes of "Beat down Imperialism of America." By this point, Monsegur was regularly using the nickname Sabu, borrowed from the professional wrestler who was popular in the 1990s for his extreme style, and who played up his minority status by claiming to be from Saudi Arabia, when he was actually from Detroit and of Lebanese descent. Sabu, similarly, claimed online to be born and bred in Puerto Rico.

Monsegur's group was called Hackweiser; it was founded in 1999 by a talented Canadian hacker nicknamed P4ntera. It counted between ten and fifteen hackers as members when Monsegur joined. His role in the group was one that would remain the same a decade later: he hacked into, or rooted, as many servers as he could. Later in 2001, after Sabu had spent several months learning the ropes with Hackweiser, P4ntera suddenly went missing. Monsegur realized that if the group's charismatic leader could get arrested, the same could happen to him. He wrestled with his ego. He loved seeing "Sabu" gain notoriety for the audacious hacks he was carrying out, but he did not want to go to jail.

"We humans suffer from egos," Sabu later remembered. "We have a need to have our work appreciated." But Monsegur decided to play it safe, and he stopped all public use of the name Sabu and went underground for the next nine years. If "Sabu" ever appeared online, it was only in private chat rooms. He also tried using his programming skills for legitimate means. In 2002 he started a group for local programmers in Python, a popular programming language. Introducing himself as Xavier Monsegur, he invited others to "integrate their knowledge into one big mass of hairy information" and said that the site he had made was "nere [*sic*] its final layout state...It'll be all about us, our knowledge, our ideas, just 'us' having a fun time and enjoying what we have and can do."

The sociable programmer went on to freelance for a Swedish IT security company called Tiger Team, then found work with the peer-to-peer file-sharing company LimeWire. He continued living with his grandmother and used his computer-hacking skills to help neighbors in the apartment block fraudulently raise their credit ratings. Money thus came sporadically from both legal and illegal sources: sometimes it was from Monsegur's legitimate work; other times it was from selling marijuana on the streets, or hacking into a computer network to steal credit card numbers.

But problems came all at once in 2010, when he was twenty-six. Monsegur's father and aunt had been released from prison, but his aunt Iris had resumed selling heroin and that year was arrested again. She left her two daughters in Monsegur's care, and he got legal custody. At around the same time, he lost his job at LimeWire after the recording-industry group RIAA hit the company with a $105 million lawsuit and it was forced to lay off workers. Worse, Monsegur's grandmother with whom he had lived since the age of fourteen died.

"That messed him up," a family member later told the *New York Times,* referring to his grandmother's death. Monsegur became more disruptive, hacking into auto companies and ordering car engines and disturbing his neighbors by playing loud music, often until 4:00 a.m. in the home where his grandmother no longer lived. Monsegur was unemployed and drifting.

Then in early December, out of nowhere, Anonymous burst onto the scene with WikiLeaks, offering a cause that Monsegur could be passionate about. He watched the first attack on PayPal unfold and saw echoes of his work with Hackweiser and his protest attack for the island of Vieques, but on a much grander scale. He would later say that Anonymous was the movement he had been waiting for all those years "underground."

On December 8, when AnonOps had its highest surge of visitors for the initial big attack on PayPal, Monsegur signed into the public chat room, using the nickname Sabu for the first time in almost a decade. It was chaos on AnonOps IRC, with hundreds of trolls and script kiddies (wannabe hackers) all talking over one another.

"We need the name of the wired employee who just spoke on cnn," he said, referring to *Wired* magazine's New York City bureau chief, John Abell. "john swell? john awell? pm me the name please.!!!" As Sabu, he repeated the request three times. Eventually he zeroed in on Tflow, who was dropping advanced programming terms. After Sabu and Tflow talked via private messages, neither of them revealing his true location or any other identifying information, Tflow showed Sabu into the secret channel for hackers, #InternetFeds.

#InternetFeds was secure and quiet. In the open AnonOps chat rooms, hundreds clamored for large, impossible targets like Microsoft and Facebook. There was little point trying to reason with the horde and explain why those targets wouldn't work, that you needed to find a server vulnerability first. It was like trying to explain the history of baseball to a noisy stadium full of people itching to see a home run. It had been the same in Chanology, when the #xenu channel was backed by the quiet planning in #marblecake. Discord grew in #operationpayback over who should feel the wrath of Anonymous next; the WikiLeaks controversy was receding from the headlines, and the hackers had grown bored with trying to attack Assange's critics. Sabu, Kayla, and the others in #InternetFeds increasingly talked about focusing their efforts on another growing news story: revolution in the Middle East.

Sabu was already interested in the region, having attended a protest march or two for Palestine when he was younger. Now he and the others were seeing articles about demonstrations in Tunisia that had been sparked by documents that WikiLeaks had released. Tunisia's government was known for aggressively censoring its citizens' use of the Internet. Websites that were critical of the government were hacked, their contents deleted and their servers shut down. Locals who visited prodemocracy e-newsletters and blogs would often be met with error messages.

In early January of 2011, the government censorship appeared to get worse. Al Jazeera reported that the Tunisian government had started hijacking its citizens' Facebook logins and password details in a process known as phishing. Normally this was a tactic of cyber criminals; here, a government was using it to spy on what its citizens were saying on social networks and mail services like Gmail and Yahoo. If officials sniffed dissenters, they sometimes arrested them. Locals needed to keep changing their Facebook passwords to keep the government out. At a time when the country of more than ten million people was on the edge of a political revolution, protesters and regular citizens alike were struggling to avoid government spies.

The hackers in #InternetFeds came up with an idea, partly thanks to Tflow. The young programmer wrote a web script that Tunisians could install on their web browsers and that would allow them to avoid the government's prying eyes. The script was about the length of two sides of paper, and Tflow tested it with another Anon in Tunisia, nicknamed Yaz, then pasted it onto a website called userscripts.org. He and a few others then advertised the link in the #OpTunisia chat room on AnonOps, on Twitter, and in digital flyers. It got picked up by a few news outlets. The hacktivist Q was one of the #InternetFeds members and also one of the dozen channel operators in the #OpTunisia channel. He began talking with Tunisians on AnonOps—the ones who were web-savvy enough to access it via proxy servers—and encouraged them to spread news of the script through their social networks.

"OpTunisia fascinated me," Q later said in an interview. "Because we actually did make an impact by pointing Western media to the things happening there." Within a few days, news of the script had been picked up by technology news site ArsTechnica and it had been downloaded more than three thousand times by Tunisian Internet users.

Sabu was impressed, but he wanted to make a different kind of impact—a louder one. Thinking back to how he had defaced the Puerto Rican government websites, he decided he would support the Tunisian revolution by embarrassing its government. It helped that Arab government websites were relatively easy to hack and deface.

Sabu and a few others from #InternetFeds discovered there were just two name servers hosting Tunisia's government websites. This was unusual—most governments and large companies with Web presences ran on several name servers, so a hacker taking down a few usually didn't do much damage. In Tunisia's case, however, shutting down just two name servers would take the government completely offline.

"It was a very vulnerable set-up," one hacker that was in #InternetFeds recalled. "It was easy to shut them off."

To take the Tunisian servers offline, Sabu did not use a botnet. Instead, he later claimed, he hijacked servers from a web-hosting company in London that allowed him to throw ten gigabytes worth of data per second at the Tunisian servers. These were broadcast servers, which could amplify many times the amount of data spam of a basic server; it was like using a magnifying glass to enhance the sun's rays and destroy a group of ants. Sabu single-handedly kept the Tunisian servers down for five hours. Soon, though, authorities on the other side were filtering his spoofed packets, like the owner of a mansion telling his butler not to bring in mail from a particular person. The traffic he was sending was losing its effect. Undeterred, Sabu called an old friend for help, someone he knew from his days of dabbling in cyber crime. While Sabu hit the first name server, the other took down the second.

Tunisia was where Sabu really got involved in Anonymous for the first time. He not only took down the government's online presence; he and a few others also trudged through dozens of government employee e-mails.

But the government fought back again. It blocked all Internet requests from outside Tunisia, shutting itself off from foreign Internet users like Sabu. Sabu wanted to deface the site of Tunisian prime minister Mohamed Ghannouchi, but he would have to do that from inside the country, and he wasn't about to get on a plane. So on January 2, he signed into the #OpTunisia chat room with its dozen channel operators and several hundred other Anons from around the world, including Tunisia. There was talk of using proxies and potential DDoS attacks; questions about what was going on. Then Sabu hit the caps lock key and made his grand entrance.

"IF YOU ARE IN TUNISIA AND ARE WILLING TO

BE MY PROXY INTO YOUR INTERNET PLEASE MSG ME." The room went almost silent. After a few minutes, Sabu got a private reply from someone with an automated username like Anon8935—if you didn't choose a unique nickname on AnonOps, the network would give you one similar to this—a man who claimed to be in Tunisia. Sabu didn't know the man's real name and didn't ask. He didn't know if Anon8935 was sitting in the sweltering heat of a city or tucked away in a quiet suburb. The man said only that he'd been a street protester and now wanted to try something different, something with the Internet. Trouble was, Anon8935 didn't know a thing about hacking. Sabu gave him some simple instructions, then said, "My brother. Are you ready?"

"Yes," the other replied.

"You realize I'm going to use your computer to hack pm.gov.tn?"

"OK," the main replied. "Tell me what to do."

Sabu sent over some brief instructions for downloading and installing a program that would let Sabu take control of the man's computer. Soon he was operating on an antiquated version of Windows and an achingly slow Internet connection.

"See me?" Sabu asked, moving the mouse cursor.

"OK!" the man typed back.

Sabu set to work while the Tunisian man sat and watched. Sabu opened up the command prompt and began typing programming code that his new friend had never seen before, a lengthening column of white text against a black background representing the back roads of the Web. About forty minutes later, Sabu brought up the official website of Tunisia's president. Sabu imagined the man's eyes growing wider at this point. Within minutes, the president's official website was gone, replaced by a simple white page with black lettering. At the top, in large Times New Roman font, it read "Payback is a bitch, isn't it?" Underneath was the giant black silhouette of a pirate ship and the name Operation Payback. The word *operation* reinforced the idea that this wasn't just a protest or anarchy; it was a mission.

In the meantime, Tflow had told Topiary that a hack on Tunisia was under way, and he asked if he could create an official deface statement. Topiary wrote it up and passed the statement to Tflow, who sent it to Sabu, who used it to replace the official site of Tunisian prime minister Ghannouchi. "Greetings from Anonymous," the home page of pm.gov.tn now read. "We have been watching your treatment of your own citizens, and we are both greatly saddened and enraged by your behavior." It carried on dramatically before ending with the tagline: "We are Anonymous, We are legion...Expect us."

Sabu stared at the new page and then sat back and smiled.

"You don't know the feeling of using this guy's Internet to hack the president's website," he later remembered. "It was fucking amazing." The Tunisian government had set up a firewall to stop foreign hackers from attacking its servers; it had never expected attackers to come from within its own borders.

"Thanks, brother," Sabu said. "Make sure to delete everything you downloaded for this and reset your connection." After a few minutes, the man went offline, and some days later, Sabu hung a Tunisian flag in his house. Sabu then heard that the man had been arrested. While he felt bad for his volunteer, Sabu did not feel guilty. A higher cause had been served. "Operation Tunisia," Sabu later recalled, "was the beginning of a serious technical advancement for Anonymous."

On January 14, Tunisian president Ben Ali stepped down. It was a landmark moment, following a month of demonstrations by thousands of Tunisians over unemployment and Ali's overarching power and culminating in a new form of online protest, an alliance of people on the other side of the world working with local citizens.

Ali fled Tunisia and took a plane to Saudi Arabia, and Sabu ended his weeks-long attack on Tunisian government servers. By February, Ghannouchi would resign too, and over the coming months, Internet censorship in the country would fall dramatically. In the meantime, Sabu, the hackers in #InternetFeds, and the Anons on AnonOps turned their attention to other countries in the Middle East. Sabu worked with hackers to take government websites in Algeria offline, then accessed government e-mails in Zimbabwe, seeking evidence of corruption. Sabu and Kayla continued doing the rooting; Tflow did the coordinating; and Topiary wrote the deface messages. Anonymous's new Middle East campaign was moving at light speed, with teams of volunteers hitting a different Arab website almost every day. They were spurred on by the vulnerabilities they discovered, the new-found camaraderie—and the resulting media attention.

Kayla in particular was on a roll, but not just because she wanted to support the revolution. The hacker had struck a secret deal with someone who claimed to be with WikiLeaks.

CHAPTER 10

Meeting the Ninja

As Anonymous turned its attention to the Middle East in early January of 2011, Topiary continued organizing and writing deface messages in #propaganda and talking to journalists in #reporter. #Command wasn't much to look at anymore—too many operators and too much squabbling. There were about twenty Anons in each publicity channel, most of them talented writers who had written Anonymous press releases in the past. Once in a while, Topiary talked to Tflow, who would drop into #propaganda to pick up a deface message; soon Topiary would see his text on an official government website for Zimbabwe. With the help of a French Anon, a French version was also posted.

Topiary liked explaining Anonymous to reporters and writing deface messages that shocked a website's visitors and owners. He also liked learning how to deal with the press, how to get them interested in a story by offering them exclusive information. He wondered if the writers and spokespeople like himself were among the more influential members of Anonymous in the world outside the collective. Soon people started inviting him into more channels that no one else talked about publicly. On

January 2, he got an important tap on the shoulder, this time from Tflow.

Sabu, via a local volunteer, had been preparing to take control of the prime minister's website, and he needed a good deface message, quickly.

"The government of Tunisia's main sites are going to be hacked," Tflow told Topiary. "Can you design the deface message?" Topiary felt an instant buzz. This was the first time anyone had trusted him with the knowledge that a hack was about to happen. Eager to help, he and Tflow discussed the timing of what they referred to as the deface, and then Topiary wrote his usual ominous message to the repressive Tunisian government.

As the hack was happening and the deface message being uploaded, Topiary and Tflow went into the main AnonOps chat rooms and gave a running commentary of the attack, to inspire the troops a little.

When it was all over, Tflow surprised Topiary again by inviting him into #InternetFeds. He was effectively trusting Topiary to collaborate and share ideas with some of the most highly skilled hackers working with Anonymous. Topiary had been a stranger to these people, but gradually he was getting their attention.

Over the next month, much of Sabu's hacking and Topiary's writing would be at the forefront of Anonymous cyber attacks on the governments of Libya, Egypt, Zimbabwe, Jordan, and Bahrain. Anonymous was not only defacing sites but releasing government e-mail addresses and passwords. Attacks also continued in other parts of the world in the name of Anonymous; two Irish hackers defaced the website of Ireland's main opposition party, Fine Gael. It was a flurry of revolutionary activity that made Anonymous suddenly look less like a bunch of bored pranksters and more like real activists.

Then on February 5, Tflow sent Topiary another private message on AnonOps IRC, this time inviting him into an even more secret IRC channel that would include just a handful of core people from #InternetFeds. When Topiary entered the exclusive chat room, he forgot he had (as a joke) set a programming script to run on his IRC client that would kick anyone out of the room who didn't use at least 80 percent capital letters. His first interaction with Sabu involved kicking him out of the chat room. Embarrassed, Topiary apologized and quickly turned off the script. But Sabu took it well, and the group of five—Topiary, Sabu, Kayla, Tflow, and Q—quickly got to talking. The topic was HBGary and Aaron Barr's article in the *Financial Times*.

Topiary couldn't get his head around who or what Kayla was. He vaguely remembered seeing the name Kayla on his old MSN chat list, a 2008 4chan flood, and articles about her on Encyclopedia Dramatica. In between lots of smiley faces and *lol*s, she talked about hacking like it was an addiction. She couldn't look at a website without checking to see if there were holes in the source code that she could exploit, perhaps allowing her to steal a database or two. She was a conundrum: She seemed to be the chattiest, most happy-go-lucky person in the group, but she was also paranoid and apparently dangerous. She had developed a cast-iron protection for her real identity, and the bold admission that she was sixteen, along with the overwhelming number of emoticons and hearts (<3), suggested she was trying too hard to come across as a girl.

Topiary knew that female hackers were extremely rare; a hacker who claimed to be female was more likely not in real life, though they were possibly transgender, gay, or at least thinking along those lines. An online friend of Topiary, nicknamed Johnny Anonymous, conducted his own ad hoc online poll in late 2010. He put a series of questions to a hundred and fifty users of the early AnonOps network. About sixty, or one-third, identified themselves as LGBT (lesbian, gay, bisexual, or transgender), while the rest said they were straight.

"We have jokes about transvestites because there are so many of them among us," Johnny Anonymous said in an interview.

Kayla was obsessive about hiding her identity, which was why Topiary later called her the ninja. She rotated her passwords almost daily. She claimed to keep all her data on a tiny microSD card, and she kept her operating system on a single USB stick that she used to boot up her netbook. Like most hackers, she used a VM (virtual machine) to do all her Internet witchcraft; it acted as a buffer between her computer and her life online, so if anyone ever hacked her, he'd only get to the virtual machine. Unlike Topiary and many other Anons, she avoided using a virtual private network (VPN). She didn't trust them, since a VPN provider could always give her details to the police. She kept a low-end cell phone with an unregistered SIM card, the most secure device she had, and she used it to note down all her passwords. She partitioned a small drive called sys on her phone that she used to store malicious code.

It sounded paranoid, but Kayla said later in an interview that she learned a terrifying lesson about the need to scrub the Web clean of her identity soon after she started attacking hacker forums. The story went that when Kayla was younger (she claimed fourteen) and trying to dox other hackers for fun, she had at one point picked the wrong target. It was a male hacker who managed to do some of his own digging, and he found one of her old e-mail addresses on another forum. He got her name, date of birth, town, and some information on her family. He called her house, and when she answered, he threatened angrily to call the police. In recounting the story, Kayla said that he refused to believe her age and that she broke down in tears. When he eventually calmed down, they arranged to meet in a nearby city. They picked a crowded mall and eventually the two found each other and sat down to talk. The man was interested in Kayla's life and why she hacked. He revealed that he had found her details from old MSN profiles and hacker forum profiles, and for Kayla, the realization was like a slap in the face: her information was out there, just waiting to be discovered.

As soon as Kayla got home, she wiped everything from her accounts, deleting every e-mail, and read more about how to become completely invisible on the Internet. Within a year, she had her almost-militaristic regime in place and had become confident enough to start hacking bigger names. She couldn't shake the lure of hacking—there was just something about having access to information that others didn't have. Her online name, after all, meant "Keeper of keys" in old English. And the attack that would seal her place in the #InternetFeds chat room and in the minds of other hackers was her assault on the news site Gawker.

Gawker had once been in Anon's good books. It had been the first news site to boldly publish the crazy Tom Cruise video that helped spark Chanology. But then the site's famously snarky voice turned on Anonymous, reporting on major 4chan raids as examples of mass bullying. After Gawker's Internet reporter Adrian Chen wrote several stories that poked fun at Anonymous, mocking its lack of real hacking skills and 4chan's cat fights with Tumblr, regulars on /b/ tried to launch a DDoS attack on Gawker itself, but the attack failed. In response, Gawker writer Ryan Tate published a story on July 19, 2010, about the failed raid, adding that Gawker refused to be intimidated. If "sad 4chaners have a problem with that, you know how to reach me," he added. Kayla, at the time, had bristled at the comment and felt her usual urge to punish anyone who underestimated her, and now Anonymous.

"We didn't really care about it till they were like, 'lol you can't hack us no one can hack us,'" Kayla later said in an interview. Though Gawker had not said this literally, it was the message Kayla heard.

She decided to go after the site. Kayla and a group of what she later claimed was five other hackers met up in a chat channel called #Gnosis, on an IRC network she had set up herself called tr0lll. Anywhere from three to nine people would be on the network at any given time. Kayla actually had several IRC networks, though instead of hosting them herself she had other hackers host them on legitimate servers in countries that wouldn't give two hoots about a U.S. court order. Kayla didn't like to have her name or pseudonym on anything for too long.

People close to Kayla say she set up tr0ll and filled it with skilled hackers that she had either chosen or trained. Kayla was a quick learner and liked to teach other hackers tips and tricks. She was patient but pushy. One student remembered Kayla teaching SQL injection by first explaining the theory and then telling the hackers to do it over and over again using different approaches for two days straight.

"It was hell on your mind, but it worked," the student said. Kayla understood the many complex layers to methods like SQL injection, a depth of knowledge that allowed her to exploit vulnerabilities that other hackers could not.

On tr0lll, Kayla and her friends discussed the intricacies of Gawker's servers, trying to figure out a way to steal some source code for the site. Then in August, a few weeks after Gawker's "sad 4chaners" story, they stumbled upon a vulnerability in the servers hosting Gawker.com. It led them to a database filled with the usernames, e-mail addresses, and hashes (encrypted passwords) of 1.3 million people who had registered with Gawker's site so they could leave comments on articles. Kayla couldn't believe her luck. Her group logged into Nick Denton's private account on Campfire, a communication tool for Gawker's journalists and admins, and spied on everything being said by Gawker's staff. At one point, they saw the Gawker editors jokingly suggesting headlines to each other such as "Nick Denton [Gawker's founder] Says Bring It On 4Chan, Right to My Home," and a headline with a home address.

They lurked for two months before a member of the group finally hacked into the Twitter account of tech blog Gizmodo, part of Gawker Media, and Kayla decided to publish the private account details of the 1.3 million Gawker users on a simple web page. One member of her team suggested selling the database, but Kayla wanted to make it public. This wasn't about profit, but revenge.

On December 12, at around eleven in the morning eastern time, Kayla came onto #InternetFeds to let the others know about her side operation against Gawker, and that it was about to become public. The PayPal and MasterCard attacks had peaked by now, and Kayla had hardly been involved. This was how she often worked—striking out on her own with a few other hacker friends to take revenge on a target she felt personally affronted by.

"If you guys are online tomorrow, me and my friends are releasing everything we have onto 4chan /b/," she said. The following day, she and the others graced the "sad 4chaners" themselves with millions of user accounts from Gawker so that people like William could have fun with its account holders.

Gawker posted an announcement of the security breach, saying, "We are deeply embarrassed by this breach. We should not be in a position of relying on the goodwill of hackers who identified the weaknesses in our systems."

"Hahahahahahha," said an Irish hacker in #InternetFeds called Pwnsauce. "Raeped [*sic*] much?" And that was *hacker,* "SINGULAR," he added. "Our very own Kayla." Kayla quickly added that the job had been done with four others, and when another hacker in #InternetFeds offered to write up an announcement on the drop for /b/, she thanked him and added, "Don't mention my name."

Gnosis, rather than Anonymous, took credit for the attack. Kayla said she had been part of Anonymous since 2008 and up to that point had rarely hacked for anything other than "spite or fun," with Gawker being her biggest scalp. But after joining #InternetFeds, she started hacking more seriously into foreign government servers.

Kayla had not joined in the AnonOps DDoS attacks on PayPal and MasterCard because she didn't care much for DDoSing. It was a waste of time, in her view. But she still wanted to help WikiLeaks and thought that hacking was a more effective means of doing so. Not long after announcing the Gawker attack, Kayla went onto the main IRC network associated with WikiLeaks and for several weeks lurked under a random anonymous nickname to see what people were saying in the main channels. She noticed an operator of that channel who seemed to be in charge. That person went by the nickname q (presented here as lowercase, so as not to be confused with the hacktivist Q in #InternetFeds). Supporters and administrators with WikiLeaks often used one-letter nicknames, such as Q and P, because it was impossible to search for them on Google. If anyone in the channel had a question about WikiLeaks as an organization, he or she was often referred to q, who was mostly quiet. So Kayla sent him a private message.

According to a source who was close to the situation, Kayla told q that she was a hacker and dropped hints about what she saw herself doing for WikiLeaks: hacking into government websites and finding data that WikiLeaks could then release. She was unsure of what to expect and mostly just wanted to help. Sure enough, q recruited her, along with a few other hackers Kayla was not aware of at the time. To these hackers and to q, WikiLeaks appeared to be not only an organization for whistleblowers but one that solicited hackers for stolen information.

The administrator q wanted Kayla to scour the Web for vulnerabilities in government and military websites, known as .govs and .mils. Most hackers normally wouldn't touch these exploits because doing so could lead to harsh jail sentences, but Kayla had no problem asking her hacker friends if they had any .mil vulnerabilities.

Kayla herself went into overdrive on her hacking sprees for q, one source said, mostly looking for vulnerabilities. "She's always been blatant, out-in-your-face, I'm-going-to-hack-and-don't-give-a-shit," the source said. But Kayla did not always give everything to q. Around the same time that she started hacking for him, she got root access to a major web-hosting company—all of its VPSs (virtual private servers) and every normal server—and she started handing out the root exploits "like candy" to her friends, including people on the AnonOps chat network.

"She would just hack the biggest shit she could and give it away," said the source, dropping a cache of stolen credit card numbers or root logins then disappearing for a day. "She was like the Santa Claus of hackers."

"I don't really hack for the sake of hacking to be honest," Kayla later said in an interview. "If someone's moaning about some site I just have a quick look and if I find a bug on it I'll tell everyone in the channel. What happens from there is nothing to do with me. :P." Kayla said she didn't like being the one who defaced a site and preferred hiding silently in the background, "like a ninja."

"Being able to come and go without leaving a trace is key," she said. The longer she was in a network like Gawker's, the more she could get in and take things like administrative or executive passwords. Kayla liked Anonymous and the people in it, but she ultimately saw herself as a free spirit, one who didn't care to align herself with any particular group. Even when she was working with AnonOps or the people in #InternetFeds, Kayla didn't see herself as having a role or area of expertise.

"I'll go away and hack it, come back with access and let people go mad," she said. Kayla couldn't help herself most of the time anyway. If she was reading something online she would habitually start playing around with their parameters and login scripts.

More often than not, she would find something wrong with them.

Still, working for q gave Kayla a bigger excuse to go after the .gov and .mil targets, particularly those of third-world countries in Africa or South America, which were easier to get access to than those in more developed countries. Every day was a search for new targets and a new hack. Kayla never found anything as big as, say, the HBGary e-mail hoard for q, but she did, for instance, find vulnerabilities in the main website for the United Nations. In April 2011, Kayla started putting together a list of United Nations "vulns." This, for example:

http://www.un.org.al/subindex.php?faqe=details&id=57

was a United Nations server that was vulnerable to SQL injection, specifically subindex.php. And this page at the time:

http://www.un.org.al/subindex.php?faqe=details&id=57%27

would throw an SQL error, meaning Kayla or anyone else could inject SQL statements and suck out the database. The original URL didn't have %27 at the end, but Kayla's simply adding that after testing the parameters of php/asp scripts helped her find the error messages.

Kayla eventually got access to hundreds of passwords for government contractors and lots of military e-mail addresses. The latter were worthless, since the military uses a token system for e-mail that is built into a computer chip on an individual's ID card, and it requires a PIN and a certificate on the card before anyone is able to access anything.

It was boring and repetitive work, trawling through lists of e-mail addresses, looking for dumps from other hackers, and hunting for anything government or military related. But Kayla was said to be happy doing it. Every week or so, she would meet on IRC with q and pass over the collected info via encrypted e-mail, then await further instructions. If she asked what Julian Assange thought of what she was doing, q would say he approved of what was going on.

It turned out that q was good at lying.

Almost a year after Kayla started volunteering for WikiLeaks, other hackers who had been working with q found out he was a rogue operator who had recruited them without Assange's knowledge. In late 2011, Assange asked q to leave the organization. Kayla was not the only volunteer looking for information for what she thought was WikiLeaks. The rogue operator had also gotten other hackers to work with him on false pretenses. And in addition, one source claims, q stole $60,000 from the WikiLeaks t-shirt shop and transferred the money into his personal account. WikiLeaks never found out what q was doing with the vulnerabilities that Kayla and other hackers found, though it is possible he sold them to others in the criminal underworld. It seemed, either way, like q did not really care about unearthing government corruption, and Kayla, a master at hiding her true identity from even her closest online friends, had been duped.

None of this mattered come February of 2011 when Kayla began talking with Tflow, Topiary, and Sabu in the exclusive new chat room that would bring them together for a landmark heist on Super Bowl Sunday: the attack on HBGary Federal. The bigger secret, which Kayla didn't know then, was that Sabu would not only get her deeper into a world of hacking that would become front-page news, but watch as her details got passed on directly to the FBI.

CHAPTER 11

The Aftermath

It was February 8, 2011, two days after Super Bowl Sunday. Aaron Barr was grabbing shirts out of his closet, quickly folding them, and placing them into the medium-size suitcase that rested on the bed in front of him. This was no mad rush, but Barr had to move. He had spent fifteen years in the military, and he and his family were now expert travelers. They made their preparations quickly and with quiet efficiency. His wife was packing a separate bag, the silence interrupted only by the occasional question about traveling arrangements. Just two hours before, Barr had been back in his study catching up on the flood of news stories about the HBGary attack and the new, disastrous view the media was taking of Barr's proposals to Hunton & Williams against WikiLeaks and Glenn Greenwald.

Learning about the Anonymous hack had been stressful for him. But the media's feast on his controversial e-mails was having a definite effect on his blood pressure. Barr longed to correct each story, but lawyers had told him to stay quiet for now. All he could do was read and grit his teeth. Occasionally, curiosity would overcome his better judgment and he would dip into the AnonOps

IRC rooms under a pseudonym to see what the Anons were saying. He was still a laughingstock for the hundreds of participants hungry to see Barr humiliated in new ways. There were calls for anyone who lived in Washington, D.C., to drive past Barr's house and take pictures or to send him things in the mail—he received a blind person's walking cane and a truckful of empty boxes. He also got one pizza. A couple of people had randomly shown up at his front door, and one had tried to take pictures of the inside of his house. Barr had been disturbed but had just sent them away, figuring this was mostly harmless. Then, a couple of hours earlier, he had visited Reddit, a snarky forum site that had become increasingly popular with people who liked 4chan but wanted more intelligent discussion. A user had posted the *Forbes* interview with Barr from the preceding Monday, and amid the analysis and machismo in the 228 resulting comments, there were a few nasty suggestions about Barr's kids. It was most likely just talk, but Barr didn't want to take any more chances. It took only one nutjob to pull a trigger, after all. Minutes later, he had talked to his wife, and the two started packing.

That afternoon the family loaded everything into their car, the twins thinking they were about to embark on some exciting road trip. Barr's wife and kids drove south to stay with a friend for two weeks while Barr hopped on a plane to Sacramento. This was where HBGary Inc. was headquartered and where Barr would get into the cleanup job and start to help the police with their investigation.

Meanwhile, HBGary Inc.'s Greg Hoglund was working on damage control. He contacted Mark Zwillinger of Internet law firm Zwillinger & Genetski. Mark would later be assisted on the case by Jennifer Granick, a well-known Internet lawyer who had previously represented hackers like Kevin Poulsen and worked for freedom-of-information advocates the Electronic Freedom Foundation. After talking to Zwillinger, Hoglund penned an open letter to HBGary customers. When he was done, he published it on the now restored HBGary website, referring specifically to HBGary Inc. and not the sister company Barr had run.

"On the weekend of Super Bowl Sunday, HBGary, Inc., experienced a cyber incident. Hackers unlawfully accessed the e-mail accounts of two HBGary Inc. employees, held by our cloud-based service provider, using a stolen password, and uploaded the stolen e-mails to the Internet."

Hoglund's letter wasn't clear about where it was pointing the finger—though that would change in time. It seemed to suggest that HBGary's attackers had gone to great lengths to access the company's e-mails, when actually the process had not been difficult at all. It was an SQL injection, the simplest of attacks. Ted Vera's password, satcom31, had been easy to crack. Only Hoglund had used a random string of numbers and letters that had no relation to any of his other web accounts. The attack could have been worse too. The hackers had gotten all kinds of personal data on HBGary employees, from social security numbers to home addresses, and photos of Vera's kids after getting access to his Flickr account. "This was when my moralfag mode kicked in," Topiary later remembered. The others agreed that no kids should be involved, and they all decided not to leak the social security numbers. "I'm thankful that we didn't."

Still, the combination of social media, blogs, and twenty-four-hour online and TV news meant the names Aaron Barr and HBGary were all over the Internet the day after Super Bowl Sunday. Topiary's fake Aaron Barr tweets had been retweeted by Anonymous IRC, a feed with tens of thousands of followers, and there were now thousands of news stories about Barr.

Barr soon found out the attack had been conducted largely by five people. "I'm surprised it's a small number," he said in a phone interview early Monday morning in Washington, D.C. "There is a core set of people who manage the direction of the organization. And those people are, in my impression, very good."

Barr sounded tired. "Right now I just feel a bit exhausted by the whole thing. Shock, anger, frustration, regret, all those types of things," he said. "You know if I...maybe I should have known these guys were going to come after me this way."

No one knew at the time that the content of Barr's e-mails would prove so controversial and would gain him as much press attention as the attack itself had, but Barr was already concerned. "The thing I'm worried about the most is I'd rather my e-mails not be all out there, but I can't stop that now," he said, adding he would be contacting all the people he had exchanged e-mails with to tell them what was going on. "It does not cause any significant long-term damage to our company so I'm not worried." About this, Barr was wrong.

As the hack on HBGary Federal was taking place, Kayla had sent a message to Laurelai, the transgender woman who a couple of years before had been a soldier named Wesley Bailey and who was now becoming a familiar face in the world of hacking. Kayla told Laurelai that she was in the middle of "owning" a federal contractor called HBGary and asked if she wanted to come into AnonOps and see.

Laurelai hopped onto the AnonOps network to find hundreds of people talking over one another about what had happened, and the wife of Greg Hoglund, Penny Leavy, appealing to the attackers in the AnonOps #reporter channel.

"It was chaos," Laurelai remembered. Laurelai was now volunteering with a website and blog called Crowdleaks, an evolved version of Operation Leakspin. This was the project that had spun off Operation Payback and gotten Anons sifting through WikiLeaks cables. Laurelai had disliked Operation Payback because, like Kayla, she believed DDoSing things was pointless. She liked sifting through data and considered herself an information broker. She came aboard Crowdleaks when a mutual friend suggested she'd make a great server admin for the site's manager, an Anonymous sympathizer nicknamed Lexi.

"There's a huge story brewing from this HBGary hack," Laurelai told Lexi, who replied that Laurelai should cover it for the blog herself. Laurelai downloaded Barr's and Greg's e-mails and started searching for terms like *FBI, CIA, NSA,* and eventually, *WikiLeaks.* A list of Barr's e-mails to Hunton & Williams showed up on her screen. As Laurelai looked through these e-mails, she stumbled on the PowerPoint presentation Barr had made for the law firm in which he suggested ways of sabotaging the credibility of WikiLeaks. Laurelai did a bit more digging on Hunton & Williams and realized that the firm represented the Bank of America. By now it was widely rumored that WikiLeaks had a treasure trove of confidential data that had been leaked to it from Bank of America and that it was getting ready to publish. That's when the penny dropped.

"Oh shit," Laurelai said she thought then. "Bank of America is trying to destroy WikiLeaks." Her next realization was scarier: Barr hadn't even tried to encrypt the e-mails about the proposal, and he hadn't seemed that secretive about it. It suggested that this sort of proposal, however unethical, was not that far from standard industry practices. HBGary Federal was not a rogue operator; it counted stalwarts in the industry like Palantir and Berico Technologies as partners. Laurelai wrote a blog post for Crowdleaks and collaborated with a journalist from the Tech Herald to report that HBGary had been working with a storied law firm and, indirectly, Bank of America to hurt WikiLeaks.

Still only a couple of days after the HBGary attack, Sabu, Topiary, and Kayla did not know about Barr's strange proposals on WikiLeaks. Topiary was still trawling through the e-mails looking for juicy information, and the team was planning to publish them on an easy-to-navigate website that they wanted to call AnonLeaks. If this sort of thing caught on, they figured, AnonLeaks could become a more aggressive, proactive counterpart to WikiLeaks. Lexi offered the server space being used by Crowdleaks, which was using the same hosting company as WikiLeaks.

Just as an Anon named Joepie91 had finished programming the e-mail viewer, the group started seeing press reports on the actual content of the HBGary e-mails from journalists who had already downloaded the entire package via torrent sites.

The group decided that the searchable HBGary e-mails would be the first addition to their new site, AnonLeaks.ru. But they had no plans for where this new site would go or how, or even if, it would be organized.

"I think the media will get confused and think AnonLeaks is separate to AnonOps or PayBack," said Kayla. "I dunno. The media ALWAYS seem to get anything Anon wrong." Still, the team spent a few days in early February waiting for HBGary Federal's tens of thousands of e-mails to compile, and Topiary suggested looking for a few choice pieces to put on the new AnonLeaks website as teasers. That way, the blank website wouldn't give the impression that the team was playing for time. It was a classic PR strategy — getting the word out initially, then developing the story with a drip feed of exclusive information. Among the teasers was an embarrassing e-mail from Barr to company employees in which he gave them his password, "kibafo33," so that they could all take part in a conference call.

Finally, on Monday, February 14, after a few news sites reported that a WikiLeaks-style site called AnonLeaks was coming, the team launched the new web viewer with all 71,800 e-mails from HBGary. They included 16,906 e-mails from Aaron Barr, more than 25,000 e-mails from two other HBGary execs, and 27,606 e-mails from HBGary Inc. CEO Greg Hoglund, including a lovesick e-mail from his wife, Penny, that said, "I love when you wear your fuzzy socks with your jammies."

Now more journalists started covering the story, and the coverage went on for more than a month. The attack had been unscrupulous, but the ends were an exposé on spying, misinformation, and cyber attacks by a security researcher. Hardly anyone pointed out that people with Anonymous were using exactly the same tactics.

In late February 2011, Barr resigned as CEO of HBGary Federal. A week later, Democratic congressman Hank Johnson called for an investigation into government, military, and NSA contracts with HBGary Federal and its partners Palantir and Berico Technologies. Johnson had read reports of the scandal and asked his staff to look into it.

"I felt duty bound to move for further investigation," Johnson said in an interview at the time. He did not like the idea of government contractors like HBGary Federal developing software tools that were meant to be used in counterterrorism for "domestic surveillance and marketing to business organizations." Spying on your own citizens, he added, was bad enough.

"If you have anything else like this come up," Laurelai asked Kayla after getting a peek at the chaos from the HBGary attack, "can you let me know so we can write about it?"

"Sure," Kayla replied. She kept her word. A couple of days later Kayla asked Laurelai if she wanted to see where some action was happening and then invited her into a new exclusive IRC channel, again off AnonOps, called #HQ. By now #InternetFeds had been shut down after rumors that one of the thirty or so participants was leaking its chat logs. This room, #HQ, was smaller and had about six people in it, at most, at any one time. It included everyone who had helped in the HBGary Federal attack.

"Hang out here and you'll see when stuff is about to pop up,"

Kayla said. Laurelai was excited about being in #HQ and wondered if she might be able to help expose other white hat security firms that were operating under their own laws and getting away with the kind of stuff that Anons were getting arrested for. Already in January, the FBI had executed forty search warrants on people suspected of taking part in the DDoS attacks on PayPal, working off the list of a thousand IP addresses the company had detected.

Though no one else knew it, Laurelai was secretly logging everything that was being said in the #HQ room, even when she wasn't in it. Having spent the last two years learning how to hack and social-engineer people, she deemed it important to document what people around her were saying—at a later date, the logs could be used to corroborate things or refute them if necessary. Logging the chat was just standard procedure for Laurelai. In the meantime, she gradually became disappointed with the standard of discussion in the room. "They were acting like a bunch of damn kids," she later remembered.

"SUCH AN AWESOME CREW HERE," the hacker known as Marduk (and also known as Q) said on February 8, the same day Aaron Barr and his family fled their home.

"An Anon Skype party should be in order," said Topiary. (It eventually happened, but only with people from AnonOps who were willing to reveal their voices.)

They threw out occasional ideas for short projects. Marduk, who had strong political views and seemed to be older than most of the others, at one point asked Kayla to scan for vulnerabilities in websites for Algerian cell phone providers. He was looking for databases full of tens of thousands of cell phone numbers for Algerian citizens that he could then hand over to the country's opposition party for a mass SMS on February 12. It would be another attempt to support the democratic uprising in the Middle East after the successful attacks on Tunisia and Egypt in January.

Kayla seemed more excited about publishing Greg Hoglund's e-mails. "Greg's e-mails are ready. Parsed and everything," she said. "The time to fuck Greg is now. :3."

That was one thing they could all agree on.

"Who is handling media?" Kayla asked.

"Housh and Barrett," Topiary said, referring to Gregg Housh from Chanology, who now spoke to the media as an expert on Anonymous, and another man, called Barrett Brown, whom Topiary would deal with more closely in the coming weeks.

Eventually, Laurelai introduced herself.

"Hi," Laurelai said when she first entered that morning.

"Ahai," said Marduk. "Welcome to where the shitstorm began." Then he got down to business. "Laurelai, we can't tie [HBGary Federal] to WikiLeaks for sure?" he asked.

"I already have," she answered. "We got enough to smear the shit out of them." That confirmation pleased Marduk.

"They are one strange company," said Marduk. "Actually I'm sure it's a government coverup."

"The government uses these companies to do their dirty work," Laurelai explained.

The WikiLeaks connection Laurelai had found conveniently segued with the modus operandi of Operation Payback, making it look almost as if Anonymous had planned it all.

"*Kayla cuddles Laurelai :3 So much <3," Kayla wrote with her usual cheerfulness.

"Haha," Topiary said. "Women on the Internet."

"You hear about HBGary being contracted by Bank of America to attack WikiLeaks?" Kayla told a rare newcomer to the #HQ chat room, proud to provide the news.

"Seriously?" the person answered. "Fuck this shit's deep."

"Fallen right off the diving board and drowned," said Topiary. "That's how deep it goes."

Eventually, the group had to talk about what they would do

next. After being away for about a week, Sabu was back online, claiming he had a new laptop and eager to discuss future hits.

"So are we going to focus on AnonLeaks, or should I start looking for targets?" he asked the group. He had been up for the last two days and was exhausted but wanted to make progress and hit more digital security firms. "HBGary was the tip of the iceberg."

Overshadowing everything was a growing sense of unease about the authorities and, worse, spies and snitches from anti-Anonymous hackers like The Jester and his crew. They came to believe that HBGary Inc.'s Greg Hoglund had come onto AnonOps under a different alias, trying to track down Topiary and Marduk.

But one of the most prominent people criticizing Anonymous at that moment was doing so through Twitter, under the username @FakeGreggHoush. No one in #HQ knew the real person behind this account, which was created on February 16, the day after their HBGary e-mails viewer went live. This person was constantly making biting remarks and even threatening to expose the real names of the HBGary attackers on a specific upcoming date: March 19. @FakeGreggHoush was actually Jennifer Emick, the former Anon from Chanology who hated the real Gregg Housh and who, after breaking away from Anonymous, had begun her own campaign against it with a few online friends.

Another five Twitter accounts soon appeared, all equally spiteful and all claiming publicly to know who Topiary really was. They were not just making these claims to Topiary, but to the whole Anon community and anyone who followed it. A few tweeted to news reporters that he was leading Anonymous. "Troll Anonymous hard enough and they name one of their own," one proclaimed. "Who will be first?" Another said, "Topiary, we are outside your flat, taking pictures, we will send you a few, just so you know we aren't full of shit." Topiary replied by asking for high-quality prints. Reading the tweets was like being poked with a blunt pencil. It didn't hurt, but it was increasingly distracting. The fact was, anyone who really wanted to dox the HBGary hackers could make himself more dangerous than the FBI, especially if driven by a personal vendetta.

"How much info do you have available on the Internet about yourself, Marduk?" Topiary asked. "I mean deep, like little personal tidbits from like 10 years."

"All, but not as Marduk," he said. "And nobody, absolutely nobody on AnonOps knows who I am."

"Just be careful," Sabu said. "Can't afford to lose any of you guys."

Sabu was also worried about his own safety. While Topiary could rest assured that his real name, Jake Davis, was nowhere on the Web in connection with him, Sabu knew that "Hector Monsegur" was dotted around the Internet. Also, from what little information the team members were sharing with one another, Sabu believed (correctly) that he was the only HBGary hacker who lived in the United States. This meant the FBI was almost certainly on his tail. He gave Topiary a Google Voice number and asked him to call it every day, without fail. The first time Topiary did, he noted a heavy New York accent and a surprisingly young-sounding voice.

"Hey," Sabu answered.

"Hello," said Topiary. It was the first time they were speaking to each other in voice, and while it was awkward at first, they soon had a normal conversation. Afterward, Sabu would always answer with a coded greeting that was an homage to an Internet meme: "This is David Davidson." Sometimes he would answer the phone while he was driving; other times he'd be at home, the sound of TV or his two daughters playing in the background. Sabu made sure his Google Voice number was bounced through several servers all over the world before it finally got to his Black-Berry. His voice always sounded clear, though.

As the immensity of their heist made Sabu feel more paranoid, he also grew increasingly mistrustful of Laurelai, the newest member to #HQ. His irritation rose when he found out Laurelai had written up a manual for visitors to AnonOps about working in teams to carry out attacks similar to the one on HBGary.

"Remove that shit from existence," he said. There were no hierarchy, leadership, or defined roles in Anonymous and so no need for an operations manual. "Shit like this is where the Feds will get American Anons on Rico abuse act and other organized crime laws."

Laurelai began arguing with Sabu about how HBGary had been carried out, saying the hackers should have taken their time to exploit more internal info from the company. But Sabu was having none of it. Keenly aware of his group's reputation and image and ever fearful of getting caught, he pointed out that an operations doc that gave guidelines for hitting other websites was no different from the proposals Aaron Barr had been creating on hitting WikiLeaks and the chamber of commerce.

"It makes us look like hypocrites," he said. "Who the fuck is Laurelai and why is he/she/it questioning our owning of HBGary? ... Who invited you anyway?" Sabu said he felt the channel was being compromised and left.

Over the coming days the group of still roughly half a dozen people became increasingly distracted by theories about their enemies, a crew of people hanging out on another IRC network who they believed were plotting to dox and expose them. Who was this @FakeGreggHoush on Twitter? Topiary got hold of the real Gregg Housh on IRC and asked him if he knew. Housh suggested it was a woman from back in the Chanology days (three years ago—almost a lifetime in Internet years) named Jennifer Emick.

Topiary had never heard the name, but he drew up a document adding Jennifer Emick and a few people allegedly working with her and showed it to the others in #HQ. When Laurelai looked at the document, she suddenly grew nervous. These were all the people who had supported her Scientology Exposed website. And while she and Emick had fought and grown apart, they still talked from time to time. Laurelai believed that Emick was being framed by someone else, probably Housh. Recently, Emick had told Laurelai privately that Housh was acting as a puppet master for AnonOps and that he was trying to create chaos in the network. If anything, this was Housh's hand at work, trying to turn AnonOps into his personal army against Emick and run things like he did in #marblecake, Laurelai reasoned. She had no idea that Emick's real plans involved tracking down the people behind Anonymous and unmasking them publicly.

"Topiary, they aren't behind it," she said. "Something a lot more sinister is going on." She called up the memories from Chanology and asked a weighty question. "Does anyone know what 'marblecake' means?"

There was silence. Nobody did. One person had vaguely heard the name and associated it with petty fighting over forums, something akin to a previous generation of Anonymous. Laurelai continued: "Jen's a little weird, but she's harmless."

While the others quietly rolled their eyes, Laurelai began formulating a theory that she eventually came to fully believe: Gregg was trying to get back at her for an old vendetta in Chanology by implicating Jennifer Emick. This meant Emick was in danger of being attacked by Anon. Laurelai couldn't help but feel convinced by the theory. She had just exposed Barr's plot against WikiLeaks, hadn't she? But she was also spending about twelve hours a day online while her mother looked after her two kids. The Internet was becoming her life, and it was hard not to let it take over.

Laurelai contacted Emick and blurted out the allegations, told her what Housh was up to, and said that she was in a private channel called #HQ with the HBGary hackers. Emick, sounding surprised, denied plotting anything.

"I don't care about what's going on in AnonOps," Emick told Laurelai on the phone. "I have no idea what's going on." Laurelai took this information back to the others in #HQ as proof that Emick was not a saboteur and that all the rumors were Housh trying to "get at me." Marduk and Topiary listened but were wary of the conspiracy theories. They were noise.

"Really this shit affects nothing," Topiary concluded.

But it wasn't over. Back on Twitter, the @FakeGreggHoush account started needling Laurelai, accusing her of being part of the group of people who had worked with Housh in the old Marblecake chat room (which was not true). That was the final straw. Laurelai wrote back on Twitter and said she had logs proving that she wasn't talking to Gregg Housh and that she could provide them, privately, in exchange for new information about Housh to help her piece the conspiracy together and exonerate Emick. "The only thing I care about is protecting Jen and her friends," Laurelai said. The Twitter account @FakeGreggHoush agreed.

Laurelai looked over the chat log she had been diligently keeping that noted everything said in #HQ for the past week and a half (from February 8 to February 19). She naively believed that if she showed them to whoever @FakeGreggHoush was, she would exonerate Emick and that no one would have to know she had leaked the chat logs. Laurelai copied the entire chat log, about 245 pages, and posted it on the web app Pastebin. She then sent a direct message on Twitter to @FakeGreggHoush, telling the person to take a look at the logs. Within a few minutes, Emick had copied the logs, and Laurelai, still oblivious, had deleted the Pastebin file.

"Holy shit," Emick thought as she stared at the screen. She quickly started skimming the enormous chat log, the prize that had just been handed to her on a plate. Bizarrely, there was nothing that truly implicated Gregg Housh but plenty to implicate Sabu, Kayla, and Topiary in the attack on HBGary Federal. She started reading the huge log much more carefully.

Emick's deceptions of Laurelai, as well as her alter ego as @FakeGreggHoush, were tactics aimed at outing the real people behind Anonymous. Emick had realized after HBGary that the best way to take Anonymous down was simply to show that people in it were not anonymous at all. All she had to do was find their real names. And thanks to Laurelai, she was about to find Sabu's.

PART 2

Fame

CHAPTER 12

Finding a Voice

In mid-February of 2011, as Jennifer Emick dug into the HQ logs that Laurelai had handed her, Topiary was enjoying a newfound popularity on the AnonOps chat network. People on the network now knew that he had been involved in the HBGary attack and that he had hijacked Aaron Barr's Twitter feed. For the Anons, this had been an epic raid, and Topiary was the Anon who knew how to make it fun, or "lulz-worthy." Now, whenever Jake signed into AnonOps as Topiary, he got half a dozen private messages inviting him to join an operation, offering him logs from the CEO of a French security company, requesting that he intervene in a personal dispute, or asking his advice on publicity.

This was sort of like what was happening to Anonymous itself. Over the course of February, the public channels on AnonOps were inundated with requests from regular people outside the network asking what they thought was a group of organized hackers to hit certain targets. The requested sites included other digital security firms; individuals; government websites in Libya, Bahrain, and Iran; and, naturally, Facebook. None were followed up.

Most attacks came from discussions that occurred directly on AnonOps IRC, especially discussions between operators like Owen and Ryan. There was no schedule, no steps being taken. People would often start planning an op, run into a roadblock, and shelve it. Everything seemed to overlap. Topiary himself would rarely finish one project before moving onto another— he'd be writing deface messages one minute and the next start reading the Aaron Barr e-mails again.

After his recent invitation into #InternetFeds, Topiary was granted unusually high status in chat channels by operators. He would sometimes spend a whole day flitting between chat rooms, cracking jokes, then segueing into some serious advice on a side operation before going to bed, feeling fulfilled. It was better than the buzz he'd gotten from doing prank calls back on 4chan and unlike anything he had ever experienced in the real world, let alone in school. Operators and other hackers confirm that he came across as "charming" and "funny." Being a talented writer was useful in a world where you communicated in text, and Topiary's style had hints of mature world-weariness that appealed to Anons.

Topiary rarely interacted with people in the real world. There was the occasional visit to his family, a trip to the store, or a once-in-a-while meeting of some old friends in his town whom he knew from online gaming. Perhaps 90 percent of all his social interaction now took place online. And this suited him fine. He liked entertaining people, and soon he'd get to do the prank call of his life.

Starting in early January, many supporters in Anonymous had suggested going after the Westboro Baptist Church, a controversial Kansas-based religious group known for picketing the funerals of soldiers with giant signs blaring GOD HATES FAGS. They claimed God was punishing the United States because it "enabled" homosexuality. Westboro seemed like an obvious target for Anonymous, even though the church was practicing its right to free speech, something that Anonymous was supposed to fight for.

But soon enough, someone laid down the gauntlet. On February 18, out of the blue, a public letter was posted on AnonNews.org (anyone could post one on the site) issuing a threat with the flourish of unnecessarily formal language. "We have always regarded you and your ilk as an assembly of graceless sociopaths and maniacal chauvinists," it told Westboro. "Anonymous cannot abide by this behavior any longer." If the message was ignored, Westboro would "meet with the vicious retaliatory arm of Anonymous." The letter ended with the "We are Anonymous, We are Legion" slogan. The first day, no one noticed the letter. The next day, however, someone from #Philosoraptors asked if anyone knew where it had come from. Nobody did. An empty threat that wasn't followed up would make Anonymous look weak if the media picked up on it. One of the operators ran a search on all the network's chat channels and found a secret, invite-only room called #OpWestboro. It looked like a couple of bored trolls had been trying to get some press attention.

To everyone's chagrin, the trolls got it. The attack on HBGary had excited news reporters so much that any hint of an Anonymous threat suddenly had a veneer of credibility. Several news outlets, including tech site Mashable, reported on the latest Anonymous "threat," updating their stories on the same day with a gleeful public riposte from Westboro. Megan Phelps-Roper, the curly-haired granddaughter of Westboro Baptist's founder, Fred Phelps, quickly tweeted, "Thanks, Anonymous! Your efforts to shut up God's word only serve to publish it further.... Bring it, cowards." The church also posted an official flyer on its website in a screaming, bold font, headlined "Bring it!" and calling Anonymous "coward cry-baby 'hackers,'" "a puddle of pimple faced nerds," and adding that "nothing will shut-up these words—ever." They were clearly reveling in the prospect of a dogfight.

About five writers in #Philosoraptors scrambled to write a new, official-sounding press release to douse the fire. "So we've been hearing a lot about some letter that we supposedly sent you this morning," they said. "Problem is, we're a bit groggy and don't remember sending it." Several news reports quickly picked this up. "It's a Hoax," cried PCWorld.com, "Anonymous Did Not Threaten Westboro Baptist Church." Now people were getting confused. Was Anonymous going to attack Westboro Baptist Church or not? This troubled Topiary. He disliked the public confusion about what Anonymous was planning to do. He had seen it in December of 2010, when Anonymous said it would take down Amazon.com and then didn't because of the squabbles with botmasters Civil and Switch. He didn't want it to look like Anonymous had failed again.

Topiary popped into #InternetFeds and noticed that one of the participants had some interesting news. The first, fake threat against Westboro had gotten him curious enough to poke around in the church's computer network, and he'd found a vulnerability. Two other hackers had found a way to exploit the security hole. If they wanted, they could take down several of Westboro's key websites, including its main GodHatesFags.com site, and deface them too.

"We might as well do something now," they said. Most of the dozen or so people in #InternetFeds, including Tflow and the AnonOps operator Evilworks, began talking about hitting Westboro, revving one another up for what could be another spectacular attack. Free speech aside, it would at least bring closure to the confusion.

"So what should we do now?" someone asked. The people in #InternetFeds were good at hacking but terrible at publicity. That's when Topiary piped up. "We should do this as an event, not just the usual defacement," he said. Then he had an idea. "Gonna check something out. Be right back."

Topiary wanted to confirm it before getting people's hopes up, but in all the talk of Westboro, he had remembered hearing about a YouTube video of a recent radio show in which Westboro spokeswoman Shirley Phelps had been talking about the alleged Anonymous threat. What if he could get on that radio show and confront Shirley himself?

The David Pakman Show was a current affairs program recorded at Greenfield Community College in Massachusetts. Set in a studio with full lighting and multiple cameras, the show was recorded for TV and radio simultaneously. At twenty-seven, Pakman was one of the youngest nationally syndicated radio hosts in America; he had gotten into the business when he started his own talk show in college. Over the subsequent six years, Pakman had invited people from the Westboro Baptist Church to be on the show about half a dozen times. Pakman knew that confrontational oddballs brought listeners, whether it was a pastor who wanted to burn the Koran on 9/11 or an anti-gay former navy chaplain who claimed he had performed a lesbian exorcism. Pakman justified giving these people airtime because he felt it was right to expose what they preached.

Westboro Baptist Church had about eighty-five members and had been founded by Fred Phelps, a former civil rights lawyer. For years, Phelps had ruled his family with an iron fist. His one estranged son, Nate, claimed the preacher abused his children, even though most of them had gone on to follow his teachings. Shirley Phelps (Fred's daughter) became something of a regular guest on Pakman's show whenever Westboro picketed a soldier's funeral or did something equally unpleasant. She would tell Pakman that he was going to hell because he was Jewish and his people had killed Jesus. He found it amusing.

"Things are gonna happen to those little cowards," she said on his latest show about the Anonymous "threat" to Westboro; she was smiling, and her face was devoid of makeup. "And it's going to cause the ears of them that hear it to tingle. They've made a terrible mistake."

After the show, when Pakman got a Twitter message from Topiary stating he was from Anonymous and wanted to talk, Pakman was skeptical. Then another thought came to his mind: "This could be a compelling piece of interview." Bringing two controversial groups onto his show at the same time seemed like too good an opportunity to pass up.

Topiary e-mailed Pakman, telling the radio host that Anonymous had access to the Westboro sites and suggesting that hacking might take place on the show. According to Topiary, Pakman replied cryptically with "If something like that were to happen, it would be my obligation to bring immediate attention to it." It dawned on Topiary that Pakman was very interested, since he later brought the subject up again, asking if the "event" was still going to take place. Pakman, who later denied that he had had any idea ahead of time that Anonymous was going to hack the Westboro websites live on the air, then arranged for Topiary to go on the show the next day. He would make sure, he added, that the show got plenty of online attention by posting links on popular forums like Reddit and Digg.

"Good job," someone on #InternetFeds said when Topiary came back into the chat room and reported that the group had a forthcoming appearance on the Pakman show, giving them the chance to do a live hack and deface of the Westboro sites. He asked around to see if anyone else wanted to do the live call, since he'd already thrown his voice around on TV news network Russia Today. But people wanted to hear Topiary versus Shirley. Many on AnonOps thought he was good at public speaking, even though his speech could deteriorate into stuttered sentences and what he considered a goofy British accent.

Resigned to his part in the verbal showdown, Topiary started writing a deface message for the Westboro website. Then he noticed something odd: most of Westboro's main sites were already down. Not defaced—just offline. It looked like someone had noticed the buzz around the fake Anonymous threat and taken the sites down himself. Topiary realized it was The Jester. He hopped over to Jester's chat room, approached the hacktivist, and asked if he could let the sites back up for at least a couple of hours. He didn't give Jester any times or say that it was for a radio show, just in case someone from his crew tried to sabotage it. He stayed vague.

Jester confirmed his involvement by refusing, adding mysteriously that he was "under extreme pressure to keep them down." A little bewildered and irritated, Topiary gave up and went back to #InternetFeds. They would have to make do with an attack on a minor web page.

He set to work writing up a defacement message in the simple program Notepad++, the same way he had done all ten deface messages for Anonymous in the last month or so. After writing the release he'd paste it into a text box on Pastehtml and write the HTML code around it. All the deface pages were plain text on a white background. Topiary had tried more complicated layouts but they never had as much impact as stark black and white, a complete contrast from the busily designed websites that were supposed to be there. Often he would explore the different chat rooms on AnonOps IRC and note down any philosophical things people said about Anonymous or the world in general, and then he'd try to incorporate them into his messages. Anons were already starting to realize their opinions mattered, as journalists quoted random comments made in AnonOps chat rooms.

Topiary was doing this partly for his own good. Leading up to

Westboro and particularly after the Pakman show, his nickname became more public. "I didn't want all that attention," he later said. Deep down he didn't want his "voice" in text and audio to become familiar to the public and authorities. When he wrote a press release, he took to posting it on Pirate Pad and imploring other supporters and Philosoraptors to edit it. "I'd leave it for 10 minutes and no one would touch it," he said. "People kept saying, no it's fine. I don't know if they were nervous or didn't want to tell me it was a bit wrong."

The next day, just before the show, Topiary asked a friend on AnonOps how he should handle the Westboro Baptist spokeswoman.

"Just let her ramble," the friend replied. "You don't need to make her look bad. She's going to make herself look bad." Topiary then spent a few minutes listening to music to try to calm his nerves, a song by the mellow techno artist World's End Girlfriend. It always left him more relaxed. Thirty seconds before the show was to start, Pakman called Topiary, who could hear Shirley Phelps-Roper in the background, grumbling in a southern drawl about camera issues.

Pakman immediately recognized Topiary's voice from the interviews he had done with Russia Today and from the Tom Hartman program. At the eleventh hour, Pakman breathed a quiet sigh of relief that he was speaking to a genuine spokesperson for Anonymous.

Soon enough, Phelps-Roper was on the line too, and the video segment showed three images: Pakman in a black blazer with his microphone; Shirley with a home printer and bookshelf in the background, her hair pulled back in a ponytail and her eyes ablaze; and a picture of a giant shark being attacked by Batman wielding a light saber—that was Topiary. Whenever Topiary spoke, his own picture glowed blue.

"Well, today we have everybody here," Pakman said, introducing Topiary as a "source within Anonymous" and then referring to him as simply "Anonymous." Did Anonymous issue a threat to Westboro Baptist Church? he asked.

"No, there was no talk of it, uh…" Topiary's deep baritone voice almost growled out onto the airwaves. He had an unusual accent—a Scottish lilt blended with a Nordic twang. He'd set his laptop on a table and turned away from it. Every prank call had been like this—he looked at simple focal points, like the ceiling or a book spine, or out the window.

"Shirley, is it your belief that Anonymous cannot harm the Westboro websites in any way?" Pakman asked.

"No one can shut these words that are…ROARING out of Mount Zion!" she cried. "I mean I'm talking to a little guy who's a Jew." David looked over at his producer and smiled.

"OK." Pakman suddenly grew serious. "So, Anonymous, can you address that? I mean, aren't all of Shirley's websites down right now?" Shirley let out a surprised laugh.

"Yeah right now," replied Topiary. "Um, GodHatesFags.com is down, YourPastorIsAWhore.com is down." He listed several more snappily named sites and explained, disappointed, that credit had to go to The Jester and not, technically, to Anonymous.

"Potatoe, potahto!" Phelps-Roper said, drowning him out for a moment. "You're all a bunch of criminals, and thugs.…And you're ALL facing your imminent destruction."

"Anonymous," David ventured, "is this riling you up to the point where you will actually take action?"

"Please do," Phelps-Roper deadpanned.

"Well…" said Topiary

"Hold on, Shirley," said Pakman.

"Our response to the 'cry-baby hackers' letter was mature," Topiary said. "Our response was we don't want to go to war with you—"

Phelps-Roper's eyes widened. "Did you just call criminals and thugs…'MATURE'?"

Topiary balked and decided to switch tacks.

"You say the Internet was invented just for the Westboro Baptist Church to get its message across, right?" he asked.

"Exactly," she said.

"Well, then how come God allowed gay-dating websites?"

"Psh. Silly." Phelps-Roper laughed. "That's called your proving ground."

"Am I going to hell?"

Phelps-Roper suddenly looked concerned. "Well, hon, I only know what I'm hearing because you're"—she raised her eyebrows—"Anonymous…and…you sound like a guy who's headed to hell I'm just sayin.'"

"Well in my lifetime I've performed over 9,000 sins," Topiary said. "So…"

"OH! And you keep track! What, you have a tally sheet?"

"Yeah over 9,000 sins. I keep track."

Pakman was smiling to himself. Topiary glanced back at his laptop and for the next thirty seconds he observed a window in AnonOps IRC, where a handful of people were watching a live stream of the show on Pakman's site. They were laughing. Pakman seemed to be waiting for Phelps-Roper to get riled up and say that nobody could hack the Westboro site before bringing things back to Topiary for the hack.

Phelps-Roper was explaining why being proud of sin did not "fit into a box with repentance….Of course you're going to hell."

"Hmm." Topiary sighed. "Internets is serious business."

"Let me bring things back to a central point," said Pakman. "Is there a next step? Does Anonymous intend to prove that they can in fact manipulate the Westboro Baptist Church network of websites? What can we expect going forward, Anonymous?"

If anything was going to happen, now was the time. Phelps-Roper tried to pipe up again but Topiary kept going.

"Actually," he said, smacking his lips, "I'm working on that right now." Topiary turned back to his laptop, clicked on a tab on his IRC windows to enter the private room #over9000, and quickly typed in *gogogo,* the signal. Tflow was ready and waiting with Topiary's HTML file.

Phelps-Roper's sarcasm went into overdrive. "He's working on that RIGHT NOW! Oh yay!" she yelled. Then her face darkened. "Hey, listen up, ladies...."

"Hold on, let's hear from Anonymous please, Shirley," said Pakman.

"No, no," Shirley said.

"No I have something interesting, I have a surprise for you, Shirley," said Topiary.

"Wait a minute," she said. "You save it for a minute!" The other voices fell silent. "This is what you've accomplished. You have caused eyes all over the world to look. All we're doing is publishing a message...a HUGE global explosion of the word of God." The others stayed silent.

With no live hack, the segment was coming to a close, and Pakman needed to steer things back to Topiary. "Anonymous, go ahead."

"I was just going to say in the time Shirley started blabbing her religious preach I actually did some business, and I think if you check downloads dot Westboro Baptist Church, I think you'll see a nice message from Anonymous."

Phelps-Roper looked unmoved. "Nice," she said, rolling her eyes.

"Dot com is it?" Pakman asked. Pakman's team already knew the exact URL for the site that was going to be hacked, as Topiary had sent it in an e-mail beforehand. "That's how his producer found it so fast," Topiary later said.

"Yes, we just put up a nice release while Shirley was preaching there," Topiary said on the show.

"Just while we were doing this interview." Pakman chuckled in apparent amazement. He looked to his producer and pointed to something offscreen.

"Yeah, we'd had enough! We'd responded maturely, saying we don't want a war. Then Shirley came on the radio, started, well…thinks I'm going to hell, so we've given her something to look at."

"So hold on," Pakman said, nodding off camera again, "I am getting a thumbs-up from my producer that there has been a message posted that appears to be from Anonymous." A screenshot of Topiary's earlier written message suddenly filled the screen: a simple white backdrop topped by the Anonymous logo of a headless suited man who was taking up what was supposed to be Westboro Baptist Church's main web page for downloads.

"Anonymous, are you taking responsibility for this?" Pakman asked again.

"Yep," Topiary said. "We just did it right now this very second."

"That is so special," Phelps-Roper suddenly interjected. "So special."

Topiary tried to explain. "You told us we can't harm your websites and we just did," he said. "I mean—"

"What I told you," Phelps shot back, "is you cannot shut us up. Thank you."

That was the end of the segment.

It wasn't the smack-down of Westboro that Topiary had been hoping for, but he was relieved he had avoided screwing anything up. Sure, Phelps-Roper had been surprised by the live defacement, but years of shooting down even the most reasonable arguments gave her a knack for barbed comments laced with sarcasm. She was a tough one to troll.

"I've encountered some nasty trolls and counter-trolls in my days, but Shirley came across with a sort of new-wave supertrolling that caught me off guard," said Topiary.

Her most withering put-downs even had some truth in them. In the end, Anonymous's main weapon wasn't all that destructive. They were defacing a little-known page on the church's network — "so special" — with the anticlimax further dampened by The Jester's confusing side campaign.

None of this mattered in the first few days after what came to be called the live Westboro hack because Topiary's face-off with Shirley Phelps-Roper quickly became one of the most popular videos on YouTube that week. Topiary watched the numbers rising each day, initially with excited fascination, then with some dread. First it was ten thousand, then two hundred thousand, and after five days, more than one million people had watched the video.

By this point Topiary had learned there was a fine line between success and failure when it came to the public side of Anonymous. "There had to be humor, so a meme or two, but definitely not too many," he later remembered. "There had to be something inexplicable—a kind of what-the-fuck-am-I-seeing.jpg, so Batman attacking a shark with a light saber." Finally there had to be something blatantly obvious to pick on: Shirley. "She's like that lady from *The Simpsons* that throws cats around, except she's talking about Mount Zion and dead soldiers." It was hard for Topiary not to look like the good guy when talking to her. "I was so, so happy I never stared into her crazy eyes," he added. "The first time I saw her face was when I clicked on the YouTube video. What the fuck, man."

A more serious thought had gripped his mind at the time, though: "More than one million people have heard my voice." Mixed in with the pride was a terrible unease—if only one person who knew him personally saw the video, his identity would be revealed. He hadn't used voice altering or changed his accent because he'd wanted it to seem real. He couldn't decide if the stunt had been a stupid mistake or his ballsiest move yet.

Pakman didn't hear from anyone in Anonymous after the show, but there was a flood of feedback from listeners, with views split on how great it had been to see the Westboro Baptist Church get taken down and others pointing out that whomever the target, Anonymous had just committed a crime. Pakman took it rather lightly. "I found the entire thing to be a kind of parody at the highest level," he recalled.

"Thinking back on everything with Anonymous and LulzSec, I see many things I regret being entangled in," Topiary later said. "But the Westboro Baptist Church attack, well…is *proud* the right word? Honored. I was honored to have been involved."

It seemed Westboro and Anonymous had some similarities. One key to Westboro's unfathomable ability to survive and maintain itself was its isolation. Its members knew their unique group as "us against the world." Their pickets at funerals were not really aimed at saving souls or spreading God's word but at stirring up anger and hatred in others—a self-serving exercise to fuel their own sense of righteousness. This culture of hate was one that only its longtime participants could truly understand. Profound acceptance coupled with desensitization to their own vicious trolling. When it came to motivation, Anonymous was often the same.

Chanology and Operation Payback had shown that Anonymous could take on unsavory characters as a group, but the live Westboro hack with Topiary signaled where Anonymous would be going next: smaller and more extreme.

Kayla had conducted her vengeful attack on Gawker; Sabu had had a revolutionary turn on Tunisia; Topiary had experienced the thrill of a live performance. Anonymous may have been a movement that could change the world, but it existed just as much for its own members as anything else. It gave them something to do, made them feel useful, and, while no one would admit it, let them carry out urges in a way that seemed justified and necessary. Gawker and HBGary had shown that Anonymous could be at its most destructive when it was taking revenge and when a small but focused group of people led operations. But it was only when a joker and public communicator like Topiary was added to the mix that the group had the makings of an even more powerful team: Sabu with his passion, Kayla with her skills, and Topiary with his silver tongue.

CHAPTER 13

Conspiracy (Drives Us Together)

A few days after the live Westboro hack, Topiary couldn't help but feel worried that more than a million people had now heard his real voice. One way to distract himself from those concerns was to plow through more of Aaron Barr's e-mails. Transfixed by what was on his Dell laptop screen, he'd come across a piece of string every few hours that seemed to lead him farther down a rabbit hole, toward what looked like a dark and dirty conspiracy. In late February, as Jennifer Emick was creating her own theories about who Anonymous was, Topiary was looking into theories that went beyond the Anonymous world and involved the American military. Sabu and Kayla weren't that interested in this subject or the e-mails anymore, but a sense of possibility kept Topiary hooked, and this was largely thanks to Barrett Brown, a blond, twenty-nine-year-old freelance writer from Texas who was passionate about exposing government corruption.

Topiary had first heard of Brown the day before the HBGary attack. Brown had published a spoof statement from Anonymous on the left-wing political blog the Daily Kos on Saturday, February 5, a day before the HBGary Federal attack. The title was

"Anonymous Concedes Defeat." Rambling and comical, it claimed Barr had discovered that the true leaders of Anonymous were "Q and Justin Bieber."

He added: "Mr. Barr has successfully broken through our over 9,000 proxy field and into our entirely non-public and secret insurgent IRC lair, where he then smashed through our fire labyrinth with vigor, collected all the gold rings along the way, opened a 50 silver key chest to find Anon's legendary hackers on steroids password." It was a word-for-word quote from Topiary on IRC, and Topiary was flattered to see himself quoted.

Brown then published a more formal "press release" on the Daily Kos after the attack, titled "Anon pwns HBGary Federal." Most Anon press releases were posted on AnonNews.net, but really, who was keeping track? What annoyed many Anons was that Brown had published the press release under his real name, and they christened him a namefag. Still, Topiary didn't mind him; in fact, from the start, he rather liked him. After the attack, Topiary complimented Brown on the spoof post. Brown was eager to see the HBGary e-mails, which at that time were still being published on torrenting sites bit by bit.

"I need some more of those e-mails so I can piece some stuff together," Brown told him.

It turned out that Brown was a big research nut. He had downloaded the first batch of Barr's 23,000 e-mails, searching for clues that would crack open a wider case of corruption that started with HBGary's misinformation campaign against Wiki-Leaks and ended with the U.S. military. After a few weeks of scanning, he picked up the phone and called William Wansley, one of the vice presidents of a military contractor called Booz Allen Hamilton and a name that had popped up in Barr's e-mails.

"Hi, is this Mr. Wansley?"

"Yes," a small voice replied.

"Hi, Wansley, this is, uh, Barrett Brown, I'm sort of a, uh, informal spokesman for Anonymous?" Brown said, hiding his nervousness. "The reason I'm calling is because we're going over some e-mails and we happened to see some correspondence between yourself and Aaron Barr of HBGary. I was curious as to what exactly the project is that you guys were working on, regarding Anonymous."

There was a long pause.

"Oh," Wansley said. "If you'd like to call our public affairs office, they should be able to help you...."

"Well, I'm not sure they would be able to help me as much as you could," Brown barked, his confidence growing, "because you were actually more involved in those discussions. I don't think public affairs offices are that good, in my experience, at, uh, you know providing, uh, actual intelligence."

There was another long pause as Wansley took in what he was hearing, then a loud roar in Houston as a plane few over Brown's house.

"Uh, basically for instance I'm looking at an e-mail right now," Brown continued, shouting to be heard over the plane. "Says you had a meeting at the offices of Booz Allen, ten thirty on, let's see, somewhere in late January with Aaron Barr. Aaron Barr of course as you know was researching Anonymous, he attempted to dig up our leadership. He was going to sell a list with my name on it to the FBI, with the names of a lot of people who aren't actually IN Anonymous. His methodology was a bit off, you might say...Um, and I'm assuming at this point you're probably not working—"

"I'm—I'm familiar with the organization," Wansley said, sounding weary. "First of all we don't comment on our client work at all, to protect the confidentiality of all our clients."

"Right."

"I can tell you we have no business dealings with HBGary anymore."

Brown paused.

"So you weren't in business dealings with them, you were just discussing the topic?" he asked.

"I can't comment on what someone else asked me to do, but we had no business dealings at all with HBGary."

"But you did have business dealings with them previously, right?' Brown tried again.

"Never."

"But you met with him not for social matters, but to discuss Anonymous."

"I have no relationship and I can't make any comment."

"You have no relationship with Aaron Barr?" Brown knew the conversation was coming to an end, and he was floundering.

"Please call my public affairs office and they'd be happy to talk to you."

"Thanks," Brown said.

"Thank you. Bye."

Click.

Brown hung up, then laughed out loud without smiling. "Tee hee hee!" He quickly wrote up a blog post titled "Booz Allen Hamilton VP Caught Lying" in which he explained: "He said he had no relationship with HBGary, which is odd insomuch as that this e-mail would seem to indicate otherwise." Brown added a link to one of Barr's e-mails, saying, "I had a meeting with Bill Wansley over at Booz yesterday."

Over the next few days, Brown kept sending messages to Topiary about HBGary. Topiary soon got the hint that Brown was serious and he invited him into a private Skype group with Gregg Housh and a few others to focus on researching the e-mails more deeply. Topiary kept the Skype group open at all times and found for the next two weeks that he was increasingly being pulled into its conversations, spending at least seven hours a day on the investigation into what Barr had really been working on. Brown gave it a name: Operation Metal Gear, after an old Nintendo game, and its goal, in a nutshell, was to find out how the intelligence community was infiltrating the Internet and social media sites like Facebook and Twitter to spy on American citizens. Cyber security buzzwords like *sockpuppets, persona management software, data monitoring,* and *cognitive infiltration* frequently cropped up, every lead branching out from the work and research of HBGary Federal and Barr. Whenever Topiary stumbled upon an e-mail from Barr's cache that could lead to new information on these issues, he'd send the link to Brown and let him know.

The project was intense, largely because of Brown himself, who seemed to never sleep. Topiary would wake up in the morning in his part of the world to find the Texan had been up all night reading through the HBGary e-mail trove. Brown would then spend the next two hours explaining what he had discovered overnight, often speaking at a hundred miles a minute. One particularly long conference call with him lasted thirteen hours, and another six hours, with Brown often using overly formal phrases like *pursuant to our investigation.* Topiary found this irritating at first, but he couldn't help admiring Brown's work ethic and passion for his activism. It seemed a level above even the most diehard moralfags in Anonymous.

The son of a wealthy real estate investor, Brown had a penchant for pin-striped shirts and cowboy boots, as well as a knack for keeping Topiary's interest piqued. "We're about to unravel something big," he'd say.

"To begin with I felt sorry for him," Topiary later remembered. "He was putting in a lot of hard work, but just came across the wrong way to Anon." It didn't help that his IRC nickname was BarrettBrown. "Everyone hated him. There were all kinds of anti-Barrett discussions in private channels, often mocking his methods and drug addiction." Brown was widely known in the Anon community to take hard drugs. One journalist who interviewed him over lunch recalled Brown starting off by smoking a joint, drinking alcohol, and shunning food throughout the meal, then taking a dose of a synthetic form of heroin—all the while speaking with extraordinary lucidity. Topiary dropped hints when he could that Brown wasn't so bad if they overlooked a few things, but Brown's rambling YouTube videos and conspiracies "just made things worse."

Chanology and Operation Payback had shown that if they were manipulated in the right way, Anons in their hundreds would suddenly want to collaborate on a raid or project. But key to that was making a raid fun and exciting. Topiary, who was becoming Brown's liaison with AnonOps, noticed that while Brown's campaign to uncover corruption had sounded sexy to the Anons at first, the fact that he had to struggle to maintain their interest demonstrated how difficult it was to harness the spontaneous, unpredictable power of Anonymous. Brown wanted Anonymous to help him carry out long-term research, but it was tough getting people in a community rooted in lulz to stick to a project for weeks, even months on end. It got even harder when Brown tried to get Anonymous on the evening news.

Between January and March of 2011, Brown's name got passed around among journalists who covered Anonymous, as he was among the rare few in the community who would consent to be on the end of a phone line, not a confusing IRC network. *Newsweek, Rolling Stone,* and CNN all wanted to talk to him. Then, on March 8, NBC Nightly News broadcast an "exclusive," a television report by Michael Isikoff, who described Brown as "an underground commander in a new kind of warfare." The interview took place in Brown's apartment and had shots of him typing into his white Sony netbook, his desk strewn with cigarette packets and other paraphernalia. Toward the end, Brown was seen leaning back in his green plastic chair and pontificating to an almost awestruck Isikoff as the Texan dangled a cigarette from his fingers.

"It's cyber warfare," he said in a southern baritone, looking relaxed. "Pure and simple." Brown was actually racked with pain throughout the interview, having stopped injecting himself with Suboxone four days prior. His bones ached in a way most people would never experience. (He would relapse in April on a trip to New York, where he would take heroin, and then get back on Suboxone when he returned to Texas.)

During the interview, the camera briefly panned over the screen of Brown's laptop to reveal a snippet of an IRC chat Brown was having with Topiary, Q, and several others, as Isikoff sat by and looked on with his TV crew. The nicknames were visible.

"Yo," Barrett had typed. "NBC is here."

"Awesomesauce," said someone called &efg. "Welcome to the internet."

"They want to talk about stuff," Brown said in the next shot. "He says he's honored. So, what's next for Anonymous?" The question appeared have been dictated by Isikoff.

The feature later showed Isikoff and Brown strolling side by side down a busy road and talking, Brown gesticulating, Isikoff's khaki-colored slacks flapping in the breeze as he listened intently. Then it was back to the apartment, and Brown once more sprawled in his chair.

"I mean we got Stuxnet off of this," he said, flicking his hand, referring to an attached file among Barr's e-mails that was in fact a defanged version of the infamous computer virus that was best known for attacking Iranian nuclear infrastructure in the early 2000s. "It shouldn't have been available by this federal contractor to get ripped off by a sixteen-year-old girl and her friends."

"And it shouldn't be in the hands of Anonymous!" Isikoff exclaimed.

"But it is," Brown replied, waving his hand again and shaking his head somberly. *"C'est la vie."*

Brown was not happy with the interview when it aired. He had hoped it would go deeper into the information revealed by the HBGary hack—the military contracts on persona management software—but instead it had focused on him and made Anonymous look like a serious organization. This hurt his reputation in Anonymous further. Here again was another example of how difficult it was to push an agenda from within Anonymous—you had to convince not only the Anons of its importance but the media too. More people were criticizing him on AnonOps and Twitter as a namefag, moralfag, and leaderfag. Other Anons posted his address, phone number, and other personal information on Pastebin.org. They hated the way he talked up Anonymous as a force for good, a fighter against corruption and evil regimes.

Brown ignored them all. "If I don't respect the laws of the U.S. imagine how I feel about the non-rules of Anonymous," he later explained. Anonymous had been born out of a half joke, after all. But both Topiary and Brown agreed Brown's reputation was making it difficult to recruit supporters for Operation Metal Gear, and they needed another approach. Brown decided to announce the project on the airwaves. In recent months, someone on AnonOps IRC had set up a digital radio station, called Radio Payback, consisting mostly of techno music played 24-7 and interspersed with occasional chatter from anonymous DJs. Brown approached one of the DJs in the #RadioPayback IRC channel to ask if he could go on the air to announce recent findings of Operation Metal Gear, with no success. Then Topiary tried.

"Barrett's not so bad," Topiary told the DJ. "We should give him a chance. It might be worth it in the end." Eventually the host relented, and Brown, Topiary, and another man from their team, nicknamed WhiteKidney, took to the digital airwaves on the evening of March 16 and spent a good hour telling any Anon who would listen about their research. Topiary had told Brown to speak slowly, repeating the word *slowly*. "Voices are not bullet trains," he tried to explain. "I don't think it worked," he later recalled. On air, Brown's voice was loud, as if he were too close to his microphone.

"Booz Allen met with Aaron Barr," he blared, with some distortion. "His specialty was this software that used social media."

Topiary explained the controversial software, the soldiers who controlled dozens of fake social media profiles, the way that could subvert democracy and warp online opinion.

"We have informants," Topiary added, referring to people who had offered information on Booz Allen.

"We won't talk about informants," Brown said quickly. There were apparently two informants. One had reached out to Brown, and the other was someone Brown had found among Barr's e-mails. "This is what we've trained for for five years," he added toward the end of their segment, before the discussion descended into jokes about Brown's penis.

Still, the presentation worked. Within a couple of days, Metal Gear's ranks had swelled to twenty regular researchers. Hundreds of people had downloaded a link to their team's current research via the radio show, suggesting that listeners may have been in the thousands. One IRC operator who had previously mocked Brown and dismissed Metal Gear as trolling was now talking it up as a success on IRC. The investigation team retreated to their private Skype group and spent many more hours trawling through e-mails, making phone calls, and listening to Brown. Brown sometimes assigned jobs, but more often people volunteered to do things.

"Once we explained about 'sock puppets' and 'robots,' everyone got excited," Topiary later remembered. There was no proof at this point—only speculation. For example, the government of Azerbaijan had recently arrested online political dissidents, and Topiary and Brown stated on Radio Payback that Booz Allen's spying software must have been used. Their reasoning: Booz Allen had an office in Azerbaijan.

It was a credible lead, but as usual, the group would struggle to find the time and concentration to follow it up. Other Anons would pick out yet more juicy leads from Barr's e-mail hoard. Occasionally someone would come with a completely new lead.

Then there was a bigger distraction, this time showing how easily a person could get the mainstream press excited about a supposed Anonymous operation. A young man nicknamed OpLeakS approached Brown on the chat network, claiming that he had acquired a trove of e-mails and needed some advice. The leak, he said, involved Bank of America.

Intrigued, Brown invited him into his secret Skype group with Topiary and WhiteKidney for a conference call. OpLeakS came on with a thick New Jersey accent and monotone voice. At first Brown and Topiary were excited by what they were hearing. OpLeakS, a staunch Anonymous supporter, said he had been contacted by a former employee of Bank of America, someone who had worked there for seven years and who had joined when the bank bought Balboa Insurance. OpLeakS and the ex-employee talked by e-mail for several days. Whenever OpLeakS asked a question about Bank of America, he was met with increasingly damning responses about how the lender had been hiding loan mistakes or how managers practiced favoritism. It all pointed to fraudulent mortgage practices, he told Brown and the others on Skype, stuff that could bring down Bank of America.

"Why don't you send them over so we can take a look," said Brown, who by now had become skeptical. OpLeakS sounded out of his depth with the subject matter.

"I can probably help you with getting the word out," Topiary offered, thinking any kind of leak involving Bank of America would generate interest after the WikiLeaks affair. He added they could host OpLeakS's e-mail correspondence on the new AnonLeaks site.

OpLeakS wasn't interested in either offer, but he forwarded a handful of e-mails in the hope of some validation. Now Brown was definitely unimpressed—the claims by the ex-employee sounded embarrassing to Bank of America, but OpLeakS had nothing that could bring down an entire multinational bank. Because of recent rumors that WikiLeaks had a cache of explosive data on Bank of America, it was easy to get confused by OpLeakS's claim and think that they were somehow related. By now, Anonymous and WikiLeaks were closely associated with each other, through the Payback DDoS attacks and then the announcement of the name AnonLeaks. But of course, OpLeakS's data had nothing to do with WikiLeaks, and it was not substantially damaging either.

"He didn't seem to have what he thought he had," Brown later recalled in an interview. Topiary remembered the man promising more information but not delivering. "He wasn't forthcoming with it," Brown added.

But in spite of flimsy evidence and limited understanding of finance, OpLeakS posted several tweets over the weekend of March 12 and 13 hinting that "Anonymous" had e-mails that exposed "corruption and fraud" at Bank of America.

Amazingly, the tweets were picked up by the media and taken seriously. "Anonymous, a hacker group sympathetic to Wiki-Leaks, plans to release e-mails obtained from Bank of America," Reuters breathlessly reported on Sunday, March 13. Blogging sites like Gawker and Huffington Post echoed the news. OpLeakS had, by happy accident, stumbled upon the big story that everyone was waiting for. In December of 2010, *Forbes* magazine had published a cover story in which Julian Assange promised to leak a major cache of secret information from Bank of America that would be highly damaging to the bank. Aaron Barr had been working off this very threat when he had prospected the bank's lawyers Hunton & Williams with proposals to discredit Wiki-Leaks. The trouble was, no one knew when the big leak would come, so when it appeared that Anonymous, attackers of HBGary, PayPal, Visa, and MasterCard, were about to hit Bank of America on their own, expectations ran high. Too high.

On Monday morning, as promised, OpLeakS posted his e-mail correspondence with the ex–Bank of America employee on a website hosted by his own Wordpress blog, bankofamerica-suck.com, and under the title "Black Monday Ex-Bank of America Employee Can Prove Mortgage Fraud Part 1." (There never was a part 2.)

"I'm OperationLeakS," the post started, "read every line and screenshots." This was followed by screenshots of the e-mails between OperationLeakS and the former bank employee. Among the questions were "Do you have proof you work at Bank of America?" "It's like a cult?" "So why do you want BoA head so bad?" "When you were fired did you take your things like pictures etc.?" This last question was followed by a photo, provided by the ex-employee, of a mangled plant, some soil, and a small American flag crammed into a cardboard box.

Traffic to www.bankofamericasuck.com was so high that morning that many people trying to access the site got an error page or found it slow to load. *Forbes*'s Wall Street writer Halah Touryalai was one of the first to check out the e-mails, and early Monday morning she put together a blog post called "Bank of America E-Mail Leaks Are Here, How Much Will They Hurt?" Within a couple of hours thirty thousand people had looked at her article. As of today it has received more than forty thousand views.

"It's tough to tell if there's anything truly damning in these e-mails," Touryalai ventured in her story. She noted that while Julian Assange had told *Forbes* in December that he had troves of data that could "take down a bank, " in February Reuters had reported that Assange was no longer sure his goods would have a truly negative impact. The bank's publicity department was already calling the OperationLeakS assertions "extravagant." The market would decide.

Touryalai and other financial reporters watched Bank of America's share price that morning. As the bell rang for the New York Stock Exchange's opening, Wall Street traders looked over the e-mails—and did nothing. The bank's share price moved down by just fifteen cents at the close of trading on Monday, suggesting investors didn't care.

The mainstream media, from CNN to *USA Today* to the BBC, had excitedly reported on the e-mails, but by the end of the week all agreed the "take-down" had been a flop. "Forgive me if I suppress a yawn," said Annie Lowrey at *Slate*. The ex-employee's comments to OpLeakS were small potatoes and too perplexing to mean much.

This was perhaps the moment when the media learned a disappointing lesson about Anonymous. The collective had done damage, to be sure, but it was just as good at creating hype about secrets it had found as it was at finding anything secret at all. Worse, the hype had come not from a group of hackers, but from one monotone-sounding man with a limited understanding of finance whose voice had been globally amplified by invoking the name "Anonymous" at the right time and with the right subject matter. If Anonymous wanted credible attention, there needed to be some semblance of central organization, as with Operation Payback and Chanology, even if they hated the idea of leaderfags.

After roughly two weeks of working with Operation Metal Gear, Topiary felt torn between his two different groups: the hackers who'd hit HBGary and the now ten or so investigators who were supporting Brown (numbers had been slowly dwindling since Radio Payback). He found he couldn't explain to either side what the other was doing. Brown's information group was too complex; Sabu's and Kayla's too secretive.

Brown's ideas also started to sound outlandish, especially after he began suggesting that someone from the military might assassinate him. Topiary thought he was joking at first, but Brown was serious.

"I'm at the center of the world of information and I'm fearful for my safety," Brown told him at one point. "I know too much about Middle Eastern governments working with the United States."

Brown confirmed this in an interview months later: "Someone else who has a semiregular dialogue with people at the State Department and is very well connected to these things was raising that possibility," he said, quickly adding, "I didn't take it that seriously."

At the time, Topiary did not doubt Brown's sense of impending danger—Topiary also felt he was in too deep. "It was intense," Brown agreed. "We were getting informants telling us much wilder things. Several of us were getting the impression that what we were looking into, and accidentally learning, was much larger than anything else, and by virtue of looking into it we were getting ourselves into trouble."

The topics they were delving into hit close to home because they encapsulated the one thing Anons had to fear: technology that was better than theirs and that could identify them. Then, in late March, Congress started a small investigation into the HBGary contracts. "Shit's getting real," Topiary observed.

"Imagine losing your anonymity," Topiary had said during the Radio Payback show to explain what persona management software was. "Imagine creating an online account under one alias and, months later, creating another...Imagine software that can correlate every login time from both of these accounts, every piece of grammar you use, every nickname...automatically finding out who you are online." Topiary knew that people could tear out an Anon's true identity by simply following a Google trail that started with the name of his favorite movie. He hated the idea of government-contracted software doing that a hundred times more efficiently.

But the stress, the stream-of-consciousness Skype discussions, the conspiracies about the military were getting to be too much. He started thinking about his other group—Sabu, Kayla, and the others in #HQ. The hack on Westboro Baptist Church, on the Tunisian government, on Egyptian government websites, on copyright alliance, on the Tunisian anti-snooping script, HBGary—it had all happened because of people from that concentrated team. Topiary thought that if this group left, Anonymous, as the outside world knew it, would die. More important than Brown's research was this other group sticking together.

"Barrett," he finally said in mid-March, "I have to step out of this. It's just getting too weird and conspiratorial."

"Okay," Brown replied. "I can't expect you to be as involved as you already have been." Brown was quietly irked, but Topiary got the feeling he understood. He closed his Operation Metal Gear documents and organized them in a folder holding about a hundred and fifty megabytes of data—text files and audio files from Brown's conference calls—that he would probably never look at again.

As he did so, Topiary was asked in an interview if he thought this "concentrated team" might ever break off from Anonymous to do its own thing.

"Not really," he answered. "I can envision it now. We could probably go on a rampage around the Web under some kind of nerdy hacker group name, get on the news a lot, leak, deface, destroy." It would get boring, he said. "Under the Anonymous banner it's done with a purpose, and a meaning, and without ego."

A few weeks later he would completely change his mind.

CHAPTER 14

Backtrace Strikes

It was late February and bitterly cold in Michigan. A blizzard had followed a false spring and covered Jennifer Emick's front lawn in several feet of snow. Squirrels were poking in her mailbox and stealing packages in the hopes they contained cookies, but Emick didn't consider going outside to check. Not only was there the muscle-spasming freeze, she was now deep into the investigation into Anonymous she had initiated. It had reached a new level after Laurelai had passed over logs from the HQ channel. Emick's goal was to show the world what Anonymous really was—vindictive, corrupt, and not really anonymous at all.

Back in December of 2010, when Operation Payback had really taken off with its attacks on PayPal and MasterCard, Emick had already pulled away completely from Anonymous. It wasn't that she didn't like the targets—it was the cruelty she was seeing more and more throughout the network, ever since Chanology. Emick had kept friendships with a few Anons, hosted some supporters in her home, and joined a Skype group sometimes called the Treehouse. She described them as "just some friends who hung out and talked." Chanology had spawned new Anonymous cells, or sometimes just friendship groups. Some of these groups died off, and many Chanology participants went off to college or stopped associating with Anonymous for good. There were a dedicated few, like Laurelai and Emick, who had come back for the next wave in 2010. Except Emick had become part of a minority that wanted to stop Anonymous.

Like Barrett Brown, Emick tended to see the world through theories, and her big one about Anonymous was that it had become just like Scientology: vindictive, reactionary, and a scam. When she watched the creation of the AnonOps IRC network, she believed operators were trying to revive "this old spirit of being intimidating." Emick saw young people who wanted to be part of a group of nameless bullies because they were getting picked on at school. Suddenly, they could be part of a group that people were afraid of, she explained.

Emick was gradually creating a crusade that was part principle, part personal. She had four children, three of them teenagers, and she resented the idea that they could fall for "some idiot story" online that romanticized bullying tactics. "Kids are dumb," she said. They weren't going to question legalities. "They're going to say, 'Ok, cool.'"

She was right about the lack of legal awareness. When thousands of people joined the AnonOps chat rooms eager to help take down PayPal, most didn't realize that using LOIC could land them in jail. Emick became indignant when she went into the chat rooms at the time and saw IRC operators telling new Anons they had nothing to fear from taking part in a digital sit-in. When Emick confronted the operators Wolfy and Owen under a pseudonym and accused them of trying to raise a personal army, they banned her from the network.

By late February, authorities in the Netherlands and Britain had arrested five people involved in Operation Payback; the FBI continued to follow up on its forty search warrants in the United

States. Later, in July, the authorities would arrest sixteen suspects. The one thousand IP addresses that PayPal had given the FBI were paying off. The operators had been wrong, or possibly lying, and what irked Emick more was that they knew how to avoid arrest better than new volunteers.

Soon after learning about the HBGary attack, Emick had started spending hours in front of her computer, egged on by suspicions that the people controlling Anonymous were criminals. She was especially interested in the nickname Kayla, and when she started searching on forums, the name appeared on a popular site for aspiring hackers called DigitalGangsters.com.

Started by twenty-nine-year-old Bryce Case, known on the Internet at YTCracker (pronounced "whitey cracker"), DigitalGangsters was founded as a forum for black hat hackers, and one of its users was named Kayla, a twenty-three-year-old in Seattle. Emick did some more digging. YTCracker was a hacker himself; he'd been programming since he was four, gaining notoriety after he hacked into government and NASA websites and defaced them. He went on to develop a taste in hip-hop music, and he founded a record label and gave concerts at the hacker convention DEF Con. DigitalGangsters had originally been a production for his club nights and raves, but he turned it into a forum for his hacker friends who were moving off of AOL chat rooms and onto IRC. It was a hub for old-school hackers and a proving ground for new ones. In 2005, one of its users, a sixteen-year-old from Massachusetts, hacked into Paris Hilton's T-Mobile account and accessed her nude photos. Four years later, an eighteen-year-old hacker got the password credentials for President Obama's official Twitter account. Another hacker got photos of Hannah Montana. The forum was a place where crackers could trade ever more ambitious bragging rights, a place where a person could get in touch with spammers (also known as Internet marketers) and sell a stolen database or two.

YTCracker didn't like Anonymous because he didn't like the way innocent people got caught in the crossfire. It had happened to him. In March of 2011, a few hackers on his forum, including one named Xyrix, attacked his site for no reason other than that he hosted some of their enemies. To get his administrative access, they called AT&T and reported YTCracker's phone stolen, got a new phone and SIM card, and were able to grab his Gmail password. From that they were able to hack into the Digital Gangsters forum, then deface it with a message that said it had been "hacked by Kayla, a 16-year-old girl."

Here's where Emick stumbled into a world of confusion. Kayla was described as a twenty-three-year-old on this site, but she had read an Encyclopedia Dramatica article saying that back in 2008, "Xyrix posed as a woman using the name 'Kayla' on the Partyvan network." Xyrix was widely known to be a heavyset twenty-four-year-old man from New Jersey named Corey Barnhill. Emick thought, incorrectly, that this meant Kayla was Barnhill.

Kayla had an explanation for why everyone thought she was Xyrix: back in 2008, she had hacked his main web account and pretended to be him to get information out of a Partyvan admin; the admin then mistakenly thought that Xyrix and Kayla were the same person and added her into Xyrix's Encyclopedia Dramatica page. The "hacked by Kayla, a 16-year-old girl" deface on YTCracker's site may well have been Xyrix taking advantage of that misunderstanding to try to humiliate YTCracker.

Emick was going down the wrong path with Kayla, but she still felt she was onto something. She started spending more time on these forums, piecing together nicknames, fake identities, and false information, being led down new trails. While many hackers varied their nicknames, a lust for credibility compelled many more to stay with one name. In many cases, all Emick needed to do was plug a nickname into Google, search for it against forums like DG and Reddit, and then talk to a few of that person's friends on IRC. She used note-taking software to cross-reference every-thing.

"You have to be anal retentive," she later explained. Soon she had amassed gigabytes of data on her computer and had enough to put real names, even addresses, to a few Anons.

Emick felt an urgency to turn her research into something that would better Barr's faulty approach. Beating Barr at his own game became a personal challenge. Realizing she would need help, she began talking to an online friend from her old Chanol-ogy days about forming an anti-Anonymous tag team.

Jin Soo Byun was a twenty-six-year-old security penetration tester who had once been an air force cryptologist but had retired when he was caught in an IED roadside bombing in Iraq. The accident left him with serious brain damage and memory loss, but he threw himself into the 2008 Chanology protests and built up a reputation for social engineering under the nicknames Mud-splatter and Hubris. He and Emick served as administrators on Laurelai's website, and the pair developed a friendship via Skype, instant-message chats, and phone calls. Often they would just gossip about the hacking scene, taking pleasure in trash-talking their enemies.

Emick told Byun about her plan. Anonymous had become an almost unstoppable mob. "Someone needs to stop them before something bad happens," she told him. He was game. For a few years, Emick and Byun had talked about starting a digital secu-rity company that used Byun's technology expertise and Emick's investigative skills. Now they had something to work with, what Emick was calling a "psychological operation."

Byun reached out to friends in the cyber security industry, gathering about six people who were willing to help their re-search. Among them was Aaron Barr.

"Right away after helping the [FBI] investigation I wanted to understand the group even more," he later explained. "Especially the ones that attacked us."

They needed to act quickly. Anonymous was being riled up to attack Sony, and to make matters worse, HBGary had made them feel they were unstoppable.

They decided to call their group Backtrace Security, a name that came straight out of the 4chan-meme machine. It referred to the Jessi Slaughter incident, when /b/ users had viciously trolled a young girl who had been posting videos of herself on YouTube, leading her mustachioed father to launch a tirade into her webcam—which she then uploaded. Choice quotes such as "I know who it's coming from! Because I backtraced it!" along with "Ya done goofed!" and the "cyber police" all became memes. Sarcastically using the word *backtrace* was meant to infuriate Anonymous because it was reclaiming one of their inside jokes.

Emick got everyone connected to a spreadsheet that they could all edit. A chat bar ran alongside it for discussing their work in real time. She provided a long list of nicknames from AnonOps IRC that they would dox. Everyone picked nicknames at random, then delved into finding their true identities. Sometimes someone in the group would get a tip-off that would lead him to add a new name to the list. Barr joined in the online discussions too, sharing general information about Anonymous that he had gleaned from his research. The most time-consuming task was sifting through the compiled data. Emick and the others downloaded reams of information, but picking through it took days.

Once her kids were out the door and on the school bus, Emick was rooted to her desk, sometimes for the next eighteen hours or until her concentration flagged. She skipped lunch and often got the kids to cook dinner. They ate a lot of pizza. Emick said her kids were supportive, though she didn't let them know what she was up to most of the time. She raised them to be self-reliant. Emick was the oldest of five kids, and her father and stepmother had been alcoholics who largely left her to cook, do laundry, and pay household bills. Although her dad sometimes cooked, her stepmom rarely left the couch.

Emick worked from a seven-foot-wide custom-built desk that was tucked in a corner of her divided living room. On it were her phone, notebooks, files, lamps, a box of Christmas cards from the last holiday season, and two computers. One was a laptop that ran on Linux, the open-sourced operating system, which she used for chatting on IRC. She needed two PCs for when she was pretending to be two people in chat channels at the same time or tweeting on more than one Twitter account. Her main one was @FakeGreggHoush. When she snooped on AnonOps and tried to weed out information, eagle-eyed operators noticed her nickname and attempted to identify her IP address. Each computer worked off a proxy server that put her in two different time zones to prevent them from getting a location match.

Many names on Emick's list only took about ten or twenty minutes to track down. Some Anons were reusing their nicknames on sites like Facebook, Reddit, YouTube, and Yelp, where some of them were openly discussing their locations or talking on a public IRC without hiding their IP address behind a VPN. Instead, their IP addresses were "naked," and linked to their home addresses. In a few cases, Emick and her crew would use different names, claim to be from Anonymous, and talk to the Anons on IRC, sometimes even convincing them to do a video chat.

The investigation really took off when her old friend Laurelai fell for the intimidation tactics that Emick was using through @FakeGreggHoush. When Laurelai handed over the 245-page log of chats from the HBGary hackers' #HQ channel, Emick couldn't believe her luck. On top of implicating the nicknames Sabu, Kayla, Tflow, and Topiary in the HBGary attack, the log gave her something even more revealing.

A tiny snippet of the chat log showed Sabu telling the other hackers that they could still log into a backdoor account he had created on HBGary Federal's server—something that could allow them to snoop on the company's e-mails again if they wanted. But when he typed out the web address, he accidentally gave away the name of his private server: www.google.com/a/prvt.org.

"Oops," he had said. "Wrong domain." He then typed out www.google.com/a/hbgary.com. "There you go."

But Sabu's server address had remained in Laurelai's log. Emick quickly highlighted it and, knowing that she was onto something, pasted it into Google. Sure enough, she came across a subdomain called ae86.prvt.org. The name ae86 was important. The subdomain linked to cardomain.com, a site for car enthusiasts, where Emick found photos and a video of a souped-up Toyota AE86. With that model number, it had to be Sabu's car. Cross-referencing the information on the car site with the YouTube video of the AE86, she eventually found a Facebook page with the URL, facebook.com/lesmujahideen, and the name Hector Xavier Montsegur. She had slightly misspelled his last name, but this was the closest anyone had ever gotten to doxing Sabu. Emick could not get his address in the Jacob Riis housing complex, but she did figure out that he lived on New York's Lower East Side.

She did some more research on Sabu's online exploits. She found that, years before, he had hacked into an obscure porn site called ChickenChoker.com and, oddly, defaced it with a message about being Puerto Rican:

"Hello, i am 'Sabu', no one special for now…lately i've been seeing ALOT of Brazilian and asian defacers just come out a leash their skills, i didn't see any Puerto Rican hacker's, or well: 'defacer's', show up, so i guess i'll be your Puerto Rican defacer for now huh? elite…"

"It was political, but pointlessly political," Emick later said. Sabu went to the top of her most wanted list. He was "megalomaniacal," and "not very bright," she added.

Eventually Emick and her team pulled together research on seventy identities and were dropping hints on Twitter and to the media that a large group of Anons would soon be exposed. When she finally wrote her stinging profile on Sabu, published on the Backtrace Security website, she concluded that he was Puerto Rican, close to thirty, and hailed from New York's Lower East Side. He'd had a "troubled" high school career and was relatively intelligent but resentful of authority and "success of people he perceives to be less worthy than himself...After suffering humiliations a decade ago following his posting of rambling, incoherent manifestos on defaced websites, he fell into obscurity until publicly associating himself with the Anonymous protest group." She got ready to announce his real name to the world.

Sabu, the notorious, well-connected hacker who had rooted national domains, had just been discovered by a middle-aged mom from Michigan.

By mid-March, Emick had organized her list of seventy names into a four-page PDF file she named Namshub. In it she listed Kayla as Corey "Xyrix" Barnhill, and Sabu as Hector Xavier Montsegur from New York's Lower East Side. Anyone who was a senior Anonymous member was listed in red. She and Byun contacted a few journalists and offered to send them the list. They offered the #HQ chat logs, naturally, to Adrian Chen, the Gawker reporter known for writing skeptically about Anonymous. Since it would be difficult to corroborate the list of names and Chen didn't want to out innocent people, he latched onto the #HQ logs. They were bursting with juicy tidbits about the inner workings of Anonymous hackers. On March 18, he published an article titled "Inside the Anonymous Secret War Room," featuring choice quotes from the #HQ channel. It showed Sabu lambasting Laurelai, the group presumptuously congratulating one another after the resignation of Egypt's president, and the suggestion that this was a leading group for Anonymous with Sabu as its head honcho.

Sabu, meanwhile, was seething.

"I'm going to drive over to his house and mess him up," he told the others. Topiary and Kayla tried to calm him down. Sabu was referring to Laurelai, noting angrily that he had always suspected that "he/she/it" would betray their trust. What was worse for Sabu, and what he wasn't telling anyone, was that Backtrace had noticed his "oops, wrong domain" comment that led to "Hector Montsegur." With a close approximation of his real name and his prvt.org server address now out in the open, Sabu had a potentially big problem. If the police followed up on Backtrace's findings, they could come to his door any day now.

But there was some upside. No one had heard of Backtrace till now, and it was possible that no one would take the doxers behind it seriously. Besides, Sabu thought, his last name had been spelled wrong; his real address had not been found; and there were probably several Hector Monsegurs on New York's Lower East Side. (This was true.) Sabu contemplated whether he could laugh this off like everyone else and continue hacking with this new team of people that seemed to get on so well. Despite all the dangers, he was tempted to keep hacking.

"All wrong," said Topiary in an IRC channel with the others after he'd read the four pages of names from Backtrace's document. Emick had named him as Daniel Ackerman Sandberg from Sweden. "I've never even been to Sweden and have no idea who Daniel Sandberg is," he said. He, Kayla, Tflow, and AVunit had met again in a new IRC room to discuss the "exposé" and get some light relief.

"They all still think im Xyrix!" said Kayla.

"It's as if Aaron Barr is working with them ;)," Tflow quipped. The group had long suspected (correctly) that Barr was secretly collaborating with Backtrace to try to take down the people who had attacked him.

"They got literally nothing right on me," said AVunit, who had been described in Emick's document as a "coder" named Christopher Ellison from Ipswich, Britain. "Well, I suppose 'coder' is right."

"I'm also a paypal scammer," Tflow joked; he had not been given a name in the document. "The only part they got right about me is 'Tflow' and 'php coder.' But yeah, I feel flattered. My name is in red."

"Is this a new trend :D to see who can make the worst dox file ever?" asked Kayla. The group was feeling confident. Aaron Barr's research had been wrong; Backtrace's appeared to be wrong. People were trying, yet no one could catch them.

What they didn't know was that while Backtrace had been wrong on many names, a few, including Sabu, had been spot-on. One hacker who spotted his real name on the spreadsheet immediately stopped everything he was doing with Anonymous and lived in terror over the next few months that the FBI was coming to arrest him.

"I still get heart palpitations," he said during a face-to-face meeting about half a year later. "It's the not-knowing that kills you, whether you'll have nothing, or twenty-five years, up in the air all the time."

Incidentally, Emick had shown no mercy for her mole, Laurelai, who also appeared on her list under her old real-world name, Wesley Bailey, and who was described as "transgender" and a "former soldier from Duncan, Idaho." Laurelai still did not believe (or at least did not want to believe) that Emick was the driving force behind Backtrace or that Emick had betrayed her. No one had proof yet of who was behind this anti-Anonymous group. That was fine with Emick. Once the spreadsheet of names and HQ logs were leaked, she continued to offer a sympathetic ear to Laurelai as the "former soldier" complained about the whole experience and about how deeply she regretted passing the chat logs to the person on Twitter named @FakeGreggHoush.

It wasn't until many months later, at the annual hacker conference DEF Con in Las Vegas, that Emick gave a speech and outed herself as the Backtrace co-founder.

"I was so pissed off [at Emick]," said Laurelai after watching the video of Emick's speech on YouTube. "Believe me, I think about this daily."

Later that year, in October, Francois Paget, an analyst at IT digital giant McAfee, would do a study on Anonymous and the effectiveness of investigative attempts by people like Backtrace's members, Aaron Barr, and The Jester, who set out in late December to unmask people in Operation Payback. His conclusion was that these attempts were largely unsuccessful, even a hindrance to the police. At the time of his study, anti-Anonymous groups like Backtrace had released about 230 names for pseudonyms, while police around the world (excluding Turkey) had made 130 arrests. In those arrests, police came up with thirty names, yet there was hardly any overlap between the names released by vigilante doxers and those discovered by the authorities.

"I imagine they were more confusing than useful," Paget wrote.

Sometimes, though, you needed just one good name. A few weeks after Backtrace's release, the FBI contacted Emick and asked for her assistance in their investigation. They were interested in the name she had discovered for Sabu, but they needed to corroborate their evidence with hers to see if this Hector Monsegur was definitely the right guy. What Emick had found so far wasn't enough to make an arrest, and the FBI wanted to make sure they didn't scare the real Sabu away. He could prove useful.

The HBGary hackers meanwhile had some hard decisions to

make about how to approach the Backtrace drop. They predicted (correctly) that there would later be other groups trying to outdo Emick's work, in the same way she had tried to outdo Barr's. If they really wanted to avoid handcuffs, Topiary and the others had to think very carefully about what they did next.

CHAPTER 15

Breaking Away

In Anonymous there were three ways to respond to a dox:

(1) You could outright deny it. This was a common tactic but didn't always work. If the information was true, most people would nonetheless deny it. It was also dangerous. The worst thing to do was state honestly what was right and wrong about the information, since that would point an investigator in the right direction.

(2) Go back to the doxers and bombard them with a stream of false information and conspiracy theories, making them think you have come around to their side while confusing their research. This is along the lines of what Sabu did. Not long after the Backtrace drop, Sabu hopped over to the chat network where Emick and her colleagues sometimes hung out and pretended to offer her a private chat of the HBGary crew. Sabu pasted all the logs of his own chat with Emick back to the crew showing how they had become friendly. The team had a good laugh.

(3) Say nothing and exit stage left.

Topiary decided that the Backtrace drop had provided the perfect excuse for a clean break from Anonymous. Once again, he was feeling the urge to learn and experience something new. In the three months he'd been with Anonymous, from December to February, he'd seen every corner of Anonymous: from writing deface messages, flyers, and press releases to watching a botnet take down PayPal.com; from humiliating a federal security contractor and watching that turn into an international exposé involving a major bank and WikiLeaks to fronting a live-on-air hack of the Westboro Baptist Church.

Though Topiary had learned and experienced so much, he was restless. Anonymous was starting to become boring. What had begun as one major operation had splintered into too many side operations. It felt milked. He couldn't tell if he was growing up or getting bored with having destroyed so much in a short period of time. And he was tired of having people expect Topiary, Sabu, or Kayla to be at the forefront of everything.

Topiary had quit his part-time job in a bike and auto shop after tiring of his boss and had signed up for welfare checks, which he was now fully reliant on. He was keen to get out of the house more and go back to school. He toyed with applying to a course at his local college in Lerwick that could lead to taking a full psychology degree. In the meantime, the government housing authority was ready to offer him a new place to live in England. In a few months, he planned to move off the remote Shetland Islands, find a new job, maybe study at college.

He wasn't the only one who wanted to break away. Sabu had talked to Topiary about wanting to go dark after Backtrace and get away from all the heat. Even Tflow had recently moved away from the AnonOps network. The small clique they had formed was the one thing Topiary wanted to take with him. He not only enjoyed their company but learned from them. Kayla taught him how to hide himself online, and Sabu taught him about what was wrong with the world—from the rumors in Anonymous that Facebook spied for the CIA to the corrupt practices of white hat cyber security executives like Barr. Pressure from Backtrace and other enemies had brought them closer together and increasingly made them isolated from the rest of Anonymous.

Their group now consisted of Topiary, Sabu, Kayla, Tflow, AVunit, and occasionally the hacktivist called Q—a concentrated group of elite Anons. AnonOps had been a gathering of the elite in Anonymous; #InternetFeds a group of even more elite; and #HQ was a distillation of that. This was the elite of the elite, Topiary thought. Sabu had once used the phrase *outside Anons* to describe Anonymous supporters in the main IRC channels and the words stuck in Topiary's mind now.

The small group was now permanently based on a small IRC network on Sabu's own server. They rarely went on AnonOps IRC anymore, a network now swarming with cantankerous operators and what they assumed were undercover Feds. Besides, their team was tight-knit. Relationships between Anons could be more important than the circumstances that brought them together when it came to deciding how successfully they would go after big targets. It didn't matter how popular a target was or how easily it could be attacked. If a group worked together well, they were more likely to achieve a good hit against an outside party. If they squabbled, they might recklessly attack one another instead, sometimes through a war of words or through doxing each other or perhaps even by trying to DDoS one another's IRC networks.

Much of the drama between people in Anonymous stemmed from fights about status on an IRC chat room. Organizing things on the network was a bit like organizing a company in a headquarters building. Some rooms, like the boardroom, were designated well-known places where executives could discuss important issues. But important, deal-breaking events were just as likely to be muttered under the breath in the bathroom or at the local bar. It was similar on IRC, except here the entire building was constantly in flux, with rooms you could create out of thin air and destroy in a moment, where you could decide who entered, how many people could come inside, and what sort of speaking status each could have. There was never one channel where all the important things were discussed, and if there had been, it wouldn't have been around for long. Anons were always switching from one network to another to prevent leaks like Laurelai's, and hackers in particular rarely met on the same servers, networks, or channels for too long, lest someone snitch on them.

"I sometimes curse at the amount of channels," said a member of the #HQ hacker team, AVunit. The hackers often needed to keep their rooms secret for security's sake, and there were sometimes hundreds floating around on AnonOps. Of course, this made other Anons feel there was a hierarchy and that operations were being directed behind closed doors. (Not entirely wrongly.) Putting a +i or invited-only mode on a channel like #InternetFeds was like waving a red flag in front of a bull. "It makes people think the weirdest things" about what was really going on, AVunit said. And despite #HQ's name, it wasn't a headquarters for all of Anonymous. It was just a name one person had picked on a whim. Making a channel was like making coffee for everyone else in the group. People took turns.

There were different ways of getting into the secret channels. One idea of Aaron Barr's had been to infect the LOIC program and then, under a new nickname, call out the infection to get himself into private coding channels. And you could be in multiple channels at once. By mid-March, Topiary himself was moving between twenty-three different AnonOps channels, including Command, OpMetalGear, OpNewBlood (for coaching new Anons), and StarFleetHQ, the channel that housed a massive botnet belonging to the AnonOps operator Ryan. Tflow was in more than fifty. People tried pretending to be one another but it often didn't work since nicknames were registered with a password.

There was an array of symbols— ~, &, @, %, and +—used to show the status and power of each person in each channel; every symbol corresponded to one of the five levels of status. These status levels were known as channel owner, super op, admin op, half op, and voice. The sight of these seemingly innocuous icons could mean everything to people who were regularly on IRC because of what they allowed you to do. If you were an op (% or above) you could mute the majority of users who didn't have a symbol by hitting +m. Someone with % could kick out anyone below their status. With @ you could edit a channel topic and ban people, while & could ban a user on sight.

The idea behind all this was to ensure IRC channels didn't turn into a spam-fest. Unfortunately, power often went to people's heads, and operators would squabble and kick out people they didn't like. The ability to threaten permanent bans gave them the power to disrupt entire operations if they wanted.

No, the name of the female operator who had told new Anons that LOIC was legal and fine to use was known for regularly booting users out of the informal #lounge channel if they were spamming too much. It wasn't clear if she did this just for kicks or because she was genuinely trying to maintain the peace. You didn't have to own servers or have technical skills to become an Anonymous IRC operator. Rumor had it that No had gained her status by flirting with other male operators.

Many Anons hated or feared the IRC operators—they were like the bosses who didn't deserve to be bosses. And the operators could get away with telling police that they were not part of Anonymous. The police came to No's house in Las Vegas at 6:00 one morning in February. Mercedes Renee Haefer, who was nineteen at the time, answered the door in her pajamas to find police officers wearing vests and wielding guns. They raided her home, took two computers (one a Mac), an iPhone, and a router, all part of a sweep by the FBI to find people involved in Operation Payback and the attack on PayPal. When they found a mock-up flyer of her little sister with revolutionary imagery, part of a family joke, they asked with dead seriousness if it was an upcoming operation for Anonymous. She laughed and almost said yes.

Other Anons had been getting arrested too, mostly men in their midtwenties. On January 27, about a week before the HBGary attack, British police arrested five men in connection with the Operation Payback attacks on MasterCard, Visa, and PayPal. Two of them were alleged to be AnonOps operators: Christopher "Nerdo" Weatherhead, a plump twenty-year-old student from the city of Northampton in England, and "Fennic," a skinny seventeen-year-old with long hair from South London whose suspected real name could not be published for legal reasons. By June of 2011, at least seventy-nine people in eight countries would be arrested in connection with Anonymous activities.

News of these early arrests in January, followed by persistent doxing by people like Emick, meant that Topiary's primary concern was no longer what would happen to Anonymous if his small group went quiet. Others would find a way to carry the movement forward. If the IRC network collapsed, they would move back to image boards. If someone was arrested, more would join. Almost nothing had happened with Anonymous for two years until #savethepiratebay suddenly snowballed into Wiki-Leaks and thousands of newcomers started seeing a solid infrastructure to Anonymous. Then the buzz on AnonOps IRC had nearly died until HBGary magically came along. It was often just a matter of circumstances—major news events like WikiLeaks or a single clarion call on /b/ to fight Scientology.

Topiary marked his split from Anonymous with an elaborate getaway. He typed up a fake IRC chat log between two friends discussing how Topiary had been arrested and then made sure it was passed around until several people bought the story.

```
<contact>  i need to talk to…someone…are you Q?
<marduk>   lol. depends. who are you?
<contact>  i was told to get on anonops and find either a Q or Tflow.
           someone you know once gave me an emergency con-
           tact. you should know that guy as topiary
<marduk>   top? haven't seen him in around the last days
<contact>  i know him in real life. i live close by. there was major
           action near his house. some people and cars gathering
           around there. since then i havent seen him
<marduk>   it wasn't police was it?
<contact>  i dont know but i dont think so.
```

The complete fake log was long and full of typos, inept questions from "contact" about AnonOps to suggest he was new to the network, along with healthy skepticism from Marduk. The idea was to make the "friend" sound scared but never push the idea that Topiary had actually been arrested. If he left enough gaps, others would come up with the rumor themselves.

Topiary leaked the log to five trusted individuals, making sure each version was slightly different—an extra punctuation mark or a tiny difference in spelling. If the log ever leaked to a group like Backtrace, he would be able to pinpoint who had done it. Topiary changed his nickname to Slevin and, with a slightly heavy heart, whittled his contacts on Skype down to three un-named people.

There was the sound of clattering as Jake put dishes in the sink, including a plate covered with crumbs from a fish pie he had just eaten. Still a frequent visitor to 4chan's "cooking" board, he enjoyed making his own meals, particularly fish or meat pies.

Turning on the water, he glanced out his kitchen window and noticed a police van parked on the road a few houses down. His heart raced. Quickly he went back to his laptop to let his small group know what was up.

"Back in 15," he told AVunit under his new nickname, Slevin. He would not manage to keep the name for long; it just wasn't how people knew him.

"Good luck and stay safe, Top."

By the time Jake had signed out of his IRC channels and put his coat on, the police van was gone. It was a sunny day, cold and brisk, with the usual wind carrying scented undertones of the salty sea. Jake put on his earphones and took the twenty-minute walk into town, his head lowered as usual, his shoulders slightly hunched. He glanced around for any sign of the police van. There was none.

He went to a café near a hill. Resplendent with leather chairs, wooden tables, and soft lighting, it was probably the most modern eatery in town. He ordered a latte to go and hiked to the top of the hill to sit in his usual thinking spot on finely cut grass, a place where he could drink and look out at the view. Next to him were a handful of iron-black cannons, used generations ago to blast holes into the ships of marauders trying to invade Shetland. Now they were quiet relics, their shells varnished with protective paint. He could have sat on one, but it felt somehow disrespectful.

He walked back. The police van was still nowhere to be seen. Most likely they had been there to check on the local druggies. Jake lived in a poor neighborhood, and the several heroin users next door often played loud music. One male resident had once been so high he had hung a heavy rug outside on the clothesline to dry even though it was raining. The next morning he wrestled it off the line and swung it around in an attempt to dry it even though it was now waterlogged beyond repair. When the drug-gies were being loutish or annoying, Topiary would redirect their wireless connection so every click would go to the Goatse shock site and then rename their WiFi connection heroin-hidden-under-the-house. In the past year, they hadn't so much as thrown a beer can on his front lawn.

Jake stepped back into his house and went to his laptop. He got online and caught site of a news headline about Anonymous. It appeared that Anonymous had just declared war on Sony, an enormous target. This time he had no idea who was driving the attack, and he was completely fine with that, even happier to have stepped away from it all.

It was April 1 and a few Anons had just published a new digital flyer. "Congratulations, Sony," it read. "You have now received the undivided attention of Anonymous." This time, while Topiary was AWOL, 4chan vigilante William had jumped into the attack with gusto, his main role being to help dox Sony executives and their families as part of a side operation called SonyRecon. All of this was happening because earlier that spring, Sony had sued a hacker named George "Geohotz" Hotz after he had figured out how to jailbreak the until-then unhackable PlayStation 2 game console and then announced on his blog how people could download games onto their own systems for free. Age twenty-one at the time, Geohotz was already well known for jailbreaking Apple's iPhone and iPad. Now Sony was accusing him of breaking the U.S. Computer Fraud and Abuse Act by hacking their console.

Over the next few days, Anons who had downloaded LOIC launched a DDoS attack on several Sony websites and its PlayStation Network (PSN) for gamers. The PlayStation Network then went offline, angering millions of gamers around the world.

William, who was usually skeptical of larger Anonymous raids, was inspired by this particular attack and the side operation he was working with. Already his team had dug up personal information on several Sony executives and their families, including Sony CEO Howard Stringer and his grown children.

"This is the most focused attack yet," he enthused at the time in an interview. "The social engineers know their place and so do the hackers. This is one of the first times I'll be working as part of a team, and knowing EXACTLY my role within that team." He reasoned that Sony had treated Geohotz ("one of our own") in a way that was anti-freedom, anti-expression, anti-individualism, and, thus, "anti-Anonymous."

William did not mind that there were obvious tiers in Anonymous, with hackers and writers at the top and social engineers and LOIC users near the bottom. Each side rode on the other's reputation—William scared his targets by claiming he was a hacker, and hackers could ride on the infamy of Anonymous because of the way less skilled people bandied the name around.

The DDoS attacks on Sony continued for several more days, and they became so unpopular that just before April 7, Anonymous announced it was calling them off.

"Anonymous is not attacking the PSN at this time," a new press release said. "We realize that targeting the PSN is not a good idea. We have therefore temporarily suspended our action, until a method is found that will not severely impact Sony customers."

Strangely, though, the downtime for the PlayStation Network continued, and gamers were furious. On April 22, Anonymous posted a new press release on AnonNews.org titled "For Once We Didn't Do It." The network had been down for almost three weeks now, and it was clearly not because of an ongoing DDoS attack.

Just as strange: Sony itself had been quiet for weeks. Finally, on May 2, the company made a startling announcement. There had been an "intrusion" to its network some time between April 17 and 19. Hackers had compromised personal and financial details of more than seventy-five million accounts with the PlayStation Network. This was a hack that affected tens of millions of people. Nobody in Anonymous was taking responsibility, and nobody on AnonOps seemed to know who had stolen all those user details. Yet by the end of that month, Sony had spent $171 million trying to patch the security breach, and within a few months, news outlets were reporting that Sony's related costs from the breach could push past $1 billion.

Sony then wrote an explanatory letter to the U.S. House of Representatives. The cyber criminals, they said, had left a file marked "Anonymous" and "We are legion" in the system. It might have been a calling card or an attempt by criminal hackers to throw police off their scent, but in any case the news quickly removed any public legitimacy Anonymous had gained from its protests for WikiLeaks and the Middle East and from the information it had uncovered during its attack on HBGary.

At first, many Anons liked the notion that hackers had damaged Sony so drastically—but the taste was bittersweet. No one knew who had performed the heist, and there had been no official Anonymous statement—only a strange file left in secret. The whole affair had a dishonorable feel to it.

To make matters worse, AnonOps soon had internal problems to deal with, as word started spreading of a major leak on the network. A rogue operator had published a list of 653 nicknames and their IP addresses, the strings of numbers that if naked could lead police, Internet trolls, and anyone who knew how to use Google straight to the individuals' doors. Once again the newbies, not the real hackers, were most at risk.

Almost immediately, AnonOps IRC became a ghost town. The hundreds of regular participants who'd been on the list were too scared to sign back on. Some retreated to other IRC networks like EFnet and Freenode, while some kept talking on blogs and forums. Anonymous was suddenly a diaspora with no natural meeting ground.

Former AnonOps admins, including Owen, Shitstorm, Blergh, and Nerdo, released an official statement saying they were "profoundly sorry for this drama" and urging visitors to stay away from the AnonOps IRC servers.

After two days the name of the culprit finally emerged. Ryan had been an IRC operator who used his servers to host two popular websites for Anonymous supporters. He was known for being a temperamental web administrator who got a kick out of hosting thousands of people on his servers, and as the guy who had told Topiary about faking the LOIC hive number back in January. He was also one of the rare handful of people who controlled a large botnet. Ryan was considered something of a loose cannon, and it seemed that as clashes with network operators became more bitter, he had gone off the rails.

Ryan should have expected repercussions, and they came when someone dredged up his real-life details. Ryan had allegedly begged Sabu to prevent his details from getting published. When that didn't get him anywhere, he used his botnet to DDoS the AnonOps network and several other Anon-related websites. Despite this, on May 11, Ryan's full name was published online, along with his home address in Essex, Great Britain, his age, cell phone number, Skype name, and the e-mail associated with his PayPal account—all presented on a simple black web page. The doxer had listed his full name, correctly, as Ryan Cleary. The top of the document said "Doxed by Evo," adding, "Shouts to Kayla, Sabu, Owen, #krack, #tr0ll and all of AnonOps." Evo was someone who frequented Kayla's IRC network, #tr0ll. As a few media outlets reported on a "civil war" in Anonymous, Ryan denied the details were true, claiming in one IRC chat that they were false details he had released himself three years prior.

Anonymous was starting to look like a joke. Operation Sony

had been called off and then apparently hijacked by hackers who had tried to use it for cover. And now a former AnonOps operator had turned against the network too. Nobody was interested in raids and operations anymore, only in gossip, politics, and defending Anonymous's reason for existing.

"Sony and Ryan may have capped an end to a crazy roller-coaster ride," Topiary observed at that time. But while he was glad to be on his break from the ongoing drama, he was also talking to Sabu again. He couldn't help feeling compelled to relive the whirlwind experience of the previous winter. If they got the HBGary hackers back together, they could show Anonymous something new, something that would be not only inspiring, but jaw-dropping.

CHAPTER 16

Talking About a Revolution

Distance from Anonymous meant Jake was getting real-life things done. His house had never been cleaner. To the left of his desk was a large notice board with paperwork and a calendar, and there was a thirty-eight-inch monitor to supplement his laptop. The couch in his living room was cleaned, and next to it was a table with cables stored neatly underneath. Psychology books were stacked on top, along with a James Patterson novel about wizards called *The Gift*. He had time to iron his clothes properly — no more creases that made him feel like he was wearing crumpled paper. Some of his recently washed clothes were hanging on a rack, soaking up the heat from a radiator that was inches away. It was spring but still bitterly cold outside.

The local college had liked his application for a preliminary psychology course and had accepted him straightaway. Having been out of the education system for four years, Jake was looking forward to the brisk twenty-five-minute walk to his new courses and pushed away concerns that someone in class might recognize his voice from the Westboro video. He had always known that Anonymous would come and go, and he didn't want it to overshadow his first real crack at college. With around seven hundred pounds now saved in the bank account that he rarely touched, he had even started treating himself to a meal every Thursday night at the Ghurka, what he considered to be the island's best Indian restaurant. Its Chicken-Madras Curry, complete with french fries, garlic naan bread, and Gurkha beer, cost £13.75 ($21.80), but he always paid with a twenty-pound note and didn't take change. He liked the waiters and the way they chatted amiably about their lives back under the scorching sun in India, while the cold Shetland wind blew outside. Inside, the restaurant was a haven, garnished in Asian decor and with calming sitar music playing in the background. Jake would mostly sit and brood by himself. Over the coming months, as he became busier again, he would visit the Ghurka more than twenty times as a form of therapy, a chance to rest his mind before climbing up the hill to his front door and opening it to see lines of text frantically moving up the screen of his open laptop.

Kayla, Tflow, AVunit, and Q had also taken a break from Anonymous, leaving just Jake (as Topiary) and Sabu in the group's private chat room. Sabu would later remember the others leaving because they had "got scared," and he and Topiary being stuck together on their "own little island."

The two were talking sometimes for several hours a day in between the other goings-on in their lives. They got to know each other a little better. Topiary never dared ask Sabu what he had done in the past, but the older hacker laid it out anyway. He told stories about hacking the Puerto Rican government, about cyber war with Chinese hackers, about his defacing spree, about going underground, and about why he had come back to support Anonymous the previous December. Topiary found himself in awe of Sabu's relentless drive to be a hacktivist after an incredible eleven years, and of his long monologues about refusing to sit down to an authoritative society. Even when Sabu was tired after a long day of work and family, he'd perk up when talk turned to politics and society.

Though Sabu loved technology and hacking, it seemed that his heart lay in social and political change. In the real world, Hector Monsegur had come from New York City, gotten into real-life punch-ups with other men, and even done some jail time. He was deeply resentful of people who abused positions of authority, holding a particular disdain for white hat IT security firms and corrupt police officers. Right up to adulthood he was regularly getting stopped and searched by the police, the feeling not much different to when his high school's head of security had taken away his screwdriver.

Monsegur claimed in one interview that, earlier in 2011, two cops, one African American and one hailing from the Dominican Republic, had stopped his car while he was driving through a wealthy part of town. One of the officers came to his window and claimed Monsegur had run a red light. Monsegur suspected it was more likely because he didn't fit in with the local area. The officer requested his license and registration then asked what he was doing there. Monsegur showed him his papers. Then he was asked to step out of the car.

"What happened?" he asked.

"Just go to the back of the vehicle," the officer said. Monsegur walked around to the back, where the second cop handcuffed him.

"What's going on?" Monsegur cried as they put him in their squad car. "I got a family. Why you handcuffing me?"

"You fit the description of someone we're looking for," one of the policemen finally said.

"Okay. All right," Monsegur said, trying to stay calm. "Give me the description." The officers hesitated at first but eventually described a man who, while slightly similar to Monsegur, had a different height, date of birth, hair color, and skin tone. They finally showed him a picture of the suspect.

"Yo, listen," he said after looking at it. "Look at me. We're different in every way. He's got tattoos on his neck. I've got short hair." Then he turned to the Dominican cop and asked in Spanish why he was being arrested.

"You do kind of look like him," the cop replied in English.

"So…where are the tattoos?" he asked, glaring at the cop.

"You could have had them removed."

Monsegur rolled his eyes and fell back into his seat, his mind blazing. It was true he had tattoos, but nothing on his neck. As they drove him away, he heard one of the officers get on the radio and tell the precinct they were bringing in a "boy" that matched their suspect's description. He heard a crackling, disembodied voice from base ask for details and if he definitely matched. As soon as one of the cops mentioned Monsegur's height and date of birth, the voice asked why they were bringing him in. The cops looked at each other. "Let him go right now," the voice continued. They shrugged and turned the car around.

Monsegur felt relief wash over him. As they pulled up next to his car, he realized his lights and radio had been left on. The battery was dead, and he was stranded at ten o'clock at night.

It was an especially maddening experience, but by no means the only one. Monsegur claimed that he was used to walking down the street, being stopped, and getting frisked, the phrase *You fit the description* echoing in his ears. Growing up on the Lower East Side in the 1990s, he had seen the effects of Mayor Giuliani's order for the NYPD to concentrate on neighborhoods with high rates of drug use, and using recently enlarged tax revenues to hire around three thousand new police officers to hit the streets, bringing the total number of NYPD cops to around forty thousand. Monsegur saw them as the city's biggest gang, authoritative thugs who made citizens like himself feel like animals. He wanted to change that. In addition to his hunger for recognition and respect as a skilled hacker, he wanted people like himself who had been brought up in the projects to know their rights.

Monsegur had not come from a family of political activists, but hacking had given him a voice. It got him noticed. Breaking into databases and disrupting servers was how you subverted the modern world's corrupt powers. As he grew older, he had become more cynical about the world around him, and more temperamental when he became the target of criticism himself. Perhaps tellingly, for instance, he hated nothing more than being called a snitch.

But his cynicism was broken for a while when Operation Payback came along in late 2010. So excited was he at its potential he couldn't help but inflate the importance of Anonymous and, later, his own importance in it.

"We give police officers in the United States the power to shoot us and get away with it. Anonymous can now stand up to that threat," he said during an interview in April 2011. "The world has allowed dictatorships and tyrants to go unquestioned for decades. Now organizations like Anonymous can ask those questions."

Sabu believed Anonymous's greatest power was its lack of hierarchy. He pointed to a U.S. government counterintelligence program in the 1960s and 1970s called COINTELPRO, which saw the FBI quietly subvert activist and political organizations. They had used HBGary-like tactics of subterfuge and misinformation to erode the power of organizations from the Black Panthers to the Puerto Rican FLN to the KKK to Mexican gangs, often doing it from the inside. The reason many of these organizations died out, Sabu believed, was that they had a structured hierarchy.

Anonymous was different. If someone arrested Monsegur, there would be ten more like him to take his place. By leaking e-mails or helping Internet users around the world bypass government filtering, Anonymous could assist people like Julian Assange and his alleged whistle-blower Bradley Manning once they were arrested. When he had first heard about Assange's arrest, Monsegur had gone online as Sabu and looked for vulnerabilities in the networks of organizations related to Assange's case, from the court that allowed Assange's warrant to those who ended up taking him to jail. Sabu claimed his research led to a wealth of information for future operations, though he never released it to the public.

"[It's] for future use," he said in one interview. "I'm sure sooner or later you'll see my results. Juicy stuff, though." A verbal teaser like this about having dirt on Assange's prosecutors was typical of the Sabu persona. Hinting at the prospect of a big operation or leak was key to how he would later hook the attention of other Anons, like Topiary, and even of major newspapers, all from the comfort of his computer. As Sabu, he would often say things like "Something big is about to go down. I've found something. You'll want to see it." He would then keep quiet on details for several weeks, and sometimes he never explained it at all.

Sabu knew that many saw Anonymous as a group of miscreant trolls. "And I'm sure some people want it to stay that way," he said. Even as AnonOps had become disorderly, Sabu believed Anons could become organized and change the world. "It lives, it thinks, it breathes," he said.

As he and Topiary reflected on Anonymous throughout April, they realized that as much as they wanted to leave, they also wanted to stay. For Sabu it was the activism and recognition; for Topiary it was the fun, the learning, and the ability to cause a stir. If Topiary was socially awkward in real life, he had become a wisecracking hero online. They wondered how they could make these experiences continue now that Anonymous had gone quiet.

One night around mid-April, Sabu told Topiary again that as much as he believed in Anonymous, he wanted to go back into hiding more permanently. Suddenly, alarm bells went off in Topiary's head. Something about that felt wrong, as if they were on the verge of missing out on something truly remarkable. He started talking Sabu out of it.

"You're already out in the open now," he told Sabu. Their team had created a media storm, meaning there was enough attention and momentum to work toward his goals, to continue the hacktivist movement. "If it doesn't happen now it won't happen ever," he added.

Sabu took this in.

"Now's a good chance to do it," Topiary pointed out. "We've got the attention, the contacts, we've got AnonOps servers up and everything running smoothly. This might be your last chance to get this out there."

In reality, Topiary wasn't interested in hacktivism the way Sabu was. He had just enjoyed chatting with his team and wanted to have fun. Their elite team had drifted apart, with Kayla, Tflow, and AVunit still on their respective breaks from hacking. But the two had reminisced frequently about how well the group had gelled before, and now Topiary was broaching the idea of getting everyone back together again. He made a convincing argument, and Sabu started agreeing that in spite of his real name now out in the open, he and the others could do something great together. Sabu later talked about reaching a point of no return, and it may well have been during these discussions with Topiary that he decided to cross a line and not turn back.

Sabu later remembered things "clicking" with Topiary when talk had turned to inspirations and aspirations. It wasn't that they suddenly wanted to hack the planet. "It was more like we both believe in Anonymous. Let's work together and go from there. And of course, he [Topiary] liked the media attention....I guess the obvious connection there is I do the hacking and you do the speaking."

Sabu had been wary of how public Topiary could be, but he admired his speaking and debating skills. This explained the unusual nature of their collaboration; though they were almost polar opposites in personality, there were ways in which the two dovetailed. Sabu seemed to like Topiary's tabula rasa worldview, which made a good sounding board for his rails against the system. Topiary hadn't had a personal beef with white hat security firms, but after enough conversations with Sabu on the matter, he soon hated them too.

Sabu was also drawn to Topiary's celebrity in the world of AnonOps IRC. His nickname had a buzz—if it appeared in a chat room, conversations stopped and people called on him to talk. It was this point that would later give Topiary pause when he thought back to why he had ended up collaborating with Sabu. It wasn't that Sabu was using him, necessarily, "but there was definitely a reason he wanted me around."

Sabu was open about this.

"When you're in a chat room, it motivates people," he told Topiary, who couldn't help but feel flattered. And Sabu would also tell Topiary that he was his "brain of reason." The tautology referred to the way Topiary would help calm Sabu down when he got too excited or upset about an issue. "I would explain things," Topiary later remembered. "I would guide him on how to go about an operation a certain way, rather than going full throttle. Don't release everything in one go. Release it bit by bit." HBGary was a case in point: the teaser e-mails, the Tweets to draw press attention. There would be much more of that in the coming months.

Within the space of two weeks, each had somehow convinced the other to stay in the game and to bring the old HBGary team back together. With their small group, maybe they could get the masses moving again. They could support Anonymous 100 percent, but they didn't have to be called Anonymous.

"This means if we want to mess with some white hat company, we wouldn't ruin the Anon image," Topiary said during an interview in April 2011, while he and Sabu were still discussing the idea. "We figured it'd be too far to call ourselves a hacking team with a cheesy banner, so we haven't decided much."

Kayla had been flitting about online, so they created an IRC channel called #Kayla_if_you_are_here_come_in_this_channel. Once Kayla came back, she said she was interested, and the three of them started throwing ideas around. One was to set up a new IRC network for Anonymous, since Ryan's leak in April had turned hundreds of users off its channels. Detractors had bombarded the network with DDoS attacks, and while regular visitors had dwindled, the number of people claiming to be operators had swelled to forty. With AnonOps now so top-heavy, there was chaos in nine different "command" channels, leader-of-leader channels, and secret channels to talk about other operators. The network was about to crash under its own weight, and Anonymous needed a safe, organized place to meet. But by early May, the AnonOps operators had got it together. They had whittled their servers down from eight to two, and their operators from forty to eight. An IRC network now looked less necessary.

"I probably would have quit if we hadn't talked so much and ended up getting Kayla back," Topiary would say many months later. "In a way I wish Sabu hadn't trusted me so much." In a few days, AVunit came back from his break and joined the group too. There were now four of the old team back together who were interested in doing something big—they weren't sure what exactly—to reinspire Anonymous. There was no turning back now.

One late morning, during a period when the team was still mulling over what they could do together, Topiary got out of bed, got on his laptop, and saw Sabu online, along with Kayla. It must have been about five in the morning in New York.

"Guys I was up all night looking at sites to go after," Sabu said. "And I found this big FBI site." Topiary's breath quickened for a moment. "I've got access to it," he added.

Sabu then pasted a long list of around ninety usernames and encrypted hashes (which corresponded to their passwords) from a website called Infragard. The list of names represented half the site's user base. Topiary and Kayla immediately started trying to crack them, excited by the prospect of "hacking the FBI." Just a few minutes in, Topiary Googled Infragard, and he realized they were dealing with a nonprofit affiliate of the FBI, not the organization itself. He thought briefly about asking how Sabu had found the security hole or pointing out that it wasn't exactly a "big FBI site." But he didn't want to dampen the team's excitement.

All the users had been verified by the FBI to gain access and all worked in the security field; some were even FBI agents. Yet their password choices were questionable, at best. One of the users had used "shithead" as a password for everything online; another had "security1." Only about a quarter of the users had passwords the team couldn't crack. It is a general rule in IT security that any password that isn't a combination of letters, numbers, and symbols is weak. It is not particularly hard to memorize "###Crack55##@@" or "this is a password 666," but both of these would be extremely difficult to crack. (The hardest passwords to decipher are phrases, which are also easier for password holders to remember.)

After someone downloaded the entire database of users and then converted it into a simple text file, Sabu loaded the 25 percent of password hashes that the team couldn't crack into the don't-ask-don't-tell password cracking service he'd used for HBGary Federal, HashKiller.com. Sometimes kids used the site to send encrypted messages to one another, with the challenge to crack them. When nefarious hackers broke into the user base of a website, they would typically dump all the so-called MD5 hashes into a database and start cracking the easy ones first, then let HashKiller's forum users do the rest.

An MD5 hash was a cryptic language that corresponded to words or files, and it typically looked like this:

11dac30c3ead3482f98ccf70675810c7

This particular string of letters and numbers translated to "parmy," so the result on the site would look like:

11dac30c3ead3482f98ccf70675810c7:parmy

That information would then be stored in HashKiller's database, so if anyone tried to crack the password "parmy" and had the MD5 hash, he could do it instantly. The result from Hashkiller.com would look like this:

Cracking hash: 11dac30c3ead3482f98ccf70675810c7
Looking for hash…
Plain text of 11dac30c3ead3482f98ccf70675810c7 is parmy

It was that simple. This was why it was a bad idea to use single-word passwords, like "parmy" or—even worse, because it is commonly known—"shithead." Each password always had the same MD5 hash. And once it was in HashKiller.com, everybody knew it. A lack of context kept things relatively secret: everyone could see the hashes and cracked passwords in plaintext but nothing else. Using the site was free, and Sabu had only to sit back and wait for the passwords to be cracked by volunteers.

Once someone cracked the admin's password, the surprisingly easy "st33r!NG," Sabu created a web page that he secretly attached to the website for Infragard Atlanta, known as a shell. It was the same sort of page that the site's administrators would use to control its content, allowing him to add new pages or delete others. The difference was that the admins knew absolutely nothing about Sabu's page. Since the page for the original control panel had been xootsmaster, Sabu named his new shell page /xOOPS.php. He could have just gone through the main control panel since he had the right password, but that would mean clicking through a series of options and a long list of directories. The shell was a more simply designed page that made it quicker and easier to mess with things.

The team lurked on the site for a few weeks while sitting on its entire username and password base: twenty-five thousand e-mails from the personal accounts of the site's users, a mixture of security consultants and FBI agents. Topiary and his friends had all their passwords, full names, and e-mails. If Topiary had been feeling malicious, he could have logged into the PayPal accounts of one of the more senior users and started splashing money all over the place.

"That would be bad," he said at the time.

They had access that could let them deface the site in seconds, but they would wait it out. The crew was still feeling the heat from HBGary, the #HQ log leaks, and Backtrace, and they weren't quite sure what they were becoming yet. So they settled for spying on the users' Gmail accounts, just watching the mails roll by. Nothing particularly significant was being discussed, but the group decided that if one of them got arrested, they would publish everything.

"Most professional and high-level hacks are never detected," one hacker with Anonymous who went on to support Sabu and Topiary's team said months later. Not long after the Infragard breach, another group of hackers broke into the computer network of Japan's parliament, stealing login information and e-mails. It had taken three months before anyone figured out what had happened. The hack had involved infecting the computers with a virus, most likely by sending employees e-mails that carried Trojans. This was how script kiddies worked, the Anonymous hacker said dismissively. It was loud, common, and didn't require much skill.

Sniffing around passively without anyone knowing always made sense. You could steal a database, sell it to spammers, and move on to other ways of hustling for money. With Anonymous, there was also that obligation to cause a stir. But it depended what you had hacked into. The Anon claimed that when he breached a network, most of the time he acted "passively." At one point, for instance, he and another team had found a hole in a large foreign-government server leading to data on various hospitals. His team did not disclose the data and instead notified the admin of the problem. They even deleted their own copy of the data, since releasing the information would be "counterproductive." On that same hack, however, they also found an administrative server for that same foreign government that contained all IP ranges for its online services. "We sure released that," he said.

The paradox for hackers who became part of Anonymous was that there was suddenly a reason to go public with their leaks to make a point. With Infragard, Sabu, Kayla, and Topiary were taking the sniffing-passively route. What the group did with this information would set them apart from other hackers who sought money, curiosity, or a sense of personal achievement. They just needed the right moment.

CHAPTER 17

Lulz Security

Soon it became clear to Sabu, Topiary, and Kayla what they were really discussing: the creation of a new hacking team. It would be, in one way, like WikiLeaks. It would publish classified information that hadn't been leaked, but stolen. The idea didn't sound as nerdy as Topiary had thought a few months back.

They decided unanimously that they did not want to be constrained by the broad principles underlying Anonymous, which were:

1. choosing targets because they were oppressors of free expression
2. not attacking the media.

The idea was to do whatever it took to inspire Anonymous with new lulz, and maybe even grab the limelight again. In Topiary's mind, this would lead to something far greater than any of the pranks he had ever pulled. The whole idea of lulz didn't sit comfortably with Sabu, who was more interested in hacking as a form of protest. But he realized Anonymous needed some inspiration, and he figured he could steer Topiary and the others toward more serious pursuits. Kayla was just happy at the chance to tear up the Internet again, and since they needed to target more than just the Infragard website, she started looking for the Web's hidden security holes the same way she had secretly done for WikiLeaks's q.

Kayla had a powerful web script that let her scan the Internet for any website with a vulnerability. This process of looking for security holes in many different websites at the same time was called automated scanning, or crawling. When she was ready to start using it, Kayla hooked the bot to Sabu's chat server and then cast it out like a net. She had only to type commands into the chat box, like *find SQLI,* to direct it. The bot constantly churned out new addresses of web pages that had vulnerabilities, then filtered them again. She had spent hours configuring the script so that certain types of URLs would show up in different colors. There were hundreds each day, and about 20 percent led to security holes. About 5 percent led to databases of ten thousand users or more. Over the course of two days, Kayla scoured the websites of hotels, airports, and golf clubs, even Britain's National Health Service, leading the team to hundreds of thousands of user details. They started stealing (or dumping) the info and came up with eight databases containing fewer than five thousand usernames and passwords and two big ones, of five hundred thousand and fifty thousand.

By now Tflow, AVunit, and the Irish hacker from #InternetFeds named Pwnsauce had joined, making them a team of six. It was a number and set of names that would remain fixed to the end. Pwnsauce was a skilled and amiable young man who had been involving himself with Anonymous since October of 2010, when he helped with the attacks on anti-piracy groups. Now he was happy to help comb the Internet for security holes.

"Sabu, I may have a lead here," he said at one point after

finding something. When asked why he was working with the team, he said that while he agreed with the aims of Anonymous, "moreso I am here because of the people."

"I've never found more respectable and hardworking people in my life than those in this group," added Topiary, who had been part of the conversation. "And likable."

Anonymous attracted hackers with a conscience, Pwnsauce explained. In a past life he had consorted with a "horrible mix" of hackers who "either did not know what they were doing or who solely wanted to steal from people." These were people who stole credit card details from small retail outlets and chains. Mom-and-pop shops and gas stations were frequently the easiest to hack when they stored credit card information at the end of the day, data that often included the security codes on the backs of people's cards—even though saving them was illegal. They saw these targets as easy pickings, but Pwnsauce had found a more interesting and varied bunch of people on AnonOps, and since they had a wider array of skills, he claimed to have learned three times as much about programming and the Internet itself from Anonymous than from darker hacking circles.

Pwnsauce was studying biology but longed to get out of Ireland. When he wasn't studying or dealing with what he would only describe as "family issues," he, like Kayla, was in front of his computer, poking around the back ends of websites in what felt like a lifelong exploration of the Web's hidden vulnerabilities.

"He's a perfect blend of technical skill and imagination," Topiary later said of Pwnsauce. The two of them once had a lengthy discussion about the best way to disrupt an airport's security system, which moved them to remotely jack into a McDonald's menu screen and import green hacker text to confuse its attendants. "We were in hysterics," Topiary remembered. "I really want to have a pint with this suave Irish gentleman."

One of Pwnsauce's friends in the hacking scene was a fellow

Irish hacker named Palladium; the two had hacked into the Irish opposition party Fine Gael and called out Anonymous as being responsible back in February. Palladium had come in when the team had found a vulnerability but needed help carefully and secretly exploiting it to take internal information.

In mid-April, Tflow had found a vulnerability in the servers of media powerhouse Fox, but he hadn't done anything with it. He showed it to Palladium, who was able to get a shell on it and break in. The two decided to collaborate on breaking into Fox. One of them eventually found a sales database that held the personal information of Fox employees and journalists and seventy-three thousand e-mail addresses and passwords for people who wanted to receive updates on auditions for the network's forthcoming *X Factor,* a talent show on American television. This was a model for how the group would later operate—keeping strategic decisions to the core six but working with a second tier of trusted supporters to help them carry out attacks.

After breaching the Fox servers on April 19, the team members stayed there for days leeching all sorts of data, from user logins to the passwords of radio station announcers. The team hadn't set out to attack Fox, but its vulnerability stood out among all others because it was a right-wing media force that most people in the Anonymous community hated. They hoped to find something funny in the trove of personal information.

It took a week for Fox's IT administrators to notice the breach, but by then the team had reams of data to sift through; it had been handed over by Tflow, who had received it from Palladium. Topiary told both of them that he would go through a list of about three hundred and fifty Fox staff members and test their names and passwords out on social media sites like Twitter and LinkedIn. It would be a slow, methodical process, but hopefully he would find the misfortunate few who had reused the same passwords (as Aaron Barr had done) so he could then hack their accounts and create another shitstorm.

Kayla's scanning script had brought in a hefty list of vulnerabilities, and Topiary, who had had only a basic knowledge of hacking five months before, also found the transaction logs of 3,100 ATMs in the United Kingdom. With normal hacker groups, none of this information would have ever seen the light of day. It would have been stored for the hackers' own personal collections or sold to spammers. But Topiary, Sabu, and Kayla were coming from the world of Anonymous, where you didn't hack just for data but to make some sort of social or political point. Their twist would be, for now at least, that there was no significance to the release all. They would publish it for shits and giggles, for lulz. It was a badge for Anonymous as much as for their small, increasingly tight-knit gang, and it meant they had a wider array of potential targets to hack into and leak. First things first: the team needed a name.

That task fell to Topiary and Tflow, who decided it was paramount that the name included the word *lulz*. They toyed with the combination of several names until they got to Lulz Leaks. It seemed to fit with their modus operandi, so Topiary created a Twitter account for the name on May 3 and put out a single first tweet: "There is much to do—prepare yourselves." A little while later, he needed to do a second tweet, but he couldn't sign into the account—he had forgotten the password.

The two went back to the drawing board. Lulz4ULeaks and Lulz Cannon were a mouthful, and the Lulz Boat, which they liked, was already taken on Twitter. Then they thought about a name that would be a twist on Backtrace Security: Lulz Security. Topiary checked and @LulzSec was free as a Twitter account. He set up a new account, this time making sure he had a record of the password, then wrote a bio that read simply "LulzSecurity® the world's leaders in high-quality entertainment at your expense."

They needed a picture, so Topiary looked through a folder of two thousand images called reaction faces. Anyone who used 4chan had a folder like this to illustrate responses on a thread. He picked the drawing of a mustached man wearing a monocle and a top hat and holding a glass of red wine. Topiary had no idea where it had come from, never considering that, given Topiary's lazy eye, the man with a single lens might be representing him.

It was time to give Anonymous a peek at what they were working on. When the names Topiary, Kayla, and Sabu suddenly appeared in a key AnonOps chat room for the first time in more than two months, there was an almost visible buzz.

"You know shit is going down when the HBGary hackers are here," someone said.

"Is that THE Sabu/Topiary/Kayla?" another asked.

Hearing that Anonymous supporters were at that time keen to attack the U.S. Chamber of Commerce, Topiary and Kayla started looking for vulnerabilities in the site right then, racing to see who could find the most. Topiary was quickly trounced. The two then started pasting the page addresses for each of the security holes in the chamber's site into the chat room. The chat room participants cheered and thanked them. Soon word got out that the core HBGary trio were up to something big.

LulzSec, as hackers, were in very new territory. Stealing data was one thing, but announcing it through Twitter so the press could report on it was odd. Topiary volunteered to the others to write a short statement to accompany the Fox and *X Factor* releases, which would otherwise have been just long lists of data. Everyone agreed. It was clear that Topiary's role would always be that of mouthpiece for the group. Nobody really thought about who should man the LulzSec Twitter feed—it was just obvious that Topiary would do it. He published the statement via the application Pastebin.

"Hello, good day, and how are you?" it started. "Splendid! We're LulzSec, a small team of lulzy individuals who feel the drabness of the cyber community is a burden on what matters: Fun." This was a world away from the grave admonishments he'd written for Anonymous press releases, the ones that had scolded PayPal for "censoring WikiLeaks" or that had warringly told HBGary "you don't mess with Anonymous." If Anonymous had been the six o'clock news, LulzSec was *The Daily Show,* publishing similar content through a similar process, but spun primarily to entertain, not to inform or encourage. They were free agents.

On May 7, he put out the first LulzSec tweet announcing that Fox.com had been hacked. "We're releasing the X-Factor contestants database publicly tonight," he said, adding, "Stay tuned. Wink, wink, double wink!" A few minutes later he let it rip.

"And here you are my lovely Internet folks, the X-Factor 2011 contestant database." Topiary added a link to a torrent file that Tflow had packaged and put up on The Pirate Bay website, as he had done months before with the HBGary e-mails. Topiary hadn't been expecting an immediate response from Twitter users or from blogs, but the silence that followed over the next few seconds, then minutes, then hours, was deafening. Three days later Topiary published four more Pastebin pages of the Fox.com data, with another lighthearted introduction and more tweets. At this point, but only for a little while longer, hardly anyone was noticing.

CHAPTER 18

The Resurrection of Topiary and Tupac

Topiary kept checking Google News for any mentions of Lulz Security or the leaked usernames from Fox and *X Factor*. He noticed there were hardly any mentions besides a few blog posts from technology news sites. No one seemed to care.

If an individual or group had thousands of Twitter followers, it was more likely to create a buzz among bloggers and journalists and, eventually, to create headlines. Topiary's imaginative writing style, honed by many hours writing for the satirical website Encyclopedia Dramatica, came into play here. He could write a series of acerbic comments soaked in the parlance of Internet subculture in just a minute or two. It came naturally.

By the end of his first day using the LulzSec Twitter account, May 7, Topiary had amassed fifty followers from eleven tweets. The tone was tongue-in-cheek, cheerful and irreverent, quoting lyrics from the tacky pop song "Friday" by Rebecca Black and taunting the official Twitter feed of *X Factor*: "We stole your shit and now we're going to release it! Thoughts?"

Twitter, despite its 140-character limits and status as a gimmicky tool for the social media elite and technorati, could be a powerful communication tool. If it was used smartly and prolifically, thousands of people could start paying attention to LulzSec. By using the @ symbol, or simply by saying a name, he could speak to anyone who had a Twitter account.

The following morning he employed Sabu's tactic of dangling the prospect of more tantalizing leaks: "Guys and girls, we're working on lots of fun right now! Here's your Sunday secret: We're nowhere near done with Fox."

On Sunday, May 9, the followers had inched up to around seventy-five, but Topiary kept up the showman-style enthusiasm, as if each tweet were being blared from a ringmaster's bullhorn. "Monday spoiler: today's leak will be significantly smaller in quantity, but vastly higher in quality," he broadcast. "You guys like passwords? So do we!"

He believed it was important to keep throwing out teasers, so then tweeted: "The show starts in a few hours, folks! This one is quite interactive with a finale you'll appreciate. We, we, we so excited! :3."

If Sabu had been doing this his way, he would have dumped all the Fox data they had when they were ready, whether that was Friday or at some point during the weekend. But Topiary figured that news outlets were more likely to pick up on stories on a Monday than on a Friday, when many were winding down for the week. It seemed to make sense that if something was released on Monday, it got more attention.

The teasers kept coming on Monday morning: "LulzSec hashtag of the day: #FuckFox—let's give it another hour or so, tell your friends. ^____^"

Then: "30 minutes…#FuckFox"

Twenty-eight minutes later: "You ready?! #FuckFox."

When the moment arrived, Topiary didn't post a long document of information but tweeted a series of URL addresses for the LinkedIn accounts of employees at a Fox TV affiliate in San

Diego, California. The first said: "Meet Karen Poulsen, Marketing Consultant at Fox 5 KSWB." Clicking on the link showed Poulsen's LinkedIn account now had the LulzSec monocled man as her profile photo. Topiary did the same for Jim Hill, an account executive at Fox, and six other members of management at the media company.

There were seven more managers who got their LinkedIn accounts hacked and Tweeted, including Marian Lai, vice president of Fox Broadcasting. In between, Topiary gave a shout-out to his old constituency still hanging out on AnonOps: "Hey, AnonOps I hear you guys are having a rough time—let's cheer you up. Anonymous wants to join in? You can very soon!"

There were more tweets to a second press release, all wrapped up in offbeat humor, using the instrument of hash tags at the end of each tweet as a kind of quasi punch line. This was definitely not your ordinary hacking group. After three days, Topiary had posted thirty-five tweets, and he continued with confident profligacy.

Soon Topiary had tweeted a more damaging "phase 2" leak from Fox: a spreadsheet of more than eight hundred Fox.com users and details of the inner workings of the company's servers.

Moving quickly, he posted a spoofed link to "Secret LulzSec IRC logs," a nod to the #HQ leak and the eagerness in hacker circles to spy on others' chats. The post contained no logs, only the images of black-and-white pirate ships made out of asterisk symbols, along with spoofed dialogue between nicknames like Bottle of Rum (the nickname for Tflow), Kraken (Kayla), Seabed (Sabu), and Whirlpool (Topiary). Topiary had decided with the others that pirates and boats would be LulzSec's theme.

"What gives guys, that boat looks like it belongs in my bath," Whirlpool says. Then Kraken uses twelve lines of the chat log to create a larger battleship, followed by a mushroom cloud. Whirlpool then claims to be "beaten," "destroyed," and "forever alone." Topiary's ditty made it clear that LulzSec was not taking any of this, or itself, seriously. "Don't tell the FBI about these pl0x," the page's subtitle said. "We will get in trouble and might be grounded."

He released another document of ATM information for British cashpoints, none of it particularly harmful but a demonstration that they could get stuff. He linked the release to a YouTube video of the *Love Boat* theme song and pasted his own lyrics that ended, "Yes LULZ! Welcome aboard: it's LULZ!"

After a few days, most of @LulzSec's two hundred and fifty Twitter followers were from the Anonymous community. People had heard something was going on and wanted to keep track. Very few people, outside of a few regulars on the Anonymous IRC channels, had any idea that these were the same hackers who had hit HBGary, the same ones who had suffered from Laurelai's reckless #HQ log leak.

Then Topiary noticed the LulzSec Twitter feed had a new follower: Aaron Barr. He couldn't help but be thrilled at this and immediately started badgering him on Twitter. "We have the legendary AaronBarr following us...we hear he had a great time with #Anonymous, so great in fact that he quit his job. #ouch. We better watch out now," he added. "AaronBarr is going to check our Tweet times with every single Facebook account login."

Then: "We're following 0 people. if we follow one person, does that mean the e-detectives will pounce on them? Should we follow AaronBarr?....Okay, we're now following AaronBarr—he is our leader. He stole those Fox databases, he compromised over 3,000 ATM machines. Wait...shit."

Topiary thought for a moment about what all this attention on Barr would look like: anyone who knew about the HBGary attack would know the same hackers were now LulzSec. He threw caution to the wind and preemptively put it all out there: "Hey e-detectives: we've taken a lot of interest in Mr. Barr, therefore we must be the HBGary hackers. Right? Of course."

The team spent the next few weeks working through data they already had to plan their next stunt. Topiary, Sabu, and Kayla now had a small clutch of potential leads to work with. In the background was always Infragard, for which they could leak the details of about three hundred usernames and deface the home page.

In the meantime, Topiary's relationship with Kayla was shifting; he was going from being her friend to being her student. Knowing that he was getting into serious activity with LulzSec, he asked her about her setup for staying so incognito. Kayla taught Topiary how to run a virtual machine, then suggested he run Linux as a virtual operating system and a chat client called X-chat through that virtual machine, which he did.

He also began to store his operating systems on a microSD card inside his encrypted MP3 player: a 32 GB SanDisk microSD, inside an 8 GB SanDisk MP3, inside an encrypted volume. Opening it now required a password and several key files, which were five MP3 songs out of thousands on his player. He had learned this entire setup from Kayla.

Despite many hours of conversations, he was still mystified by Kayla. She would sign off at around four or five a.m. U.K. time most nights, suggesting that was when she was going to bed. She had told Topiary she was not in the United States or the U.K. But in conversation she often made references to things like Lemsip, a cold and flu medicine found in British stores, and beans on toast, a very British snack favored by debt-ridden students.

On another occasion, when Kayla had agreed to meet online for an interview on U.K. time, she missed it, and then apologized that she had "got the time zones mixed up." In May, Kayla also created a Twitter account, under the name @lolspoon, and it served as another way to confuse people about her true whereabouts. At 2:00 p.m. U.K. time, she would tweet, perhaps tongue in cheek, "Just woke up, early morning XD."

Topiary had seen screenshots of her desktop, which featured a clock saying 8.41, GMT -8 hours. She had claimed it was a virtual install, which meant the clock wasn't set up properly. Topiary's virtual OS was also set to GMT -8 hours. Kayla's desktop had been very girlie. She had colorful stars as one background for her host operating system; rainbows for her virtual OS; and an anime girl as another one for a terminal window. It may have been too girlie to be girlie—but then Topiary's desktop was arguably too manly: it featured one collage of comics about sharks and another of a large Slenderman character—a mythical creature spawned on an image board a few years prior—in a black suit and red tie.

The online world has plenty of elaborate liars. Topiary recalled a girl on an old IRC network who fooled everyone online into thinking she was skinny by providing fake photos and acting defensively when talk turned to eating disorders. Once, she told a group of people in an IRC channel that she was going out to get a tattoo. Three hours later she came back online and uploaded a photo of a skinny human back completely covered with tattooed wings.

"This is it," she said.

Topiary was immediately suspicious. He uploaded it to a website called tineye.com and did a reverse-image search to see where else the image had appeared on the Web. The tattoo was already all over the Web, so it wasn't real. Eventually it led him to a video site and an account that included another image avatar (a painting) that the girl had used on her Skype account. One of its videos featured an obese girl playing the ukulele. The voice and alias details matched up.

Topiary had laughed a little but didn't reveal the details. He didn't want to destroy her online life.

*   *   *

Though he knew it could make his arrest more likely, Topiary started thinking about bringing his nickname back onto the public Web by using it on Twitter and on AnonOps IRC. But he needed some convincing, in the same way Sabu had needed convincing to get the team back together.

"Why have you kept 'Kayla' after all this time?" Topiary asked her.

"No one has ever doxxed me," she replied. "It makes sense to just keep it." People were always going to try to dox the nickname Topiary, she added. "But if your dox aren't known you should just be Topiary and say 'fuck you' to all the haters." Kayla's mantra was to do all you could to be technically secure, then go out there and dismiss anyone who doubted you.

"Kayla's words had really sunk in that day," Topiary later said. "I loved her simplistic yet compelling argument: nobody knew who she was, so why should she feel pressured into changing her name? It was a sassy kick in the teeth to the doxers. A kind of 'Yes, I'm still here, bitches, what of it?' I was inspired."

For the past two months, Topiary had been constantly changing nicknames to things like Slevin and Mainframe and trying not to say anything that would make people think he was the original Topiary. He was tired of the stress; maybe it would be nice for his online name to get some of the credit for what was about to go down, and he didn't like people thinking that Topiary had been arrested and had turned snitch.

So he opened up his old personal Twitter account, called @atopiary, and posted a single tweet. People in the #anonleaks chat room on AnonOps IRC went into a frenzy. Some suggested that the person behind the account was a spy. It was classic Anonymous. Topiary knew the rumors would die down soon enough. They always did.

*   *   *

In mid-May, the PBS news program *Frontline* showed a documentary about WikiLeaks that Sabu didn't like one bit. It painted Julian Assange in a bad light. When he talked about it to the group, everyone else agreed. By chance, Kayla had found a vulnerability in one of PBS's websites a few weeks earlier with her auto-scanning bot. Now Sabu asked the team if they agreed to make PBS their next big target. Never mind that it was America's public broadcasting service and home to *Sesame Street.* There was no question—everyone was up for it.

As usual, Sabu entered the PBS network through a security hole Kayla had found, and then he started removing user data—a database of thirty-eight staffers here, hundreds of pressroom users there. Sometimes it was hard to know what was being taken. It didn't matter. They'd publish it anyway. The team used a tool called Havij to more quickly download the databases for easy viewing. While Sabu and Kayla did the grunt work of hacking, Topiary and AVunit worked on some dramatic calling cards, something that would make Anonymous laugh. The group worked through the night, adding several new pages to the PBS website, starting with www.pbs.org /lulz/, which went to a page with a giant picture of Nyan Cat. This was a cartoon image of a cat flying through space and pooping a rainbow, one of the most famous Internet memes of all time.

They made another page, www.pbs.org/ShadowDXS/, featuring the photo of a fat man eating an enormous one-foot-tall hamburger with the caption "LOL HI I EAT CHILDRENS." This was a shout-out to another Anon nicknamed ShadowDXS, a man of ample proportions who looked like Hugo from the TV series *Lost.* (Topiary went on to tweet something about Hugo from *Lost,* but then deleted it, thinking it was too silly. The Jester came to believe this signified a cover-up, that Sabu was someone actually named Hugo.)

Before the PBS hack, Topiary, Shadow, Pwnsauce, and about fifteen Anons whom they knew from AnonOps had all gone on TinyChat on Saturday night and gotten drunk while chatting via text, with a few on voice and even fewer on webcam. Topiary ended up posting a series of drunken tweets to several thousand followers through his personal account, including, "dudd, you have no idea how uch hotgowg repeat the same proces as the nigger behing barry shadow exx rainbows ubunche fa..." People kept sending him telephone numbers, hoping for a good show, and Topiary kept prank-calling them.

The next morning Barrett Brown woke up to several voice mails from Topiary saying he was "pursuant to being pursuant" as well as messages from a few raunchy transvestites who'd been given Brown's number and promised a "booty call." Topiary slept through most of Sunday, then, out of curiosity, dialed one of the many random U.S. numbers on his call history from the night before. He got an angry man with a Southern accent who said, "If you call me again you stupid Indian prick I'll chop your fucking head off." Topiary couldn't remember the man at all but figured he'd had a good time with him. The fun that night seemed to overlap with LulzSec itself. Booze had put Topiary on a high when he was doing prank calls. LulzSec's small audience and the team's capabilities did the same when they were hitting PBS.

To Sabu's later annoyance, Topiary's Nyan Cat page seemed to say that this hack wasn't about Assange but about lulz. To drive the point home, in the early hours of Monday British time, Topiary got into *NewsHour*'s content management system, essentially the system PBS used for publishing stories to its website, and realized he could publish a legitimate-looking news story directly on the PBS *NewsHour* website.

At first he wanted to make it about Obama choking on a

marshmallow. But when he suggested it to the others in the group, they decided a better story would be about Tupac Shakur, the American rapper who had been fatally shot in Las Vegas in 1996 but who in death had enjoyed Elvis-like rumors that he was still alive. In about fifteen minutes Topiary had written up an elaborate story, paragraph by paragraph, in the IRC chat, titled "Tupac Found Alive in New Zealand":

Prominent rapper Tupac has been found alive and well in a small resort in New Zealand, locals report. The small town—unnamed due to security risks—allegedly housed Tupac and Biggie Smalls (another rapper) for several years. One local, David File, recently passed away, leaving evidence and reports of Tupac's visit in a diary, which he requested be shipped to his family in the United States.

"We were amazed to see what David left behind," said one of [his] sisters, Jasmine, aged 31. "We thought it best to let the world know as we feel this doesn't deserve to be kept secret."

David, aged 28, was recently the victim of a hit-and-run by local known gangsters. Having suffered several bullet wounds on his way home from work, David was announced dead at the scene. Police found the diary in a bedside drawer.

"Naturally we didn't read the diary," one officer stated. "We merely noted the request to have it sent to a U.S. address, which we did to honor the wishes of David."

Officials have closed down routes into the town and will not speculate as to whether Tupac or Biggie have been transported to another region or country. Local townsfolk refuse to comment on exactly how long or why the rappers were being sheltered; one man simply says "we don't talk about that here."

The family of David File have since requested that more action be taken to arrest those responsible for the shooting.

"David was a lovely, innocent boy," reported his mother. "When he moved to New Zealand, he'd never been happier."

His brother Jason requested that one part of David's diary be made public in an attempt to decipher it. "Near the end," Jason says, "there's a line that reads 'yank up as a vital obituary', which we've so far been unable to comprehend."

David's girlfriend, Penny, did not wish to make a statement.

The final line in the elaborate story was a nod to HBGary's Penny Leavy, while the phrase *yank up as a vital obituary* was another calling card: an anagram for *Sabu, Kayla, Topiary, AVunit.*

PBS's IT admins were scrambling in vain to reaccess their system; Sabu and Kayla were hitting them with a Denial of Service attack, so they were paralyzed. Topiary added a photo of Tupac Shakur to the story and clicked publish. Then he tweeted links to a Pastebin post of passwords for almost every journalist who worked with PBS, then to a post of all login passwords for PBS affiliate stations, then to a post of MySQL root passwords for PBS.org (the root password for the database), so that people could hack into the site whenever they wanted, or at least until someone patched the security hole. There was more: login details for anyone who worked on PBS's *Frontline* and a map of the PBS server network. For the most part, he didn't want to push the idea that their hack had been motivated by WikiSecrets or that their fun was founded on politics. But he made the point at least once on Twitter. "By the way," Topiary added, "WikiSecrets sucked."

Almost immediately, readers started sharing the Tupac story with their friends, posting it on Facebook and Twitter, and latching onto the rumor that Tupac was alive. PBS's content management system might have been woefully unprotected, but it was still a reputable news source. Teresa Gorman, PBS *NewsHour*'s social media and online engagement worker, scrambled to reply to a dozen readers publicly asking her on Twitter about the story's veracity: "No it's a hack." "No it's a hack, thanks." "It's a hack." Then to four people at once: "It is a hack, not a PBS story, apologies." Within the same hour, @LulzSec had received a hundred and fifty tweets and re-tweets.

"Dudes. Of course Tupac is alive," the LulzSec account tweeted. "Didn't you see that official @PBS article? Why would they lie to their 750,000+ followers?

"u mad, Frontline?" he added.

Within three hours, four thousand people had hit the Facebook Like button beside Topiary's fake article. The PBS publishing system was so outdated that the hackers could make updates to content being stored on thirty different servers by interfacing with just one server. The result was that when the IT admins deleted the Tupac story, LulzSec deleted every single blog on the PBS *NewsHour* website. Fortunately for PBS, the admins had backed up the blog content elsewhere and could replace the deleted posts in a few hours. Until then, anyone who tried to click on another story got a 403 error—but the Tupac story was still showing up on the PBS home page. The hackers had deleted all of the site's user and admin login data and declared themselves administrators, which made it almost impossible for the real admins to initially regain control. When the admins made changes, the hackers were always there to change things back. And when PBS *Frontline* posted an official statement about the hack on its website, LulzSec replaced it with a blank page saying only "FRONTLINE SUCKS COCKS LOL."

It was Labor Day, a slow day for news, and mainstream outlets like the *New York Times* and the *Wall Street Journal* picked up on the Tupac spoof and the hacker group Lulz Security for the first time. By 10:30 a.m. on Monday in London, Google News showed that it had logged fifty-three articles about the hack. It was unclear what the group was officially called at this point, and some reporters referred to it as Lulz Boat and later, in a misreading of the autocue on Rupert Murdoch's Sky News on TV, the Louise Boat. When one news outlet reported that the hacker group was Anonymous, Topiary posted a tweet saying, "We aren't Anonymous you unresolved cow-shart." An hour or so later, that tweet alone made the news, with the respected tech news site Venture Beat posting a story with the headline "PBS Hack Not Anonymous." To Sabu's surprise, the members of the press weren't that interested in the leaked user data or the fact that the hack had been done in retaliation for the Assange documentary. They were mostly enthralled by the fake Tupac Shakur story.

LulzSec gave a single interview after the attack, to *Forbes,* saying they had gone after PBS for two reasons: "Lulz and justice. While our main goal is to spread entertainment, we do greatly wish that Bradley Manning hears about this, and at least smiles."

"Some people would say that you went too far in attacking a media company—not to mention a public service broadcaster," *Forbes* said in the interview with Topiary, who was answering questions under the nickname Whirlpool. "What's your response to that?"

"U mad bro."

In a moment of candor afterward, Topiary said that LulzSec wasn't after fame as much as they wanted to make people laugh.

He started taking requests on Twitter for pages to add to the PBS site, the same way he had taken random numbers from people during his drunken night on TinyChat. One Twitter user requested a web page showing unicorns, dragons, and chicks with swords. All this was possible because the team still had admin access to the site.

"Sure thing," the LulzSec feed said. "Wait a sec." Topiary and Tflow scrambled to put together an image, and about half an hour later posted the link to the gaudy-looking new web page, pbs.org/unicorns-dragons-and-chix-with-swords.

Topiary wanted to respond to some of the group's detractors who were accusing it of using simple SQL injection techniques to get into PBS. He wrote up a note explaining how the hack was done and published it to Pastebin with a tweet saying, "Dear trolls, PBS.org was owned via a 0day we discovered in mt4 aka MoveableType 4." It went on to describe in detail how the hack had been carried out with a shell site and how the hackers had gained root control of the PBS servers. They had been able to take over the network because a number of staffers at PBS with access to its most secure parts had used their passwords more than once. He had then pasted a list of those fifty-six staffers. They could have permanently destroyed the site's entire contents and defaced its home page, but they didn't.

Topiary felt exhilarated. He was uninterested in food, sleep, or anything beyond the bubble he now inhabited with Sabu, Kayla, Tflow, AVunit, and Pwnsauce, a team more elite than any he had been part of before. With the help of Topiary's prodigious communiqués to the outside world, LulzSec was starting to look less like a hacker team and more like a rock band. Topiary began monitoring LulzSec's Twitter followers and press mentions on a website called IceRocket and saw everything suddenly shoot up after PBS. The following day, LulzSec appeared in most major printed newspapers for the first time. A group of hackers had taken over "the U.S. public-television broadcaster's website and posted an article claiming the late rapper Tupac Shakur had been found alive in New Zealand," the *Wall Street Journal* reported. "The group posted a string of Twitter messages in which it took credit for the breach."

Topiary started requesting donations for LulzSec and used Twitter and Pastebin to provide the thirty-one-digit number that acted as the group's new Bitcoin address. Anyone could anonymously donate to their anonymous account if he converted money into the Bitcoin currency and made a transfer. Bitcoin was a digital currency that used peer-to-peer networking to make anonymous payments. It became increasingly popular around the same time LulzSec started hacking. By May, the currency's value was up by a dollar from where it had been at the start of the year, to $8.70. A few days after soliciting donations, Topiary jokingly thanked a "mysterious benefactor who sent us 0.02 BitCoins. Your kindness will be used to fund terror of the highest quality."

He used Twitter to drop hints about whom LulzSec would hit next. "Poor Sony," he said innocuously on May 17. "Nothing is going well for them these days." The papers picked up on this immediately, saying that Sony looked like the group's next target.

On Twitter, Backtrace founder Jennifer Emick publicly criticized LulzSec through her @FakeGreggHoush account, and was joined increasingly by other online colleagues who didn't like Anonymous or this apparent splinter group. A day after the PBS hack, one of these detractors tweeted the *yank up as a vital obituary* phrase in the faked Tupac article. It was "an anagram for 'Topiary, Kayla, Sabu, AVunit,'" they added. "What did [Topiary] mean by that? Taking credit? Red herring?" Very few people outside of the LulzSec team and a few of their closest online friends knew that LulzSec was made up of the old HBGary hackers, and the anagram question was quickly drowned out. Hundreds of people on Twitter were talking excitedly about this new hacking group and its audacious swoop on PBS. Many more started following the @LulzSec Twitter feed to hear communiqués directly from Topiary. Almost at once, he was getting tens of thousands of followers.

CHAPTER 19

Hacker War

The victory of the PBS attack had left Topiary in a daze of newfound fame and hubris. He knew he wasn't leading the hacks or really even partaking in their mechanics, but acting as the mouthpiece for LulzSec certainly made it seem to him, and sometimes to the others in the group, like he was steering the ship. That meant speaking on behalf of LulzSec when he got into verbal tiffs with some often impassioned enemies on Twitter.

The PBS hack had ushered a blast of attention from the media and earned the group a sudden wave of fans, with even the administrators of Pastebin, the free text application that LulzSec was using to dump its spoils, apparently happy with the extra web traffic they got with each release. But in a world already steeped in trolling, drama, and civil war, there were plenty of eager detractors. Jennifer Emick flung a few diatribes at the LulzSec Twitter feed, as did the Dutch teenager Martijn "Awinee" Gonlag, who had been arrested in December of 2010 when he used the LOIC tool against the Netherlands government without hiding his IP address.

Awinee and many other "Twitter trolls" appeared to align themselves with The Jester, the ex-military hacker who had DDoS'd WikiLeaks in December of 2010, then taken down the Westboro Baptist Church sites in February. He was never as dangerous as the actual police, but he was certainly a source of drama and distraction. The Jester hung out in an IRC channel called #Jester, on a network aligned with the magazine *2600: The Hacker Quarterly*.

The name 2600 came from the discovery in the 1960s that a plastic toy whistle found inside certain boxes of Cap'n Crunch cereal in the United States created the exact 2,600 hertz tone that led a telephone switch to think a call was over. It was how early hackers of the 1980s, known as phone phreaks, subverted telephone systems to their desires. Unlike AnonOps IRC, on the 2600 IRC network, any talk of illegal activity was generally frowned upon. If people talked about launching a DDoS attack, they were discussing the technological intricacies of such an attack. If 2600 was a weapons store where enthusiasts discussed double- and single-action triggers, AnonOps was the bar in a dark alley where the desperadoes talked of who they'd like to hit next.

After hitting PBS, LulzSec's founders decided that as attention to LulzSec grew, they would eventually need their own IRC network just like AnonOps and 2600. Sabu also wanted to create a second tier of supporters, a close-knit network beyond the core six members that could help them on hacks. The team had decided from the beginning that their core of six should never be breached or added to, and when Topiary heard Sabu's plans, he felt skeptical. Just look what had happened in #HQ when Kayla had invited Laurelai. But Sabu argued they needed at least a fluid secondary ring of supporters. These were people that Sabu already knew from the underground and trusted 100 percent or they weren't in. Sabu had started talking to some of his old crew and he invited them into an IRC chat room they had created for these new supporters, called #pure-elite, named after a website he had created for his hacking friends in 1999. These were genius programmers and people with powerful botnets, veteran hackers from the 1990s who had gotten into the networks at Microsoft, NASA, and the FBI. The combined skills of the group were almost frightening. Topiary reminded Sabu that he wasn't comfortable with all the new people—it seemed risky. Who knew; one of these people might leak logs, as Laurelai had done so devastatingly in #HQ. It also brought up the question of why Sabu even needed him anymore.

All the same, he could hardly believe the company he was now in. He focused on picking up tips from the others. If they used hacker terminology he didn't understand, he would Google it: jargon like virtual machines, hacking methods like SQL injection, various types of attack vectors and programming terminology. If he hit a brick wall, they could give him a quick summary.

Soon there were eleven supporters in #pure-elite to learn from, plus the original six. Sabu was still the main person to ask about finding exploits; Kayla about securing yourself. AVunit and Tflow were still the experts in infrastructure. For Sabu, the extra supporters weren't there to teach him anything—he believed he and LulzSec were training them. Sabu tended to think of everyone in the subgroup as a student and he told Topiary privately that he hoped this could lead to the start of another anti-security, or Antisec, movement. The last time Antisec had been in the headlines was the early 2000s, when the Web's disrupters were a few hundred skilled hackers, as opposed to the thousands of Internet-savvy people joining Anonymous today.

By now Kayla and the others who had been scanning for big-name websites with security vulnerabilities had hundreds to work from. But each one had be checked out, first to see if it could be exploited so that someone could enter the network, and second to see if there was anything interesting to leak from it. All these things took time and were often done sporadically without roles being assigned. People would volunteer to check a vulnerability out. LulzSec now had a raft of much bigger targets beyond PBS and Fox that they could potentially go after, some with .mil and .gov web addresses. None of them corresponded to any particular theme or principle; if hackers found a high-profile organization that looked interesting, they would go after it and explain their reasoning later. Knowing that Sabu had a tendency to inflate his rhetoric about targets, Topiary did not yet understand what hitting some of these websites actually meant.

The associates were hackers like Neuron, an easygoing exploit enthusiast; Storm, who was mysterious but highly skilled; Joepie91, the well-known and extremely loquacious Anon who ran the AnonNews.net website; M_nerva, a somewhat aloof but attentive young hacker; and Trollpoll, a dedicated anti–white hat activist. In the most busy periods of LulzSec, both the core and secondary crew were in #pure-elite or online for most of the day and sometimes through the night. Some were talented coders who could create new scripts for the team as their own side projects; Pwnsauce, for instance, had been working on a project to create a new type of encryption.

In the end, Topiary never invited anyone he knew into #pure-elite, and while Kayla had recommended a few friends, Sabu wasn't comfortable with letting them in either. According to Topiary, about 90 percent of the hackers who ended up in #pure-elite were Sabu's friends or acquaintances from the underground. The #pure-elite chat room was an invite-only hidden command center, but the original founders would occasionally retreat to an even more secretive core channel to talk about the new recruits, the enemies, and, on rare occasions, strategy. The atmosphere in #pure-elite was often buzzing as the crew celebrated over the latest attack and resultant media attention. When M_nerva entered the room, he seemed to be noticing this for the first time.

"Lots of news coverage," he said on the evening of May 31.

Topiary showed him a photo of the front page of the *Wall Street Journal*'s Marketplace section. The lead story had the headline "Hackers Broaden Their Attacks" and the subtitle: "Almost Anyone Is a Target."' Underneath it was a large image of the cartoonish Nyan Cat image they had uploaded to the PBS website, and the LulzSec monocled man. Above the rainbow emanating from Nyan Cat's butt as it flew through space was the Internet meme "All your base are belong to LulzSec." It was a most surreal combination of old media and Internet subculture.

"Fucking Wall Street Journal printed a Twitter name and a fucking cat in space," said Topiary, incredulous.

The group was shooting the breeze mostly, chatting about the technical intricacies of Internet browsers, while Topiary would drop updates on the group's Bitcoin donations. Participants would report on leaks they were being offered by other hackers outside the group and, increasingly, on what LulzSec's enemies were up to. These antagonists were made up of online colleagues Backtrace and hackers like The Jester; both camps often chatted together on the 2600 IRC network. There was no requirement to being invited into the #pure-elite room and no rules other than the obvious one to keep everything that was said there secret. The channel topic, set by Sabu, always said: "NO LEAKS— RESPECT EACH OTHER—RESEARCH AND EXPLOIT DEV!" The one policy of #pure-elite was that no one was to store chat logs from the channel.

The secondary crew generally knew their place, aware that directions would come from Sabu, Topiary, and Kayla, and they were meant to be followed. Overall, they were happy to be coming along for the ride, though a few were shocked at the backlash LulzSec was getting.

"By the way," Storm said one evening. "FailSec? WTF is this shit?" He was referring to another Twitter account with a few hundred followers that had been set up to publicly heckle

LulzSec with messages like "Load fail cannons!" and ominous hints that the team would soon be in jail.

"Storm, we've had stalkers like that for months," said Topiary. "They follow us everywhere we go. They monitor everything we do. They make parodies of our accounts." He thought for a moment then added, "We're kind of like a rock band." With stardom came infamy. Some of their detractors were so obsessed with heckling LulzSec that when Topiary blocked one on Twitter, the detractor would create two or three more accounts to keep talking.

Kayla pointed out that Adrian Lamo, the hacker who claimed to have outed the WikiLeaks alleged mole, Private Bradley Manning, had even registered the web address LulzSec.com to stop the team from using it as a website. Lamo, age thirty and diagnosed with Asperger's syndrome, had been called the "world's most hated hacker" for passing information on Manning to military intelligence.

Storm offered to find a different URL, but Topiary declined. He and Tflow were already designing a simple-looking official site for LulzSec in their spare time. Naturally, the background would be of the Nyan Cat flying in space and would borrow the design template of HBGary.com.

"Night guiz," M_nerva suddenly said.

"Night," said three of the others. M_nerva signed off. It was nighttime in the United States, but LulzSec and its supporters were bored and looking for things to do.

"Wanna find something to hit?" Topiary asked the room.

"Sure," said Storm.

"There's a shit cool site, FBI.gov," said Topiary jokingly. There was a pause.

"Are you really that open to just going to jail?" Storm said.

"I suppose we could piss off some IRC for lulz," said Topiary, pointing to a less risky target.

"Sure," Storm said. Topiary and Kayla decided that, high on

their victory against PBS, it was time to go after their biggest detractor, The Jester. They would not just spam his channel #Jester and boot off his so-called Jesterfags but flood the entire 2600 chat network with junk traffic and take all of it offline. It may have housed hundreds of participants, but it was still The Jester's hideout, and Topiary hoped that the result would be the 2600 admins getting angry not at LulzSec but at The Jester for provoking them. Topiary was sure that The Jester's supporters included people like Emick and Byun from Backtrace and considered sending spies into his channel at some point to see what they were up to, maybe profile some of its members. If Jester's people were trying to provoke, it was working. Topiary and the others had become increasingly irritated by The Jester over the past few days and now were set on attacking his crew for both fun and revenge.

"Best thing to do when bored," said Kayla in #pure-elite, "go to 2600 irc and just cause drama :D."

"Should we just go on over to 2600, flame them, and then packet it?" Topiary said, already getting ready for the action. He connected to the 2600 network to get a firsthand view of the network going down.

Storm's role was to launch a Denial of Service (DoS) attack on the 2600 network. This was like a DDoS but without the extra *D* for "distributed," since Storm was sending junk packets from a single computer or server, not from multiple machines. (It was a loose term in any case—if your computer was running a virtual machine, or VM, and you launched a DoS attack, that could be considered more than one computer and thus a DDoS attack.) How could one computer launch a DoS attack against an IRC network? It would need a server or two to help amplify the data transfer. Sabu had used a similar method for his attack on the Tunisian government, though to a much greater degree, with the help of broadcast servers that he'd claimed to secretly hijack from a hosting company in London. Storm rented a basic server, so while his attack wasn't as powerful, it could easily take down a small IRC network. Many people in Anonymous and in hacker circles, particularly those who acted as operators for AnonOps IRC, rented or owned servers. Controlling a server was more common than controlling a botnet; it was like owning a nice car. You paid good money for it but were happy to let other people ride in what was a status symbol as much as a useful tool.

Storm could use his server to fling a hundred megabytes of junk traffic per second to a target. The process was not that different from uploading a picture or movie to Facebook or to a file-sharing site. In that case, you are uploading something useful at perhaps four megabytes a second. Storm's extra server acted like an electric guitar amplifier, but increasing data speed, not sound.

Storm would use his server to aim junk packets at certain sections of the 2600 chat network, server nodes of the network known as leaves. If you're sending junk packets instead of useful data, it can overload a server and take it offline. An IRC network was like a tree, and 2600 had three so-called leaves. Instead of attacking the whole network at once, Storm flooded each individual leaf. Using this plan, he could needle the hundreds of participants to scramble from one leaf to another instead of disconnecting altogether and waiting for the network to come back up. The ultimate goal was to annoy them as much as possible.

Through the IRC command map, the LulzSec group could watch how many users were on each of their enemy network's leaves. Before Storm's attack there had been about six hundred people on all leaves, and then the number started dropping. In just over ten minutes, one of the leaves went down.

"It's nulled," said Storm.

"Haha," said Kayla.

After seven minutes, as the users were jumping around to stay connected, Storm took down another leaf and kept it down for about fifteen minutes. He let it up again for twenty minutes so participants would think everything was okay, and then he took it down again.

"I can't even connect to 2600," reported Kayla. Storm laughed.

"These guys are so fun to fuck," said Topiary.

"Wait :D let us troll the shit out of them first :D," said Kayla, "then we can PUSH/SYN/ACK/UDP them to oblivion haha-hahahahaha." That was a reference to different types of junk packets. Attacking an entire network to get back at one annoying clique didn't seem to strike anyone in the group as an abuse of power or an act of bullying. Instead, with Storm now getting the limelight, Kayla couldn't help but mention her own successful attacks of the days of Chanology, and she started reminiscing about how she had DDoS'd three Chanology sites for three weeks back in 2009—the incident where she had been stumbled upon by Laurelai.

"Ahaha that was you?" asked Topiary.

"Yes :D," said Kayla.

"Gregg Housh was bitching about that."

"A lot of people were bitching about it."

"Sending packets of size 40…" Storm reported. Another server leaf was nulled. "Dude, they're not gonna have anywhere to chat." Now three key servers hosting the 2600 chat network were down. He and Topiary started trying to connect to the network and couldn't.

"Lolz," said Storm.

"We should do this everyday until they refuse to house Jester," said Topiary. He pointed out the small clique of people communicating with Jester on Twitter, and Awinee, from Holland, was being especially vindictive. "These are the same guys who specifically went after Sabu and our crew back in February with HBGary," Topiary added. "They're a lovable bunch of scoundrels."

Topiary sent some messages from the LulzSec feed: "What's wrong with irc.2600.net AKA Jester's hideout? Oops, I think we just fucked it. Sorry, Awinee and crew. Have fun explaining to the 2600.net admins that we just took down the entire network because of Jester people. Uh-oh!"

Back on #pure-elite, weapons were still firing at the 2600 servers. "Should I let it back up?" Storm asked Topiary.

"Whatever you want."

When he saw more criticism from Jester's people on Twitter, Storm switched to a different type of junk packet. And as Awinee kept up his rhetoric, LulzSec kept attacking. LulzSec was behaving like other hacker groups with its tit-for-tat behavior, except that more traditional hackers wouldn't have been riled up by a few relatively unskilled hecklers on Twitter. Perhaps it was because LulzSec was so open and public, but it was the critics who spoke the loudest that seemed to get under the group's skin the most.

Storm was proving a useful supporter with his DDoSing ability. In front of the crew, Topiary called him the LulzSec "cannon-fire officer," working in tandem with Kayla, who was the group's assassin and spy. "We dock in ports and she immerses, and eliminates."

"I also bake cookies," she added.

Everyone was laughing. They were all game for more attacks when Sabu finally entered the room. By now it was early in the morning New York time.

"I wake up to Storm packeting, and Kayla excited," he said. "What you niggas been doing without me?" There was a pause. His tone was lighthearted, but the crew knew about his hot temper from the #HQ channel with Laurelai and about his general tendency to blow up at others who disagreed with him. His presence made some a little anxious. If this had been real life, everyone might have been glancing at one another or at the floor.

"Owning 2600.net," said Storm. "About it."

"Lol, they're going to end up losing some servers," said Sabu. "I want to own 2600 servers themselves."

"That would be awesome," Topiary said.

"Topiary my brother, how are you?" Sabu asked.

"Good Sabu, what's up?"

"Nothing broscope. Just woke up, tired as balls." Sabu took a break from the discussions, and people went back to planning ways to mess with Jester's crew or configuring software tools and scripts for future hacks.

Quickly the group was splitting into all manner of channels to find new leads for hacks or flush out spies. Hopping from channel to channel and network to network was no trouble for these guys, some of whom were used to jumping around twenty-five IRC networks at the same time.

When 2600 came back online, Topiary, Joepie91, and others started hopping over to the network to spy on its participants before coming back to report new gossip. Rather brazenly, they then set up their own #LulzSec channel on the 2600 network. Pretty soon it was teeming with dozens, then more than a hundred people. It was impossible to tell at first who they all were, but enough observation showed they were a mixture of Anons, script kiddies, general fans who had heard about LulzSec from media reports, and white hat hackers. Over time the LulzSec crew came to believe that around half the makeup of that channel, which anyone could access, was a mixture of spies from enemy groups like Jester's and Feds. In their new, public #LulzSec chat room on 2600, the crew were disguised by their maritime-related names: Whirlpool for Topiary, Kraken for Kayla, and Seabed for Sabu.

As Sabu observed these developments, he grew concerned that the crew was getting too excited about having fun on the 2600 network—a place they had attacked but where they had also set up their own public meeting room. It was impossible to distinguish the real fans from the spies who wanted to manipulate the crew for information and access. At one point it looked like Kayla had gone back into Santa Claus mode and offered some stolen voucher codes from Amazon to someone outside the crew. When Sabu found out about the conversation, Kayla explained that she had merely given someone a few of the coupons so they could be tested and eventually sold on the black market. Sabu, who was already wary of Kayla's connection to Laurelai, was perturbed.

"Ok guys," he suddenly said. "I don't have to say this more than once I hope. But people on 2600 are not your friends. 95% are there to social engineer you. To analyze how you talk and make connections. Don't go off and befriend any of them."

He didn't mind that the reprimand pierced the lighthearted atmosphere. Four other secondary-crew members quickly insisted that they were being careful about hiding their identities, doing so by speaking in broken English so they would appear to be foreign. But Sabu added that if anyone gave them private info, they should log it and show it to the team. If they were sent a link, look at it from a secure connection.

"Be smart about shit," he concluded. "If any of you get owned, I'll LOL."

Kayla then piped up, as if she wanted to show the others that she was on the same page with Sabu. "Another protip," she said. "Even if you are American, don't spell it 'color,' use 'colour,' which is wider used around the world. Just saying 'color' means you are American."

Sabu didn't seem to be listening and gave Kayla a new order. He wanted her to change the topic of the public #LulzSec chat room to say that anyone with 0days and leaks should message her new pseudonym in the channel.

"Make sure we take advantage of that," he said. "See what niggers got access to." Kayla signed out. Sabu enjoyed the banter that took place in #pure-elite between the organizational talk, but he was constantly reminding the group to stay focused on finding new exploits and keeping the group as tight-knit as possible. It made for a tense atmosphere, but it was necessary. The team's profile was rising faster than they had ever expected. Googling the name LulzSec on June 1 had yielded twenty-five thousand mentions on the Internet. In less than twenty-four hours, that number had risen to two hundred thousand.

CHAPTER 20

More Sony, More Hackers

By the first of June, the LulzSec team and its associates had gathered a long list of vulnerabilities found by team members like Kayla, Pwnsauce, and Sabu. None were stored on an official group document since that was too risky—instead, whoever found a vulnerability kept it on his or her own computer and shared it with the group when needed. Here LulzSec was setting itself apart from Anonymous, not just because it was picking media companies but because of its focus on stealing data. HBGary had shown that stealing and selectively leaking data could be far more damaging—and "lulz-worthy" with all the attention it was getting—than a straightforward DDoS attack.

When the team found a vulnerability, the hope was that it would lead to critical secret data they could publish. Often following up a lead would happen spontaneously. Kayla had found the PBS security hole earlier in May, but the group had only followed it up because of the WikiSecrets documentary. Finding the security hole was one thing, but exploiting it took more work, and they would have to have a good reason to turn it into an operation. With one vulnerability they had recently found, though, the target company itself was reason enough.

Sony's lawsuit against George Hotz in April, the resultant DDoS attack from Anonymous, and the devastating data theft by a small group of black hat hackers had snowballed into a new craze among hackers to hit Sony in any way possible. It meant that Sony had become something of a piñata for hackers. Partly the black hats found it funny to keep hitting the company over and over, and partly they believed Sony deserved it for waiting two weeks after the original data breach had been discovered before reporting it.

The PBS heist was finished, and the 2600 network was still smoldering from the attack, but Sabu and Topiary were now knee-deep in organizing data stolen from Sony's servers: hundreds of thousands of users, administrators, internal upcoming albums releases from Sony, along with 3.5 million music coupons. Three weeks prior, the group had been poking around looking for vulnerabilities in Sony websites, finding and publishing the security vulnerabilities in the website of Sony Japan but also looking at Sony's Hong Kong site and others. Whenever someone found a vulnerability, he would paste the web address in his private chat room, and someone else would go into the source code to see how it could be exploited. There was no order to this; people simply contributed when they were around.

Just for the heck of it, Sabu checked SonyPictures.com, the main website for Sony's $7.2 billion film and television franchise. To his astonishment, there was a gaping hole in the innocuous Ghostbusters page that left the network wide open, once again, to a simple SQL injection attack.

"Hey guys, we need to dump all this now," he said excitedly. He rushed to map out the area and gather everyone together so they could start taking different sections. "We've owned something big here. Sony are going to crash and burn."

When the group entered the network they found a massive vault of information. It took a while to make sense of the data, but soon they had found a database with two hundred thousand users.

More shocking was that all of the data, including passwords, were stored in plaintext. The only encrypted passwords were those of server admins, and the team managed to crack those anyway.

It was a damning indictment of Sony's security, just weeks after the big PlayStation Network data breach. Small schools and charities had better database encryption than Sony. In fact, by this time, rumor had it that the PlayStation Network had been hacked because a disgruntled employee at Sony had given hackers an exploit; the breach had occurred two weeks after Sony had fired several employees responsible for network security. Rumor also had it that those hackers had sold the database of more than a hundred million users for $200,000.

Kayla stumbled upon another Sony database that looked exploitable but did not bother to look inside. As per the usual custom, she pasted its location into the chat room for someone else to scan. When Topiary finally opened the database, he found a table with rows and rows of names and numbers that seemed to go on forever. Looking around he finally noticed a counter at the top with the number 3.5 million. It looked like coupons of some sort. It felt like getting an exceptionally good Christmas present.

"Sabu, this one is pretty massive," Topiary called. Sabu came over and proceeded to poke around the new, massive database before coordinating the team's gathering of it all.

"Wave bye-bye to Sony," one of the team remarked.

"Kayla can you take users?" Sabu asked. He assigned one person to take care of the music codes, another the 3.5 million coupons, and Sabu himself took the admin tables. There were four core members and two other secondary-crew members help-ing out.

This was the kind of labor that would have put off a single hacker toiling alone. It involved downloading reams of data, sometimes manually. The work was monotonous and could take days. But as a group effort, the whole process suddenly became faster and more compelling, the team members motivated by the fact that this was a target they were about to publicly embar-rass. The tasks of compiling the databases—one of 75,000, one of 200,000—took each person between a day and several days to complete, depending on how detailed the information he or she was dealing with was. Each member then set up a computer to download each database. The files were so big that it would take three weeks to download them, typically in the background of whatever else was being done online.

The team eventually decided they wouldn't keep any of the coupons—they had tried taking them and got to only 125,000 when they realized the downloads were happening at the glacial rate of one coupon a second; all told the whole thing would take several more weeks. They didn't have the time or resources to cope with such a huge download. Instead, they took a sample of this and a sample of that to demonstrate that they had gained access. They would also publish the exact location of the server vulnerability in the Sony Pictures site that led to the data (the Ghostbusters page) so that anyone who wanted could dive in to loot the bounty before Sony's IT admins patched the hole.

Sabu gathered all the data together, and Topiary dressed the numbers and passwords up to make everything look palatable to a mass audience. "We have a lot of different files for various Sony sites," he explained. "Press—less smart press—will get confused. Gotta have a summary document." He would publish several documents revealing the heist in one big folder. He created a file called For Journalists that explained what they had found, using words that would grab headlines, such as *compromised* instead of *stolen*.

Topiary had been up since six o'clock that morning to keep up with Sabu's time zone, but he wasn't feeling tired. On Twitter he was counting down to their official release time, building anticipation among followers and the media. Gawker's Adrian Chen quickly posted a story headlined "World's Most Publicity Hungry Hackers Tease Impending Sony Leak."

Topiary had gone through the Sony Pictures database looking for anyone with a .gov or .mil e-mail address. He found a few and started posting their names and passwords on Twitter. Then At 5:00 p.m. eastern time on the same day that Sony finally restored its PlayStation Network, Topiary published everything.

"Greetings folks. We're LulzSec, and welcome to Sownage," he said in the introduction. "Enclosed you will find various collections of data stolen from internal Sony networks and websites, all of which we accessed easily and without the need for outside support or money." LulzSec was kicking Sony just as it was getting back up.

Thirty-eight minutes after the release, Aaron Barr tweeted that LulzSec had released stolen Sony data. "The amount of user data appears significant." In forty-five minutes fifteen thousand people had looked at the message, a rate of eighteen people a second, and two thousand had downloaded the package of Sony data from file-sharing website MediaFire.

Topiary didn't have time to sit back and watch the fallout. He and Tflow were putting up the new LulzSec website, complete with a retro–Nyan Cat design and the soft tones of American jazz singer Jack Jones singing the theme song of *The Love Boat* in the background. The home page showed Topiary's revamped "Lulz Boat" lyrics as plain black text in the middle. A link at the bottom offered viewers the option of muting it—when clicked, the link raised the volume by 100 percent. Sabu initially hated the website and yelled at Topiary and Tflow for creating something that had the potential to be DDoS'd, which would make the team look weak. Eventually Topiary convinced him that they should keep it.

They moved quickly to put the site in place, then worked to ensure it didn't collapse under the weight of thousand of visitors and the inevitable DDoS attacks from enemy hackers. They also made sure the torrent file of Sony data stayed up, that there weren't any more LulzSec Bitcoin donations (they totaled $4 so far), and that everything else was in check. The LulzSec Twitter feed now had 23,657 followers, and there were dozens more people pouring into the public #LulzSec chat room. Topiary would go to bed and find it difficult to sleep knowing that he was getting new tweets every two minutes. It was chaotic, but satisfying. He would go back onto Twitter with greater confidence each day, dismissing his detractors with withering put-downs and keeping the followers enticed. If LulzSec announced a new operation, it was now guaranteed to get on the news.

Often they didn't need to go into the details of what they were about to do—the media and the public often assumed that LulzSec was causing more damage than it really was. But as people's expectations rose, the stakes went higher.

"We don't want to be the hacking group that just leaks once a week some little thing," Topiary said at the time. "We will only do big things from now on…Unless we find someone we don't like."

One of those "big things" was imminent. The time had come for LulzSec to play its ace card and announce the hack on Infragard. "Welcome to FuckFBIFriday, wherein we sit and laugh at the FBI," Topiary announced on Twitter. "No times decided, but we'll cook up something nice for tonight. <3."

As the group scrambled to prepare the Infragard drop, a few from the team decided to pay particular attention to one person in the database of usernames and passwords they'd taken from the FBI affiliate site: a digital security entrepreneur named Karim Hijazi. Hijazi was thirty-five and ran a start-up called Unveillance. When the team checked Hijazi's Infragard password against Gmail and found a match, they started snooping around his e-mail account to see if they could expose some dirty laundry, as they had with Aaron Barr.

Sabu hated white hat security firms. That much Topiary knew. And now he was talking about the subject more than ever in private, particularly about a revival of the anti-security movement. Sabu's beef with white hats went back a long way. Anti-security got going in 1999, when a vulnerability in widely used Solaris servers that was known to only a couple hundred hackers in the world led to their hacking into a wide range of companies and organizations. Then they started stealing e-mails from white hat security firms. The reason was they hated a new edict in cyber security called full disclosure. The idea was that if cyber security experts (white hats) publicly disclosed a website's vulnerabilities quickly, they got fixed more quickly. But black hats preferred to keep the flaws hidden so that they would stay within the underground community and continue being exploited.

Antisec had seen its share of hacktivist groups like LulzSec, and one of the first was a notorious clique called ~el8. The shadowy hackers would target white hat security researchers and companies, steal their passwords and e-mails, and publish them in a regular e-zine. It was a single white page with *el8* elaborately spelled out in symbols at the top, not too dissimilar from the Pastebin posts of LulzSec and filled with new web scripts, exploits, stolen e-mails, and jeering commentary. The group called its work project mayhem, or "pr0j3kt m4yh3m." The phrase was borrowed from the movie *Fight Club,* and their e-zines heavily referenced the film. The bulletins never spelled out ~el8's motivations, but project mayhem appeared to be a violent incarnation of the Antisec movement. Many in the white hat industry figured ~el8's real motivation was to fight full disclosure so that black hats and gray hats would be the only people who knew about the Internet's secret vulnerabilities.

"One of these days, these kids are going to have to pay a mortgage and get a job," said Eric Hines, an executive of one of the white hat firms that was attacked, in a *Wired* article. "And they're not going to become lawyers or doctors—they're going to do what they're good at. And that means getting a career in the security industry."

Sabu had nurtured a dislike for white hats even after the 1999 Antisec movement dwindled. Emick believed Sabu was simply resentful after getting turned down for a job in IT security. Either way, the sentiment was rubbing off on Topiary as the two had more one-on-one discussions. Sabu would point out that white hats charged $20,000 for penetration testing, stuff that the LulzSec crew could do for free. He explained that Topiary himself could have done what HBGary was charging $10,000 for. The message was that white hats were like unscrupulous car mechanics, tricking people into believing they needed to pay thousands when the real cost was much lower.

This line of reasoning was very different from the original Antisec argument over full disclosure. That's because a decade later, the Web was now so chock-full of websites, data, and vulnerabilities that white hats weren't pushing for full disclosure anymore. The view had flipped, and fully disclosing server flaws was veering into a criminal offense. The notorious Internet troll Andrew "weev" Auernheimer, who had come up with the meme "Internets is serious business," had learned that the hard way. In 2010, he and a few hacker friends from their trolling group Goatse Security poked around in AT&T's website and found a security hole that led to internal data on 114,000 iPad users. Weev "fully disclosed" it, albeit through mainstream media and not a cyber security newsletter. The following January, six months after journalists at Gawker did an exposé on the AT&T security flaw for iPad users, the U.S. Department of Justice announced that it was charging weev with fraud and conspiracy to access a computer without authorization.

A successful revival of Antisec could keep the authorities busy with more people like weev. Sabu wanted to keep the focus on white hats, like the old days, so it was crucial to find some real dirt on Hijazi's tiny firm Unveillance. The company made money by hunting for malicious botnets, but digging around in its e-mails, Sabu and the others thought they found evidence that he was working with others to snoop on Libyan web users. They decided to confront him on IRC under different guises to let him know they had all his e-mails and that they could do worse. On May 26, they e-mailed him his password, with the subject line, "Let's talk," and said they wanted to see his botnet research.

Hijazi immediately picked up the phone and called the FBI. When he finally got through to someone and tried to explain what was happening, Hijazi got the impression the people on the other line weren't interested, or perhaps didn't understand what he was talking about. They referred him to an agent in his local office. When he called that number and told a local staffer that malicious hackers were trying to access his botnet research, he was surprised when that individual replied, "What's a botnet?"

Eventually, an agent advised Hijazi to start logging all of his conversations with the group and to play along to see if he could get any information on them. On the other side of the fence, Sabu, Topiary, and Tflow were trying to position Hijazi to admit that he wanted to hire the hackers to attack his competitors. Both sides ended up lying to each other to obtain information, which made for a confusing encounter filled with misinterpretation.

"The point is a very crude word: extortion," Topiary had told Hijazi under the name Ninetails, adding that Hijazi would be paying for their silence. "You have lots of money, we want more money."

The team kept offering to help Hijazi by attacking his corporate competitors. Playing along like he was supposed to, he eventually replied: "I can't ask you to get someone and stay a 'legit' firm. Agreed?" When Topiary read this he believed that Hijazi was falling into their trap and that it was proof of yet another corrupt white hat, just as Sabu had predicted.

"Can I take a guess at who you are?" Karim had later asked.

"Karim, we've been expecting you to be secretly guessing since day one," Topiary replied under a second nickname, Espeon. "Do share."

"808chan."

Sabu burst out laughing. "Are you serious bro?" he asked, using the nickname hamster_nipples. "How dare you call us a fucking chan."

"Then tell me," replied Karim, who was keeping his responses as measured as possible while playing their game.

"If we tell you who we are, you will shit yourself and shut the fuck up," Sabu said. "But yes we are very well known." The group kept prodding Hijazi, calling him dense and warning him about what they could do with his e-mails. But Hijazi had to pretend to be oblivious—he knew just as well as Sabu and the others that playing stupid was one of the most effective ways to social-engineer someone. It could sometimes trick him into revealing facts about himself.

"Why be hostile? Just curious," Hijazi said.

"We're not a chan," replied hamster_nipples, who seemed to have an issue with status. "Don't refer to us as a chan. We are security researchers."

"No worries," said Hijazi. "You're not a chan."

"Heh," hamster_nipples said. "You're testing my patience."

Though Sabu came across as menacing in the resulting chat

logs (released by both LulzSec and Hijazi himself), Hijazi's press officer later said in an interview that the most aggressive hacker in the team had been Ninetails, the alias of Topiary. "He is very blunt," Michael Sias said, "and forceful about the extortion." Hijazi, he added, had been trying to do the right thing.

"It was tough, not pleasant," Hijazi remembered a few weeks later. "I'm not sure what their motivation is. They're just name-calling, which seems very juvenile. I thought at minimum there would be some belief system and there didn't seem to be anything behind it. It was petty."

Of course none of that struck Topiary and Sabu, who figured they were gradually picking up proof that white hats were bad, and black hats were their avengers.

"There are a lot of companies that overcharge and abuse the fact that people know nothing," Topiary said excitedly in an interview after a recent conversation with Sabu on the topic of Antisec. "Computers aren't our intelligence. Buy a book or two and learn it yourself. That's what I find." The message Topiary was getting from Sabu was the same: that the white hat security industry was keeping regular people in the dark about how to navigate the Internet, undermining and emasculating the public when they could easily learn things on their own, just as he had.

With LulzSec unveiling these apparently new and hitherto unspoken corruptions, Anonymous was starting to look irrelevant. LulzSec had quickly racked up fifty thousand Twitter followers and was gearing up to spread the Antisec message. AnonOps IRC was a mess; everyone was on edge. There was no thrilling atmosphere anymore, no humor. Where there had once been eight hundred regular participants in a chat room like #OpLibya, there were now fifty or a hundred at most. The hot-tempered operators had gone back to fighting one another and kicking out participants on a whim. Feds were crawling all over the network. It

wasn't friendly, or safe. Topiary and Sabu figured they were creating a far better world in LulzSec and its public chat network.

As Sabu nursed ambitions to revive a crusade against white
hats, he encouraged the group in #pure-elite to seek leads from
black hat hackers in the public LulzSec chat room, now being
hosted on a new IRC network called luzco.org. The crew were
still getting ready to drop Infragard, and in the meantime Topiary, Joepie91, and others were hopping over to their channel to
suss out some of its visitors. Later that day, a hacker named Fox
came in the room and approached Topiary. It seemed he had
some leads for future hacks.

"You got a messenger?" Fox asked. "I'd be happy to toss exploits and business back and forth." Topiary had never heard of
the guy but figured it could lead to something.

"We got people offering us exploits," Topiary announced to
the team when he came back to the #pure-elite channel. "He's legit, but not so sure we can trust him." There was no chance Fox
would be invited into their channel, unless Sabu said the words
100 percent trusted. Instead, the team invited Fox into a new, neutral channel where the others could feel him out. It was hard not
to be paranoid.

"He's probably a spy," Topiary told the others. Sabu suggested
he might be Jester himself. "If he is then we can throw them off
course. If he isn't, free exploits."

Often when the group started talking to a new contact, they
used it as a chance to practice their banter and have some fun.
When Sabu joined in the chat with Fox, he pretended to be a
LulzSec hacker from Brazil. The team members were hopping
back and forth, from chatting in the neutral channel to chuckling over their antics back on home base, particularly at Sabu's
Brazil act.

"Have you guys ever talked to a real hardcore Brazillian
hacker?" Sabu quickly asked the crew. Sabu knew many Brazil-

ian hackers, to the extent that he could impersonate the way they spoke, in very basic English mixed with hacker slang, and in text chat rather than voice.

"HEUHEAUEHAUHAUEHAHEAUEHUHheuheush-HUAHUehuuhuUEUue." Sabu had quickly typed out a typical Brazilian online laugh.

"Fox, a gentlemen never tells," Sabu had told the new hacker, still playing the part of a Brazilian.

"Ah, I love that answer," Fox had replied.

The LulzSec crew seemed to fall over laughing. "Sabu, you are a god," said Neuron.

"Thanks, sir," Sabu replied. "Consider yourselves lucky no one really gets to see me work in action. No one is trustable outside our crew. Remember that, Neuron."

The crew kept jumping from the public #LulzSec to the private #pure-elite where they would report more openly (though never completely openly) about what was happening. New participants could instantly tell who was important to talk to because the LulzSec crew all had operator status, teetering at the top of the long list and with special symbols prefacing their names.

At one point Joepie was privately approached in the teeming room by someone named Egeste, a name that was familiar to anyone who had been on Kayla's #tr0ll IRC channel. "So, I want to play with you guys and this channel is like, gayer than gay and full of newfags," Egeste said. It was true that LulzSec now had more participants than all of the 2600 network. "Where's the real lulzsec?"

"Play in what sense?" answered Joepie, who was using the name YouAreAPirate.

"You know what I mean. I know you guys don't know me, but you probably know people that do. Xero, venuism, e, insidious, nigg, etc etc." Then he added, "Kayla."

Joepie reported all of this verbatim back to the crew in #pure-elite. Those nicknames were very well known, pointed out a secondary-crew member called Trollpoll. Another laughed.

"He's just name dropping," said Sabu. Neuron, a friendly and analytical Anon, suggested asking Egeste to provide a zero-day as proof of his skills. Also known as a 0day, this referred to an as-yet-unknown server vulnerability, and finding one meant big kudos for any hacker, white hat or black hat.

Sabu asked Kayla if she'd heard of Egeste, and it turned out the new guy had also been in the #Gnosis channel when she had coordinated the hack on Gawker, but "he did not do shit," she said. For all the names he had mentioned, Egeste was just another distraction. Soon the encounter was just a drop in the ocean of dozens of others with potential supporters and trolls.

Once in a while the #LulzSec chat room was graced with the presence of a disgruntled company employee who was eager to leak some internal data via a charismatic new group. Not more than a day after LulzSec's first attack on Sony made headlines, a new visitor to the #LulzSec chat room approached secondary-crew member Neuron, offering what appeared to be source code for the official website for Sony developers. Neuron reported it to home base.

"Just looked at this guy's source for 'sonydev.net,'" he said. "It seems ligit. php file etc. Still investigating."

"Neuron, that source you got," said Sabu. "[Post it on] pas-tee.org so we can analyze also." Neuron sent the others a link to the fifty-five-megabyte file along with a thirty-three-digit password to access it.

"Downloading," said Sabu. "Which site is this for? Sony-dev.net?"

"Aye," said Neuron. "I'm sure we can find the pass somewhere on Sony."

"Analyzing 'scedev' source codes now," said Sabu. Neuron checked in about ten minutes later.

"What's the word on that source?" Neuron asked.

Sabu seemed to approve of it. "Should we just leak the source code?" he asked Topiary and Neuron.

"I wouldn't suggest it just yet," Neuron replied. "We could use more of his shit. He's a Sony developer."

"You serious?" asked Sabu.

"If we keep quiet we can get more," said Neuron, who took the view that it was better to lurk than dump everything at once like a script kiddie.

"So tell him to give us access into [the] Sony network."

"I'll see. He said he was an ex-Sony developer but has access."

"Social engineer him into that shit," said Storm, who was listening in.

"Ok," said Sabu. "So bro. What are you doing here talking to us? Social his ass. Haha." Neuron had gone to try to talk to the source again but it was already too late.

"He logged off," said Neuron.

"Gay," Sabu said, a little disappointed. "So he messaged you, gave you source, logged off?"

"Yeah," said Neuron. "He likes us or something."

This was how it often went. The promise of leaks and exploits would come from gray and black hat hackers or anyone who had something worth offering. Often the data wasn't as exciting as originally promised, but in the end, the team used the source code that the ex–Sony developer had passed them. And over time they stopped being surprised that so many outside people wanted to pass them vulnerabilities to exploit—it seemed like everyone in the IT security field, itself a medley of white hats with a darker past, was talking about LulzSec. A few secretly wished they could be a part of the fun.

One hacker had a particularly unusual way of demanding to be let in. One afternoon, the LulzSec crew found themselves getting individually kicked out of the public LulzSec chat room.

"Wow, bro," Storm suddenly said on #pure-elite. "People are trying to down our ops." Someone was sending junk packets and bumping each LulzSec crew member off the IRC channel. It wasn't affecting their computers, but the virtual machines or virtual private networks being used to displace their true locations were getting hit. DDoSing someone's IP could make him disappear from the Internet for a while, but if you did it enough he'd be booted from his hosting service altogether.

"We gotta get off that server," said a second-tier member called Recursion.

"We're getting hit," cried Neuron. There was a general hub-bub among the secondary crew as they floundered over a response to the attack.

Sabu almost rolled his eyes. "Neuron, so sign off? Look guys." No one was listening.

"The whole room is hit," Storm exclaimed. "He's hitting random people." It seemed a lone mercenary who went by the nick-name Xxxx was trying to disrupt LulzSec's attempts to meet with its fans.

Then Joepie received a private message: "Hi Kayla or Sabu or Tflow." It had come from Xxxx. Joepie ran a search on the user's IP and realized it was Ryan, the botnet-wielding temperamental operator from AnonOps.

Neuron received the same private message, then others in the secondary crew did too.

"Everybody shut the fuck up," Sabu said. People were still talking excitedly. "EVERYONE. SHUT THE FUCK UP." That seemed to get their attention.

"Relax," he continued. "As for Ryan, ignore him. He doesn't know it's us. Jesus."

"Relax," said Joepie, adding a smiley face.

"Ryan, huh?" said Topiary.

"The situation is getting horribly stressing," said Trollpoll.

"I know, Jesus," said Sabu. "Look. From now on, no one goes on 2600 unless you prep yourself for the social engineering."

Everyone was listening now. "If you don't know how to social engineer do not get on 2600," he said. "If you do not have a DDoS protected IP, do not get on 2600. That's it."

"Aye," said Neuron.

"Exactly," said Storm.

"Aye-aye, Storm," said Recursion. "Err, Sabu. I meant to say aye-aye Sabu, not Storm."

"Ok," said Sabu. "Sony was leaked. We got bigger projects." He pointed to Neuron's work on the new Sony development source code. "How about those who are not too busy work on auditing that source code." Everyone got back to work.

CHAPTER 21

Stress and Betrayal

As LulzSec's targets got bigger, Kayla started drifting away a little from operations, more interested in taking revenge on enemies like Jester and Backtrace. She had always been a free spirit, loyal to her friends but never aligning herself too closely with any particular cause for too long. Sometimes, she just got bored. She also wasn't as interested in reviving the Antisec movement as Sabu or Topiary. Instead, she started developing an elaborate plan to creep into the #Jester chat room as a spy, embed herself, then infect the computers of its members with a key-logger program so that she could monitor their key strokes, learn a few key passwords, and take them over. It was called a drive-by attack, and while in this case it was an elaborate operation, typically the attack was just a matter of enticing someone to visit a website and installing malware on their system as a result. It meant she was now spending just a couple of hours a day chatting with the crew before disappearing for a day or more.

In the meantime there was some surprising news coming from the United States. The Pentagon had announced that cyber attacks from another country could constitute an act of war and that the U.S. could respond with traditional military force. Almost at the same time, a draft report from NATO claimed that Anonymous was becoming "more and more sophisticated" and "could potentially hack into sensitive government, military and corporate files." It went on to say that Anonymous had demonstrated its ability to do just that by hacking HBGary Federal. Ironically, it stated that the hackers had hit Barr's company and hijacked his Twitter account "in response" to Bank of America hiring the security company to attack adversaries like WikiLeaks. Even NATO seemed to be inflating the abilities of Anonymous, seeing reason and connections where there were coincidences. The hackers hadn't known about Barr's plans with WikiLeaks until after they had attacked him. Even so, the news got everyone's attention.

"Did you read the NATO doc about anonymous?" asked Trollpoll in the #pure-elite hub. Trollpoll did not sound like he was from the United States, though it was impossible to be sure of anyone there. "They will put tanks on our houses?"

"Obama will be like 'Lol you just DDoS my server?'" said Kayla, "'Nuke.'"

With the world's attention now moving to LulzSec and the fighting words from the U.S. administration, it seemed as good a time as any to drop the FBI affiliate Atlanta Infragard. They'd had the site under their control for months and felt they now had enough on white hat Hijazi to expose him at the same time. This would bring more heat than ever on LulzSec, but the group was on a roll and felt safe.

LulzSec's founding team members would carry out the final Infragard swoop. As they got ready to deface the site, Sabu entered the shell, the administrative page he had set up called xOOPSmaster, opened his terminal program so he could start playing with the source code, and, on a seeming whim, typed *rm –rf /*. It was a short, simple-looking piece of code with a notorious reputation: anyone who typed it into his computer's back end could effectively delete everything on the system. There was no window popping up to ask *Are you sure?* It just happened. Web trolls famously got their victims to type it in or to delete the crucial system 32 file in Windows.

"Oops," Sabu told the others. "Just deleted everything. rm –rf /*." Kayla made the face-palm gesture, and everyone moved on. On top of everything they had already done, deleting the Infragard website contents didn't seem like a big deal. They then used the /xOOPS.php shell to upload a giant image and title onto the Infragard home page—their deface. It was no serious admonishment of the FBI but another prank aimed at Jester's crew. The team had replaced the Atlanta Infragard home page with a YouTube video of an Eastern European TV reporter interviewing an impeccably drunk man at a disco. Someone had added subtitles spoofing him as a wannabe hacker from 2600 who didn't understand what LulzSec was doing. Above the video was the title "LET IT FLOW YOU STUPID FBI BATTLESHIPS," in a window captioned "NATO—National Agency of Tiny Origamis LOL."

Topiary's official statement was a little more serious—but not much. When everyone was ready, he hit publish.

"It has come to our unfortunate attention that NATO and our good friend Barrack Osama-Llama 24th-century Obama have recently upped the stakes with regard to hacking," Topiary had written in their official statement. "They now treat hacking as an act of war. So, we just hacked an FBI affiliated website (Infragard, specifically the Atlanta chapter) and leaked its user base. We also took complete control over the site and defaced it." Of course, LulzSec had not hacked Infragard in the past day or two or in response to the Pentagon's announcement, but news outlets reported the attack as a "response."

Infragard's web contents had been deleted, the site defaced, and details of 180 people in its user base had been published on the Web, along with their passwords in plaintext, their real names, and their e-mail addresses. Topiary had signed off the missive, declaring, "Now we are all sons of bitches."

Since Topiary had been reminding the world for the past day on Twitter that an FBI hack was imminent, mainstream news agencies jumped into the story, leading a whole new stream of people to follow the group on Twitter. Their website had now received more than 1.5 million views. Despite the damage LulzSec had done to the 2600 network, the actual magazine *2600* sounded impressed. "Hacked websites, corporate infiltration/scandal, IRC wars, new hacker groups making global headlines," its official Twitter feed stated, "the 1990s are back!"

Television news stations were racing to find security experts who could explain what was going on and offer some lucid opinions. "We are facing a very innovative crime, and innovation has to be the response," said Gordon Snow, the assistant director of the FBI's cyber division in an interview with Bloomberg right after the Infragard attack. "Given enough money, time and resources, an adversary will be able to access any system."

Yet LulzSec's hack into Infragard had not cost that much in terms of "money, time and resources." All told, the operation had cost $0, had been carried out with the relatively simple method of SQL injection, and was made worse because an admin's cracked password, "st33r!NG," had been reused to get administrative access to the Infragard site itself. As for time, it had taken the team thirty minutes to crack the admin's password and twenty-five minutes to download the database of users. Within two hours, the LulzSec team had complete administrative access to an FBI-affiliated site, and for several weeks no one from the FBI had had a clue.

Of course, along with the Infragard drop had been LulzSec's condemnation of Hijazi. The team had kept some of their chat logs with the white hat and published them online as evidence that he was corrupt. And while the group members had told Hijazi that they wouldn't release his e-mails, they published them too.

"We have uncovered an operation orchestrated by Unveillance and others to control and assess Libyan cyberspace through malicious means," Topiary announced, meaning by *assess* that Unveillance wanted to spy on Libyan Internet users.

"We leaked Karim because we had enough proof that he was willing to hire us as hitmen," Topiary added on Twitter. "Not a very ethical thing to do, huh Mr. Whitehat?"

Hijazi also released a statement immediately after, explaining that he had "refused to pay off LulzSec" or supply them with his research on botnets. Topiary shot back with a second official statement saying that they had never intended to go through with the extortion, only to pressure Hijazi to the point where he would be willing to pay for the hackers' silence and then expose him publicly. It was a war of words built on the gooey foundations of lies and social engineering.

Topiary still called on journalists and other writers to "delve through" Hijazi's e-mails carefully, hoping for the same kind of enthusiasm there had been around Aaron Barr's e-mail hoard. But there was none. For a start, Hijazi just didn't have enough dirty laundry. More, the infamy of LulzSec was overshadowing any more sobering, sociopolitical points the group was dimly making with each attack—that it didn't like Fox, or that WikiSecrets "sucked," or that NATO was upping the stakes against hackers, or whatever Unveillance might have been doing in Libya. It was quite an array of targets; LulzSec seemed to be attacking anyone it could, because it could.

This was getting to some of the secondary-crew members. The hacker Recursion came into the #pure-elite room late on June 3 after watching the Infragard events unfold. He hadn't taken part in the hack and was shocked when he read the news reports.

"Holy shit," Recursion told the others. "What the fuck happened today?"

"A lot," said Sabu, adding a smile. "Check Twitter."

"LulzSec declared war on the U.S.?" Joepie offered sardonically.

"I caught the jist of it," Recursion answered before seeming to trail off. He didn't say anything more on the subject, but twenty minutes later, after presumably holding a private conversation with Sabu, he left the channel, for good.

Sabu was disappointed in anyone who bailed on him in battle. It felt disrespectful. But he moved on quickly to guide the remaining troops. Sabu came back to the room and addressed the handful of participants. "Well guys. Those of you that are still with us through this, maintain alert, make sure you're behind VPNs no matter what. And don't fear. We're ok."

"Sabu, did we lose people?" asked Neuron.

"Yeah."

"Who?"

"Recursion and Devurandom quit respectfully," he answered, "saying they are not up for the heat. You realize we smacked the FBI today. This means everyone in here must remain extremely secure." It was a grave reminder of the potential charges LulzSec was racking up if its team members were to get caught.

A few of the members started describing how they were strengthening their security. Storm was getting a new netbook and completely wiping his old computer. Neuron was doing the same. He used a virtual private network called HideMyAss. This was a company based in the United Kingdom that Topiary used and had recommended.

"Did you wipe the PBS [chat] logs?" Storm asked Sabu.

"Yes. All PBS logs are clean."

"Then I'm game for some more," said Storm. Sabu typed out a smiley face.

"We're good," he said. "We got a good team here."

Not everyone was good though, and not all logs were clean. The aloof LulzSec secondary-crew member known as M_nerva, the one who had said "good night" to the others just a few days before and not said too much else afterward, had just gathered together six days' worth of chat logs from the #pure-elite channel and repeated Laurelai's frantic act in February. He leaked it. On June 6, the security website seclists.org released the full set of #pure-elite chat logs held on Sabu's private IRC server. The leak revealed, embarrassingly, that not everyone in #pure-elite could be "100 percent trusted," and that for all its bravado, LulzSec had weaknesses. The team jumped into action, knowing that they had to send a message that they did not accept snitches, even if M_nerva had allegedly been persuaded to leak the logs by another hacker, named Hann. They knew they could find out who M_nerva really was because among the other black hats supporting LulzSec was someone who had access to pretty much every AOL Instant Messenger account in existence. Since many people had set up an AIM account at one time or another, they only needed to cross-check the nickname and IP to come up with a real name and address. It turned out M_nerva was an eighteen-year-old from Hamilton, Ohio, named Marshall Webb. The crew decided to hold on to the information for now.

With Sabu's trust betrayed, the older hacker was now more paranoid than before. Topiary felt vindicated. He had known that a leak could happen if Sabu kept inviting people into #pure-elite, and it did. But he didn't push the point. When he brought it up with Sabu, the hacker brushed off the topic quickly. He had nothing to say about it. Instead, Sabu worked on making the wider group more secure by separating it into four different chat rooms. There was a core channel, which now had invited fifteen participants, and #pure-elite, then chat rooms called upper_deck, for the most trusted supporters, lower_deck, kitten_core, and family. Members could graduate up the tier system depending on how trustworthy they were. Neuron and Storm, for instance, eventually were invited into upper_deck, so that they could be phased into the main channel for LulzSec's core six members: Sabu, Topiary, Kayla, Tflow, AVunit, and Pwnsauce.

The heat wasn't coming only from the media attention; Topiary was seeing hackers with military IP addresses trying to compromise the LulzSec IRC network and users every day. Already, rumors were spreading that LulzSec had been founded by the same crew that had hit HBGary. Enemy hackers were posting documents filled with details they had dug up online about each member, much of it wrong but some of it hitting close to home. LulzSec's members needed to switch their focus from finding targets to protecting themselves.

Kayla suggested a mass disinformation campaign. Her idea was to create a Pastebin document revealing that Adrian Lamo owned the domain LulzSec.com; then to add details of other Jesterfags and claim they were members of LulzSec; then to spam the document everywhere. It was a classic social-engineering tactic, and it sometimes worked.

"But saying more or less that LulzSec is CIA," Trollpoll offered. It was outrageous, but some people would see sense in the idea that the CIA was using freelance hackers to hit Iran or Libya and would build their own conspiracy theories around it.

Topiary and Kayla wrote up a document titled "Criminals of LulzSec," under the guise of a fictitious social engineer called Jux who claimed to have been invited into the group's private channel, saying, "I believe they are being encouraged or hired by CIA." In the document, Jux claimed Lamo was a key member of the group, along with a Pakistani hacker named Parr0t, a Frenchman named Stephen, and an unnamed hacker from the Netherlands. The document was viewed more than 40,000 times, retweeted by notorious hacker Kevin Mitnick, and mentioned in a few tech blogs as a rumor.

When Gawker's Adrian Chen started reaching out to LulzSec via Twitter to try to investigate them, the crew, still bitter about his exposé on the #HQ log leak, decided to aim a separate misinformation campaign directly at him. They invited him into a neutral IRC channel, where Sabu posed as an ex–secondary-crew member of LulzSec who had run away and wanted to spill some secrets. The crew made their hoax on Chen especially elaborate, drawing up fake logs, fake web attacks on the fake persona's school, and fake archives of data as proof for the journalist. Sabu then started feeding Chen a story that LulzSec was a tool of the Chinese government in a cyber war with the United States, that Kayla was working with Beijing, and that Topiary was funneling money from the Chinese government into the group.

"If he publishes, that old sack of crap is completely ruined," Topiary said. They were planning to let the story do the rounds for five days, then deny it on Twitter, posting a link to all their logs with the journalist. But Chen never published anything. Like Hijazi, he had been playing along with LulzSec's story in the hope of teasing out some truth, which he realized he wasn't getting. The lack of a story was disappointing for LulzSec's members, but they were managing to keep outsiders from getting too close; for now, at least.

By early June the members of LulzSec were working flat-out on several different misinformation campaigns and the odd operation and trying not to think about the potential damage caused by M_nerva. One light in the darkness was that they had racked up five hundred dollars in Bitcoin donations. Topiary controlled the Bitcoin account and was passing some of the money to Sabu to buy accounts with virtual private networks, like HideMyAss, to better hide their ring of supporters and also to get more server space. Turning that money into untraceable cash was a drawn-out task but relatively easy. The Bitcoins bought virtual prepaid cards from Visa, with the help of fake names, addresses, personal details, and occupations at fake companies, generated in seconds on the website fakenamegenerator.com. As long as the contact address matched the billing address, no online store would question its authenticity. The Visa account was used to get in the online virtual world Second Life and buy the in-game currency Lindens. Convert that money into U.S. dollars via a currency transfer site (recommended by Kayla) called VirWoX, then put those dollars into a Moneybookers account. Finally, transfer that money into a personal bank account. That was one method. Another more direct route, which Topiary often used, was to simply transfer money between a few different Bitcoin addresses:

Bitcoin address 1 → Bitcoin address 2 → Bitcoin address 3 → Liberty Reserve (a Costa Rican payment processor) account → Bitcoin address 4 → Bitcoin address 5 → second Liberty Reserve account → PayPal account → bank account.

If even the hint of a thought occurred to him that there weren't enough transfers, he would add several more paths.

Then on Monday, June 6, Topiary checked the LulzSec Bitcoin account. *Holy shit,* he thought. He was looking at a single, anonymous donation of four hundred Bitcoins, worth approximately $7,800. It was more money than Topiary had ever had in his life. He went straight into the core group's secure chat room.

"WHAT THE FUCK guys?!" he said, then pasted the Bitcoin details.

"NO WAY," said AVunit. "LOL. Something has gone wrong."

"Nope," Topiary said. He pasted the details again.

Suddenly they all stopped what they were doing and talked about splitting the money: $1,000 each and the rest to invest in new servers. They started private messaging Topiary with their unique Bitcoin addresses so he could send them their shares. Topiary had no intention of keeping quiet about the money or cutting a bigger slice for himself. Everyone was funneling the money through various accounts to keep it from being traced. Who knew if the donation had come from the Feds or opportunistic military white hats?

"Guys be safe with the Bitcoins please," said AVunit. "Let it flow through a few gateways.... Use one bit to get out of financial trouble and then sit on the rest."

"Okay, beginning the sends," Topiary said. "All of you are now $1,000 richer."

"Excuse me while I light up a victory cigar," said Pwnsauce.

"I'm just going to stare at it," said Kayla. "Let it grow as Bitcoin progresses." So volatile and popular was the value of the Bitcoin crypto currency that by the following day one Bitcoin had risen to $26 in value, making their big donation worth $11,000. Three months prior it had been one to one with the dollar.

"I'm honestly sorry you guys aren't here," said AVunit, "because I'm going to open a bottle of great whiskey. One of the Highland Scottish." Topiary barely noticed the reference to where he lived.

"Now let's all have some sex," Tflow said.

Everyone was beaming inside, forgetting the enemies and the heat. Sabu took the chance to congratulate his crew. "Thanks, team," he said. "We all did great work. We deserved it."

For Sabu, the celebrations would not last long. The next day, Hector "Sabu" Monsegur finally got a knock on the door from the FBI.

It was late in the evening on Tuesday, June 7, and two agents of the Federal Bureau of Investigation had entered the Jacob Riis apartment building and were heading for the sixth floor, where

Hector Monsegur lived and often partied with his family and friends. The FBI had been trying to pin down Sabu for months, and a few weeks prior they had finally managed to corroborate Backtrace's pronouncment: Sabu had inadvertently signed into an IRC channel without hiding his IP address. Just the one time was all they needed. To make sure he cooperated, the Feds needed evidence that Monsegur had broken the law. So they subpoenaed Facebook for details of his account and found stolen credit card numbers he'd been selling to other hackers. That alone carried a two-year prison sentence. Knowing that he had two daughters and a family, the FBI now had some leverage.

The FBI had watched and waited for the right moment. Then on Tuesday, the agents got the call to move in. Amid the growing number of small groups who were, like Backtrace, trying to dox LulzSec, one had published the name Hector Monsegur, along with his real address. Sabu had recklessly kept hacking till now, perhaps reasoning that he had come too far already and that arrest was inevitable. But the FBI didn't want to take any chances. They needed him.

The agents knocked on Monsegur's maroon-colored door, and it swung open to reveal a young Latino man, broad-shouldered and wearing a white t-shirt and jeans.

"I'm Hector," he said. The agents, who were wearing bulletproof vests as a standard precaution, introduced themselves. Monsegur, apparently, balked. According to a later Fox News report that cited sources who had witnessed the interaction, he told the agents that he wasn't Sabu. "You got the wrong guy," he said. "I don't have a computer." Looking into the apartment, the agents saw an Ethernet cable and the green, blinking lights of a DSL modem.

They probed Monsegur further, launching into a traditional good cop/bad cop routine. They told him that they wanted him to work with them as a cooperating witness, to help them corroborate the identities of the other LulzSec hackers. Sabu refused at first. He wasn't about to snitch on his own team.

Then they told him about the evidence they had from Facebook that showed that he had sold stolen credit cards and told him that this alone would put him in jail for two years. What would happen to his girls if he went to prison? The good cop told Monsegur he could get a lesser sentence if he cooperated; he had to think of his kids. Monsegur was still holding back. That's when bad cop piped up.

"That's it, no deal, it's over," the other agent said, storming out of the apartment. "We're locking you up." Sabu finally relented.

"It was because of his kids," one of the agents later told Fox. "He'd do anything for his kids. He didn't want to go away to prison and leave them. That's how we got him."

The following morning at ten, Monsegur appeared in the Southern District Court of New York with his new lawyer, Peggy Cross-Goldenberg, and agreed before a judge to let the FBI monitor his every movement—both online and in real life. It would take a few more months for prosecutors to formally charge him on a stream of other counts related to computer hacking, but his punishment would be agreed as part of a settlement. From Wednesday, June 8, on, Sabu was an FBI informant.

Monsegur, who had climbed to the pinnacle of the international hacker community thanks to his technical skills, charm, and political passion, was now feeding information about his friends to the FBI.

As Hector Monsegur was being arrested in his secret New York apartment, thousands of people were talking about his crew of audacious hackers. Twenty-five thousand more people had started following LulzSec's Twitter feed after the Infragard hack, and it now had seventy-one thousand followers. The name was getting 1.2 million hits on Google. Topiary found that he would spend a few seconds thinking of something silly to tweet, then he would tweet it to find it immediately quoted in a news headline. When he tweeted a link to the group's public IRC channel, irc.lulzco.org, one Sunday evening at six, more than 460 people quickly piled in for random chatter and a chance to rub virtual shoulders with the most famous hackers on the planet. "Join the party," he had announced. "We're enjoying a peaceful Sunday."

"LulzSec, you guys rock!" said one visitor.

"I need someone to take down my school's cheap ass website, for the lulz," said another.

"Hey can anyone hack this douche for me?" asked someone else who then posted an IP address. Each time another group of twenty or thirty people joined the chat, someone would shout, "Here comes the flood!"

"You guys released my mom's e-mail," said another fan on Twitter. "I LOL'ed."

Meanwhile journalists were struggling to keep up with the fast-paced developments. No sooner had LulzSec released Sony's development codes than it uploaded the user database for porn site Pron.com, pointing out users who had .gov and .mil e-mail addresses with the note, "They are too busy fapping to defend their country." One American fighter pilot had used the password mywife01 while the e-mail address flag@whitehouse.gov had used karlmarx.

Australian IT security expert and the blogger behind cyber security blog Risky.Biz, Patrick Gray, wrote up a blog post called "Why We Secretly Love LulzSec." It got re-tweeted hundreds of times and said, "LulzSec is running around pummeling some of the world's most powerful organizations into the ground...for laughs! For lulz! For shits and giggles! Surely that tells you what you need to know about computer security: there isn't any." His kicker at the end voiced what many in the cyber security industry were thinking: "So why do we like LulzSec? 'I told you so.' That's why."

LulzSec's flagrant use of often simple SQL injection methods had brought home how vulnerable people's private data was, and done it more compellingly than any IT security's marketing campaign had. Cisco even capitalized on the interest, at one point sponsoring promotional tweets at the top of any search results for the group on Twitter.

Then a white hat security company did the same. The next morning Topiary woke up to see news reports of LulzSec's supposed latest attack, defacing the home page of digital security company Black & Berg. Its home page had a large title saying "Cybersecurity For The 21st Century, Hacking Challenge: Change this website's homepage picture and win $10K and a position working with Senior Cybersecurity Advisor, Joe Black." Directly after that was: "DONE, THAT WAS EASY. KEEP YOUR MONEY WE DO IT FOR THE LULZ." Under the title was a photo of a U.S. federal building covered by the black-and-white image of LulzSec's ritzy monocled man. The *International Business Times* quickly posted a story headlined "LulzSec Wins Hacking Competition, Refuses $10K Award," then quoted Joe Black himself commenting, "What can I say? We're good, they're better." When the *Times* asked Black how LulzSec had done it, he replied: "I'm going to go with reconnaissance, scanning, gain access, maintain access, and cover tracks."

But when Topiary asked the team about the Black & Berg attack, nobody knew anything about it, and this deface message didn't have any of the nutty creativity that marked their other attacks. Topiary didn't know it at the time, but Black had most likely defaced his own site to get the white hat firm some much-needed clients. (A year later the business had shut down and its founder had aligned himself with Anonymous and Antisec.)

In another part of the world, the hard-core hacker community in Brazil was forming its own version of LulzSec, called LulzSec Brazil. Another hacker group calling itself LulzRaft briefly emerged. Other black hat hackers sent over more leads. Each day the LulzSec crew members were sent dozens of links to web pages that could infect them with viruses, but among them there were a few genuine security exploits, and plenty of data dumps left and right; 1,000 usernames and passwords here, another 500,000 there. Often they were from gaming companies, a paradoxically popular target for hackers, since so many of them were gamers too. They wanted to leak through LulzSec because they were often too scared to do it themselves and didn't want the data or exploit they had found to go to waste. The team had to be choosy about what it leaked—Topiary had learned from his time with AnonOps not to say yes to every request.

Though Topiary was finding it hard to keep a steady hand on things with so much happening at once, LulzSec was about to ramp up the pace of announcing hacks. The team was sitting on a mound of unused data, mostly provided by other hackers, that needed to get out. The Pentagon had given them a reason to finally drop Infragard, but soon they wouldn't be waiting for the right moment. It would just be a fire sale of attack after attack.

Feeling the strain that Wednesday night, June 8, Topiary sent a message to Sabu asking if he was around and wanted to talk. He was hoping for a simple chat about security or maybe life in general. But Sabu didn't respond. Just a few hours earlier, Monsegur had been in court signing agreement papers with the FBI. With Sabu offline for several hours now, Topiary battled a strange sense of foreboding.

"I'm starting to get quite worried some arrests might actually happen," he remarked that evening, U.K. time, in a rare expression of emotion. It wasn't the enemy hackers, Jester, or even the Bitcoin donation that had come out of the blue. Backtrace had just published the document claiming to dox the team members of LulzSec, though again, he was sure that all the names of his colleagues were wrong. "I just have a weird feeling something bad is inbound for us, I don't know why."

He remembered how he had mentioned similar concerns a few days earlier to Sabu after the M_nerva leak, and how Sabu had suddenly seemed more worried too. (This had been before Sabu's arrest.) Topiary had always been the calm one in their group, Sabu's brain of reason. Once Topiary started to get nervous, it was perhaps another signal to Sabu that they were in too deep. As the two had continued talking, they both decided that in spite of all the heat they were inviting, they could not just stop now. Momentum was too strong, expectations too high. They would carry on and run on faith in their ability to stay hidden. A small part of each of them had also accepted that arrest would probably happen at some point.

Did Topiary now fully trust Sabu and Kayla? In answering that question Wednesday night, he said that he trusted them "more than anyone else" in the group, and Sabu in particular.

"I treat Sabu as more important to me than mostly anyone online," he said. "If I get arrested, I'm not snitching on them."

But the niggling feeling came in part from knowing that Sabu had been social-engineering people for more than a decade and the weird fact that Sabu trusted him so much despite having known him for only a few months. For instance, Sabu had told Topiary his first name, Hector, a month before, had trusted him with his Google Voice number, had told him the names of a few of his friends, and even mentioned that he lived in New York City. When Topiary had asked a few weeks prior what Sabu knew about him, wondering if he had the same amount of information, Sabu had replied: "A U.K. guy that does good accents, which makes me think you're not really from the U.K." Topiary, who had an unusual Scottish-Norwegian accent developed from playing online games with Scandinavian friends, had never told

Sabu his real first name or confirmed that he lived on the British Isles or named any of his friends. It was almost as if Sabu didn't really care anymore about hiding his own true identity.

Topiary considered himself to be less reckless in that regard than Sabu. Plus, living in such a remote part of the world had made him feel safe. He doubted the police would even bother traveling up to the Shetland Islands.

Topiary went to bed. Getting to sleep was difficult. He tossed and turned, then had a strange nightmare and woke up at 5:00 a.m., shouting. He hadn't done that in years. It was still dark outside, but he got out of bed and went into his living room anyway. He sat in his gaming chair and signed in to #pure-elite. Suddenly, he was bombarded with messages.

"Sabu is gone," one of the crew members said. The LulzSec team finally noticed that he had been missing for more than twenty-four hours.

CHAPTER 22

The Return of Ryan, the End of Reason

Topiary was anxious and confused. He was sure someone was lying. First Kayla had reported rumors on a public IRC network that Sabu had been raided. Then someone else had said his two daughters were sick and in the hospital. Then another person whom Topiary knew as a real-life friend of Sabu's also claimed he had been raided. Then he heard the hospital story from yet another source. There was a fifty-fifty split on what had happened. Topiary wanted to believe the hospital story. Typically, in paranoid hacker circles or Anonymous, if someone disappeared from a public IRC for a while and without reason, people assumed the worst (an FBI raid). But if Sabu had suddenly wanted to go back underground, he would have told a few trusted people to say different things.

Topiary started calling Sabu's Google Voice number every hour but got no answer. It was unusual for him not to be online for more than half a day. Topiary waited and hoped Sabu wasn't in a cell being questioned or, worse, snitching. On IRC, Sabu was still logged on. Once his nickname had been idle for twenty-four hours, the team killed it, just in case Feds were watching.

"I'm quite worried," Topiary said that morning.

Sabu had given him instructions the week before that if he was ever caught, Topiary should access his Twitter feed and tweet as normal while the team should keep announcing hacks. If the Feds did have Sabu, this could be his ticket to avoiding some charges. Topiary's heart sank when he looked at Sabu's Twitter account and was reminded of how much the hacker had motivated him. The short bio read: "To all Anons: you all are part of something amazing and powerful. Do not succumb to fear tactics that are so obvious and archaic. Stay free." Sabu may have been hot-tempered, but he could also be inspiring.

Kayla was just as concerned. "I'm gonna turn the Internet upside down if I find out Sabu's been hit," she told Topiary.

Still, the team was in a catch-22. If Sabu had been caught and forced to divulge information, then there was a large chance the Feds could monitor what they were doing. If they did nothing or fled, that would immediately implicate Sabu.

As evening fell, Topiary rang Sabu's number again. Suddenly, someone picked up the phone. There was no voice. "Uh, who's this?" Topiary asked.

"David Davidson."

It was Sabu. Topiary let out a sigh of relief. Sabu sounded like he had a cold or had been crying. Sabu explained that his grandmother had died and that he had had to help with funeral arrangements. He then asked if the rest of the team was around and if Topiary could inform them that he was back. Topiary at first didn't care that Sabu might have been lying—he was just glad to speak to him again. Not long after, Sabu changed his story and said that it had actually been the anniversary of his grandmother's death. When they had first spoken, Sabu had probably changed his voice deliberately to make his story sound more genuine. By then, the FBI was logging everything that Sabu said online to LulzSec's members, as well as everything he said on the phone to Topiary.

Sabu would end up being offline more than usual for the next few days as he began collaborating with the FBI, even working out of their office on a daily basis. Sabu occasionally kept his group abreast of other developments, but the still oblivious Topiary took more responsibility for the team.

As a precaution, Topiary deleted more files, then he redid all his passwords and encryptions to make them ultra-protected. He kept all passwords in a file on an encrypted SD card, with one character in each swapped around. Only he knew which characters were swapped. Still, he couldn't help constantly looking outside his window and jumping whenever a van drove past. For the first time, he started seriously wondering if a couple of men in police uniforms would splinter his door at dawn the next morning.

A few days earlier when he had been out to buy some food, one of the local druggies had approached Topiary on his way home. "Hey," the man had said, waving as Topiary took out his earbuds.

"There were some police knocking on your door the other day," the man said in a thick Scottish accent. Topiary's heart had started to pound.

"Really. What did they do?"

"They drove by in their car. Then a couple of them came out and knocked on your door, but there was no answer," he said, shrugging. Topiary played it cool. The druggie might have been lying, but the police might also have stopped by while he was at his thinking spot, looking over the sea. And it was just as likely that they were doing a drug sweep of the area. Still, he resolved to wipe every shred of Topiary and Anonymous from his laptop, encrypt whatever he kept, and send it to all to himself in an e-mail via Hushmail. Eventually he would wipe his laptop completely.

If the police came to his door, they'd find a clean house with one rarely used desktop computer and his innocuous-looking

Dell laptop, a couple of extra monitors for watching films, and one phone line going over his living room with clips. None of the empty pizza boxes associated with basement-dwelling hackers. Any documents the police might find about Anonymous on either of his computers could be passed off as research Topiary was doing for a book. They'd find some pirated music and a handful of databases holding a few hundred thousand names and passwords he had acquired from acquaintances or from his own scanning for LulzSec. Topiary called it his personal collection. Sometimes he used it for his own attempts at doxing people, but for the most part it was just nice to have.

He tried not to think that his virtual private network provider, HideMyAss, would ever turn him in to the authorities. His logic was that if customers of HideMyAss ever found out the company had turned in one of its users, they'd leave in droves, and HideMyAss would go out of business. They would surely never give him up.

As Sabu remained offline on the pretext of dealing with family matters, a familiar face came back into the LulzSec fold: Ryan. It made little sense at first, considering Ryan's temperamental behavior in the past and his cyber attacks on the LulzSec communication channels, but that was hacker life for you. Even the most explosive of disputes could be remedied when someone needed something. In this case Ryan needed some friends, and LulzSec could use Ryan's mammoth botnet, which infected computers via a rogue Facebook app. Ryan was well connected in the underground hacker scene and served as an administrator of Pastebin, the text application tool that LulzSec used to publish all its leaks, and Encyclopedia Dramatica. Ryan was like the kid in school that people didn't necessarily like but whom they were compelled to befriend because he had a brand-new Hummer and a house with a pool. Ryan wasn't rich in real life, but online he seemed loaded; he had spent years building up an impressive array of assets, from servers to his botnet. His servers helped host Encyclopedia Dramatica, and after he had reconnected with a member of the LulzSec crew in the previous week, they also hosted LulzSec's new IRC network, lulzco.org.

After Topiary first reconnected with Ryan on IRC, he wanted to hear what the new ally sounded like in voice to better suss him out, so the two became contacts on Skype. When Ryan's voice came through, his English accent was so strong, he sounded almost Australian. Ryan spoke at a rapid-fire pace, openly bragging about his botnet, his hacking, and how he was making money on the underground; he littered his prose with swearwords then described at great length a farmhouse-bread ham sandwich his mother had once made him. Ryan seemed pretty unhinged and insecure, but Topiary's opinion of him softened when he explained why he'd leaked hundreds of names from AnonOps months before. The network operators had been hassling him, and then someone else had gathered all the data and given it to him to leak. It was water under the bridge. Oh, he added, and that dox of his full name, address, and phone number that had been posted online? That was based on fake information he had created four years ago. Ryan assured Topiary that he had made the false documents and spread them everywhere so that his real information would remain hidden.

Topiary figured he could tell when someone was bullshitting, especially when it was in voice. Ryan, he believed, was genuine. In fact, Topiary started to feel sorry for the guy. People on AnonOps had accused Ryan of being a perpetually angry cretin who logged and attacked everything. But he wasn't really angry; he was just passionate. Perhaps he came across as rude, but he worked hard and got into things, Topiary thought. With Sabu gone, Topiary missed having someone passionate and a little crazy to talk to, to counteract his laid back personality.

Ryan promised not to log any of the chats, and said he would give the LulzSec crew complete control over his logging ability. He also said the team could use his botnet any time they wanted. He had used it in the past to prank DDoS sites of the U.S. Air Force and then call them afterward to mock them. He could also make hundreds of dollars a day by subletting the botnet to others who wanted to use it for nefarious purposes like extortion and hacker skirmishes. But LulzSec could use it for free. This was like fresh meat to a ravenous dog: with Ryan's botnet, LulzSec could bring down almost any website it wanted at the drop of a hat.

During one of Sabu's occasional drop-ins on IRC, he mentioned to Topiary that he did not like having Ryan as a supporter. LulzSec was making too many contacts, he added. (It is unclear if this was the case, or why that might have concerned him now that he had started working as an FBI informant.) Topiary argued back that Sabu himself had been inviting his trusted associates into #pure-elite, including log leaker M_nerva. Topiary won the argument, and Ryan stayed. With Sabu mostly away now, Topiary was enjoying the funnier side of what LulzSec could do with its growing stable of Twitter followers. After he released the administrative passwords of fifty-five porn sites and twenty-six thousand porn passwords, he got replies from people on Twitter saying they had used the data dump to hack into other people's e-mails or, in one case, find out a guy was "cheating on his girlfriend."

Topiary realized he could start making things more interactive. He could send a hundred thousand people to a YouTube video and grant the account holder a huge increase in views, or he could send the horde to crash a small website or IRC network. LulzSec's attacks would become a lot more fun. He and Ryan started talking and doing some prank calls on Skype with some of Ryan's friends as an audience. Then Ryan set them up with a joint Skype Unlimited account so they could call anywhere in the world, dropping eighty dollars in credit without blinking an eye.

Topiary had an idea. Instead of making prank calls, what if they got LulzSec's Twitter followers to call *them*? Topiary suggested setting up a Google Voice number so that anyone in the world could call LulzSec (or at least himself). He wanted the number to spell out the group's name, as in 1-800-LULZSEC, but he couldn't find an area code where the number would work. Eager to prove himself, Ryan spent hours going through every possible U.S. number till he found that 614, the area code for Columbus, Ohio, was available with the corresponding digits. They now had a telephone hotline: 1-614-LULZSEC.

It was a free Google number that directed to their new Skype Unlimited-World-Extra number that in turn could bypass to two other potential numbers registered to fake IP addresses. The pair created two voice-mail messages, using voice alteration and over-the-top French accents for the fictional names Pierre Dubois and Francois Deluxe, saying they couldn't come to the phone because "We are busy raping your Internets."

Once Topiary announced the hotline on LulzSec's public chat room, they got several calls a minute; they answered a few and joked with their callers. Without giving any hints, Topiary stated there would be a $1,000 prize for anyone who called in with the magic word—*lemonade*—but nobody guessed correctly, and around forty people thought it was *please*. At the end of the day they'd received 450 calls.

In between fielding calls, Topiary wrote up an announcement of the group's latest drop: a directory listing of every single file on the U.S. Senate's web server, which had come to them thanks to another black hat. This was a serious attack that could earn someone five to twenty years in prison, but Topiary was mostly eager to get back to his LulzSec hotline.

"This is a small, just-for-kicks release of some internal data from Senate.gov," Topiary had written. "Is this an act of war, gentlemen? Problem?"

Along with that release was a dump of the source code and database passwords of the gaming company Bethesda—a topic totally unrelated to the Senate, just one of the leaks they were sitting on. They also had a database of two hundred thousand users stored on the servers of gaming company Brink, but they wouldn't release that because "We actually like this company and would like for them to speed up the production of Skyrim. You're welcome!" At the top of each release was now a short list of contact and donation details for LulzSec, including the telephone hotline and the IRC chat room.

"It is unclear why LulzSec decided to attempt to embarrass yet another video game company other than to show off," said Naked Security journalist Chester Wisniewski. "It is difficult to explain random acts of sabotage and defacement, so I am not going to attempt to get into the heads of those behind these attacks." Yet this was not a matter of motivation, but of circumstance. Back when Kayla had used her botnet to scan the Web for vulnerabilities, hooking it up to an IRC channel and using basic chat commands to run it, she had stumbled on a vulnerability in the network of Bethesda that had given her access to its servers. Since the company was so big, the team chose not to root around for databases right away, using Bethesda's bandwidth to help search for other sites to hack into and using it as a safe location to hide bots. The gaming company had no idea it was effectively being used to hack other sites. When the servers outlived their usefulness, it was time to dump the data stored on them.

Now the hacks were about to get even more arbitrary. Knowing that Ryan's botnet could take out anything, Topiary announced the LulzSec hotline on Twitter and told the public: "Pick a target and we'll obliterate it." The hotline was suddenly inundated with calls, and the three people that initially got through all requested gaming companies: Eve, Minecraft, and League of Legends.

Within minutes, Ryan's botnet had hit all three, as well as a site called FinFisher.com, "because apparently they sell monitoring software to the government or some shit like that." DDoSing sites like this was nothing new, and neither was one or two hours of downtime, but it was the first time anyone had boasted about it to a hundred fifty thousand Twitter followers or referred to it as a DDoS party called Titanic Takeover Tuesday.

"If you're mad about Minecraft, we'd love to laugh at you over the phone," Topiary announced. "Call 614-LULZSEC for your chance to reach Pierre Dubois!"

When Topiary started thinking about the Internet meme phrase "How do magnets work?" made famous by the hip-hop duo Insane Clown Posse, he called up the offices at Magnets.com. He asked the woman who answered that question and got a bemused response, hung up, then redirected the LulzSec hotline to the main switchboard of Magnets.com.

"Everyone call 614-LULZSEC for a fun surprise," he tweeted. About three minutes later he called the number again and heard dozens of phones going off at the same time with answers of "This is Magnets.com...Uh..." He asked to speak to a manager. When a man's voice came on, Topiary explained the reason for the flood of strange calls. To his credit, the manager took it in good humor.

"How did you do it?" he asked.

"We're testing out our new Lulz Phone Cannon," Topiary said. "How are you feeling?"

"I'm a little out of breath." Magnets.com had been getting more than two hundred calls a minute to their customer support center.

"Okay, I'll get it to stop," Topiary said.

"Good, because I feel like I'm about to pass out."

With a few clicks he stopped the hotline from redirecting, and he heard all the phones in the background suddenly go silent. It was like a DDoS attack by telephone. It made sense to keep this going. Soon he was redirecting the LulzSec hotline to the World of Warcraft online game, then to the main switchboard for FBI Detroit, and then, naturally, to the offices of HBGary Inc.

"You take care of the horde while we're gone, AaronBarr," Topiary tweeted to its former executive. "Thanks mate. Bye for now." In the next twenty-four hours, in between his talking with the other LulzSec hackers and manning a Twitter feed, Topiary's busy switchboard had received 3,500 missed calls and 1,500 voice mails; the following day, 5,000 missed calls and 2,500 voice mails.

Soon, though, Ryan started to get restless. He wanted to do more than just play around with hotline callers; he wanted to go back to hitting websites, bigger ones. He had a rapt audience now, and a gang of people who were willing to go after the big names under this banner of LulzSec, or Antisec, or Anonymous. Whatever. On his own initiative, he hooked up his botnet, then called up most of his bots and aimed at the main website of America's Central Intelligence Agency. Then he fired.

Within a few minutes, CIA.gov had gone down.

"CIA ovened," Ryan said on Skype before beginning a monologue about how he disliked the United States. Topiary was stunned. He visited the CIA's main site and saw it really was down. He couldn't help feeling a little uncomfortable. This was big. But he couldn't leave it unannounced. Through Twitter he said, almost quietly:

"Tango down—cia.gov—for the lulz."

News outlets on television, print, and the Web instantly took notice and published screaming headlines that LulzSec had just hit the CIA. A few said, incorrectly, that the CIA had been "hacked." LulzSec was clearly provoking the authorities now, almost inviting them to come and arrest the group.

At around the same time Aaron Barr came onto Twitter to send a new, public message to HBGary Inc.'s chief, Greg Hoglund. "Damn good to see you," Barr said. "Let's grab some popcorn. I feel a show coming." Topiary saw the remark, and it seemed out of the blue.

"Hello Aaron," Hoglund replied in his first-ever tweet, which he also directed to LulzSec. "I created my Twitter account because I wanted a ringside seat for what is about to go down." Topiary's gut feeling was to be skeptical of the veiled threat—he was getting them almost every day now—and he responded with sarcasm.

"What does kibafo33 mean?" he asked Barr on Twitter. "Is it a Turkish/Portuguese combination of 'that' and 'breath?' Are you a 33rd degree Freemason also?"

Besides, Topiary had other, bigger distractions. About three hundred miles away in London, WikiLeaks founder Julian Assange had heard about LulzSec's takedown of the CIA website, and he was chuckling to himself.

For Assange, a simple DDoS attack on CIA.gov was some much-needed comic relief. Since Anonymous had leaped to his defense in December, he had spent the last few months fighting the threat of extradition to the United States and accusations of treason over WikiLeaks's release of diplomatic cables. Swedish authorities had doubled his problems by charging him with attempted rape, which meant he was now fighting extradition to Sweden too. In the meantime, he was staying in the countryside manor of an English journalist, wearing an electronic tag, and trying to keep up with developments in the world of cyber security. It had been hard not to notice LulzSec. On the one hand, the group looked like fearless comedians. On the other, it clearly had skilled hackers on the team.

Impressed and perhaps unable to help himself, Assange had

opened the main WikiLeaks Twitter account and posted to its nearly one million followers: "WikiLeaks supporters, LulzSec, take down CIA…who has a task force into WikiLeaks," adding: "CIA finally learns the real meaning of WTF." Soon after a few news agencies and websites reported that WikiLeaks was supporting LulzSec, he deleted the first tweet. He didn't want to be publicly associated with what were clearly black hat hackers. Instead, he decided it was time to quietly reach out to the audacious new group that was grabbing the spotlight. On June 16, the day after Ryan set his botnet on CIA.gov, an associate of WikiLeaks contacted Topiary.

"I've got a contact in WikiLeaks that wants to talk to you," the person said, then directed him to a new IRC server that could serve as neutral ground for a private discussion. The network was irc.shakebaby.net and the channel was #wikilulz. Topiary was immediately skeptical and believed the contact was trolling him. When he finally spoke to a WikiLeaks staff member known as q, who was in the channel under the nickname Dancing_Balls, he asked for someone to post something from the WikiLeaks Twitter account. Assange, who allegedly had sole access, did so, putting out something about eBay, then deleting the post. Topiary did the same from the LulzSec Twitter feed. But he needed more proof, since the WikiLeaks feed could have been hacked. q said he could do that. Within five minutes, he pasted a link to YouTube into the IRC chat, and he said to look at it quickly.

Topiary opened it and saw video footage of a laptop screen and the same IRC chat they were having, with the text moving up in real time. The camera then panned up to show a snowy-haired Julian Assange sitting directly opposite and staring into a white laptop, chin resting thoughtfully in his hand. He wore a crisp white shirt and sunlight streamed through a window bordered with fancy curtains. q deleted the twenty-two-second video moments later. Also in the IRC channel with Topiary and q was

Sabu, now likely with very interested FBI agents monitoring the discussion.

"Tell Assange I said 'hello,'" Sabu told q.

"He says 'hi' back," q said.

At first Topiary was nervous. Here was Julian Assange himself, the founder of WikiLeaks, reaching out to his team. He couldn't think why he wanted to talk to them. Then he noticed what q and Assange were saying. They were praising LulzSec for its work, adding that they had laughed at the DDoS attack on the CIA. With all the flattery, it almost felt like *they* were nervous. For a split second, LulzSec seemed to be much bigger than Topiary had ever thought.

By now a few others from the core team knew about what was happening and had come into the chat room. Sabu had given them a quick rundown of what was going on, then said it could mean hitting bigger targets.

"My crew seems up for taking out traditional government sites," he told Assange and q in the chat. "But seeing as that video was removed, some of them are skeptical."

"Yes I removed the video since it was only for you, but I can record a new one if you want :)," q said.

"If we need additional trust (mainly my crew) then ok," said Sabu. "But right now we seem good."

Then q went on to explain why he and Assange had contacted LulzSec: they wanted help infiltrating several Icelandic corporate and government sites. They had many reasons for wanting retribution. A young WikiLeaks member had recently gone to Iceland and been arrested. WikiLeaks had also been bidding for access to a data center in an underground bunker but had lost out to another corporate bidder after the government denied them the space. Another journalist who supported WikiLeaks was being held by authorities. Assange and q appeared to want LulzSec to try to grab the e-mail service of government sites, then look for evidence of corruption or at least evidence that the government was unfairly targeting WikiLeaks. The picture they were trying to paint was of the Icelandic government trying to suppress WikiLeaks's freedom to spread information. If they could leak such evidence, they explained, it could help instigate an uprising of sorts in Iceland and beyond.

The following day, q and Assange wanted to talk to LulzSec again. Perhaps sensing that Topiary was still skeptical, q insisted on uploading another video. It again showed his laptop screen and the IRC chat they were having being updated in real time, then a close-up of Assange himself, head in hand again, but this time blinking and moving the track pad on his laptop, then him talking to a woman next to him. The camera was then walked around Assange before the video ended. The video had been filmed and uploaded in less than five minutes. Topiary, who was experienced with Photoshop and image manipulation, calculated that doctoring the IRC chat and Assange in the same video image within such a short space of time would have been incredibly difficult, and he veered toward believing this was all real.

But q was not asking LulzSec to be hit men out of the goodness of their hearts. There was potential for mutual gain. q was offering to give the group a spreadsheet of classified government data, a file called RSA 128, which was carefully encrypted and needed cracking. q didn't send it over, but he described the contents.

"That's pretty heavy stuff to crack," Sabu told q. "Have you guys tried simple bruteforce?" q explained they had had computers at MIT working on the file for two weeks with no success. Topiary wanted to ask if Assange was going to give the team other things to leak, but he decided not to. Part of him didn't want to know the answer to that. It was already starting to look like LulzSec was on the road to becoming a black hat version of WikiLeaks. If WikiLeaks was sitting on a pile of classified data that was simply too risky to leak, then it now had a darker, edgier cousin to leak it through.

Topiary decided to mention that LulzSec had been the same team behind the HBGary attack. Assange said he had been impressed with the HBGary fallout but added, "You could have done it better. You could have gone through all the e-mails first."

"We could have," Topiary conceded, "but we're not a leaks group. We just wanted to put it out as fast as possible."

"Yes but you could have released it in a more structured way," Assange said.

"We didn't want to go through 75,000 e-mails looking for corruption," Topiary countered again. He remembered how he had trawled through those e-mails looking not for scandal but for Penny Leavy's love letter to Greg Hoglund and for Barr's World of Warcraft character.

The team decided to invite Assange and q over to their IRC network on Sabu's server. Topiary created a channel for them all to talk in and called it #IceLulz. q said he wished WikiLeaks could help the group more with things like servers or even advice, but they didn't want to link the organization too obviously to LulzSec. In fact, when Topiary told q to go ahead and send the RSA 128 file over any time, q seemed to back off.

"Yeah, maybe in the future we'll see how this goes," q said. He never did send the file, at least not to Topiary.

Still, Sabu was "the most excited he had ever been," Topiary later remembered, over the moon that WikiLeaks was asking for his help. It is unclear if Sabu was in reality haunted by the fact that he was now also helping to implicate Assange. Six months prior, he had believed so passionately in the WikiLeaks cause that he was willing to risk bringing his hacker name out into the public for the first time in nine years. Another possibility: the FBI was encouraging Sabu to reach out to Assange to help gather evidence on one of the most notorious offenders of classified government data in recent times. It seems probable that if Sabu had helped, for instance, extradite Assange to the United States, it would have improved his settlement dramatically.

"It's our greatest moment," Sabu told the crew. He and q started talking in more depth about various websites, and then Sabu sent links to two government websites and a company to the rest of the team, tasking them with finding a way to get into their networks and grab e-mails. Over the next few days, Topiary passed the job of staying in contact with WikiLeaks to Sabu, and for the next few weeks, Assange visited LulzSec's chat network four or five more times.

Topiary left the #IceLulz IRC channel open on his laptop and kept it open. Pretty soon, though, it became just another one of the thirty other channels demanding his attention, another page of flashing red text.

CHAPTER 23

Out with a Bang

LulzSec was now so big that it made Anonymous and its fountainhead 4chan look like harmless pranksters. Over on 4chan, hardly anyone wanted to talk about the group. "Literally no one cares about LulzSec enough to post about them," William noted at the time. "These guys are getting fame for the things that we're used to getting fame for." At one point, Topiary had made a /b/ thread asking what the locals thought of LulzSec. He got a fifty-fifty response, and the thread capped at 350 posts after a few minutes before disappearing. When he confirmed the legitimacy of the first post as OP from the LulzSec Twitter feed, the board was in uproar.

But the newfags, the folks who were always eager to be part of a raid organized on 4chan and who were now angry that LulzSec was stealing their site's thunder, wanted to lash out at the new champions of Internet disruption. When Topiary and Ryan saw a thread on /b/ plotting to "hunt" the LulzSec hackers, the board, which hated outsiders knowing that it existed, was the next to look like fresh meat.

"Everyone go to /b/ and post stuff about Boxxy, LulzSec sending you there, and triforces," Topiary commanded the Twitter followers. He promised to publish several thousand assorted e-mail addresses and passwords in return, not mentioning it would come out of his personal collection. Going after 4chan didn't mean LulzSec was hitting Anonymous, as a few blogs suggested. "That's like saying we're going to war with America because we stomped on a cheeseburger," Topiary said.

The image board was soon overrun by LulzSec fans. "As always, LulzSec delivers," the account tweeted: "62,000 e-mails/passwords just for you. Enjoy." Within about ten minutes Topiary's database had been downloaded 3,200 times, and people were using it to hack random web accounts from Facebook to World of Warcraft. One person found an e-mail and password combination that had been reused on an Xbox account, PayPal, Facebook, Twitter, YouTube, and "The whole lot!" he cried on Twitter. "JACKPOT."

"Y'all were the inspiration I needed to mess with my room-mate's Facebook beyond all repair," said another.

"Good to see some refreshing carnage," Topiary told the horde, whom he now referred to as lulz lizards; he called their intended victims peons. "Releasing 62,000 possible account combinations is the loot for creative minds to scour. Think of it like digging a very unique mineshaft." Pretty soon more than forty thousand people had downloaded the database and were using it to hack all manner of social media accounts.

LulzSec's 220,000 Twitter followers had become a community for Topiary as much as an audience. For the next few days he was constantly joking with them on Twitter, telling the FBIPressOffice Twitter account that "we pissed in your Cheerios," then funneling more requests to hit other smaller websites and sending the Twitter followers to a funny video and watching the site crash.

Anyone who had met Topiary would see hardly any similarity

between his real-life persona and the cocksure voice he used as LulzSec's front man. It was all an act, and to him it felt like acting. A few times he would try to sound like Sabu or Kayla so that it would look like more than one person was manning the feed, but for the most part he was speaking for the monocled man with the top hat. And dozens of people constantly asked how they could join in.

"We've got all this attention now," Topiary said quietly to his core team, "and people asking to join us. How about I write something about the new Antisec movement attacking governments and banks? Is everyone up for that?"

The others in the team, including Sabu, said yes. With a respected name like WikiLeaks now silently behind them it made sense to, for once, put a serious face on what they were doing. Straightaway Topiary wrote up a new official statement saying that Antisec would "begin today," calling on more people to join the cyber insurgency LulzSec was spontaneously reviving. On the evening of Sunday, June 19, he published a statement inviting white hats, black hats, and gray hats, and just about anyone else, to join the rebellion. Later he said that writing it was, as usual, like writing a piece of fiction:

"Salutations Lulz Lizards," it started. "As we're aware, the government and whitehat security terrorists across the world continue to dominate and control our Internet ocean...We are now teaming up with Anonymous and all affiliated battleships....We fully endorse the flaunting of the word 'Antisec' on any government website defacement or physical graffiti art....Top priority is to steal and leak any classified government information, including email spools and documentation. Prime targets are banks and other high-ranking establishments."

Not really that interested in hitting banks and governments but more interested in how people would respond to the call to arms, he posted the official statement and headed to bed. His mind was still racing after another chaotic day keeping up with the media, his constantly changing passwords, the fast-paced operations, the new supporters, the tweets, the reactions, the uproar, the chaos of seeing more than a thousand news and blog posts written over a Pastebin post he'd typed out on Notepad. He had never expected this much to happen when he and Sabu had first discussed getting the team back together. It did not feel like things were spiraling out of control, at least not yet. If anything, Topiary was starting to feel that old, familiar itch in the back of his mind. A sense that this latest experience in disrupting the Internet through LulzSec had run its course and was becoming tedious. It was an echo of the restlessness he'd felt with AnonOps only a few months ago.

In the meantime, Ryan had become increasingly annoying to Topiary with his lonely and desperate bids for attention. A couple of days earlier, after twelve hours away from his computer because he'd been asleep, Topiary found more than a dozen messages from Ryan on his laptop asking why he was being ignored.

Of course, there was no way Topiary could stop. He was the main mouthpiece of LulzSec and a prime motivator for the team and its supporters, and leaving would be an enormous practical and emotional effort.

It was hard to sleep. Topiary now habitually glanced out of his window whenever he heard a car drive past. He said privately that he was expecting a raid any day. Acceptance seemed the best way to deal with these things. His emotions lurched from the high of an outrageous new leak to the gut-wrenching paranoia that he was about to get doxed or, worse, raided. Ryan thought the same. He claimed he often went to sleep each night expecting to be raided the next day.

"I've given up caring," Topiary said. Was he imagining what jail might be like? "I don't like to think about that," he answered. He also couldn't help thinking about the second, stiffly worded tweet that Greg Hoglund had added just few days before, the one he had blithely dismissed at the time.

"Aaron," Hoglund had said. "I wanted to be here to see the fruits of our labour over the last two months. LOL."

Topiary woke up on Monday, June 20, to a surprise. There had been a much bigger response to his Antisec statement than he had anticipated. Tens of thousands of people had read it (eventually almost a quarter of a million accessed the page) and the media was eagerly reporting the line that LulzSec had "teamed up with Anonymous" and declared war on just about everything in a position of authority in the hope of rooting out corruption. It seemed that cyber anarchists everywhere were running amok. That day CBS local TV news for San Diego reported on some mysterious black graffiti that had appeared on the boardwalk along Mission Beach: a crudely drawn man in a top hat and mustache and the words "Antisec" in a speech bubble.

"I was taken aback," Topiary later remembered. "My Notepad-forged declaration of Antisec had the AnonOps servers teeming with users. It was like Operation Payback's prime on steroids. For a while I felt horribly guilty for some reason. The words were almost fiction to me, just another piece of writing, but it got through to so many people, who were now putting their necks on the line for the cause. Someone had even gone out and tagged beach walls with Antisec, getting on the news."

Ryan was also galvanized by the new mass enthusiasm for Antisec. Naturally, he became more eager than ever to put his botnet to good use. Later that day he started trying to lash out at other major targets: Britain's Ministry of Finance, then the NSA, then the FBI. Finally, he successfully hit the site for the U.K.'s Serious Organised Crime Agency (SOCA). Anything ending in .mil or .gov, he wanted to get. Topiary watched, transfixed, and after a while decided it would be good to calm Ryan down. He didn't want things getting out of hand. Even so, he didn't want to let LulzSec's credit for the SOCA hit go to waste, so he announced it on Twitter, again without the usual loud flair. "Tango down — soca.gov.uk — in the name of Antisec."

Compared to the CIA, this felt like a minor attack, and it hadn't even completely worked, since the SOCA site was down only for certain visitors. But moments later, someone at SOCA sent an e-mail to London's Metropolitan Police saying the website had been brought down. Ryan had been launching DDoS attacks from his computer for many months, but now, finally, the police were spurred into action.

Later that same Monday, at around 10:30 p.m., while Ryan was still DDoSing the website of the Serious Organised Crime Agency, ten police cars quietly pulled up outside his house. The address they'd been given belonged to Ryan Cleary, a nineteen-year-old computer nerd who lived with his parents in a nondescript, semidetached house in Essex, England. It turned out the dox that Ryan had claimed was fake was real. He really did live at that address, and he really had been using his actual first name this whole time. When the police entered his rectangular bedroom, they found windows covered in foil to block out any sunlight, a single bed, a messy desk covered in potato chips, and allegedly about £7,000 (about $11,340, based on the exchange rate that day) in cash in his desk drawer. Ryan was pale, had a boyish wisp of a mustache, and was a little on the chubby side. The last time he had been outside the house was Christmas — six months earlier.

The police questioned Ryan for five hours, then said they were arresting him. At around 2:00 a.m. he signed off from MSN with the quit message "leaving." It wasn't the "brb Feds at the door" inside joke, but neither was it the leaving message he normally used. The police drove him in the early hours of Tuesday morning back to Charing Cross police station in Central London for further questioning. At that moment, agents from the FBI were on a plane headed for London, and Topiary was fast asleep in his bed, completely oblivious to what was happening.

That morning, London's Metropolitan Police announced that an eighteen-year-old had been arrested and charged with launching DDoS attacks on several organizations. Within hours, Britain's tabloid newspapers had picked up the news, followed by major media outlets in the United States. Though the police hadn't mentioned LulzSec in their release, several newspapers reported, strangely, that the "mastermind" of LulzSec had been arrested.

When Topiary signed in to the LulzSec private chat rooms the next morning, there was the same kind of frightened chatter that had accompanied Sabu's disappearance. Topiary slowly realized what was going on. Still, Tflow and Sabu said they were relieved. They had heard about the arrest on the news and each said they thought it was Topiary.

"Ryan is now fucked beyond all belief," Topiary said. He felt numb. Eventually Ryan's name was released and a newspaper got hold of his family. They interviewed his mother, who talked about how she had to leave plates of food outside his door because he would never leave his bedroom and how he had once almost killed himself when she tried to take his computer away. It printed a photo of Ryan as a doe-eyed schoolboy, along with a picture of his room. The photo had captions and arrows pointing out everything from the foil covering his windows to the spoof-motivational poster on his wall of two semi-naked women and the title "Teamwork." Topiary recognized it all from their video chats. The newspapers didn't seem to know the half of Ryan's eccentricities. The windowsill was where Ryan had grown weed a year before. His desk was now clear of litter and potato chips and had probably been cleaned by his mother. Just a week earlier Ryan had grabbed a hypodermic needle and started stabbing his toe in front of the webcam. On top of all that, the idea of arrest now felt much closer to home.

Sabu and Topiary spoke on the phone. They agreed to change their e-mail addresses and their public nicknames and everything Ryan knew about because Ryan would snitch. They talked about finding new servers to host their IRC networks and the LulzSecurity website. And for the public face, Topiary played it cool. "Seems the glorious leader of LulzSec got arrested," he said on Twitter. "It's all over now…wait…we're all still here! Which poor bastard did they take down?"

There was one other errand to take care of: M_nerva. They had always known that the hacker who had leaked the #pure-elite chat logs had worked with Ryan on some of his money-making schemes. With Ryan out of the picture, there was no need to hold back from M_nerva anymore. It was safe to finally take revenge. Topiary published an official statement on Marshall "M_nerva" Webb, addressing it to the FBI as a helpful offer of new information. "Snitches get stiches," he had written, unaware that his closest confidant, Sabu, was a far more dangerous snitch. The public was keen to see who had been the snitch, and the page got more than a thousand views in twenty seconds. It took a few weeks for the FBI to follow up on the M_nerva information, but in late June, federal authorities would raid Webb's home in Ohio.

In the meantime, there were now more than three hundred thousand people following LulzSec on Twitter, more than 135 eager people in LulzSec Brazil, hacker groups in Spain and Iran wanting to join forces, constant offers of database dumps, control of a few dozen government sites, and more than a gigabyte of data to release. It included twelve thousand passwords from a NATO website, hundreds of random internal police documents, government documents, a video of the police accidentally dropping a dead body from a plane, photos of human flesh scattered across pavements; "/b/ would love this stuff," Topiary thought.

He tried not to think about the fact that doing more would pile on a greater jail sentence. He convinced himself that LulzSec had become like WikiLeaks—it was just leaking information that other people had handed over.

The FBI, in the meantime, was racing to keep up with their new informant, who was plugged into this fast-moving world. As hackers offered vulnerabilities to Sabu in secret IRC meetings, he passed them on to his new overseers so that those security holes could be fixed. Sabu was deftly pulling the strings of LulzSec, putting on the face of genuine complicity while secretly helping the authorities prevent many of those potential attacks from happening. With things moving so quickly, Topiary, Kayla, Tflow, and the others had no time to track how many of them led to dead ends, thanks to Sabu. They were always on the lookout for the next big hit.

"We are challenging ourselves to progress to bigger things," Topiary said at the time. "Funny, bigger targets." There was no turning back now.

Among the stream of offers Topiary and Sabu got for exploits and data, one stood out. It had been evening in Topiary's part of the world when a hacker who had been talking to Sabu and had then been unable to get through contacted Topiary to say he had access to hundreds of secret files and user info after hacking into the Arizona police department network. He was an activist, passionately against the racial profiling that took place in the state, and he wanted to release the data as retribution. Topiary recognized the name, since Sabu had mentioned it before. After the hacker had uploaded the data to a secret server, Tflow, Pwnsauce, and Topiary all grabbed it to see what was inside. It was a folder containing more than seven hundred documents. There were embarrassing e-mails complaining about a scared officer who had run and hidden in a ditch during a recent shootout, innocuous details about a new safe-driving campaign, and home addresses and contact details for Arizona police officers. Given enough digging, the hacker hoped his cache of documents could shed light on corrupt practices in the department. The hacker made a convincing argument about systemic prejudice in the border police, and Topiary, employing his usual carefree outlook on things, figured that the hacker should write his own press release—the first time anyone but Topiary would write one for LulzSec. Tflow created a torrent file.

There hadn't been much time to check over the press release, and there was no editing. Once everything was ready, Topiary published it. The press release was titled "Chinga La Migra" and next to it were the words "Off the pigs"; beside that was the image of an AK-47 machine gun fashioned from keyboard symbols. Topiary did a double take. When he reread the press release, now public for everyone to see, he didn't see LulzSec's usual lighthearted dig at a large, faceless institution but an aggressive polemic against real police officers that revealed their home addresses. When he Googled *Chinga La Migra,* he learned it was a Spanish phrase for "fuck the police." He immediately regretted posting the other hacker's statement. It was almost encouraging people to attack cops. It turned out Tflow had also Googled *Chinga La Migra* and felt exactly the same way.

He sent Topiary a message. It was too much. The statement had made him feel "radicalized."

"We don't want to get police officers killed," Topiary replied, agreeing. "That's not my kind of style." It wasn't Tflow's either.

Topiary had just set up an interview via instant message text with the BBC television news program *Newsnight* that evening, June 24. It was one of his few media interviews while LulzSec was still active. Putting on his acting hat, he made grand statements about anti-security and the corruption his group was fighting. "People fear the 'higher-ups,'" he told BBC producer Adam

Livingstone, "and we're here to bring them down a few notches."
But the words stuck in his throat.

When he really thought about what LulzSec had turned into,
he realized it had moved far from being a group that simultaneously entertained and fixed the world. It did neither of those
things. It was chaos. Every day now the core group was spending
more time dealing with internal issues, conspiring against trolls
like Jester and Backtrace, rooting out snitches, or worrying about
what Ryan might say to the police. It had been more than a week
since the team had really gotten together and worked at something as an original leak. Just hours before Topiary's interview
with BBC Television, the *Guardian* newspaper had gotten hold
of the #pure-elite logs leaked weeks before by M_nerva and published a story saying that LulzSec was "a disorganized group
obsessed with media coverage and suspicious of other hackers."
The glow surrounding LulzSec seemed to be fading.

"This is annoying now," Topiary exclaimed in an interview.
"Two months ago we were a small team working on operations
with no outside hassle. Now there's other people coming and going, 'enemy' groups, press saying stupid things, people trying to
toss around politics, people starting drama all the time. Kind of
out of control." Even the Wikipedia page on LulzSec was clut-
tered with rumors.

The distractions from enemy hackers, trolls, the press, and
misunderstandings across the blogosphere had become overwhelming. Recently someone had copied and pasted the LulzSec
logo on a Pastebin post and claimed (posing as LulzSec) that they
had hacked the entire U.K. census database of more than seventy million people. The national press breathlessly reported it
as another legitimate LulzSec threat. LulzSec was becoming like
Anonymous: anyone could lay claim to the name and be taken seriously.

"People are pretending to be us everywhere," Topiary said. Ignoring the trolls wasn't enough because when Topiary signed in to the private LulzSec chat rooms with his crew, he could see that people in the room had spent the past hour talking about snitches and enemies. It was often impossible to look away, and when Topiary stayed quiet in those conversations, Sabu would ask him why he wasn't saying anything, and the conversation would become awkward.

Topiary finally made up his mind. On the evening of Friday, June 24, four days after Ryan's arrest, he decided to tell the others in LulzSec that he wanted out. It would be hard because, as the mouthpiece of LulzSec, Topiary leaving meant the team itself would probably have to call it a day. As he entered the LulzSec private chat channel, Tflow beat him to the punch. "Guys. Topiary, AVunit, you here?" Tflow asked.

"Yeah," Topiary replied.

"Well, I need to leave LulzSec / Anon / etc. for some time. I need to hand over any site-related stuff to you guys, including domains."

Topiary felt a sudden rush of relief. The very idea of leaving LulzSec seemed to make all the other distractions and anxieties melt away. It was possible there was an end to this. He wanted Tflow to lay out why he was leaving so the group could have a discussion about it. Maybe others would say they wanted to stop too.

"Any reason for your departure?" he asked.

"I'll be honest," Tflow replied. "The 'off the pigs' remark in the last release, which I did not know the meaning of before, is making me feel radicalized and depressed, so I need a break. Feds probably are going to leave no stone unturned now, so I'm going to wipe my hard drive and start fresh."

Another glimmer of optimism. It would be hard to let go of the name and the action, but there was something appealing about starting over. He threw in his agreement.

"I was thinking kind of the same," Topiary said. "Like you said, heat is insane...I mean, a friend that has nothing to do with us saw Ryan on the front page of a shitty local newspaper. I know I don't want to be on the front page of a shitty local newspaper. And neither do you guys." Besides, he added, "All our leaks come from other people."

"So do you think we should all just quietly split up for a while or what?" asked Tflow.

"I think it would be classy to sail off into the distance and never be caught," Topiary mused. "In 10 years we will be the greatest hacking group in the entire world. Ever." It was tongue in cheek, but the thought of leaving on a high note, like rock stars disbanding while they were still on the charts, suddenly made ending LulzSec seem like a good idea. Obvious, even.

Topiary and Tflow started discussing their final, explosive release of some of the pile of data they had been sitting on for weeks. An American hacker had given Tflow a cache of stolen business documents from AT&T's servers. There were login details for a NATO bookshop, as well as other .gov and .mil logins. Tflow had thought the AT&T documents were valuable enough to save for a separate release, but Chinga La Migra had opened his eyes to how futile things really were.

"I don't give a shit anymore," he said. "Release everything." Then Tflow checked his calendar and saw this all made even more sense. "On Monday it will be exactly 50 days that have passed," he added. They could call the final release Fifty Days of Lulz. It might almost look like this had been planned from the start.

Sabu appeared online. "Yo yo," he said.

Topiary felt a twinge of anticipation but continued discussing practicalities with Tflow as Sabu read over their conversation. "Wow," Sabu finally said. "I understand your point of views, but there's no turning back. We've passed the point of no return."

Topiary was getting tired of Sabu's point-of-no-return line and wanted to remind him that he and LulzSec weren't as powerful as Sabu thought.

"Sabu, when was the last time we, as LulzSec, leaked anything that was ours?" Topiary asked. He listed leaks for Fox, Sony, NATO, Senate.gov—all targets of cyber attacks handed over on a plate by other hackers. Only Infragard and PBS had truly been carried out by LulzSec hackers. In the end, LulzSec had become just like Anonymous, a brand that other cyber punks could exploit for their own purposes, whether it was to make themselves look more important or to cower under. While that had brought them fame and respect, it was vastly increasing their culpability to the police.

"You guys can go," Sabu finally said. "I'm fucked sooner or later, so I got no choice but to continue." Despite the heat, it had never truly felt like Topiary and Tflow were trapped in LulzSec. Then, when Sabu changed tack and began telling them to stay, adding that they were abandoning him, it suddenly was like trying to crawl out of a spinning barrel. Soon AVunit and Pwnsauce had entered the chat room and added their agreement that it was time for a break. Even Kayla showed up and said that while she didn't mind—"I just let it flow" were her words—she saw the reasoning in wanting to stop.

Topiary sighed to himself. "You know I'm all for this nihilistic 'we have to go on' theory," he said, "but I like my life, bros. I don't want to be arrested." Encouraged by Tflow, he started talking about how the Antisec movement would carry on without them anyway; they'd sail off in the distance, leaving behind a trail of mayhem and the revival of a movement against white hats, governments, and corporations. But no matter how hard he tried, he couldn't pacify Sabu, who seemed to be laying on the guilt as thick as IRC allowed: "That's alright, you guys leave. I'll be the only faggot left," he said.

It looked as though Sabu had gone through several stages of intention with LulzSec, initially excited at the prospect of creating the group, then even more enthusiastic as he took on support from other older hackers and Julian Assange himself. Topiary started to think Sabu was almost acting suicidal. More likely: Hector Monsegur had nothing more to lose, and the FBI needed more evidence on the LulzSec hackers.

"Sabu, we're leaving behind the LulzSec public face with a classy ending," he tried. "The movement you strive for is continuing." It was no use. After a few minutes, Sabu started talking to each of the hackers individually. He was enraged.

Soon enough Topiary saw flashing text on his screen that indicated Sabu wanted to have a private conversation. Reluctantly he opened it, and Sabu started venting. Topiary kept saying that ending LulzSec had turned out to be a majority decision. It wasn't just him—the whole team wanted a break. But Sabu saw a team that had been turned against him by Topiary's manipulation. When the heat increased, Topiary told Sabu to get off the computer and get a drink of water so he could calm down.

"Don't fucking talk down to me like you're elite," Sabu shot back. "I treat you with nothing but respect, but I destroy kids like you instantly. Don't forget this point. So treat me with respect."

"Sabu what are you thinking?" Topiary said. "You've got kids and need to stop this. At least change your nick from Sabu."

"It's too late anyway," Sabu said, simmering.

"What do you mean? You can't say it's too late. You don't want your kids to grow up with their dad in jail. Change your nick, wipe all your stuff and come back under a different name. If I had kids I wouldn't be doing this." Sabu replied again that it was too late. The team was abandoning him.

"We're not abandoning you," Topiary countered. "We're just stopping LulzSec. We're still here as friends." Instead of mollifying Sabu, this made him more angry. Topiary gave up trying to reason with him. It was impossible to explain why things happened in LulzSec or in Anonymous other than to say that so much had been done on a whim: creating the group itself, picking the targets, suddenly reviving the Antisec movement. LulzSec had never planned its activities more than twelve hours in advance. The media and the authorities were giving LulzSec too much credit and not seeing it for what it really was: a group of people with all the right talents that had come together at the right time and had then lost control of what they had created. Now even Topiary was starting to get bored with it all.

Sabu began hinting that he saw less whim, and more conspiracy. He opened up private discussions with AVunit and Tflow, who later passed on details of these conversations to Topiary. Sabu talked with each of them about how Topiary had been using him and Kayla to hack into websites like PBS. He argued that when his grandmother had died and he had to go on a break, Topiary had effectively tried to wrest LulzSec from his control, then take off with the Bitcoin donations. Sabu's brain of reason was now his fall guy. It was almost as if he were trying to get the other team members to implicate Topiary as much as possible before they split for good.

When Topiary got wind from the others about Sabu's private discussions, he suddenly realized the other reason why he wanted out: Sabu's uncanny ability to get inside his head. If Sabu was a good hacker, he was an even better social engineer. Despite his fierce temper, he could coax love, admiration, and guilt out of just about anyone. Often it had been based on something intangible—the promise of a bigger hack on the horizon or the devotion that the LulzSec members had for one another as a team. The harsh reality was that the members now all had to fend for themselves.

Topiary tried to ignore Sabu's protestations and began writing his final press release, titled "50 Days of Lulz."

"Let it be known in an entirely sexual way that we love each and every one of you," Topiary told the more than 325,000 followers on Twitter, "even the trolls." Ten minutes later he published the release:

"For the past 50 days we've been disrupting and exposing corporations, governments, often the general population itself, and quite possibly everything in between, just because we could," it said. "All to selflessly entertain others." These were Topiary's words, not Sabu's. It wasn't the rousing address he and Tflow had discussed but a metaphor of what LulzSec had been over the past month: rambling, cocksure, and reaching for a sense of serious conviction about some issue while never seeming truly committed to it. It called on more people to follow the Twitter account Anonymous IRC. Controlled by several hard-core hacktivists who did not wish to be named, it had more than 125,000 followers and was slowly looking like an official line of communication for Anonymous.

The final leak was a mishmash that included a technical document for AOL engineers, internal documents from AT&T, and user info from gaming and hacker forums. The statement revealed for the first time that LulzSec had been a "crew of six." Topiary had said it loud and clear: LulzSec was over.

CHAPTER 24

The Fate of Lulz

LulzSec's significance had not been completely manufactured. For those who spend most of their time in the world of breathable air, traffic lights, and bimonthly paychecks, it meant the companies that stored their personal details on flimsy databases reconsidered how well those details were protected. LulzSec had pointed to an important fallacy held by companies like Sony—that customer data was safe because their own IT specialists couldn't hack into them. Now any company could suddenly become a random target of someone else's whims; it didn't take an army of hackers to steal more than a million passwords, but a merry crew of six. LulzSec was doing what full disclosure had done in the late 1990s: widely publicizing flaws that companies might have left bare and allowed black hats to steal from if they hadn't been embarrassed into patching them up.

For those who spend more time looking at screens, immersed in the world of browsers, IRC, and new web scripts, LulzSec had revived an interest in disrupting the Web. You didn't need to wait for a raid interesting or funny enough to get a few hundred supporters on /b/ or for an incident like WikiLeaks to spark a cyber insurgency with thousands of participants. You just needed a handful of talented, motivated people with a few good connections in the black hat community. LulzSec had reminded Anonymous that small groups could make a lot of noise. They didn't always need big resources or connections with the press. Topiary had journalists contacting him every day via Twitter, but he had given only a handful of interviews as LulzSec. He had not used any special software, just the anonymous web tools of Twitter and Pastebin, Notepad to write all his missives, and a simple, retro-designed website that used a design template borrowed from HBGary Federal.

Anonymous, as an idea, had been around for thousands of years. At some point, a few cavemen must surely have smeared buffalo blood over the rocks of a rival in the dead of night and then run away giggling, Topiary thought. With the dawn of the Internet and anonymous image boards, the process reached beyond a handful to dozens and then to hundreds of people reacting, thinking, and contributing to a collective thought process within very short spaces of time. Anonymous had become a joint psychological state, a sanctuary where a person's mind could be relieved of the responsibilities that came with identity, or of baggage like guilt and fear. It spawned a new wave of creativity—memes and figurative writing—unhindered by social conventions. When that hive-thought turned to action, it created energy, a mass force that could not be contained. A few could occasionally direct it, but for the most part that nebulous force, as Topiary called it, seemed to have a life of its own.

For those who wanted more control and more glory, there were the splinter groups. A month after LulzSec disbanded, several new hacker groups had popped up to launch their own ops, often in the name of Antisec and web activism. In July a group called the Script Kiddies hacked into the Twitter feed of Fox News to say that President Barack Obama had been assassinated, and then it defaced the Facebook page of drug giant Pfizer and claimed to have stolen data from Walmart. Groups from the Philippines, Colombia, Brazil, and Peru launched attacks in the name of Antisec, mostly publishing data of government or police officials. More groups followed suit. Through no clear objective of their own, Topiary, Sabu, and Kayla had inspired a trend for anarchic hacktivism.

It was often not to the benefit of hackers, though. While Sabu had seemed disappointed with the end of LulzSec, the revival of Antisec meant that hackers and script kiddies were still approaching him with vulnerabilities that he could pass on to the FBI. He was fast proving himself to be a valuable informant. Days after the final release from LulzSec, there were more than six hundred people in the AnonOps chat room Antisec discussing both legal and illegal forms of protest against various targets. They were now looking to Sabu for direction, hanging on his every word, trying to impress him with their ideas for hacks.

"I'm doing the same work, more revolutionary," Sabu said in an interview on July 1, a few days after his bitter send-off with the LulzSec team members, and of course now secretly working for the FBI. "No more 'FOR THE LULZ' as Topiary and Tflow turned it into. I'm doing real work with real motivations." With Topiary out of the picture, Hector Monsegur's alter ego Sabu could comfortably take the virtual reins of what looked like a resurgent global movement. Even if it was on false pretenses, he could continue living the life of a revolutionary. Perhaps in an act of self-justification for turning on his old colleagues, he professed nothing but contempt for Topiary and Tflow. "They had me breaking laws and putting myself out there, and when the heat got too hot for them they copped out," he said. "They're fucking frauds."

Sabu dismissed the idea that he had ever controlled Topiary with intimidation. It's "bullshit," he said. "Never once have I mistreated anyone. I…I feel if they did get caught they'd point all fingers at me. When in reality it's them organizing this bullshit. Don't mind me. I'm just angry about this. I feel used."

If Sabu felt an ounce of guilt, he didn't show it. It seemed that his perception of the world was that it had always been against him. In his version of events, the idea for LulzSec had started as a joke and to get the old crew back together. Then Topiary had motivated him to get involved, then it had turned into an organization, then something far more serious, with a website, servers, and press releases. Then Topiary had turned himself into the leader of LulzSec and closed up shop.

"They wanted me to hack for them," he said. "Then after I did that, they got too scared. It's that simple." Ironically, he claimed that the incident that hurt him the most was when he had gone offline for more than a day, and Topiary had worried that Sabu had been raided. In retrospect, it seemed he hated the idea that his colleague on the other side of the Atlantic might have correctly suspected the truth.

"The truth is for a few days I took a break because I needed one and my family had some issues," he explained, now giving a different version of what really happened that day. "And [Topiary] concocted some story in his mind that I got raided or something more sinister. He hurt me deep with that act. I would love to speak to him, mainly to see him apologize."

Sabu claimed that he resented having to clean up the reputational mess Topiary had left behind in the hacker community, responding to comments that LulzSec members were "shit scared about being nailed by the authorities" and had "run away." After a couple weeks, Sabu finally cooled down, and, perhaps unfortunately for Topiary, he reconciled with the Shetland teenager. The two started speaking to each other regularly on IRC. It was awkward at first, but both accepted that they had been under tremendous pressure and tensions had been running high.

Topiary had meanwhile taken a break from Anonymous and was trying to spend less time online. He was selling more of his stuff, things like his cooker, fridge-freezer, and bed frame, packing his books, playing his Xbox. His mother and brother had moved to a suburb in England, and he was planning to join them, then find his own place in the southeast region of Kent. He'd bought a sixty-five-liter backpack to prepare for his big move, and he would fit everything else into his laptop bag and a small suitcase. He chatted frequently with Kayla, with whom he was still good friends. She claimed to be on vacation in Spain with her dad and a friend, and on Twitter she dispensed extraordinarily detailed stories about hearing noises from the hotel room above her and splashing in the pool. Between these anecdotes, Kayla would teach Topiary more about hiding himself online and "reverse trolling." He had set up an e-mail address, Topiaryhatemail@gmail.com, and posted it on the bio of his personal Twitter account. If anyone sent a malicious link to the account, he and Kayla would grab it and reverse-engineer it, then embarrass whoever was trying to infect him. It was a bit of lighthearted fun.

After a week, he signed back onto AnonOps IRC and was inundated with about fifteen private messages. People asked him questions about LulzSec. They showed him website vulnerabilities, invited him into secret channels.

"Fuck, it's THE Topiary," someone said without any hint of sarcasm. The Anons were desperate to get him to respond to their comments and questions, and several followed him from channel to channel. One person sent him seven hundred FBI logins. Another asked for advice on destroying a few lawyers. He was asked to help with five different operations. Everything seemed to have gotten a bit more loopy since he'd left, even the operators.

"Topiary, you worm. You anarchist. I love you, bro," said the AnonOps operator Evilworks. "I bet my left nut that government is DDoSing us....But I have news for you. AnonOps ain't going down. NEVER EVER."

"My private message windows were flying," Topiary remembered. "People I'd known from the writing channel back in January were reminding me of who they were, even though I remembered them perfectly." One anonymous user even mashed his keyboard in excitement when Topiary started talking back to him, saying he didn't expect "someone like Topiary" to respond. "This made me feel mindfucked to say the least."

If he came up with a new channel, named something like #BananaEchoFortress, within minutes it would have a dozen people in it simply because so many were making /whois requests on his name to see which channels he was in.

"I couldn't help but wonder what I had done to deserve this much praise," he said. "I'm far from the most skilled hacker or comedian, writer, or designer." Topiary came to the conclusion that, throughout the first half of 2011, he was simply in the right places at the right times, supported by the right people.

Topiary eventually came across a new op that he couldn't say no to. He didn't want to get too involved, but a hacker with ties to LulzSec had found a vulnerability in the website for the *Sun,* a tabloid that was the most popular newspaper in the United Kingdom. It was also a staple title in News International, the media powerhouse owned by Rupert Murdoch. Around this time, the issue of hacking was all over the news—not computer hacking, but phone hacking. The British government had just launched an investigation into reports that journalists from the Murdoch paper the *News of the World* had hacked the phone of a murdered British schoolgirl and then hindered the case after deleting some of her voice mails. Phone hacking was an open secret in the British press, used most often on celebrities. In fact, the way to listen to someone else's voice mail was well known across 4chan and other image boards: you simply waited for a dial tone, then held down the # key and hit the common password of "0000." But news that reporters had hacked a murdered schoolgirl's phone got the public baying for blood. With Murdoch himself soon to be questioned by a parliamentary committee, it seemed a fitting time to cut Murdoch down to size.

The hackers who had contacted Topiary on AnonOps wanted him to write a spoof news story reminiscent of his Tupac article on PBS. It was a simple job, and Topiary agreed, thinking it was a good idea. The hackers had managed to take almost absolute control over theSun.co.uk and on July 18 broke into the tabloid's network and redirected every link on the *Sun*'s website to Topiary's story. It was headlined "Media Moguls [*sic*] Body Discovered" and detailed how Murdoch had been discovered dead in his garden. Topiary couldn't leave it without a calling card for himself and one of the hackers, adding that Murdoch had "ingested a large quantity of palladium before stumbling into his famous topiary garden." When News International released an official statement about the attack, the hackers reconfigured the page so it linked to the LulzSec Twitter feed.

Major news outlets picked up the story immediately, sending it to the top of Google News and saying that LulzSec had struck again. Topiary got messages from the BBC and TV news reporters in the United States, Canada, and Australia seeking voice interviews, but he declined every one. Sabu capitalized on the interest by announcing on Twitter that he was also sitting on a huge cache of the *Sun*'s e-mails, then announced, "We're working with certain media outlets who have been granted exclusive access to some of The News of the World e-mails we have." None of this was true, but several mainstream press outlets' ears perked up in envy and they reported on the claim.

LulzSec had successfully made the world's most powerful media man the butt of a joke that millions of people were laughing at. The day after the *Sun* hack, Murdoch appeared before the parliamentary committee, and a rogue comedian took things a step further by shouting "You naughty billionaire!" before throwing a shaving-cream pie at Murdoch's face.

Rebekah Brooks, former editor of the *Sun* and the *News of the World,* was also being investigated for her knowledge of phone hacking. In the midst of the police investigation, a police officer found that her husband had tried to discreetly dump her laptop in a black garbage bag back behind their home. They retrieved it. Topiary read the story and thought that the couple should have melted the laptop. He considered that was something he should do too but figured he could put it off. He was ready to turn over a new leaf, find a new apartment, and even meet his online girlfriend for the first time. She was planning to fly over from Canada in September. But he wouldn't wipe his laptop or say good-bye to Anonymous just yet.

Then on July 20, two days after the *Sun* hack, Topiary was reading the news, and his heart leaped into his throat. According to a Fox news report, British police had arrested a suspected core member of LulzSec in London, a man who went by the nickname Tflow. The official statement said that the male they had arrested was sixteen. Topiary read that again. Tflow, the genius programmer who had written the Tunisian anti-snooping web script, configured their website, compiled all that data, was just sixteen years old. He checked his IRC client and saw the last message he'd received from Tflow had been just four hours before his arrest:

"Nice work with Sun. Do you guys have everything you need for a proper e-mail release? I don't want to leave you guys hanging." And that was it. Tflow had been the most reserved member of LulzSec. Mysterious, mature, and quiet, he was assumed by most people on the team to be in his twenties. He was a level-headed programmer and evaded most questions about himself and his personal life—the complete opposite of Kayla. And yet there was the Metropolitan Police statement in an article titled "Youth Arrested under Computer Misuse Act" that added that computer equipment had been taken in for analysis.

"If that's really him, I'm really worried now," Topiary said at the time. "I'm on the same ISP as him and everything." Topiary was on a twelve-month contract with his Internet service provider, and he couldn't afford to break the clause by paying for the entire year.

Topiary saw a pattern with the arrests. He went to Sabu and suggested that Ryan and Tflow might have been on the police's radar for months but were arrested only after a big U.K. hit, Ryan after the SOCA attack, Tflow after the *Sun* (though he had not taken part in the hack). Since several LulzSec members were located in Britain, "we should stop hitting U.K. targets now," Topiary said.

Sabu was indifferent. "So it's ok for us to stop U.K. targets because you gimps are in the U.K., but not to stop hitting USA targets because I'm in the U.S.A.? Thanks." Topiary gritted his teeth. He felt he had a right to be worried, considering that he was in the U.K. too when the arrests had occurred, but Sabu was suggesting it was selfish to avoid British targets.

"I've missed you, brother," Sabu then added, before asking if Topiary might give him the password to the LulzSec Twitter feed. Topiary declined and left the chat room.

Topiary hated to admit it, but the lulz were slowly coming to an end. The music had stopped; the harsh lighting had flickered back on. By the time LulzSec officially ended in late June, police across eight countries, including the United States, Britain, Spain, and Turkey, had arrested seventy-nine people in connection with activities carried out under the names Anonymous and LulzSec. Most of the arrested were male, and the average age about twenty-four. Being part of the large crowd hadn't helped. Fourteen, including twenty-year-old Mercedes "No" Haefer, had been arrested for taking part in the LOIC attacks on PayPal and were now on trial.

As people increasingly saw Anonymous and Antisec as a movement, the people arrested were painted as martyrs. The absurdity of the pranks had evolved into an exaggerated significance, even delusions of grandeur, but its shaky foundations were revealed when people like Ryan finally had to confront the grim faces of a courtroom. People like Topiary and even William had joined 4chan, Anonymous, Antisec, or LulzSec for the lulz, but stayed when it looked like they were part of something even greater that they could not put into words.

On July 27, seven days after Tflow's arrest, two officers from the Metropolitan Police got out of a four-seater private plane they had hired for about £8,000 and walked gingerly down its steel steps onto the asphalt below. The sun was shining and there was a slight breeze. They were met by local Scottish police officers, who rarely had much crime to deal with, let alone a chance to meet their counterparts from London. The two officers got into a car and were driven down the island's narrow, winding roads.

Topiary was in his gaming chair, his laptop on his knees, his mind on other things. He faintly heard a car driving near his house and the whine of brakes as it came to a stop. Then the sound of several car doors opening and shutting in a series. He stopped what he was doing, lifting his fingers from the keyboard. He looked over toward the front door, willing it to stay silent. His heart started to pound. There was a long moment of quiet and the sweet, merciful possibility that car had been for his neighbors. Then there was a knock.

PART 3

Unmasked

CHAPTER 25

The Real Topiary

Call it a gut feeling or common sense, but as soon as he heard that knock on the door, Jake knew it was the police. He clung to one hope: that they had not come to arrest him. Police conducted raids around his neighborhood all the time, thanks to the druggies. There was every possibility they were just doing another sweep.

When he opened the door, six plain-clothed people were standing on his doorstep.

"We're with the Metropolitan Police," one of them said. "We're here to search this address."

In the hope that they were looking for drugs, he asked, "What for?"

"Computer equipment."

Jake's heart sank. If Aaron Barr had ever hoped one of his adversaries would experience the same kind of dread he had felt less than a year earlier, Jake just had.

"Are you Jake Davis?" one of them asked after they had all flashed badges and identified themselves. Jake nodded. "Yes." They added that they were also there to arrest him.

"What for?" Jake asked.

"Conspiracy to DDoS the Serious Organised Crime Agency." Jake waited for them to mention something else, but they did not. It almost seemed like the DDoS attack on SOCA had been the final straw that made the authorities fly all the way up to the Shetland Islands.

There were no handcuffs, no guns; there was no shouting, just polite conversation that made the encounter completely surreal. A woman officer from the Met's e-crime division walked straight to Jake's Dell laptop and started to engage the track pad. Before he could even try to make a move, she told him not to touch it.

Despite everything that had happened, Jake had not yet wiped his laptop as he had intended. Incriminating documents, notes, and databases were still on there, albeit on an encrypted hard drive. But that was no trouble for the police. They had only to ask Jake for his password; he gave it to them. The woman tried to see what was on the hard drive, but she couldn't find it. She motioned for Jake to come over and allowed him one final interaction with his computer: a click of the mouse to reveal his hidden hard drive so the officer could get a look inside. He had forty programs running at the same time.

Just as Barr had kicked himself for reusing the same password, Jake silently regretted not deleting everything the way Kayla had been encouraging him to, the way he had been telling himself to.

The officers moved ahead with brittle practicality. They told Jake he had to leave with four of them, now, while the two others remained in his home to close down his laptop and search the house for other items they could use as evidence. There was no time to pack a bag or grab a book or call his mother. He was allowed to bring two changes of clothes. They opened his front door and led him down the steps to the car with no ceremony. If the local druggies had been watching, they might have thought their young, hermetic neighbor was headed out to town with a few family friends, not being arrested for helping lead one of the world's most notorious cyber gangs.

At exactly the same time, several hundred miles south in the northern English town of Spalding, Jake's mother, Jennifer, was across the street from her house, chatting to a neighbor. A policeman showed up at the neighbor's door and asked Jennifer to come home. Confused, she did, opening the door to her house to find it bustling with e-crime detectives and other police officers who were going through the family's things while questioning her other son, seventeen-year-old Josh. They took all the family's computer equipment.

Back in Shetland, as the private plane that had carried the detectives up north now sped down the tiny runway and took off for London, Jake thought about the inevitable headlines. Till then, the Shetland Islands had been merely a blip in the British public consciousness. A distant land of Scots with strong accents who were partial to sheep-rearing. The biggest local news until that point had occurred that very week, with his town's hosting of the Tall Ships Races of 2011. Many of the island's seven thousand residents had taken part as dozens of large sailing ships manned by young people had docked in the bay at Lerwick. Jake remembered how he had stepped out of his reclusive life for a spell, strolling down to the harbor and watching with wonder as thousands of people bustled between tents, food, and live music.

He was brought back to reality with a jolt as the plane landed. Though it had once taken an eighteen-hour bus trip plus a ferry to get to his home in Shetland, the flight had taken just forty-five minutes. Within another hour Jake was being driven up to the clean white stucco walls of Charing Cross police station in central London and then led into a tiny holding cell. There was a bed with a blue gym-style mat, a thin blanket, and a toilet in the corner. It was a warm summer's day outside, but the cell was cold. The sounds of singing and banging by other inmates echoed down the hall. Eventually he had a chance to speak to his mother, who was beside herself with worry. He told her he was all right and asked if she could bring him some clothes, books, and fruit. The food being served in the custody cells was mostly take-out: fried chicken or sausage and chips.

The following day, a woman wearing brown corduroy trousers and leather flip-flops walked up the white stone stairs into Charing Cross police station. Jake's mother, Jennifer Davis, had dark brown hair that had been dyed a subtle shade of red, and she was carrying a cloth satchel with embroidered flowers along with a large blue duffel bag stuffed with clothes and fruit that she had brought down on the train from her home in Spalding. She had been expecting to see her son in a few months' time when he moved down to England to live with her again; not like this. Jake's mother was required to attend all of his interviews, since, owing to Jake's age, an adult needed to be present.

The interviews went on for hours at a time, and Jake looked forward to them. It was a chance to get out of his cell. He was shocked at the amount of detailed research the police had carried out on Anonymous and LulzSec. They had thorough chronologies of cyber attacks, with exact times, and tables of suspects going back to 2006, often spread across giant sheets of paper. Thanks to recent extra funding from the government, there was now a dedicated team of about a dozen detectives working on tracking Anonymous. They had arrested him in connection with the SOCA attack and on suspicion of several other offenses. Eventually, the police said that based on their interviews and what they had found on Jake's laptop, they were planning to charge him with five specific offenses. The police were using innocuous things as evidence: printouts of his browser window being open on a ten-minute e-mail service; another window showing Nyan Cat. Jake was cooperative where he could be, giving the police the passwords to the LulzSec Twitter account and everything on his laptop.

Word spread that the police had arrested the person they believed to be Topiary and were questioning him in London, and the world of Anon was in uproar. The AnonOps chat rooms were ablaze with rumors about what had happened.

Sabu quickly posted "RIP Topiary," on his Twitter feed, which had several thousand followers, equating the arrest to a death in the world of hacking. "I'm pretty fucking depressed," he said in an interview that day. But that quickly morphed into anger at governments and, perhaps, at his new overseers. "The problem is not hackers. It's the thinking of our governments. They need to show their citizens that the government can retaliate against civil disobedience."

It is still unclear how the police managed to track "Topiary" to Jake Davis's yellow wooden home on the remote Shetland Islands. Sabu may have helped, since he had been arrested a month before. But there are other possibilities. Like Sabu, Topiary wasn't always as careful as he should have been. For just a few seconds, the name Jake had popped up on the AnonOps chat network. It happened just after December 8, 2010, when Anonymous was launching its pro-WikiLeaks attacks. Though Jake had layered two or three VPNs to conceal his computer's address, a temporary connection error to his broadband that coincided with a failed connection of one of the VPNs left him briefly unmasked. He'd had no idea this had happened.

Then there were rumors that a friend of Jake's from his days of hanging out on Xbox forums had recognized his voice on the Westboro Baptist Church video and had started posting messages on Twitter that Topiary was "Jake from Shetland."

Another more likely reason relates to the VPN company that Jake paid a monthly subscription fee to to hide his IP address. Both Topiary and Sabu had endorsed VPN provider HideMyAss to the core and the secondary crew of LulzSec, with Topiary spending a few hundred dollars from the group's donations on seven online accounts. When someone needed an extra VPN, Topiary would lend him a login name and password and cross it off his list. Some time after the #pure-elite logs were leaked, showing the world that LulzSec was using HideMyAss, British police served the British VPN company with a court order. HideMyAss later admitted it had divulged information on one of the LulzSec accounts in response. The company explained that it regularly logged its users' IP addresses and login times to help weed out abusive users. Its customers were up in arms, but a court order was a court order, business prospects be damned.

Among the things Jake noticed during his interviews with detectives was that the police seemed to see Anonymous as an organized criminal group, which was precisely the thing that Sabu had been worried would happen when he had railed against Laurelai for writing a user guide. When the detectives questioned Jake, they seemed to want answers that fit that point of view. Jake tried to explain that Anonymous was not a group, was not organized, and did not have a structure. It was more of a culture or an idea than a group.

Yet in explaining that, Jake realized that the police were right in one sense. In less than a year, Anonymous had indeed become more organized. In November and December of 2010, during Operation Payback, there had been no stable chat network and more than two dozen IRC operators entangled in a bureaucratic mess. By July of 2011 there was a lean, solid chat network with about six operators far more in sync with one another. The Twitter accounts @AnonymousIRC and @anonymouSabu by then had more than a hundred thousand Twitter followers in aggregate, not as high as LulzSec's but enough still to grab mass attention. Pastebin had been popularized as a quick and easy way to publish stolen data. More people knew which hackers to approach to get things done. There were servers around the world, and Bitcoin donations were still coming in. In fits and starts, a system was being created.

American authorities were in agreement with the Met. In early August of 2011, the Department of Homeland Security said it expected more significant attacks from Anonymous in the coming years, and there was the possibility of a "higher level actor providing LulzSec or Anonymous with more advanced capabilities."

From the front lines and sidelines, Topiary, Sabu, and Kayla, along with William on 4chan, had watched Anonymous grow from nothing to a nebulous, possibly dangerous entity with pockets of significant power and influence. Like some petulant teenager, it remained volatile and misunderstood. From WikiLeaks in December of 2010 to Tunisia in January of 2011 to Aaron Barr in February of 2011, operations had popped up almost randomly. There had been no funding, no planning, and no leaders. No one knew anyone's name or had ever met in person. Anonymous had come out of nowhere to create the mirage of a criminal organization that police were only just starting to rope in.

Now at least they had a face to show the world. The police kept Jake in custody for as long as they could—ninety-six hours. After that, it was time to announce his real name.

On Sunday, July 31, London's Metropolitan Police announced on their website that they were hitting a Shetland teenager named Jake Davis with five charges related to computer hacking, including violating the Computer Misuse Act and conspiring to attack the U.K.'s Serious Organised Crime Agency. Now, for the first time, the name Jake Davis was publicly associated with Topiary. Later that day, Britain's *Daily Mail* published an article headlined "Autistic Shetland Teen Held over Global Internet Hacking Spree Masterminded from His Bedroom." It was typical British tabloid fare, now with the suggestion that Jake Davis was the "mastermind" of LulzSec (instead of Ryan Cleary) and with no explanation of how anyone knew that Jake was autistic. (He was not.) The media that Topiary had courted so successfully before, that he had almost held in the palm of his hand, was turning on him, gleefully invoking the hacker clichés of mental disorder and social ineptitude.

The following day, Jake was driven to Westminster Magistrates' Court for his first hearing, which was in the same brightly lit room where Ryan Cleary had stood just a month before. Outside the court, cameramen with long lenses reached up to the windows of any police van that drove in and took photos through the tinted windows. They would check what they got, then take more. About two dozen journalists were there to report on the news, including editors from the *Guardian,* the BBC, and the *Financial Times*. They huddled together to talk about what a "soap opera" the LulzSec story had been.

"I expect he'll be pale and windswept, skinny or fat," said the technology editor of the *Guardian*, which had published the #pure-elite logs. That editor, Charles Arthur, had been the target of Topiary's trolling at one point, getting his cell number tweeted and quickly getting two hundred voice mails before the mailbox was filled and Jake deleted the tweet. "If they had just been corporations it would have been 'Ok, bring in some sandwiches,'" Arthur said as he mused on LulzSec, "but to hit SOCA...." He trailed off, giving a whaddya-expect shrug.

Inside the courtroom, people readjusted their seating as Jake walked into the octagonal dock wearing a denim shirt and holding a book, his head bowed. He glanced around as he confirmed his name and address to the judge, then took a seat and scratched his head. He looked over toward the journalists, who were straining to see the book he was carrying, then looked down again. For the most part he appeared calm and collected.

"Sir, the picture that emerges is not a skilled and persistent hacker," Jake's barrister, a tall, bespectacled man named Gideon Cammerman, said, "but someone that sympathizes and publicizes, and acts as a repository for information hacked by others."

The government's prosecutor, a portly woman in a dark suit, disagreed. Referring to Jake's group as "luke sack," she insisted he remain in police custody till further notice. When he'd heard enough, district judge Howard Riddle, a stern, red-faced man with short gray hair in a bowl cut, looked at Jake for a moment and then back at the prosecutor. This was the same judge who had ruled earlier that year that Julian Assange be extradited to Sweden.

"Make it explicit for me if you would," he said, looking over his glasses, "the nature of the harm that he has caused." Jake's mother looked on from the public gallery.

"Sir, he's compromised personal information of hundreds of thousands of members of the public," the prosecutor said softly as she looked up at the judge. "People who have used the National Health Service, the bank accounts and personal details of the users of Sony Entertainment systems." She mentioned the ten-minute e-mail they had found on Jake's laptop and the fact that the computer had a 100 GB encrypted hard drive with sixteen separate "small computers"—his virtual machines—operating independently of one another.

Judge Riddle asked Jake's lawyer what his "temperament" had been like in police custody. "He was perfectly charming," Cammerman answered, then took the opportunity to point out that Jake's mother and brother had just moved to Spalding, England, and still had no broadband. No Internet access at all. The lawyer suggested Jake be bailed and sent to stay with them on condition he wear an electronic tag and not access the Internet. For someone like Jake who had gone online almost every day since he was eleven, this would be the coldest of cold turkey. But it beat a jail cell.

In just a few minutes, the judge made up his mind. "It is clear that there is strong evidence that you have been involved with a group that has committed very serious offenses," he intoned as Jake nodded. "The objections to bail I understand. But I bear in mind the following." He stared at Jake more intently. "You are still only eighteen. You've not been in trouble before." In spite of his tough appearance, the judge granted Jake bail, with a list of conditions that included a 10:00 p.m. curfew. The guard came up to Jake with a clipboard. Jake offered him a small smile and signed it.

"You're a lucky man," the guard said quietly as he led Jake out. "I didn't think they'd give you bail." The guard led Jake down a corridor and into a small room where he met once again with his mother and another solicitor who worked with Cammerman. Knowing there were cameras waiting outside, their small group wondered how best to leave the courthouse. The solicitor reported that members of the media were waiting at both the front and back entrances to the building for Jake to emerge. If they went out the front, where most of the cameras were, they would at least exit onto a main road where a London black cab was already waiting. If they went out the back, they would need to walk around to hail a cab and would risk meeting more media. Jake's mother decided it was best to go out the front, together as a family.

With his hands in his pockets, his book tucked under his arm, Jake walked down to the courthouse's bright entranceway and stood in front of the main door. Looking out the windows, he could see it was a perfect day outside, spots of sunlight dancing around the sidewalks and through giant deciduous trees across the road. At the bottom of the front entrance steps a throng of photographers and TV cameramen stood waiting in a semicircle, all of them stock-still in expectation. Jake's mother eyed them warily from inside the building. Jake put on a pair of sunglasses, which his mother had brought along, to hide his amblyopia.

"Shall we go?" she asked.

"Yeah." He let out a breath as the glass doors opened in front of him, then stepped through the doorway. The dark mass of photographers erupted into flashing lights, accompanied by an eerie silence. There was no shouting and almost no talking, only the passing of cars and rustling of wind through the trees. When they all got down to street level, Jake flinched as he became engulfed by the crowd. He started slowly shuffling toward the black cab that was waiting for him on the other side of the street. Just inches away from his face, the cameras were exploding in flashes. The photographers soon enough were shouting to get Jake's attention, knowing the cab was near and their time was short.

"Jake! Jake!" It was the *Guardian*'s Charles Arthur, who was jostling against the photographers to get Jake's attention. "What's the book?" Jake stopped to look at him, then held up the paperback for everyone to see, the one he'd been reading in his jail cell. The cameras flashed and clicked frantically. It was called *Free Radicals: The Secret Anarchy of Science,* about how scientists would do anything—lie, steal, or cheat—to pursue new discoveries. For the first time, as Jake looked through his sunglasses into one of the cameras, he gave a tiny, almost imperceptible smile.

After his court appearance, Jake took a train up to northern England to the house he would be living in with his younger brother, his mother, and her partner. The police would fit an electronic tag onto his ankle to notify them if he ever broke his curfew. He never would, becoming so paranoid about breaking his bail conditions that he refused to listen to a YouTube video over the telephone when someone offered it. Photos of Jake's face after leaving the courthouse were shared across the Internet. How did Anons react to seeing the real Topiary for the first time? They presented him as a martyr, superimposing his face onto movie posters from *The Matrix* to make new propaganda images. Sabu, Kayla, and many others changed their Twitter avatars to read "Free Topiary." Other hackers with Anonymous who were still at large followed the developments of Jake's trial and wondered how he would fare. But since phone numbers were rarely given out in Anonymous, none of the hundreds of people Topiary had chatted to on AnonOps knew how to get in touch with him after his arrest. This meant that once he got home, Jake was met with complete silence.

Three months after his court appearance, a few letters had come through the door—some from journalists and one or two pieces of fan mail. Jake had gone from communicating with hundreds of thousands of people every day online to opening the occasional piece of mail, talking mostly to his immediate family, watching TV, playing computer games, and trying to use a typewriter to express his thoughts.

Then there came a chance for something different. After a few months of his new, sequestered existence, Jake was offered the unique opportunity to talk to someone from Anonymous face to face. It was not someone he had collaborated with or even met in person. It was William.

Like William, Jake Davis would never have found his way to the front lines of the Anonymous phenomenon if he hadn't first found 4chan. This seemingly innocuous website, still mostly unknown to the mainstream but beloved by millions of regular users, was at the heart of what had driven Anonymous to get the world's attention. Despite the headline-grabbing actions of hackers, the roots and lulz ethos of Anonymous was still firmly in image boards.

From the time he was fourteen, Jake had been learning how to maneuver the hordes on 4chan and entertain them on other websites. William was different. From fourteen right up until he was twenty-one, his age in 2012, William still rarely left the world of /b/, the ever-popular random thread on 4chan. There were many like him—oldfags who believed they were the true Anons. The site continued to be a home to twenty-two million unique visitors a month, 65 percent of whom were male, ages eighteen to thirty-five, and living in North America or Western Europe. Like many other web forums, 4chan was a place to discuss a wealth of subjects both crass and sophisticated, from camera lenses on the photography board to Victorian authors on the /lit/ board. But thousands of visitors each day still went straight to /b/, hoping to discover an "epic thread" that saw 4chan make its mark on the real world, anything from ruining someone's life to raiding a website to finding a kidnapped girl.

William was still pulling all-nighters on 4chan, terrorizing the enemies of his beloved /b/ and trying to improve his hacking skills. News of Topiary's arrest had been disappointing—he had liked the guy on that Westboro video—but it had also made him more determined to become a hacker himself. William reasoned that since his emotions were so extreme, prison would be either mind-numbingly boring (which wouldn't matter because he was so depressed at home anyway) or "a laugh." Either way, he did not care about the consequences.

"I won't get caught, I am certain," he explained.

William's online exploits had become bolder, sometimes including a gang of others from /b/ to help him torment a wider group of people. For example, a few days before Christmas 2011, William was browsing what he lovingly referred to as "my /b/" when he saw a thread that started: "Post their contact info if you hate them." These types of threads were common on /b/ and often heralded a night of fun for William.

Among the responses, one user had posted the phone number and Hotmail address of a sixteen-year-old girl in Texas named Selena, adding, "Make this girl's life hell. She's a slut." When William looked her up on Facebook, he saw she had more than three thousand friends on the network. He decided to try to hack her account.

He wrote down Selena's e-mail address on a piece of paper, went to Hotmail, clicked on the link that said "Can't access your account?," and then hit "Reset account." He put in Selena's e-mail address, then answered the security question: "What is your father's hometown?" Selena's Facebook page showed that she lived in Joshua, Texas, which was the correct answer.

It then asked: "What is your grandfather's occupation?"

William sighed. He signed into one of his fake Facebook profiles, Chrissie Harman, and sent Selena a direct message.

"There's a group of hackers after you," he told her without bothering to introduce himself. He pasted a screenshot of the thread from /b/ with her contact details as proof. William said he was part of this fictitious hacker gang and that they were dangerous. He was willing to help but would need to be paid.

"How do I pay you?" Selena asked, worried.

"Take a photo of yourself with a shoe on your head and a time stamp." In the past he would have wanted nude photos, but by now William had plenty and couldn't be bothered to ask. Sure enough, within a few minutes, Selena had taken a self-portrait and sent it over. William felt a small victory.

"OK. Now I'll ask you questions to help secure your account," William said. He could have just told her to remove her security questions. Instead he bombarded her with technical-sounding gibberish about "randomized answers," "servers," and "a database string input," a deliberate tactic in social engineering. Distract someone with enough misinformation and that person will forget what you are really trying to get, or to hide. "Pick a number between 1 and 100," he said. "What's your mother's middle name? Mine's is Deborah." After every answer of hers, he replied, "Yes, that will work very well."

Then he asked, "What does your grandfather do?"

"Oil," Selena said. William opened his other window and quickly typed *oil* into Hotmail. Nothing. He tried *oil operative, oil technician,* and *oil executive.* They didn't work either. He would have to try something else.

"Ok. My questions will get more technical now, but don't worry," William said. "This will really secure it. After this you'll be un-hackable forever." He asked Selena how many e-mail accounts she had and how many characters were in her average password. Then he asked her to type out her Hotmail password backward.

"Here's mine," he offered, pasting gibberish. Selena hesitated, then she typed it out. Within a few minutes, William had gotten into her e-mail account, and then he activated a series of steps that allowed him to reset her Facebook account too, still asking her questions so she wouldn't get suspicious.

Before she could answer his last question, he went into her account settings and signed her out. He set up secure browsing to mask his IP address, then changed the password again. He went back to /b/.

"I'm in this girl's account," he said, starting a new thread and pasting a link to her Facebook profile. "Give me ideas for things to do." One person suggested talking to Selena's boyfriend, a local boy named James Martinez. William decided that was a good idea. He went ahead and changed Selena's relationship status from "in a relationship" to "single" then sent boyfriend James a direct message.

"OMG I accidentally made us single!" he told him, now in the guise of Selena. "Can you give me your password so I can log into your Facebook and accept our relationship status again?" James agreed, but when he sent over the password *boobies1,* it didn't work.

Exasperated, William passed the work on James off to another prankster on /b/. That was the benefit of having a /b/ behind you — if you got stuck on a problem, someone else could help you fix it. A couple of /b/ users had by now contacted William via their own fake Facebook profiles, and one, who used the fake name Ben Dover, offered to get James's correct password. Soon enough, James realized he wasn't talking to his sixteen-year-old girlfriend, Selena, but a malicious hacker. The Caps Lock went on.

"I'M GOING TO KICK YOUR HEAD IN," he told William, who laughed.

"It was possibly the funniest moment of the night for me," William later said. "I really like it when people get angry without realizing how helpless they are. It's like walking up to the biggest man in a nightclub and saying 'I'll knock you out.' It's just not going to happen."

James's tirade had continued. "I'm going to slit your throat you faggot," he wrote. In another window, Ben Dover reported that he was almost in James's Facebook account.

"I'm going to do it now," Ben finally said.

"Ok do it now," said William.

There was silence from James for about ten minutes. Then came a new message from James's account in the same chat window: "I'm in." It was Ben. William smiled. After chatting to Ben more, William realized he was a /b/rother who understood the art of trolling softly. This was a more subtle form of pranking. For example, it was funny to hack someone's Facebook profile and post porn on his wall, but funnier still to make it seem that the person had accidentally uploaded a porn link himself.

William and Ben set up a private Facebook group and pasted a link to it on /b/. After half an hour about fifty other fake Facebook profiles, all linked to /b/ users, had joined. The group discussed ideas for what to do next.

For now, William wanted to keep Selena's Facebook login credentials to himself. Selena, with her network of three thousand Facebook friends, was the jewel in his crown. As soon as he signed in to her account, ten tabs of chat messages flashed up from boys trying to talk to her. It was a reminder of how big a magnet teenage girls could be online and how blinded a man could become when he thought he was talking to one. This was the benefit the person behind Kayla found in being a sixteen-year-old girl online. William picked one of the boys trying to chat to Selena, Max Lopez, and sent a reply.

"Hey, babe :)," William wrote, still as Selena. "What you up to?" Max responded, and the two embarked on inane small talk, Max oblivious of the fact that he was actually talking to a twenty-one-year-old man in the United Kingdom.

"I'm kinda horny :D," William typed out. The conversation that followed was like hundreds William had had before. Weeks later, when William described it in a quiet café, he looked off to the side, his hands held firmly together. As he searched for the memory, he seemed to enter a trance, suddenly reciting an oddly seductive dialogue as if he were Selena again:

"Sorry," he had told Max Lopez, "I shouldn't have said that. It's terrible."

"It's alright," Max had replied.

"My boyfriend never does anything these days and I just want to be really slummy."

"You shouldn't do that if you have a boyfriend."

"I know. It's terrible…Sometimes I find a guy that's up for it."

"Oh. You found guys that have done stuff before?"

"Yeah."

"Well I hope you find someone."

"I was kinda hoping it would be you." Pause. "I feel dumb."

"No, don't worry."

"Do you send pictures normally?"

"Not really."

"Well, if it's not too weird maybe I could send you a picture. And if you don't like it, that's ok." William then dug through his collection of downloaded porn and found a photo of a young woman's breasts that he figured would pass for Selena's, based on what he could see from her profile picture. Then he sent it over.

The goal was to get Max Lopez to send back a photo of his own genitalia. Like a charm, it worked. As soon as William sent over the photo of breasts, Lopez promptly sent back a photo of his own penis. "They're all desperate to be complimented on their penises," William said. "I don't know why guys think girls want to see that but it works."

"Oh my God this is so hot," William had written back as he opened another window and posted Max's photo in the private Facebook group with his /b/rothers. "Everybody add Max Lopez," he told them.

Soon Max was being bombarded with friend requests from the fifty other fake Facebook profiles. Apparently not too suspicious, Max accepted friendship from fifteen of them. William and his /b/ cohorts went to Max's profile page and looked for Facebook friends that had the same last name, Lopez.

When the group thought they had identified an account that was Max's brother, William corroborated the information with Max directly. "Oh, I think I went to high school with your brother," he said, still as Selena. "What's his name again?" Max replied that it was Kevin. Now William and the /b/rothers had mapped out Max's immediate family. It was time to pounce.

"Don't block me," William suddenly said. Even in text, the tone had changed as his charade as Selena came to an end. "I have your penis picture and I'm going to send it to all of your family if you don't give me your Facebook password."

Max Lopez was stunned, and soon enough, distraught. He was seventeen. He worked for his local church. This wasn't going to look good.

"I felt bad, but I just laughed," William remembered. Out of desperation, Max gave his password, but William had no qualms about going back on his deal. Once he was in Max's account, he took the penis photo and posted it on the Facebook wall of Max's mother, along with the message "Hi, mom. Here's a picture of my cock. Tell me what you think. LOL." Other /b/rothers from William's private Facebook group had been given access to Max's account too and were now posting the photo to around ten of Max's friends and family members. The benefit of posting from different accounts was that it was almost impossible for a person to block all of them. As others in the Facebook group took over spamming Max's social network with his genitalia, William moved on to other boys in Selena's chat list and did the same thing all over again.

It had been months since William had laughed as much as he did that night. It was "a perfect evening" that finished at around nine the next morning. In the end, his team hacked into more than ten different Facebook accounts, all thanks to his access to Selena.

"We split up several boyfriends and girlfriends and appalled many people's mothers," William remembered. "That's one of the bits I enjoy more. Sending a picture of someone's cock to their mum. The idea of it happening to me is so unimaginably embarrassing it makes me laugh."

What he loved doing even more, from the time he'd begun pedo-baiting, at fifteen, was getting another man online highly aroused and then suddenly dousing the moment with the threat of exposure to family and friends or police. As his victim shot from one end of the emotional spectrum to the other, William was offering him a brief glimpse into what he felt all the time. What he called a "bleach shower, a reactive depression, a hot flush and shiver at the same time." Hacking into people's Facebook accounts wasn't exactly life-altering, but he got a buzz from knowing that at least for a moment, his victims felt their lives crumbling around them.

"I'd be lying if I said there was any great reason," he said, leaning back in his chair and stretching his arms to reveal a large hole in his sweater, near the armpit. "I don't feel guilty, it makes me laugh and it wastes a night. That's all I want from 4chan. I want something that's going to leave me not depressed and give me something to focus on. And it's fun to make someone feel that awful from such a distance. I could never do it face-to-face."

William spent the next few nights keeping hold of Selena's credentials, meeting with his new Facebook group of /b/ pranksters, and terrorizing people on Selena's social network, including posting comments on the photos of her female friends and calling them fat. The mother of one of Selena's Facebook friends, who happened to be a police officer, eventually sent harassment papers to the real Selena's home address. Selena, William said, was "the gift that keeps on giving." At one point he posted a status update on Selena's Facebook profile, announcing to her friends that her account had been hacked but that everything was back to normal—then followed that up with another update purporting to be from a friend, saying Selena had been hit by a drunk driver and died. This was how William liked to cause a stir. Not by entertaining an audience of thousands on Twitter, like Topiary did, but by embarrassing others to entertain himself. Still, there were things that William and Topiary had in common, not least that both had found Anonymous through 4chan.

Two months after hacking Selena's account, he accepted the chance to meet Jake Davis, who was now on bail, over an organized lunch to talk about Anonymous. It would be the first time they would talk, offline or online, and the first time either would meet another Anon face to face and discuss the impact of Anonymous on his life.

William and Jake both bought train tickets to a nondescript town in England where they would meet. Though Jake would learn William's real first name and see him face to face, he would not ask for any other identifying information and would never know his full name. The morning of their meeting, William's train snaked through the countryside, past green and beige fields, dawdling sheep, and brown rivers that shimmered in the harsh winter sun. He couldn't help but feel nervous. Jake felt the same. His train was headed south, the electronic tag snugly reminding him to be home by 10:00 p.m. When Jake's train arrived at the station, he stepped out, walked over to a wall in the main concourse, and waited.

Fifteen minutes later William's train squealed to a stop along the opposite platform. He walked into the station's entrance, wading through a large crowd of commuters, then saw Jake standing by a wall in a small stream of sunlight. Jake wore a black coat, had a five o'clock shadow, and was small. He looked up and smiled. William was expressionless. The two said their hellos and shook hands before quickly looking away.

Anons almost never met in person since, naturally, it defeated the point of anonymity. So William and Jake's meeting was awkward at first. What made it harder was the fact that William was going through a particularly dark phase in his mind, and in recent days he had been constantly fighting thoughts of suicide. Jake, who wanted to speak to people outside his immediate family, especially those he had something in common with, was eager to talk.

As the pair sat in a local pizza restaurant for lunch, Jake chatted amiably about his court case and some recent news he had seen about Anonymous on television. William was quiet and sullen. When Jake told a funny story from his LulzSec days, hoping it might generate a laugh, William greeted it with stony silence. The meeting was not going well.

Finally, when talk turned to 4chan, William opened up a little. He talked about his frustration with the site he visited so much, and how it had become a community filled with "newfag cancer," eager young participants who did not understand the culture or how to cause real mischief.

Jake, like William, was not a skilled hacker, but he knew a little about programming languages. When William mentioned that he was interested in developing those skills, Jake pulled out his netbook. The small laptop had been stripped of its wireless card and Ethernet, so that there was no way it could connect to the Internet. But Jake could still play around with Zalgo script, a type of programmable font that packed lots of digital bytes into each letter. If you were looking for fun, you could use it to send someone a message over Skype; it might crash his or her program.

Jake started typing. "If you put that into Skype it'll reverse your text," he said.

William looked visibly impressed. "Your memory is amazing," he said, shaking his head and leaning forward in his seat.

Jake kept going. "Just load up the character map in Windows, dump that anywhere, and it messes it up," he said, now typing furiously.

"So I could do this on Windows?"

"Yeah, it's kind of complex."

"So eight bytes is equal to...one bit," William said, hesitating.

"Eight bits is equal to one byte." William was getting a short lesson in programming basics.

"Yeah, yeah," William said, laughing a little, now more relaxed. "I don't know any of this."

"I'm kind of enthusiastic about Unicode," Jake said, shrugging. Once the netbook had been closed and put away, the two started talking about Anonymous and how it had changed them.

"It's made me a more extreme version of myself," William said. "I used to sleep badly. Now I sleep terribly. I used to be sarcastic; now I can be an asshole." He didn't just "like" tormenting people; he loved it. He didn't just "like" porn; he looked at it every day. "None of it bothers me," he added. "I don't care about anything." William had said in the past that he had no moral code; everything was case by case, his decisions based on a gut reaction. Ernest Hemingway had said it best: "What is moral is what you feel good after, and what is immoral is what you feel bad after."

Jake was nodding. "I have to agree with all of that," he said. "It desensitized me. You can have Japanese dubstep playing to the Twin Towers falling. It might seem horrific, then it seems like a natural thing you see every day." That was the culture that so many outside of Anonymous could not understand. Acting out with crowds of people on the Internet had created a detachment from reality and a sense of obliviousness to certain consequences. Anonymous did bad things, but its members were not bad people, per se.

As if to illustrate the point, a woman sitting nearby suddenly turned to Jake and William and asked if they knew how to access the restaurant's WiFi on a phone. The two looked at each other blankly then quickly explained that neither had a mobile that could go online. Genuinely apologetic, they tried to help the woman with some advice.

"Maybe you could ask the staff downstairs?" suggested William. "Sorry."

The woman smiled and turned back to her panini. She would never have guessed this pair of polite young men had been two notorious members of Anonymous. There was a common misconception about the lack of morals on /b/ and in Anonymous. "It doesn't mean you do bad things," said William. "It just means there's no rules. We don't revert to being bastards at every opportunity."

"It's also nice to just be nice," Jake added.

Many of /b/'s most hard-core users, like William, didn't care about jobs, family, or life's typical milestone events. Both Jake and William relished the idea of living a life that had no impact on real people. If William could scrape enough money together from blogging—he had a clever web script that allowed him to exploit Google Ads without his having to do too much writing—he would fly to mainland Europe later that month and sleep rough in a major capital. He was tired of being a burden to his father and brother, tired of playing his guitar and knowing they could hear him.

"To have as little impact on anywhere as possible is a really appealing thought, which is like never being born," said Jake. No legitimate home, no name on a piece of government paper, no fingerprints. To be nameless, with no identity, not bogged down by any system but to "lightly live everywhere" was something they both craved in real life.

Did that craving come from what they'd experienced with Anonymous: vandalizing things often with little consequence?

"It's Anon and Internet culture," said Jake. "Online you see everything. Gore, disgusting things, and you realize you don't care. Let's stop fussing over little things. There's always something bigger or smaller or worse or better. Most of what we do is what people have done before."

Nothing that occurred on /b/ was meant to be taken seriously, William added. They were just things that happened. "Nothing matters."

"Exactly," said Jake. "That's the main thing about life. People think we are superior to animals. And they're looking for this missing link, but what if we are the link to animals and real human beings haven't evolved yet? It's pretentious to think we're superior in the universe because we can communicate with each other."

"It's so arrogant," said William.

"Bees found out that the earth was round before us," said Jake. "So bees are more clever than us."

"They don't kick up a fuss," William added.

Did people take Anonymous too seriously?

"Anonymous takes Anonymous too seriously," William said quickly. "When I started getting more involved it was 50 percent fun and 50 percent passing the time and that's it. Now there are all these political messages and I just don't care about it. It bothers me it's a bunch of rich kids whining about being oppressed. There are much worse things going on in the world than copyright law [one of the big causes cited by the recent Anonymous attacks]. But I don't think we should kick up a fuss anyway."

"I struggle with that," Jake admitted. "Sometimes I care so much about something, but the next minute I don't. When I try and explain that to people in the real world they attribute that to schizophrenia."

"Sometimes something will happen and then you suddenly care about it," said William. "It matters for thirty seconds." Though this sounded unusual at first, it was not all that different from the twenty-four-hour news cycle or the hype that surrounded popular new stories; they faded just as quickly from the public's short-term memory.

"That's what it was like writing press releases for LulzSec," said Jake. "'I care, I care, I care.' Then it causes a shitstorm in the news, and then I think, 'Whatever.' I feel bad that people are getting arrested and inspired and I don't care afterwards. Like the Antisec movement."

"Opinions on stuff like that are so fluid," said William, "maybe because we're young and impressionable. Maybe we're just honest when we change our mind."

"We care suddenly about something because we're more enriched by the sense of victory," said Jake, referring to the large-scale attacks by Anonymous and the big LulzSec hits. "Then it goes and you don't care anymore."

Did either of them ever feel like he had been manipulated by Anonymous?

"Not at all," said William.

Jake looked down for a moment, then answered. "Not manipulated, but influenced," he said. "When you're in a mob mentality with lots of others. You have a 'mob extreme' version of yourself too, this one, unified mind-set where you don't care that anything exists and you want to wreck something." William was nodding now.

"I've said no but the mob thing rings true," he said. The issue of mental health meant a lot to him personally, but sometimes he'd see a thread on /b/ where the original poster has said, "I'm really depressed and want to kill myself." If the thread's participants leaned toward telling him to commit suicide, William would join in, posting a picture of a can of cyanide and reminding the OP to do it properly. "Which is something I don't even believe. I don't want people to die, but"—he shrugged—"it's something to write and something to do."

Of course, both William and Jake had done their fair share of manipulating too. William was dismissive of the younger "goombie" users and newfags on 4chan who cared about the *V for Vendetta* revolutionary symbols of Anonymous, and sometimes he would rile them up for fun.

"They want to think the world is against them so there's something to justify their angst," he said. That's why it was almost easy to get people to join the revolution in Anonymous. "You can just make stuff up [about government or corporate corruption] and they buy it." To write a rousing post on /b/, for instance, you just needed to write in a way that would appeal to the Anon crowd, using linguistic devices like alliteration, repetition, sound bytes, and dramatic words like *injustice, oppression,* and *downtrodden* to describe corporations and governments, and *justice, freedom,* and *uprising* when referring to Anonymous.

"You could inspire some fifteen-year-old, or someone with a fifteen-year-old's mind-set, to hate whoever you want them to hate," said William matter-of-factly. In having no clear goal, Anonymous was like any other modern-day movement that had become fragmented by the user-generated, crowd-sourced nature of a web-enabled society. Movements like the Tea Party and Occupy Wall Street had the same issue; they were often vague in their goals, but their supporters fought passionately against rival ideologies. Anonymous was a new movement, and a new process for fighting perceived oppressors. And it could be manipulated.

"It's easy to come up with examples of ways that we're oppressed, and some idiot, some gobby student who has a political awakening at fourteen or fifteen who thinks they're clever will buy it!" William was almost shouting now. He stopped in a moment of self-reflection, as if taken aback by the strength of his own opinion, then laughed a little. "I'm only five years older than these guys and I feel like I'm their dad."

But Jake was nodding again. If you knew how to communicate with the Anons, sometimes you could direct them. "It's just so easy," he said.

As Jake and William walked back to the train station through a biting wind, they swapped stories about elaborate trolling, barely noticing how their earlier tensions had disappeared. Jake ran through one of his favorite incidents as William listened: Years before, he and a friend had convinced an online enemy to perform a sexual act in front of his webcam in the middle of the night. They had filmed it, then told the boy they would show the video to the local police and his school if he didn't wake up his mother so they could show it to her. At four in the morning, he did, and he cried most of the way as his mother watched, horrified. Jake and his friend had laughed.

"We decided to let him off by just showing his mum," he said, raising his voice to be heard over the strong wind.

William looked shocked. "That's what you call letting someone off?" he asked, incredulous.

"Yeah," said Jake, shrugging. William blew air through his lips, as if impressed.

William's train pulled up and it was time to go. There followed an unceremonious good-bye, the weighty discussion and baring of souls quickly forgotten in the final, awkward handshakes. Jake and William each nodded quickly to the other and then glanced in the opposite direction. William got on the train without turning around. Jake went back to wait for his own train.

They had found Anonymous in the same place and adopted similar perspectives on life, but they were on divergent paths. Even after meeting Jake and seeing the consequences of getting arrested for hacking, William still wanted to learn to do more than just trick someone into giving him her Facebook password. He wanted to know how to break into a computer network. For weeks afterward, he continued downloading free e-books and reading sections about programming on Encyclopedia Dramatica. Gradually he started testing popular hacking techniques like the Cain and Abel password cracker, SQL maps, Googledorks, and Backtrack5. Then on March 10, 2012, William reached a milestone. After five hours of tinkering, he cracked the password of his neighbor's WiFi, and started using it.

"Next I'll try and steal their shit," he said hopefully, "but I think they're old, so I'm not holding my breath for n00dz." William had no plans to stop disrupting other people's lives, and just like Jake, Sabu, and Kayla before him, he was sure he'd never get found out.

Jake, by March of 2012, had been banned from using the Internet for eight months. If his case went to trial, the thousands of pages of chat logs and complex computer configurations that served as evidence meant it could easily last a year. It was hard for him to think about his future and what he might do when he got out of jail. He still liked the idea of "lightly living everywhere," traveling to places where no one knew who he was. He hoped that one day, he would get a job where he could work outdoors, maybe drive around. He most definitely did not want to work with computers. He was tired of all the stress they had led to in the past. Even without the Internet, it was hard to escape those fraught, paranoid memories. But that month, they would come flooding back stronger than ever, when he found out why Sabu had been at large for so long.

CHAPTER 26

The Real Sabu

What ended up happening to Hector "Sabu" Monsegur? After the arrests of Topiary and Tflow, he continued leading the revived Antisec movement, tweeting from the account he had labeled "The Real Sabu" to a growing stable of tens of thousands of followers. Sometimes he incited revolution—"I love the smell of cyberwar in the morning #fuckisrael"—and sometimes he funneled supporters into the Antisec chat channel, "irc.anonops.li payload is coming soon!" When his handlers needed him to pull in the reins, he complied, cautioning Anonymous on September 21, 2011, that attempts to DDoS Wall Street financial firms was "a fail…Not because of lack of manpower, but rather, wrong direction. Own them, don't waste resources DDoSing."

For someone who had been so loud about hating the police, it had not been all that hard to get Sabu to work for the FBI. On June 8, 2011, the day after he had gone missing from LulzSec and caused distress among his clique of hacker friends, Sabu went to court, where a judge decided to release him from police custody on bail. The condition was that he let the FBI supervise his every movement online and in real life.

For the next two months, as LulzSec finished its hacking spree and the group's founding members, Topiary and Tflow, were arrested, Sabu continued to quietly work with the Federal Bureau of Investigation. According to later reports, he proved to be a devoted informant. He continued to stay up until the early hours most nights, talking to other hackers and finding out about upcoming attacks. If rumors swirled that Anonymous or LulzSec were about to hit a government or company, he would try to talk to the hackers involved to corroborate the attack was about to happen. Perhaps for once Monsegur felt like he was getting the respect that he deserved—this time from the police.

On August 15, he stood before a judge at a second secret hearing in the Southern District Court of New York and pleaded guilty to twelve charges, mostly related to computer hacking. Sabu agreed to help the FBI, and federal prosecutors agreed not to try Sabu for several other crimes he had committed outside the world of hacking. These included carrying a handgun, selling one pound of marijuana in 2010 and four pounds of weed in 2003, buying stolen jewelry and electronics, and running up $15,000 in charges on the credit card of a former employer. And there were plenty of other misdemeanors Sabu had carried out online; detectives found out he had hacked into an online casino and, in 2010, had hacked into a car parts company and shipped himself four car engines worth $3,450. Given how enthusiastically Sabu had boasted about his decade "underground" in which he had "owned entire governments," there was possibly plenty more the police missed. But the Feds were more interested in the other prosecutions that Sabu could help them with.

"Since literally the day he was arrested, the defendant has been cooperating with the government proactively," U.S. district attorney James Pastore, the prosecuting lawyer, told the judge during the August hearing. "He has been staying up sometimes all night engaging in conversations with co-conspirators that are helping the government to build cases against those co-conspirators." Pastore read out the charges and said they could lead to a total maximum sentence of a hundred and twenty-two and a half years in prison. If Monsegur followed his "cooperation agreement" with the federal government, he could get a shorter sentence.

The judge then turned to Monsegur and asked if he was willing to plead guilty.

"Yes," he answered. Monsegur could now skip any sort of trial. He read out a statement in which he admitted to a stream of illegal actions between 2010 and 2011.

"I personally participated in a DDoS attack on computer systems, PayPal, MasterCard, and Visa," he said. "I knew my conduct was illegal." He repeated the admission after listing every count on his indictment, from accessing the servers of Fox, to PBS, to Infragard Atlanta.

"Very well," said the judge. "The plea is accepted." The judge agreed to delay publishing the court docket because Monsegur could be in "great personal danger" if he were identified. Among the apparent risks laid out in court: hackers could send hundreds of pizzas to Monsegur's apartment or have a SWAT team sent to his home (tactics well known to 4chan users like William).

"It's actually called swatting," District Attorney Pastore had explained.

After the hearing, Sabu continued to collaborate with the FBI, working sometimes daily from the FBI offices. The Feds replaced his laptop, which was so old it was missing the Shift, L, and 7 keys, with a new laptop that contained key-logging software that monitored everything he typed. They put video surveillance in his home to monitor his physical movements. They allowed him to continue the public charade of being America's most wanted hacker, encouraging others to join the Antisec movement for which he had positioned himself as its leader, even taunting the police and his critics.

"Sources inside Interpol tell me (besides 'They like butter on their toast') that I'm next to get raided," he announced on Twitter in August. "Is everyone excited by this news?" Later he added: "Message to Interpol: SUCK MY DICK."

But many people in Anonymous had their suspicions about Sabu. Why had everyone else who had founded LulzSec been caught while the loudmouthed ringleader who was widely known to live in New York and be of Puerto Rican descent was still at large?

Among the more suspicious was Mike "Virus" Nieves, a hacker whom Sabu had collaborated with during LulzSec. On August 16, a day after Sabu's second court appearance, where he had agreed in writing to work for the FBI, Virus accused Sabu outright of being a snitch. The conversation started when Sabu first approached Virus and made the veiled accusation that a friend of Virus's was an informant. Virus saw through this deliberate tactic straightaway. It was a typical strategy among hacker informants: to faze someone who suspected you of being a snitch, you accused *him* of being a snitch. Their long and eventually hostile chat took place two weeks after Jake Davis had walked out of his first court appearance.

"Regarding Topiary," Virus told him. "You ratted him out. It's so obvious, Sabu."

"You better watch your fucking mouth because I'm not a rat," Sabu wrote back. "And I definitely didn't rat my own boy." Virus wasn't listening.

"I can spot a rodent a mile away," he said, adding for good measure, "'Antisec,' what a fucking joke."

"For a fucking joke it's doing more mayhem than it did a decade ago," Sabu retorted.

"You don't even get what Antisec was about," said Virus. "You're not owning whitehats. Just dumbass foreign .govs."

"I was actually involved," said Sabu. "Big difference man. I don't sit here and run automated tools. I'm a seasoned security researcher going back to mid-to-late 90s."

"You're a low-level blackhat that got owned," Virus shot back. "I'm done being your friend. You're way too shady and I'm too old for this childish crap. Your lame-ass Antisec movement is hitting anything it can." In truth, Sabu's Antisec followers were often thwarted when they tried to hit out at "anything they could." The FBI was taking advantage of Sabu's cult-leader status by following up each hacker who presented a vulnerability to his mentor in the hope of a pat on the head. Sabu sometimes received more than two dozen vulnerabilities a day, and each time he would alert his FBI handlers. By August of 2011, he had helped the FBI patch a hundred and fifty vulnerabilities in computer networks that other hackers were targeting or was at least helping to mitigate the damage. Over the coming months, he would reportedly assist in alerting about three hundred government and corporate organizations about potential attacks by hackers with Anonymous, allowing them to patch flaws in their networks.

As Virus brought his standoff with Sabu to an end, he waxed pragmatic about what Sabu was probably doing. "Quite frankly, I don't care if you're working with the Feds to clean up the mess you created and getting your so called 'friends' arrested," he said. "It's human nature."

"My nigga," said Sabu. "You seriously need to stop saying that."

"Or?"

"We'll meet up in Manhattan and talk it out face to face."

"I know your tactics, and you won't gain access to any of my shit," said Virus.

"Bro, you know me less than the Feds do," Sabu said, momentarily hinting at his working relationship the FBI. "But let's be real."

The two went back and forth about how offensive *snitch* was before Sabu observed, "You're talking a lot of shit, like you have some issue with me. I always gave you mad love even from the first day I met you."

"I don't care for your love," said Virus with finality. "There is no 'love' on the internet." This seemed to ring true above all else. Sabu may have been a skilled rooter who could find network vulnerabilities and exploit them, but his greatest skill was hacking into people's minds. He lied to the very team members he had brought together and led, all the while helping the police build up charges against them and corroborate their identities. All the more impressive was that Sabu's charisma and lies were so effective that other hackers continued working with him, even after Topiary, Tflow, and Kayla were arrested, and even as other hackers remained suspicious of him. It was even said to be an open secret among hackers in New York City that "Sabu" was Monsegur, with one rumor doing the rounds that local hackers had sprayed graffiti on his building.

On the same day as Sabu's confrontation with Mike Virus, a group of self-styled anti-Anonymous investigators published a blog post claiming to dox Sabu. This time it included a photo of a large Latino-looking man in his late twenties, wearing a leather jacket and a hat. The photo was of Monsegur. It also showed a detailed history of his exploits, and his IP address. It was perhaps the most comprehensive dox to date. The following day, August 17, Sabu posted a cryptic message on Twitter, invoking a quote from the movie *The Usual Suspects* about the film's mythical bad guy, Keyser Söze: "The greatest trick the devil ever pulled was convincing the world he did not exist. And like that...he is gone." For the next few weeks, nobody heard a peep from Sabu on public IRC or Twitter. Most assumed that he had either fled or been caught. Then exactly a month later, on September 17, he started tweeting again, starting with:

"They tried to snitch me out, troll me, dox every one around me, bait me into endless arguments but there's one thing they can't do: STOP ME!"

All at once, Sabu dived back into the world of Anonymous and Antisec, jumping into conversations on public IRC channels and asking to hear reports from other Antisec hackers. For the most part, he didn't join in any attacks. Other hackers close to Sabu at the time do not remember him hacking anything for the months after he came back. They knew that he was bragging publicly on Twitter about attacks he had carried out but assumed this was part of his role as a mouthpiece for Anonymous and Antisec. Sabu instead pushed the "younger ones" with Anonymous by praising them and offering to help facilitate attacks, one source said.

At one point, for instance, he offered to help Anonymous hackers in Brazil get root access to government servers. (Hacktivism is extremely popular in Brazil, in part because the country has the highest rate of Twitter usage and also because of long-standing controversy over government corruption.) Sabu acted as the mediator, talking to the Brazilian hacktivists, then telling his crew of hackers what the Brazilians wanted to deface. His crew rooted the Brazilian servers and then sent Sabu the login credentials to pass on to the Brazilian hackers.

"We can't remember one [hack] he did, even before he got busted," said one hacker who had been working with Sabu from at least late 2011. "He liked to say he did it all. He did not."

It is unclear to what extent Sabu was allowed to hack with impunity during his time assisting the FBI. There are different accounts. Some say that in his role to corroborate the public claims by Anonymous that a company or government agency had been hacked, he would enter the targeted network and check that the vulnerability was there. Others have said he would simply check the claims out by talking to other hackers in private IRC rooms. It was probably a bit of both. For the most part, he was either giving advice, barking orders, or trying to keep on top of what was going on. For instance, he asked a hacker named Sup_g who had stolen data from nychiefs.org in December of 2011, "What's the latest with that nychiefs ownage? You done with it or?"

That month, Sabu helped the FBI get a glimpse inside one of Anonymous's biggest attacks and bait that same hacker. The attack was on Stratfor, an Austin-based intelligence service that made money selling a newsletter to clients who included the Department of Homeland Security.

On December 6, Sup_g approached Sabu about Stratfor, excitedly, in a private IRC channel.

"Yo, you round? Working on this new target," he said.

"Yo," said Sabu. "I'm here." Sup_g pasted a link to the admin panel for Stratfor.com, saying that it could lead to credit card data that he was confident he could decrypt.

Sabu notified his FBI handlers. Over the next few days, Sup_g and other hackers dubbed the Stratfor hack *lulzxmas* and deemed it a landmark attack for Anonymous and Antisec. A week later, Sup_g spent around eight hours getting into the company's network, and the following day, December 14, he told another hacker that he was now in Stratfor's e-mails.

"We in business baby," he said. "Time to feast upon their [e-mail] spools.... I think they'll just give up after this goes down." As the FBI looked on, apparently helpless, the hackers stole 60,000 credit card numbers, along with records for 860,000 clients of Stratfor, staff e-mails and financial data, and a whopping 2.7 million confidential e-mails. At the FBI's direction, Sabu told the crew to store it all on a New York server.

On Christmas Eve, December 24, the hackers defaced the Stratfor site and published the credit card details of 30,000 Stratfor clients, claiming they had used them to donate $1 million to charity—even publishing receipts. The FBI later confirmed that the credit cards had been used to make at least $700,000 in fraudulent charges. Stratfor had to stop charging a subscription for its all-important newsletter and it estimated the breach cost it $2 million in damages and lost revenue.

Sabu might not have stopped the breach, but he did help the FBI identify the person behind the Stratfor attack, Sup_g. He did this by corroborating that Sup_g also went by another nickname, Anarchaos. On December 26, Sabu approached Sup_g online, going perhaps a little over the top in playing the role of the still-outlawed hacker.

"Yo yo," he said. "I heard we're all over the newspapers. You mother fuckers are going to get me raided. HAHAHAHA."

"Dude it's big," said Sup_g.

"If I get raided anarchaos your job is to cause havoc in my honor," Sabu said, subtly dropping Sup_g's other nickname, anarchaos, and adding a heart—<3—for good measure.

"It shall be so," Sup_g replied, unaware that he had just implicated himself. Over the next few months, as the Feds pored over chat logs with Sup_g on Sabu's computer, they pieced together enough personal information to build up a picture of who the hacker really was. It led them to twenty-seven-year-old Jeremy Hammond, a political activist from Chicago who wore long dreadlocks and was a practicing freegan—federal agents reported seeing him looking in dumpsters for food once they started physical surveillance. His mother later told reporters that Hammond had been a computer genius who couldn't stop his urge to "get the goat of America."

The FBI may well have had a bigger target in mind than the dreadlocked Hammond: Julian Assange. Soon after the hackers breached Stratfor's e-mails and started rummaging through them, they noticed that many e-mails talked about WikiLeaks. The hackers decided it made sense to pass them over to the whistle-blower organization and that WikiLeaks would do a better job at disseminating them anyway.

It is possible, though not conclusive, that as the FBI watched what was about to happen, they hoped to take advantage of the Stratfor hack and gather more evidence against Assange so they could finally extradite him to the United States. The FBI later denied to the *New York Times* that they "let [the Stratfor] attack happen for the purpose of collecting more evidence," going on to claim the hackers were already knee-deep in Stratfor's confidential files on December 6. By then, they added, it was "too late" to stop the attack from happening. Court documents, however, show that the hackers did not access the Stratfor e-mails until around December 14. On December 6, Sup_g was not exactly "knee-deep" in Stratfor files: he had simply found encrypted credit card data that he thought he could crack.

It is also telling that Sabu, the man who had jumped into Anonymous to help avenge Assange, suddenly seemed very keen to talk to the WikiLeaks founder once his FBI handlers were watching. Beyond the initial contact he made during LulzSec, hacker sources have said, Sabu tried especially hard to speak to Assange again and again after the Stratfor hack, "bugging" Assange's assistant to talk to him.

"Sabu was trying to contact [Assange] for a long time," one hacker said. Others add that when Sabu first heard that Anonymous was planning to give the Stratfor e-mails to WikiLeaks, he "freaked out," then called WikiLeaks by telephone and demanded to speak to Assange directly. It is unclear if he got through to Assange himself or just his assistant, but according to several sources, Sabu then asked for money in exchange for the Stratfor e-mails. Assange apparently said no.

When the Stratfor hackers got wind of news that Sabu had asked for money for the e-mails they had stolen, they were shocked, and quickly transferred the e-mails to WikiLeaks's server for free. WikiLeaks has not denied, publicly or in private, that Sabu asked for money from the organization. But if Wiki-

Leaks had paid for them, American authorities might have had a much stronger case against Assange. It seems doubtful that the FBI had the time or inclination to decide from the top down that it wanted to play along and try to nab WikiLeaks, but perhaps an agent somewhere had the idea to nudge Sabu to ask Assange for money, and see what came of it.

Once WikiLeaks had the Stratfor e-mails, it formed partnerships with twenty-five media organizations, including *Rolling Stone* and *Russia Reporter,* and published a drip-feed of confidential information. WikiLeaks called them the Global Intelligence Files.

News commentators noted that this marked the first time WikiLeaks was sourcing files from data that had been hacked by Anonymous. Till then, hardly anyone outside of LulzSec's hacking community, WikiLeaks, and the FBI had known that Assange had been dealing to Sabu and other Anon hackers since June of 2011. That of course did not mean there was a solid partnership in place. Two separate hacker sources said that for a long time, Assange did not trust Sabu. Exactly why is unclear, but Assange would not have been the only one to sense that something was off.

"There is one thing that really struck me as funny after he came back," said another hacker, referring to when Sabu had returned to LulzSec after going missing for twenty-four hours (his secret FBI raid in June 2011). "He suddenly talked about his family. He mentioned in a private chat to me that he had two kids." This was deeply unsettling. Despite the unspoken rule in Anonymous to never talk about your personal life, Sabu was suddenly saying things like "My family is the most important thing." Before then, he had never talked about his two daughters. Another oddity: when others from Anonymous were questioned by police and then allowed to come back online, they mentioned to other hackers how strange it was that the authorities never asked them about Sabu.

Sabu was unflinching when he denied to hackers, and in interviews, that he was "Hector Monsegur," using the implausibility of the situation to his advantage and tweeting on June 26, 2011, "How many of you actually fell for that bad whois info? Haha. First off 'hector montsegur' has been posted every day for the last six months." He repeated this line to others in private.

Surprisingly, though, Sabu admitted to his closest hacker friends that the several acts of doxing him—and there were others besides Emick who came up with Hector Monsegur—were correct. This, again, was bizarre, but many assumed it was Sabu's usual nihilism, the guy whose favorite saying was, "I've gone past the point of no return." Sabu seemed to relish the trouble he was getting himself into and at some point down the line, they figured, he would get busted.

In late November of 2011 and then again in January of 2012, a hacker confronted Sabu about not hacking into any targets himself. "Man, get your hands dirty for once," the hacker told him in exasperation, adding that it was the only way to prove to others that he was not a snitch. Sabu responded with histrionics, claiming he had done plenty for the cause already, then adding that "haters" wanted to hunt him down. As Sabu ranted, the hacker typed out an emoticon for weariness, -.- , and went back to work.

Despite their suspicions, most of Sabu's associates never really believed that this veteran revolutionary hacktivist who was so passionate about his cause could really be a snitch.

"The idea was so horrid. And we weren't sure who to trust to talk about it," the same hacker said. Sabu had such a strong psychological hold on his crew that they actually feared asking around about his true intentions lest the volatile figure suddenly flip out on them.

While Sabu was an informant, his lies were aimed at not only other hackers but also journalists. Together with his FBI handlers, he would lie to reporters who hoped for an online interview. Sometimes the reporters were speaking to federal agents, other times it was Sabu but with the agents looking over his shoulder. In the end, it was just another disinformation campaign.

Throughout his volatile year with Anonymous, Sabu had proved himself to be a masterful liar. But there was one thing he could not seem to fabricate: his name. At one point in 2011, before his FBI arrest, Hector Monsegur dropped the nickname Sabu online and started trying to use the new nickname Kage or Kaz in private IRC channels. The goal was to start anew, burn the old Sabu name, and avoid arrest and doxing. Had he maintained the new names, he might never have been raided by the FBI and might still be living with his two kids in his Lower East Side apartment today, watching YouTube videos and paying the bills with stolen credit card numbers. But Monsegur couldn't manage the new online identity. After a few weeks, he went back to using Sabu.

This was the dilemma for hackers in Anonymous. There were practical problems when someone who was well connected in the hacker underground, like Sabu, took on a new name. He would lose his contacts and the trust he had with them. Sabu had brought in dozens of useful contacts from his time underground to work with LulzSec, Anonymous, and Antisec. Hector Monsegur could never have orchestrated all that collaboration without the name Sabu. In the end, ego and a thirst for control got the better of him.

By early 2012, FBI administrators had begun to go back and forth over when they should out Sabu as their informant. So far, he had helped fix a number of vulnerabilities in targeted networks, helped identify Jeremy Hammond, and helped bring charges on Donncha "Palladium" O'Cearrbhail, from Ireland. In early January of 2012, O'Cearrbhail (a Gaelic name that's pronounced "Carol") had hacked into the Gmail account of a member of the Irish national police, an officer who routinely sent e-mails from his official police account to his Gmail account. One of the e-mails contained details of a conference call that was to occur on January 17 between FBI agents and Britain's Metropolitan Police to discuss the LulzSec and Anonymous investigation. Palladium quickly notified Sabu that he would be listening in and recording it.

"I am happy to leak the call to you solely," he said excitedly. "This will be epic!"

After recording the eighteen-minute call, Palladium passed the audio file to Sabu, who then passed it to the FBI to corroborate that it was real. It was. When Sabu didn't publish the file online, someone else put it up on YouTube, much to the delight of the Anon community and embarrassment of the FBI. Behind the scenes, the FBI went on to identify Palladium (thanks to a search warrant they'd gotten on a friend's Facebook account) and level a significant charge against the hacker (thanks to Sabu's chat logs). Sabu had helped gather evidence against five people, all told: Topiary, Kayla, Tflow, Sup_g (Jeremy Hammond), and Palladium.

In early 2012, police on both sides of the Atlantic got ready to press charges against the five Anons. The time to out Sabu was soon, but choosing a date wasn't easy.

"There were constant problems with the relationships between the British authorities and the FBI," said one person with knowledge of the FBI investigation into LulzSec and Anonymous. Though Sabu was in New York, at least four LulzSec hackers lived in the British Isles, which meant Britain's Metropolitan Police were more eager than their American counterparts to pull the trigger and charge them. While the Americans had a major informant who could help them grab more hackers at large, the Brits had four hackers they were ready to send through the court system.

The FBI wanted to capitalize on their Lower East Side snitch as much as possible. He had helped patch those flaws, and the announcement of his arrest and the revelation of his duplicity would devastate the socially disruptive ideas of Anonymous and Antisec. But the Feds could not know for sure how useful Hector Monsegur would continue to be. Though he was smart and well connected, he was also a loose cannon. One evening in early February, a cop from the NYPD encountered Hector at another apartment in his neighborhood. He asked Hector for his ID.

"My name is Boo. They call me Boo," Hector replied. "Relax. I'm a federal agent. I am an agent of the federal government." It seemed that Hector had started to believe that he was both Sabu and a bona fide FBI agent. That same evening he was charged with criminal impersonation.

Just as complicated: In monitoring Sabu, the Feds were getting a look at how quickly things moved in the worlds of Anonymous and Antisec. Sabu saw scores of ideas for attacks floated every day, and while some got thrown out, others were followed up faster than the FBI's red tape might allow. Hackers bragging on Twitter, Internet drama, lulz—this was all new territory for the FBI.

When London's Met finally told the FBI that they had a "drop-dead" date of March 7 to arrest and publicly charge the person alleged to be Kayla, a date from which they could not budge, the Feds agreed to out Hector just before that deadline too. Everything would come out into the open at the same time: the suspected identities of Kayla, Pwnsauce, Palladium, and Stratfor hacker Sup_g, and the news that Sabu had been working with the FBI for an extraordinary eight months. It was a bombshell, and the police were about to drop it squarely on Anonymous.

CHAPTER 27

The Real Kayla, the Real Anonymous

Seven months earlier, on September 2, 2011, British police had pulled up to a family-sized house in the quiet English suburb of Mexborough, South Yorkshire. It was a cold and gray morning. One of the officers had a laptop open and was watching the @lolspoon Twitter feed, waiting for the hacker known as "Kayla" to post another tweet. When she did, several more burst in the house through a back entrance, climbed the stairs to the bedroom of Ryan Mark Ackroyd, walked in, and arrested him. Ackroyd was twenty-five and had served in the British army for four years, spending some of that time in Iraq. Now he was unemployed and living with his parents. Appearance-wise he was short, had deep-set eyebrows and dark hair in a military-style crew cut. When he spoke, the voice that emerged was a deep baritone, and the accent strongly northern English. Ackroyd's younger sister, petite and blond, was, perhaps tellingly, named Kayleigh.

In the same way police had simultaneously questioned Jake Davis's brother, detectives also synchronized Ackroyd's arrest with that of his younger brother, Kieron, who was serving in the army in Warminster, England. After questioning Kieron, the police released him without charge. Kieron and Kayleigh Ackroyd seemed close as siblings, with Kayleigh regularly posting on her younger brother's Facebook wall, encouraging him at one point on a forthcoming driving test. "You'll get the hang of it," she said in January 2011. But their older brother, Ryan, never appeared in their public conversations.

"He is the archetypal English infantryman," said one person who knew of Ackroyd. "He will stand to attention and if he's told to jump he'll ask how high—that type of personality. He's either exceedingly clever to pull this off, or it genuinely isn't him."

"She's a soldier in the UK," Sabu said quietly during a phone interview on November 5, when asked who he thought Kayla was. "It's a guy." Then he seemed not to be sure, saying he'd heard it was someone who shared the "Kayla" identity with a group of transgender hackers. "I don't know what the fuck it is. They're all weird transvestites and shit. I'm brain-fucked about it."

In any case, on that cold morning in September 2011, Kayla's once-prolific Twitter feed as @lolspoon went quiet. (It has remained inactive ever since.) Then in March of 2012, as the FBI got ready to go public with the truth about Sabu, British authorities got the go-ahead to charge Ryan Ackroyd with two counts of conspiracy to hack a computer network.

On March 6, 2012, Fox News, the subject of multiple taunts by Anonymous and LulzSec and at least one hack in 2011, announced to the world that Sabu, the "world's most wanted hacker," was an FBI informant.

"EXCLUSIVE: Infamous International Hacking Group LulzSec Brought Down by Own Leader," the headline read. Fox had been working on the story for months and sourced much of its info from FBI officials and a few hackers who knew Sabu. It outed Sabu as Hector Monsegur and reported that police were arresting and charging five other men, largely based on evidence that Hector "Sabu" Monsegur had gathered.

"This is devastating to the organization," the story quoted an FBI official as saying. "We're chopping off the head of LulzSec."

Every major news outlet picked up on the item, most of them sourcing the Fox story. Journalists descended on the Jacob Riis housing projects, taking pictures of Sabu's apartment door; knocking on it but hearing nothing. Others talked to the neighbors, who gave Hector Monsegur mixed reviews. He had been quiet but friendly, they said, and would smile at people he passed by in the hall. One elderly neighbor who lived below confirmed she had complained to the Manhattan community board about the sounds of "shouting children, barking dogs, screaming and 'pounding'" that came from his apartment, usually lasting until four o'clock in the morning.

The snitch revelations stunned thousands of people who followed or supported Anonymous. Some of the more popular Anonymous Twitter feeds simply tweeted the news, unable to provide much comment. One suggested the arrests were like cutting off the head of a hydra; more would grow back. Anonymous, the implication was, would bounce back from this.

Jennifer Emick had a field day, pointing out on Twitter that Anonymous was now as good as dead.

Gabriella Coleman, a Wolfe Chair in Scientific and Technological Literacy at McGill University in Montreal, was one of the rare few to meet Sabu in person while living in New York. He was not so different from his online persona, she remembered. Though she'd studied Anonymous for years, Coleman was in shock. She had suspected Sabu was up to something (why else would he meet?), but on the day the news came out she claimed it was "an all together different thing to experience it and know it." Just before he was outed, Sabu had been allowed to notify family and friends by telephone of what was about to happen. Coleman was one of the people he called. When recounting that final conversation, Coleman described it as "part apology, part 'It-is-not-what-it-seems.'"

When key people in Anonymous and Antisec heard the news, there was shock at the extent of Sabu's cooperation. But there was just as much surprise at what the FBI had been privy to during their exploits on Stratfor, the intercepted FBI-conference call, and other attacks.

"If I was Stratfor, I'd be pretty pissed off at the FBI," said one hacker. "They were basically sacrificed to arrest one guy [Jeremy Hammond]. What the fuck man...what kind of investigation is this?" Other hackers who had consorted with Sabu were now "freaking out" and many said they would go dark for some time.

"I knew something was shifty," Jake Davis said soon after hearing about the extent of Sabu's betrayal against the people he had started LulzSec with. Jake was, as usual, cool about the news. He did not seem angry at Sabu, perhaps because he had already built up resentment against the former friend who had pushed him to take up the Antisec cause. What shocked Jake more was how the FBI had apparently carried out their investigation by monitoring cyber attacks as they happened. "I didn't think the FBI were that insane."

Now it was clear: Sabu, Topiary, Kayla, Tflow, and Pwnsauce, five of the six core members of LulzSec (it is not known what happened to AVunit) had been arrested. It seemed almost impossible to become a hero in Anonymous and avoid handcuffs. But did that spell the end of Anonymous? Jake's final tweet as Topiary had been "You cannot arrest an idea," and it rang true. In Anonymous, there were no real leaders but symbols and smaller groups who occasionally worked together. There were even different cultures: the old-school EFnet hackers like Sabu who had embraced the vision of Antisec, the 4chan users like William who loved Anon because it helped him "waste a night." And there were those who fell somewhere in between, like Topiary, Kayla, and Tflow, who saw Anonymous as a broad means to find fulfillment, have new experiences, and make a difference in the world in a way that suited their enjoyment of computers and the Internet. Tying Anonymous all together and destroying it was impossible.

This was a phenomenon that came from the nascent world of memes, crowd sourcing, and social networks, things that had a viral-like quality that could not be predicted, controlled, or stopped. As some members were arrested, others joined. The FBI said that they were "chopping off the head of LulzSec," but by March of 2012, after LulzSec had been disbanded for more than nine months, other hacker cells were taking up the Antisec cause; in February of 2012 alone, supporters of Anonymous had taken credit for attacking the websites of the CIA, Interpol, Citigroup, and a string of banks in Brazil, among other targets.

Then there was the growing international movement called "Occupy," which emerged in September 2011 and saw tens of thousands take to the streets in major capitals to protest social and economic inequality, often using the slogan "We are the 99%." Activist-style supporters of Anonymous largely showed their support for Occupy, promoting it on Twitter and blogs and wearing the *V for Vendetta* masks at protests. Police had arrested more than 6,800 people in connection with the Occupy movement as of April 2012, by which time it had gone into hiatus. But as observers marveled at how this apparently leaderless global crowd could organize itself so extensively online and in physical demonstrations, they only had to look at Anonymous to see it had already been done before.

For the FBI, getting Sabu as an informant had been a coup, but chasing the day-to-day glut of bragging, secret discussions, conspiracies, and threats probably soon turned into a bureaucratic nightmare. Although they had Sabu working for them for eight months, it is not clear how instrumental he was in initially identifying any of the five hackers that were charged on March 6—at most, he may have helped drum up charges.

Sabu was outed, but Anonymous seemed to refuse to be destroyed. Later that evening on March 6, a group of hackers announced that Anonymous had hacked into and defaced the website of Panda Securities, the same IT company that had observed the Anonymous DDoS attacks on PayPal in December of 2010. Their message: it isn't over.

Then, over the subsequent days, the hackers who had worked with Sabu brainstormed about new ways to work together.

"Sabu's shit makes things different now," said one. "We mistrust a lot more." By mid-March the hackers were discussing other methods of talking to one other besides IRC and how they could raise standards for new people to join private discussions. Anonymous as an activist movement would stay public, but the hacking activities would go farther underground. Anonymous had emerged from the shadows, the hacker added, and it would go back into the dark for a while. "But don't worry. We exist."

Anonymous had already been changing. The software tools its supporters used, for instance, were becoming easier to disseminate. When members of Anonymous launched DDoS attacks on several companies in January of 2012 to protest the shutdown of Megaupload, a video-streaming site, they didn't use the traditional LOIC program. There was no need to download anything. By then, supporters could launch LOIC directly from a web browser. That meant that by posting a link on Twitter or Facebook, organizers tricked hundreds, perhaps thousands, of oblivious web surfers into joining the attack. The attack method, dubbed mobile LOIC by digital security company Imperva, was used as early as August of 2011 in the first of several DDoS attacks against the Vatican and became more popular over the following months.

By early 2012, Anonymous attacks were no longer carried out by thousands of volunteers, as with the Payback attacks for Wiki-Leaks. Just like Chanology's real-world protests, they were a one-off, as if Anonymous was learning what worked and what didn't. Anonymous was shifting from mass gatherings and DDoS attacks to small groups stealing data, like LulzSec. For this, more were using the web tool Havij. After LulzSec used it to collate data during the PBS heist, a splinter group called CabinCr3w used Havij (or something like it) to expose the personal data of five hundred police officers in Utah, while other Anons used Havij to try to steal data from the Vatican in August 2011. Imperva's studies showed that only a year after its creation by what are believed to be Iranian programmers, Havij had become, by the summer of 2012, one of the most popular tools for SQL injection attacks. The program was so simple that one Imperva executive taught his eleven-year-old how to use it in fifteen minutes. The free-to-download tool performed SQLi automatically, even filtering data into helpful categories like "Passwords" and "Credit card numbers." With the right free programs and just a few clicks, it seemed almost anyone could be a hacker.

Of course, keeping the idea of Anonymous alive would be complicated. The media, police, and even the hackers themselves had their own concepts of what it really was: an idea, a movement, a criminal organization, and other things besides. By March of 2012, the public and parts of the media still seemed to think that Anonymous was a very large group that made plans and carried them out in an orderly way. Though the notion was deeply misguided, it was understandable. A newfangled phenomenon like Anonymous, born of the Internet itself, was something society would struggle to make sense of at first. On top of that, the mystery surrounding what really happened inside the hive-mind had left just enough room for the public to create its own versions of the Anonymous narrative, just as when Topiary had spun a vague tale about getting raided when he wanted to leave AnonOps. Anonymous wasn't just a group or a process; it was also a story that people were telling themselves about how the Internet was fighting back. Anons could grab headlines by simply tweeting a threat, which is why the power of Anonymous spoke to the power of myth. Anonymous was another example of social engineering, on a mass scale. It was not too dissimilar from Kayla herself.

Over the past few years, the online entity Kayla had been telling her friends different stories about who she was in real life, tempting them to try to piece together a puzzle of her real identity. A teenage girl who hated her father; a teenage girl who loved him. In the end, though, her hacker colleagues stopped being interested in the truth.

"We told her we'd prefer her to lie to us," one longtime friend remembered. "We all loved the story. I don't think we cared if it was true or not." Like children wanting to keep the magic of Santa Claus alive a little longer after starting to doubt his existence, to her hacker friends, Kayla's story had become more important than the truth itself.

This spoke to the constant struggle within Anonymous: weighing the ethos of anonymity and lies that came with it against the need for trust and truth. Anons have spoken of how persistent lying detached them from reality and "warped" their ethics. It was hard for someone to remember what he was ultimately trying to achieve when he was constantly lying to others. Even Sabu started to believe his own lies by openly claiming to the police that he was a federal agent.

During Operation Payback, thousands of new volunteers had trusted AnonOps operators who claimed that using LOIC would not lead to arrest. That was naive of the volunteers, but there was also manipulation at work, or at least a major split in motives. The operators in #command had quietly latched onto the idea of avenging WikiLeaks, because it would lead to publicity for their new chat network. They hungered for the kudos of having thousands of people visit their channels and follow their orders. Then the botmasters hit PayPal, MasterCard, and Visa to show off their power. The thousands of volunteers were oblivious to this, believing they were part of a digital sit-in, for a cause they cared about. Similarly, in 2008 Gregg Housh and his #marblecake team had thought they were spearheading the mother of all pranks, but Chanology had turned into serious activism. In many ways, Anonymous could be like a scam—with people attracted to the camaraderie, learning, and new experiences, but coming away disillusioned by the disorganization, big egos, and sobering reality of arrest. But Anonymous was something else too: a gateway to political activism, a strange but compelling elixir to the apathy among young people in today's real-time society.

These were issues Anonymous would deal with over time. No single person would make a final decision about how it evolved; it would be a collective effort. People from this current generation of Anonymous would leave, having had enough of the Sabu drama. But plenty of newcomers would take their places and make changes. And a few, including hackers that were there during #InternetFeds or even Chanology, would stick around. A few have indeed stuck around so far.

"They still haven't caught Kayla," said Emick on March 6, the day Sabu was outed. "It's an 18-year-old boy in California." She laughed, then went back online. Emick was still carrying on with her investigations, trying to track down who Kayla really was. She was sure it was a composite name that more than one person had used and that while Ryan Ackroyd was getting charged for some of her offenses, others remained at large. If Anonymous could share a collective identity, why couldn't Kayla?

As for Jake, the Internet ban gave him a chance to reflect on the Web itself, a new entity that has become an integral part of everyone's life. In February 2012 he put a USB flash drive in the mail, and on it was this short missive—his view of how the Internet looks at us:

Hello, friend, and welcome to the Internet, the guiding light and deadly laser in our hectic, modern world. The Internet horde has been watching you closely for some time now. It has seen you flock to your Facebook and your Twitter over the years, and it has seen you enter its home turf and attempt to overrun it with your scandals and "real world" gossip. You need to know that the ownership of cyberspace will always remain with the hivemind. The Internet does not belong to your beloved authorities, militaries, or multi-millionaire company owners. The Internet belongs to the trolls and the hackers, the enthusiasts and the extremists; it will never cease to be this way.

You see, the Internet has long since lost its place in time and its shady collective continues to shun the fact that it lives in a specific year like 2012, where it has to abide by 2012's morals and 2012's society, with its rules and its punishments. The Internet smirks at scenes of mass rape and horrific slaughtering followed by a touch of cannibalism, all to the sound of catchy Japanese music. It simply doesn't give tuppence about getting a "job," getting a car, getting a house, raising a family, and teaching them to continue the loop while the human race organizes its own death. Custom-plated coffins and retirement plans made of paperwork…the Internet asks why?

You cannot make the Internet feel bad, you cannot make the Internet feel regret or guilt or sympathy, you can only make the Internet feel the need to have more lulz at your expense. The lulz flow through all in the faceless army as they see the twin towers falling with a dancing Hitler on loop in the bottom-left corner of their screens. The lulz strike when they open a newspaper and care nothing for any of the world's alleged problems. They laugh at downward red arrows as banks and businesses tumble, and they laugh at our glorious government overlords trying to fix a situation by throwing more currency at it. They laugh when you try to make them feel the need to "make something of life," and they laugh harder when you call them vile trolls and heartless web terrorists. They laugh at you because you're not capable of laughing at yourselves and all of the pointless fodder they believe you surround yourselves in. But most of all they laugh because they can.

This is not to say that the Internet is your enemy. It is your greatest ally and closest friend; its shops mean you don't have to set foot outside your home, and its casinos allow you to lose your money at any hour of the day. Its many chat rooms ensure you no longer need to interact with any other members of your species directly, and detailed social networking conveniently maps your every move and thought. Your intimate relationships and darkest secrets belong to the horde, and they will never be forgotten. Your existence will forever be encoded into the infinite repertoire of beautiful, byte-sized sequences, safely housed in the cyber cloud for all to observe.

And how has the Internet changed the lives of its most hardened addicts? They simply don't care enough to tell you. So welcome to the underbelly of society, the anarchistic stream-of-thought nebula that seeps its way into the mainstream world — your world — more and more every day. You cannot escape it and you cannot anticipate it. It is the nightmare on the edge of your dreams and the ominous thought that claws its way through your online life like a blinding virtual force, disregarding your philosophies and feasting on your emotions.

Prepare to enter the hivemind, motherfuck.

Since 2008, Anonymous had destroyed servers, stolen e-mails, and taken websites offline. But in the collective act of social engineering, its greatest feat was in getting people to believe in the power of its "hivemind." This was what attracted the supporters, what got them arrested, and what inspired others to avenge their arrests. Anonymous was how a new generation of computer-savvy individuals could show the world that they had a voice, and that they mattered.

What they do next has yet to be written. These small groups of young people from around the world, often male, often poor and unemployed, who mostly just talk together in Internet chat rooms, have finally managed to grab hold of the public consciousness. They are still holding on, and they will not let go.

Acknowledgments

This book would never have happened were it not for the contributions of several key individuals. First and foremost is Jake Davis, who has given unceasingly helpful and clear insights into the bewildering world of Anonymous, LulzSec, and Internet culture generally. There is more from Davis than I could fit in this book, and I maintain that he should, at some point, write a book of his own. I would not have first started talking to Davis back in December of 2010 were it not for a crucial e-mail introduction from Gregg Housh, whose own role in the history of Anonymous is detailed in chapter 5. At that time I had just started covering Anonymous for *Forbes* on its new blogging platform, but, being based in London, I was interested in speaking to a U.K. representative. I asked Gregg if he could recommend anyone, and he gave me a general e-mail address for AnonOps. It turned out that one of the people manning that address was Jake "Topiary" Davis. As I exchanged e-mails with this address, I became even more intrigued. This representative spoke confidently as "we" when referring to Anonymous, yet maintained that theirs was a fluid system, allowing jobs to be carried out by "anyone and everyone."

Acknowledgments

I asked how he had found Anonymous and I was told about image boards. I'd never heard of them. "I know it sounds a bit silly," he added, "but it really is a whole different world once you're refined to it. You start seeing things differently in life." I found this fascinating. When this person then revealed that his nickname was Topiary, I Googled the word and found references to gardening. Who were these people?

After covering the HBGary attack, I struggled to figure out where to take the story next and called *Forbes* managing editor Tom Post seeking answers. After listening to me ramble on about social media vulnerabilities, he gave me what was probably the most valuable advice I received all year: "Marshal everything you have on Anonymous that has not been reported, then let's find a focus there." He told me to find out more about the people behind Anonymous, like Topiary. I took his advice and ran with it. The idea for a book came to me after some initial encouragement from staffers at *Forbes* in February of 2011, including the magazine's cyber security writer, Andy Greenberg. Andy would later become a brother in arms as we both grappled with the book-writing process—he has written a book about WikiLeaks, and hacktivism, published in 2012. From there I went on to gain invaluable advice and mentoring from Eric Lupfer at William Morris, whom I cannot thank enough for having helped me write and then rewrite a decent book proposal.

By now I had met (via e-mail) the extraordinary young man referred to in this book as William. That started when he first tried to friend me on Facebook, then sent a cryptic, direct message: "Hello. What would you like to know? In return for answering what you ask, may I ask some questions of you? I'd really appreciate a response, negative or otherwise. Thank you, Chelsea." Not knowing who or what this "Chelsea" was, I ignored the message. A week later another message came: "Please don't ignore me, it's rude." And then: "Is it really too much to ask to get a simple dialogue going?" Today I am grateful that I did, not only because I might have otherwise ended up on the receiving end of one of his "life ruins," but because I eventually discovered someone far more articulate, helpful, and forthcoming than William's original message suggested. Though he will come across to many as a somewhat vindictive individual, William has answered almost every question I have ever asked him about 4chan, Anonymous, his life, and even the darker corners of his own mind. For that, and for helping to give this book an important insight into 4chan culture, he deserves enormous thanks.

Among the other key people who deserve acknowledgment: *Forbes*'s chief product officer, Lewis D'Vorkin. He met some skepticism when he first established the *Forbes* contributor platform in the summer of 2010, which completely changed the way journalists at the publication posted online stories. But this book would never have happened if D'Vorkin had not made that bold and rather brilliant move. It gave journalists like me the freedom to pursue the stories that truly intrigue us, and then the ability to measure how much our readers are intrigued by them, too. Thanks to D'Vorkin's complete revamping of the architecture of *Forbes,* I could see there was a healthy appetite for stories about the world of Anonymous, and now had an unprecedented opportunity to chase those stories down. The *Forbes* technology editor, Eric Savitz, who is also my boss, has given me a wealth of helpful encouragement on this book. Coates Bateman, *Forbes*'s executive producer of product development, has been an invaluable collaborator with this book's publisher, Little, Brown, while *Forbes*'s legal counsel Kai Falkenberg has also offered me sound advice on legal matters.

I am grateful to all the other people associated with Anonymous that I spoke to for this book, including LulzSec's core members Hector "Sabu" Monsegur, Kayla, Tflow, AVunit, and Pwnsauce, along with Barrett Brown, Laurelai Bailey, Jennifer

Emick, and a number of others who have asked to remain, fittingly enough, anonymous. Though some of these people, particularly hackers, were not always completely forthcoming, or honest, when speaking to me, I was fortunate, as a journalist, that they would speak to me at all. Many have asked how I was able to get access to people who frequented such hard-to-reach corners of the Web, and the answer is that I had enormous help from sources who made introductions and vouched for me. I also believe that people, no matter how sociopathic, narcissistic, or duplicitous they may seem to be, have a genuine urge to tell their stories and carve out some sort of legacy. I believe that is why it helped that, when I first started speaking in March 2011 to the hackers who hit HBGary and then formed LulzSec, I told them their interviews would be contributing to a book I was writing about Anonymous.

In addition, Gabriella Coleman, now Wolfe Chair in Scientific and Technological Literacy at McGill University in Montreal, Canada, regularly provided me with a refreshing dose of clarity on who Anonymous was as a collective and how it worked. Coleman has shown extraordinary dedication to studying the Anonymous phenomenon. She has spent more time speaking to a broader base of regular Anons on IRCs than I likely did for this book, and she is rightly seen as the expert on Anonymous and its evolution. Be sure to keep an eye out for her forthcoming book on Anonymous in the next year or so.

Sincere thanks goes to my former colleagues at *Forbes* Anita Raghavan, who offered some smart advice on my book proposal, and Stephane Fitch, who also introduced me to David Fugate of Launch Books. David has proved himself to be a brilliant and continually supportive agent who helped me find the best possible publisher in the form of Little, Brown. From the beginning of my relationship with Little, Brown, I have been impressed with the company's genuine, solid championing of this book and with the clear and incisive editing by John Parsley. Given the subject's intricacies and complexities, its multiple identities and sometimes unreliable storytellers, I can imagine that *We Are Anonymous* might have been a troublesome manuscript for some editors, but John did a masterful job of keeping me focused. He helped me tell the story as clearly as possible, and aided me with just the right amount of editorial intervention.

I must finally acknowledge my wonderful circle of friends and family, whose constant support and encouragement kept me going through the sometimes ulcer-inducing process of researching and writing this book through most of 2011 and early 2012. Those friends include Miriam Zaccarelli, Natalie West, Luciana and Elgen Strait, Victor Zaccarelli, Nancy Jubb, Il-Sung Sato, Anthea Dixon, Leila Makki, and ethical hacker Magnus Webster. My father has been my number one cheerleader for writing this book, while my husband has shown unbelievable support and patience as I worked my way from idea to proposal to manuscript. Another member of my family who did not know about the book but has been a guiding light in spite of that fact was my grandmother, who died on the day I finished revising the final draft of the manuscript and to whom this book is dedicated. Though she was ninety-six years old and hailed from a farming village on a remote volcanic island in the Azores, I think even she would have found something familiar in the stories that underlie Anonymous and its adherents. Despite their modern, mysterious world, steeped in jargon and technobabble, I think she might have seen, as I did, that Anonymous is a very human story.

Timeline

November 5, 1994—In one of the first known acts of hacktivism and cyber disobedience, a group called the Zippies launches a DDoS attack on U.K. government websites, taking them down for a week starting on Guy Fawkes Day.

1999—The Anti Security movement is spawned, as a post on the anti.security.is website calls to end the full disclosure of known website vulnerabilities and exploits.

September 29, 2003—Christopher "moot" Poole registers 4chan.net. (It is now 4chan.org.)

March 15, 2006—Jake Brahm, twenty years old, posts fake threats on 4chan about detonating bombs at NFL stadiums; two years later he is sentenced to six months in prison.

July 12, 2006—Users of 4chan's /b/ raid Habbo Hotel, a

virtual hangout for teens. They join the online game en masse and flood it with avatars of a black man in a gray suit and an Afro hairstyle, blocking the entrance to the virtual pool and forming swastikas. This spawns the "pool's closed" meme.

January 2007—Controversial blogger and radio show host Hal Turner tries and fails to sue 4chan after users on /b/ launch a DDoS attack on his website.

June 7, 2007—Partyvan's /i/nsurgency site is founded as an information hub on raids and, later, communications through the establishment of the Partyvan IRC network.

July 2007—A Fox News affiliate in Los Angeles describes Anonymous as "hackers on steroids" and an "Internet hate machine."

January 15, 2008—Gawker posts a video of Tom Cruise that the Church of Scientology has been trying to suppress. The church issues a copyright violation claim against YouTube. In response, an original poster on /b/ calls on 4chan to "do something big" and take down the official Scientology website. Using a web tool called Gigaloader, /b/ users manage to take down Scientology.org, keeping it down sporadically until January 25, 2008.

January 21, 2008—A handful of Chanology participants publish a video on YouTube of a robotic voice declaring war on Scientology. The following day thousands more people join in the IRC channel where Chanology attacks are being discussed.

Timeline

January 24, 2008—Anonymous launches a bigger assault on Scientology.org, taking the site offline.

February 10, 2008—Anonymous supporters don masks from the film *V for Vendetta* and hold protests outside Scientology centers in key cities around the world, such as New York, London, and Dallas, Texas.

Late 2008—Protests and cyber attacks against the Church of Scientology wind down as supporters lose interest in the cause.

January 25, 2010—Anonymous supporter and engineering student Brian Mettenbrink pleads guilty to downloading and using the Web tool LOIC to attack Scientology as part of Project Chanology and is sentenced to a year in prison.

September 17, 2010—Supporters of Anonymous launch a DDoS attack on Indian software company Aiplex after it admits to launching its own DDoS attacks on BitTorrent site The Pirate Bay. Anonymous launches several more attacks against copyright companies under the banner Operation Payback. Supporters collaborate on an array of IRC networks.

October 2010—The FBI starts looking into the Anonymous attacks on copyright companies ahead of what will become a full-blown international investigation.

November 3, 2010—Anonymous supporters with server resources set up AnonOps IRC, a more stable chat network to host discussions about Operation Payback and other Anonymous operations.

November 28, 2010—Five newspapers begin publishing U.S. diplomatic cables that have been fed to them exclusively by whistle-blower organization WikiLeaks. Over the next few days, a hacktivist known as The Jester launches a DDoS attack on WikiLeaks.org, taking it offline.

December 3, 2010—Online payment giant PayPal announces on its blog that it is cutting off funding services to WikiLeaks, which relies on donations. Shortly thereafter, a few organizers in the #command channel on AnonOps IRC coordinate a DDoS attack on the PayPal blog.

December 4, 2010—An announcement posted on Anonops.net states that Anonymous plans to attack "various targets related to censorship" and that Operation Payback has "come out in support of WikiLeaks."

December 6, 2010—Organizers on AnonOps launch a DDoS attack on postFinance.ch, a Swiss e-payment company that has also blocked funding services to WikiLeaks. Roughly 900 people join in the #operationpayback chat room on AnonOps and around 500 join in the attack by using LOIC.

December 8, 2010—AnonOps launches a DDoS attack on PayPal.com, using 4,500 volunteers with LOIC but only becoming successful when one person using a botnet takes the site fully offline. Some 7,800 people have now joined the #operationpayback chat room. Later that day they hit MasterCard.com and Visa.com, which have also nixed funding services for WikiLeaks, taking both sites offline for about twelve hours.

Timeline

December 9, 2010—Botnet controllers who had previously helped take down PayPal.com, MasterCard.com, and Visa.com turn on the operators of AnonOps and start attacking the IRC network, upsetting a planned attack on Amazon that day.

December 11, 2010—Dutch police arrest nineteen-year-old Martijn "Awinee" Gonlag for using LOIC to participate in an Anonymous DDoS attack, among the first of scores more arrests in Europe and the United States over the next year.

December 15, 2010—A member of PayPal's cyber security team gives a USB thumb drive to the FBI that contains the IP addresses of 1,000 individuals who had used LOIC to attack PayPal.

Mid-December 2010—AnonOps administrators grapple with maintenance as their network is continually attacked, leaving them unable to oversee strategy. As a result, Operation Payback splinters into several side operations, such as Operation Leakspin, Operation OverLoad, and an attack on Sarah Palin's official website.

Mid-December 2010—A few technically skilled supporters of AnonOps create a private IRC channel off the network called #InternetFeds, where about thirty black hat hackers—such as Sabu, Tflow, and Kayla, along with other interested Anons who have been offered invitations to the channel—can discuss future operations.

Early January 2011—The hackers in #InternetFeds discuss raids against websites of repressive Middle Eastern regimes like Tunisia, where popular democratic uprisings are currently taking place. The hacker Tflow writes a Web script that allows Tunisians to circumvent government Web snooping, while Sabu hacks and defaces the website of the Tunisian prime minister with a message from Anonymous.

Mid- to late January 2011—Members of #InternetFeds continue to collaborate on hacking and defacing the websites of other Middle Eastern governments, including Algeria and Egypt.

January 27, 2011—British police arrest five men in connection with the Operation Payback attacks on PayPal, MasterCard, and Visa, including AnonOps operators nicknamed Nerdo and Fennic.

February 4, 2011—A small group of hackers from #InternetFeds meets in another private IRC channel to discuss an attack on IT security firm HBGary Federal, after its CEO is quoted in the *Financial Times* that day as saying that he was investigating Anonymous and had uncovered the true identities of its core leaders.

February 6, 2011—News breaks that "Anonymous" has stolen tens of thousands of Aaron Barr's corporate e-mails, as well as those of two executives at sister company HBGary Inc.; it also takes over his Twitter feed and DDoSes and defaces his site.

Early to mid-February—The same group from #InternetFeds publishes Aaron Barr's private e-mails on an e-mail viewer. Journalists and supporters discover Barr had been proposing controversial cyber attacks on WikiLeaks and opponents of the U.S. Chamber of Commerce. Barr resigns.

Timeline

February 24, 2011—Anonymous conducts a live hack and deface of a website belonging to the controversial Westboro Baptist Church, while Anonymous supporter Topiary confronts a Westboro representative on a radio program. The resultant YouTube video receives more than one million hits.

Mid- to late February 2011—Jennifer Emick, a former supporter of Chanology turned anti-Anonymous campaigner, decides to investigate the true identities of key Anonymous hackers and supporters and uncovers details about Sabu, aka Hector Monsegur.

Mid-March 2011—Emick and a handful of colleagues publish a list of seventy names, including Monsegur's, under the guise of a cyber security company called Backtrace. Soon after, Emick is contacted by the FBI.

April 1, 2011—Supporters of Anonymous publish a digital flyer declaring war on Sony after the company sues a hacker named George "Geohotz" Hotz. They follow this up with a DDoS attack on Sony websites and the Sony PlayStation Network, greatly upsetting gamers.

April 7, 2011—Organizers with Anonymous call off the DDoS attacks on Sony, saying they do not wish to disrupt the PlayStation Network, but the network remains offline for the rest of the month.

April 2011—Topiary and Sabu discuss breaking away from Anonymous, then decide to get the team of attackers behind the HBGary assault back together to collaborate on more raids. The hackers Tflow and Kayla rejoin Topiary and

Sabu, along with another Anonymous supporter named AVunit and, later, an Irish hacker nicknamed Pwnsauce. The group of six forms a hacker splinter group that is not constrained by even the loosest principles of Anonymous— such as not attacking media companies. They call the group LulzSec. They begin scouring high-profile websites for vulnerabilities that "rooters" like Sabu and Kayla can then exploit to steal and publish data.

May 2, 2011—Sony announces an intrusion to its network in mid-April, which has compromised the personal and financial details of more than 75 million PlayStation Network accounts. Though Anonymous has not taken responsibility, Sony later claims that the hackers left a file marked with the words "Anonymous" and "We Are Legion."

May 9, 2011—A former operator within AnonOps goes rogue, publishing a list of 653 usernames and IP addresses, which, if not protected with VPNs or other proxies, could identify the people behind them.

May 7, 2011—LulzSec announces on Twitter, via the new account @lulzsec, that it has hacked Fox.com and published a confidential database of potential contestants in the TV talent show *The X Factor*.

May 30, 2011—LulzSec hacks into the computer network of PBS after its *PBS NewsHour* program broadcasts a documentary on WikiLeaks that the group claims to dislike. LulzSec publishes a list of e-mail addresses and passwords for PBS employees, while Topiary writes a spoof news article about the murdered rapper Tupac Shakur being found alive, publishing it through the *PBS NewsHour* website. The group's founders discuss forming a second-tier network of trusted supporters, many of them hacker friends of Sabu's.

June 2, 2011—LulzSec announces its hack on SonyPictures.com and says that the group has compromised the personal information of more than one million of the site's users.

June 3, 2011—LulzSec defaces the website of Atlanta InfraGard, an FBI affiliate, and publishes a list of e-mails and passwords for 180 users of the site, some of whom are FBI agents.

June 6, 2011—LulzSec receives a donation of 400 Bitcoins, worth approximately $7,800 at the time.

June 7, 2011—Two FBI agents visit Hector "Sabu" Monsegur at his home in New York and threaten to imprison him for two years for stealing credit card information if he does not cooperate. Monsegur agrees to become an informant while continuing to lead LulzSec.

June 8, 2011—The LulzSec hackers notice that Sabu has been offline for twenty-four hours and worry he has been "raided" by the FBI. Later that night, U.K. time, Topiary makes contact with Sabu, who claims that his grandmother has died and that he will not be active with LulzSec for the next few days.

June 15, 2011—LulzSec claims responsibility for launching a DDoS attack on the official website of the CIA. The attack has been carried out by former AnonOps operator Ryan, who wields a botnet and now supports LulzSec.

June 16, 2011—A representative of WikiLeaks contacts Topiary to say that core organizers want to talk to LulzSec. He and Sabu eventually hold an IRC discussion with a WikiLeaks representative and someone purporting to be Julian Assange. The representative "verifies" Assange's presence by temporarily uploading a YouTube video that shows their IRC chat happening in real time on a computer screen, then panning to show Assange on his laptop. The group discusses ways in which they might collaborate.

June 19, 2011—LulzSec publishes a press release encouraging the revival of the Anti-Security (or Antisec) movement and advocating cyber attacks on the websites of governments and their agencies.

June 20, 2011—Galvanized by the surprisingly large response to the Antisec announcement, Ryan uses his botnet to DDoS several high-profile websites, including Britain's Serious Organised Crime Agency. Later, at 10:30 p.m. that evening in the U.K., he is arrested in his home.

June 23, 2011—LulzSec publishes sensitive documents stolen from Arizona law enforcement, including the names and addresses of police officers. Feeling that they have gone one step too far, LulzSec members, including Topiary and Tflow, discuss ending the group.

June 24, 2011—Topiary and Tflow tell AVunit and Sabu that they want to end LulzSec; a heated argument ensues.

June 26, 2011—LulzSec announces it is disbanding after "50 Days of Lulz."

Timeline

July 18, 2011—LulzSec comes back for one more hack, uploading a spoof article about the death of News International owner Rupert Murdoch on the home page of his leading British tabloid, *The Sun*.

July 19, 2011—British police announce they have arrested a sixteen-year-old male who they claim is LulzSec hacker Tflow.

July 27, 2011—Police arrest Shetland Islands resident Jake Davis, whom they suspect of being LulzSec's Topiary.

September 2, 2011—British police arrest twenty-four-year-old Ryan Ackroyd, whom they believe to be Kayla.

December 24, 2011—Anonymous announces that it has stolen thousands of e-mails and confidential data from the U.S. security intelligence firm Stratfor under the banner of "Lulz Christmas." Sabu, who claims to be still at large while other LulzSec members have been arrested, keeps tabs on the operation from private chat channels and feeds information about the attack's organizers to the FBI.

March 6, 2012—News breaks that Hector Monsegur has been acting as an informant for the FBI for the past eight months, helping them bring charges against Jeremy Hammond of Chicago and five people involved with LulzSec.

Notes and Sources

Part 1
Chapter 1: The Raid

The opening pages, including descriptions of Aaron Barr's early career, home, and
family life, are based on interviews with Barr conducted both on the phone
and in a face-to-face meeting in London. Further details about his work
with HBGary Federal came from an investigative feature article on *Wired*'s
ThreatLevel blog, which dug through his published e-mails and pieced together a picture of his plans for the company along with the proposals he
was making to Hunton & Williams. The article was entitled "Spy Games: Inside the Convoluted Plot to Bring Down WikiLeaks," by contributor Nate
Anderson. The *Financial Times* article in which Aaron Barr revealed his
forthcoming research was entitled "Cyberactivists Warned of Arrest," by San
Francisco reporter Joseph Menn, and was first published Friday, February
4, 2011, then updated the following day. Further details on e-mails between
Barr and Greg Hoglund of HBGary Inc. prior to the attack came from the
HBGary e-mail viewer published by the hackers in mid-February.

The details about Sabu hacking computers as a teenager come from interviews
with the hacker conducted via Internet Relay Chat in April 2011, two months
before he was arrested and became an FBI informant. Further details about

being born and raised in New York come from court documents after his arrest later that year.

Throughout the book, personal details claimed by Kayla stem from interviews with the hacker conducted between March and September of 2011 via e-mail and Internet Relay Chat. The rumor about stabbing her webcam with a knife came from an online interview with Topiary. Also throughout the book, details about Topiary come from online, phone, and face-to-face interviews with him (Jake Davis) between December of 2010 and the summer of 2012. Details about Tflow come from interviews with Topiary and Tflow himself; the information that Tflow had invited Sabu and Topiary into the secret IRC channel come from Topiary, one other hacker who wished to remain anonymous, and Sabu himself. Details of how the hackers planned the HBGary attack, including how they used the website HashKiller to crack the company's passwords, came from interviews with Topiary conducted via IRC and Skype (voice only).

Details of Barr's research on Anonymous, including the "hasty notes like 'Mmxanon—states…ghetto,'" came from his research notes, which were posted online by the hackers.

Dialogue between Barr and the hackers, including with CommanderX, comes from chat logs that were published online—partly via the Web tool Pastebin, and also on the Ars Technica article "(Virtually) Face to Face: How Aaron Barr Revealed Himself to Anonymous," by Nate Anderson. The dialogue between Barr and Topiary, which ends "Die in a fire. You're done" comes from a snippet of the chat log that was cut and pasted to a Skype conversation between me and Topiary a few days after the attack. Further details about the attack came from interviews with Jake Davis, as well as online interviews with Sabu, Kayla, and other hacker sources. Details of the February 2011 Super Bowl come from various news reports and from my viewing of the actual game while I was following online developments of the HBGary Federal attack. Although I had already been interviewing Topiary on a regular basis, the attack led to my being introduced to others in the group—first Kayla, then Sabu, then Tflow.

SQL reads like a stream of formulas. An example is: "Select creditcard from person where name=SMITH." If someone were to perform an SQL injection attack, they might inject code saying, "Select a from b where a=SMITH."

How did the hackers know that Barr was CogAnon? Topiary later explained that, almost immediately after seeing the *Financial Times* story and breaking into the HBGary Federal network, one of them had seen that his internal e-mail headers listed the IP address of his VPN (virtual private network). Barr had used this same VPN connection to log into an Internet Relay Chat network used by Anonymous, known as AnonOps. The hackers only had to hand over the IP address to one of the chat network operators, who ran a quick search. Sure enough, the name CogAnon popped up.

Chapter 2: William and the Roots of Anonymous

Details about how Christopher Poole created 4chan come from an interview that Poole gave to the *New York Times* Bits blog. The article, entitled "One on One: Christopher Poole, Founder of 4chan," was published on March 19, 2010.

I sourced the information on Japan's 2chan from the 2004 *New York Times* article "Japanese Find a Forum to Vent Most-Secret Feelings" and *Wired*'s May 2008 story "Meet Hiroyuki Nishimura, the Bad Boy of the Japanese Internet."

Further details about the development of 4chan, such as its "TWO TIMES THE CHAN" announcement on Something Awful, come from an article on 4chan history by Web developer Jonathan Drain, on jonnydigital.com. Moot's referral to /b/ as a "retard bin" comes from an announcement on the 4chan "news" page, 4chan.org/news?all, on October 2, 2003.

Though the story of Shii's enforcement of anonymity on 4chan is relatively well known among image board users, the details come from testimony provided on Shii's website, shii.org.

Details about the life, viewpoints, and exploits of the young man named in this book as William come from scores of e-mails and several face-to-face meetings, all taking place between February of 2011 and the summer of 2012. After telling me—in a meeting that took place in July of 2011— the story of hacking "Jen's" (not her real name) PhotoBucket account, William e-mailed me photos of Jen and "Joshua Dean Scott." I have the images on file. Scott's photo, for instance, shows him holding a piece of paper reading "'Jen' owns my ass 3/2/11." He wears a black baseball cap, a lip ring, and a black Converse shoe on top of his head, along with a slight smile. On several occasions William e-mailed me screenshots of the conversations he was having with the people he trolled on Facebook, as well as the raid threads he sometimes participated in on /b/, to corroborate his stories. The pranks and online intimidation of individuals described

in this book are only a small fraction of the many nightly exploits that
William alerted me to.

Further details about /b/ and 4chan were sourced from the meme repositories
Encyclopedia Dramatica (now redirecting to ohinternet.com) and
KnowYourMeme.com, as well as interviews with Jake Davis.

Chapter 3: Everybody Get In Here

The vast majority of details about Topiary's early childhood and life on Shetland
come from online and face-to-face interviews with Topiary (Jake Davis) himself, with further details and corroboration coming from discussions with his
mother, Jennifer Davis, after his arrest. As of mid-April he was living in
her home on bail, awaiting a plea and case management hearing at a British
crown court on May 11, 2012. A few key details, such as the death of his stepfather, Alexander "Allie" Spence, were corroborated by newspaper reports.
Descriptions of the scenery and lack of modern shops in Shetland come from
my own one-day visit to Lerwick, where I first met Davis in late June 2011.

Details of Davis's frequent prank calls to the Applebee's restaurant in San Antonio, Texas, are a result of interviews with Davis himself. Though he could
not provide recordings of the Applebee's calls, he did provide audio files of
other similar prank calls.

A common feature of /b/ raids was a "surge" of users against an online target,
the idea usually being to overwhelm them. Among the examples provided
are spamming shock photos on a forum; this is a common tactic of /b/ users,
and was most recently perpetrated on the comedy site 9gag. The raid in
which /b/ warped the votes for *Time* Magazine's "Person of the Year" took
place in 2009, when 4chan users famously teamed together to program a bot
that would crank out fake votes that put Christopher "moot" Poole at the
top of *Time*'s ranking. As well as giving him an unfeasible sixteen million
votes, they gamed the system so that the first letters of the following twenty
names in the ranking spelled out the words "Marblecake also the game." This
was thought to be a reference to the IRC channel in which much of Project
Chanology was organized in 2008 (see chapter 5). *Time* magazine provided
details of the hack in a video and quoted moot as saying that he had no idea
who was behind the vote rigging.

The stories of the Habbo Hotel raid and Operation Basement Dad come primarily
from Davis's testimony, but are also corroborated by online news reports,

such as ReadWriteWeb's April 16, 2009, article "Operation Basement Dad: How 4Chan Could Beat CNN & Ashton Kutcher" and, in the case of Habbo Hotel, the April 8, 2009, Fox News article "4Chan: The Rude, Raunchy Underbelly of the Internet."

Details of the origins of Internet Relay Chat come from the online article "History of IRC" by computer consultant and hacker Daniel Stenberg, posted on his website, http://daniel.haxx.se/. Some extra descriptions, such as the numbers of IRC channels and numbers of users in channels, come from my own exploration of IRC. The source for the common "Everyone get in here" feature is Jake "Topiary" Davis, and I have verified the phrase's frequent use through repositories for image board content, such as chanarchive.org.

Chapter 4: Kayla and the Rise of Anonymous

Main sourcing on the backstory that Kayla claimed about her childhood and parents came from online interviews with Kayla herself (I refer to the online entity as "her.").

The source for the notion that Kayla lied about being a sixteen-year-old girl comes from my own observations and discussion with other hackers, with further evidence coming from the Metropolitan Police's arrest of Ryan Ackroyd in September 2011. As of mid-April 2012, I cannot confirm that the person I was interviewing on Internet Relay Chat between March and September of 2011 was Ackroyd. As far as rumors that Kayla was "a transgender hacker," Ackroyd did not appear to be transgender when he first appeared in Westminster Magistrates' Court, then aged twenty-five, on March 16, 2012.

The quote "Kayla seemed to have a deep need to tell stories to prove her value to others" comes from reading comments by Kayla in the leaked chat logs from #HQ and #pure-elite during the days of LulzSec, including those in which she boasted about attacks she instigated during Project Chanology. So elusive has Kayla been online that phone and face-to-face interviews conducted with Hector Monsegur, Jake Davis, Aaron Barr, Gregg Housh, Jennifer Emick, Laurelai Bailey, and other anonymous sources yielded little more than speculation about who she really was.

Background information on the tendency for some men to claim to be women online comes from conversations with hackers and general knowledge from the world of memes and Internet culture. The phrase "There are no girls on the Internet" has its own entry in KnowYourMeme.com, from which some of this context is sourced, while the popular /b/ comment "Tits or GTFO" comes from my own exploration of /b/ and discussions with William. Incidentally, the list of 47 Rules of the Internet has been widely published online.

In my explanation of IP addresses, I am referring in this instance to IPv4 addresses (which have now sold out). The latest IPv6 addresses are a combination of numbers and letters that are segmented by colons.

Details about Partyvan were sourced from interviews with an organizer from the time of Chanology who wished to remain nameless, interviews with Kayla, and content on the partyvan.info website, also known as the /i/nsurgency W/i/ki.

Details of the Fox L.A. television news report from July 2007 were sourced from a YouTube video of the report.

Chapter 5: Chanology

Details about the publication of the Tom Cruise video come from interviews with anti-Scientology campaigner Barbara Graham and e-mails exchanged with journalist Mark Ebner. Patty Pieniadz wrote her own detailed account, entitled "The Story Behind the Tom Cruise Video Leak," and posted it on the forum WhyWeProtest.net under the nickname "pooks" on September 4, 2011; some of the first part of this chapter is also sourced from this account. Descriptions of the video come from watching the video itself on YouTube. According to Ebner, ex-Scientologist and TV journalist Mark Bunker had originally uploaded the video to his YouTube account and notified several of his media contacts. Then, a few hours later, he took the video down.

The detail about Viacom's $1 billion copyright lawsuit against YouTube parent Google was sourced from various news articles, including the *New York Times* story, "WhoseTube? Viacom Sues YouTube Over Video Clips," published March 14, 2007.

Text from the original discussion thread on /b/ about a raid on Scientology on January 15 come from 4chanarchive.org. The rumor that the original poster on /b/ for the first anti-Scientology thread was female come from an interview with Gregg Housh.

Details about DDoS attacks come from numerous Web articles about how such cyber attacks work, along with background discussions with IT security professionals and hackers from Anonymous. The Graham Cluley analogy about "15 fat men" originally comes from an August 6, 2009, article by Cluley on the Naked Security blog of the research firm Sophos. Background on the 4chan attack on Hal Turner comes from numerous blog posts, as well as from archived 4chan threads. The point that one could download "at least a dozen free software tools" from 4chan's /rs/ board to take part in some sort of DDoS attack comes from an interview with Housh. Details of phases 1, 2, 3, etc., and how /b/ was hitting Scientology.org, specifically with Gigaloader, come from an archive of the actual thread. Details about Gigaloader come from piecing together and corroborating various Internet forum discussions about the Web tool.

Details later on in the chapter about the hundreds of people that piled into the #xenu channel on IRC, then the move to physical protests and establishment of the #marblecake organizational hub, come from a phone interview with Gregg Housh and e-mails exchanged with one other Chanology organizer who wished to remain anonymous. There also exists a timeline of the main Chanology events on the aptly named chanologytimeline.com.

Housh confirmed in an interview that he had been arrested for copyright violations. Further details were sourced from a "motion for booker variance" filed through the U.S. District Court of New Hampshire on November 23, 2005. The motion showed that Housh had pled guilty to one count of conspiracy to violate copyright laws, related to creating a computer program in the summer of 2001, which automatically searched for new software. Details about Housh's family background were sourced from the court motion and the section "The History and Characteristics of the Defendant." The motion also states Housh was approached by the FBI about the case in 2001, and that he sought to mitigate his offenses by cooperating with the Bureau "for four years." Further details about Housh serving three months in federal prison come from Housh's interview with the *Huffington Post* in the story "Anonymous and the War Over the Internet," published on January 30, 2012. Housh's age of thirty-five was also mentioned in the interview.

The factoid about 25,000 Scientologists in America in 2008 originally comes from the American Religion Identification Survey, cited in a report by the Associated Press.

Information on the posting of internal church documents by the newsgroup alt.religion.scientology is sourced from the January 2008 *Globe and Mail* article "Scientology vs. the Internet, part XVII."

The detail that XSS is the second most common hacking technique after SQL injection is sourced from the Web Hacking Incident Database (WHID) of 2011, an online database that tracks media-reported security incidents and is led by Ryan Barnett, senior security researcher on Trustwave's SpiderLabs Research Team.

Details about the technical impact of Anonymous DDoS attacks on Scientology's website come from research by Arbor Networks, along with court documents related to Brian Mettenbrink's case; these documents provide, among other things, the date when Scientology hired Prolexic Technologies.

Details on LOIC come from numerous online articles about the Web application, screenshots of the interface, news reports from tech site Gizmodo, and research from the IT security firm Imperva. Details on Praetox come from the programmer's own website, http://ptech.50webs.com/, which appears to have been created in 2007 but was abandoned around 2009 or 2010. The emergence of NewEraCracker as another programmer to develop LOIC comes from details on GitHub, a Web-based hosting service for software projects.

The anecdote that Time Warner would profit from the *V for Vendetta* mask comes from an August 2011 article on the *New York Times* Bits blog.

The example of a channel topic in #marblecake came from a chatlog provided by Jennifer Emick's Backtrace Security, via logs obtained from a leak among Chanology organizers.

The vast majority of details about Brian Mettenbrink come from a phone interview conducted with him on December 16, 2011, as well as from court documents and an FBI transcript, both of which were published on the Partyvan website. A few extra details came from an archive started when Mettenbrink uploaded a scan of his driver's license and photo, along with the business card of one of his visiting FBI agents, to WhyWeProtest.net, as well as from comments in that thread made by Mettenbrink and others. Mettenbrink was banned from using the Internet for a year after his jail sentence and, at the time of this writing, still had to receive e-mails through a friend.

Chapter 6: Civil War

The vast majority of details about the experiences of Jennifer Emick are derived from phone interviews with Emick herself, as well as from a few interviews conducted over Skype text chat. Extra details about the methods of intimidation used by Scientology representatives against Anonymous protesters come from the testimony of Emick, Laurelai Bailey, various Web reports, and YouTube videos.

Notes and Sources

Details about the life and experiences of Laurelai Bailey (formerly Wesley Bailey) come from phone interviews with Bailey herself, along with several discussions held via Internet Relay Chat and Skype text chat.

The details of "simultaneous worldwide protests on February 10" come from Bailey's and Emick's own testimonies as well as from various blog posts that reported on the events afterward. Details about playing an audio version of OT3 at protests come from testimony by Laurelai Bailey as well as from the *Der Spiegel* article "Tom Cruise and the Church of Scientology," published on June 28, 2005.

The point about an alleged list of "murdered Scientology defectors" came originally from conversations with Jennifer Emick, who also pointed me to discussions on the anti-Scientology message board ocmb.xenu.net, also known as Operation Clambake. A number of campaigners on this board, for instance, believe that former Scientologist Ken Ogger, found dead in his swimming pool on May 29, 2007, was murdered.

The description of Chanology as "full-blown activism" comes from interviews with multiple participants in the raids and protests, including Emick, Laurelai Bailey, and an anonymous Chanology organizer, with viewpoints split on whether the veering toward activism was a good thing or not. The notion that Scientology "stopped coming out to play," i.e., stopped responding defensively to the antics of Anonymous, is sourced from testimony by Bailey and Emick, as well as from various online forums in which Chanology is discussed, such as WhyWeProtest.net.

The rows between IRC network operators, including the quote "you have no idea who you're fucking with," are sourced from Emick's testimony, and the squabbles are also chronicled in detail on the main Partyvan website. Details of Scientology's litigation against Gregg Housh are sourced from various news reports, including an October 2008 article in *The Inquirer* entitled "Anti Scientology Activist Off the Hook. Sort of." Scientology's perspective on receiving "death threats" is sourced from a CNN video from May of 2008, in which the news network's John Roberts spoke to a Scientology spokesman who claimed that Anonymous was "terrorizing the church."

Details about the way Emick "outed" Bailey's online nickname, Raziel, leading to their falling-out, come from the accounts by both Emick and Bailey.

The information about SWATing a house comes from testimony from Emick as well as from interviews with William, who directed me to websites that showed the steps one needs to take to "SWAT" someone.

Details of Laurelai's first online meeting with Kayla come primarily from interviews with Bailey. The extra context on transgender hackers comes from e-mails I exchanged with Christina Dunbar-Hester, PhD, Affiliated Faculty, Women's & Gender Studies, at Rutgers, the State University of New Jersey.

Chapter 7: FIRE FIRE FIRE FIRE

The introductory paragraph, which suggests that Anonymous went quiet between Chanology in 2008 and WikiLeaks in late 2010, comes from interviews with various key players, including Jake Davis, Jennifer Emick, Laurelai Bailey, and conversations with other Anons, along with my own observance of a drop in news coverage about Anonymous between those dates.

The interview with Girish Kumar from Aiplex that is referred to at the start of this chapter is sourced from the September 8, 2010, article "Film Industry Hires Cyber Hitmen to Take Down Internet Pirates" in the *Sydney Morning Herald*. Kumar was quoted as saying similar things in the TorrentFreak.com article "Anti-Piracy Outfit Threatens To DoS Uncooperative Torrent Sites," published on September 5, 2010. It is unclear if Kumar or Aiplex were ever prosecuted for launching DDoS attacks; there are no press reports since that suggest the company was.

Details of the discussion of Aiplex on /b/ and then the creation of an IRC channel to coordinate a raid were sourced from an online interview with the hacker Tflow in April of 2011, and from the TorrentFreak.com article "4chan DDoS Takes Down MPAA and Anti-Piracy Websites." I gleaned some context on the attacks from a timeline of events that was posted on the Partyvan.info website. The story that Anonymous supporters were herded between IRC networks, along with the names of the main IRC channels, was also sourced from the interview with Tflow. Extra details about Aiplex and MPAA attacks come from other online articles, such as TechCrunch's "RIAA Goes Offline, Joins MPAA As Latest Victim of Successful DDoS Attacks," from September of 2010, and a blog post by IT security firm Panda Labs entitled "4chan Users Organize Surgical Strike Against MPAA," published on September 17, 2010.

Details about Tflow's alleged real age and location come from the later announcement (in July of 2011) of his arrest by the U.K.'s Metropolitan Police. The description that he was quiet and "never talked about his age or background" comes from discussions with other hackers as well as from my own observations of Tflow in interviews, in chat rooms with others, and in leaked chat logs. Details of the way Tflow approached people in IRC channels with more technical knowledge than he, and the way that group turned Copyright Alliance into a repository for pirated material, come from an interview with Tflow as well as from a September 2010 news article entitled "Wave of Website Attacks Continues—Copyright Alliance Targeted" on Skyck.com. Details of the attacks on Gene Simmons and other DDoS attacks come from various online news reports, while the notion that the campaign "went into hiatus" comes from testimony by Tflow and Topiary. Tflow claimed that the SQL injection attack on copyrightalliance.org was the first of its kind under the banner of Anonymous, though it is possible that similar attacks were carried out during Chanology.

Among the technical remarks that Tflow saw in the #savethepb channel that led him to collaborate with more skilled individuals was, verbatim, "LOIC does not overwhelm its targets with packets. It's a matter of flooding port 80. Most web servers can not handle a vast amount of open connections."

The account of the creation of the AnonOps IRC network comes from interviews with Jake Davis, Tflow, and one other key organizer of AnonOps, as well as from the "History" page on the AnonOps website: AnonOps.pro/network/history.html. There, organizers describe the original "cunning plan" of late 2010, adding that they had wondered, "How about a ship for Anons, by Anons?"

Testimony from Topiary about first "checking out" Operation Payback, and then hearing about the suicide of his father, come from interviews with Topiary himself.

References to WikiLeaks and the leaking of 250,000 diplomatic cables come from a wealth of mainstream news reports that were published in November and December of 2010, such as a November 28 article in the *Guardian* entitled "How 25,000 U.S. Embassy Cables Were Leaked," as well as the *New York Magazine* story "Bradley Manning's Army of One," published on July 3, 2011. The assertion that State Department staff were barred from visiting the WikiLeaks website came from my discussions with an anonymous State Department source. The description of the attack by The Jester on WikiLeaks comes from various news reports, such as "The Jester Hits WikiLeaks Site with XerXeS DoS Attack," by Infosec Island, published on November 29, 2010, as well as from testimony by Topiary and references in leaked chat logs. The account of the subsequent nixing of funding services by PayPal,

MasterCard, and Visa to WikiLeaks comes from a range of mainstream news reports.

Details throughout this chapter about the discussions that took place in the #command channel on AnonOps—e.g., first going after PayPal to stoke up publicity; operator names like Nerdo, Owen, and Token; or the collaboration with botmasters Civil and Switch—were originally sourced from Topiary, who had been invited into the channel and was friends with several AnonOps IRC operators. Much of this information was corroborated by news reports as well as by blog posts written by Panda Securities researcher Sean-Paul Correll, who closely tracked the PayPal attacks. Though Correll has been on sick leave from Panda Securities for much of 2011 and was unavailable for interviews, one of his colleagues e-mailed me additional, never-before-published details of his conversations with the botmaster Switch on IRC. The operator names Nerdo, Token, and Fennic were associated with real names and faces when the four young men accused of cyber crimes under these names appeared in Westminster Magistrates Court on September 7, 2011: Peter David Gibson (accused of computer offenses under the nickname Peter), Christopher Weatherhead (accused of offenses under the name Nerdo), and Ashley Rhodes (Nikon_elite). Because he was a minor, the real name of the seventeen-year-old known as Fennic could not be revealed for legal reasons. Further details, such as the nickname BillOReilly, came from screenshots of AnonOps IRC published on Encyclopedia Dramatica.

Details about the numbers of people piling into AnonOps IRC during the PayPal and MasterCard attacks were sourced from Sean-Paul Correll's research as well as from testimony by Topiary in the month or two after the attacks.

Dialogue from the public #OperationPayback IRC channel, such as "Do you think this is the start of something big?" came via an online database of AnonOps chat logs from December 8, 2010, searchable here: http://blyon.com/Irc/.

Content from the digital flyer that contains instructions for using LOIC was taken directly from the flyer, which is still available online. The LOIC message to PayPal servers was cited in the Ars Technica article "FBI Raids Texas Colocation Facility in 4chan DDoS Probe," published in late 2010; the exact date is not shown on the online article, which cites log entries in a search request by the FBI.

The notion that operators probably did not want public attention focused on botnets because it could lead to heat from the authorities comes from a conversation with academic and Anonymous expert Gabriella Coleman.

Details about Ryan and the use of his botnet on OpItaly, and about the manipulation of numbers, come from testimony by Topiary. Information about the fourteen people arrested for using LOIC against PayPal comes from wide-ranging news reports, including the *Financial Times* story "FBI Arrests 14 Suspects in PayPal Attack," published on July 20, 2011. The detail about Ryan's mental health was sourced from the testimony of his lawyer, Ben Cooper, who told a court hearing on June 25, 2011, that his client had been diagnosed with Asperger's syndrome since his arrest.

A note about lying to the press: did supporters of Anonymous lie to me in interviews? Sometimes, yes. Was I aware this was going on? Yes, though admittedly not always to start with. Over time, if I was not sure about a key point, I would seek to corroborate it with others. Such is the case with statements presented as fact in this book. My approach to Anons who were lying to me was to simply go along with their stories, acting as if I were impressed with what they were saying in the hope of teasing out more information that I could later confirm. I have signposted certain anecdotes in this book with the word "claimed"—e.g., a person "claimed" that a story is true. Not everyone in Anonymous and LulzSec lied all the time, however, and there were certain key sources who were more trustworthy than others and whose testimony I tended to listen to more closely, chief among them being Jake Davis.

Tflow created the #reporter channel for AnonOps, according to Topiary. Some dialogue that refers to the #over9000 channel comes from the leaked #HQ logs.

Chapter 8: Weapons that Backfired

Much of the detail in this chapter about the bugs inherent in LOIC comes from online and face-to-face interviews with a programmer and former supporter of Anonymous who does not want to be identified. Additional descriptions of IRC, such as the topics at the top of chat channels, come from my own observations when visiting the chat network and from rumors about "Feds" crawling the network, which were mentioned by Topiary and other Anons that I occasionally chatted with, as well as from online articles about the general usage of IRC and the role of operators, such as "The IRC Operators Guide" on irchelp.org. Some dialogue about the legalities of using LOIC comes from the online database of AnonOps chat logs, http://blyon.com/Irc/. Extra statistics about the numbers using LOIC and about AnonOps IRC can be found on Pastebin (http://pastebin.com/qQgxtKaj) and in the section about Operation Payback on the website opensecuritylab.org. Further details come from the TorrentFreak article "Behind the Scenes at Anonymous' Operation Payback," published in late 2010 (the article does not give the exact date of publication).

There was a wide range of news reports on the arrest of Martijn "Awinee" Gonlag, including "They're Watching. And They Can Bring You Down," published in the *Financial Times* on September 23, 2010.

Regarding the sentence about using LOIC behind "anonymizing software": users could not fire the tool from behind an http proxy because their "packets" would hit their own proxy, taking them offline; so it was VPN or nothing.

Details of the FBI's initial investigation into Operation Payback were sourced partly from an article on *Wired*'s ThreatLevel blog entitled "In 'Anonymous' Raids, Feds Work from List of Top 1,000 Protesters," published on July 26, 2011. Additionally, details about the initial contact between PayPal and the FBI agents, along with the passing over of one thousand IP addresses on a USB thumb drive, are sourced from an FBI arrest warrant filed on July 15, 2011, and available online.

Owen's quote "Switch is basically under a shoot on sight watch list" comes from screenshots of the #InternetFeds chat room made by freelance journalist Matthew Keys, which were e-mailed to me by Keys in early 2011. Keys was invited to observe the goings-on in InternetFeds from December of 2010 to January of 2011. He used the nickname AESCracked.

Details of the DDoS attacks on AnonOps IRC, and the details about Operation Leakspin and Operation Leakflood, come from testimonies by Anonymous supporters, including Topiary, as well as from various blog posts and news reports. The account of splitting into operations, such as the DDoSes of Sarah Palin's website and the Venezuelan government sites, comes from a variety of news reports on websites such as Panda Security's blog, ABCNews.go.com, and KnowYourMeme.com.

Details about #InternetFeds gradually usurping #command as an organizational hub popular with Anonymous hackers come from Topiary, Kayla, and two other hackers who were in the channel. Further description of dialogue and content from discussions in the channel comes from scores of screenshots provided by Matthew Keys.

Chapter 9: The Revolutionary

At least two people have corroborated that Tflow first invited Sabu into #Internetfeds; Sabu also claimed this. Details about Sabu's views come from dozens of online interviews I held with him both before and after his arrest by the FBI on June 7, 2011. My phone interviews with Monsegur provided insights into his accent, his way of speaking, the background sounds I heard when I was speaking with him, and his skills for lying and manipulation. At times they yielded little in the way of reliable insights since the phone interviews took place after he started working for the FBI and had been encouraged to feed misinformation to journalists. Further details about his life, upbringing, and address come from a series of court documents that were unsealed after the FBI revealed that he had been acting as an informant since soon after June 7, 2011. Additionally, I have sourced some details from a three-part series of Fox News stories about Monsegur published in March of 2012, one of which is entitled "Inside LulzSec, a Mastermind Turns on His Minions." Another helpful source for corroborating personal details on Monsegur was the *New York Times* story "Hacker, Informant and Party Boy of the Projects," published on March 8, 2012, in which reporters spoke to Monsegur's neighbors to piece together a picture of the man. Interviews with sources close to Hector Monsegur and the FBI investigation also contributed to the information in this chapter.

Details about the incident at Monsegur's high school with the head of security were sourced from an essay purporting to be written by Sabu on August 14, 2001, and bearing all his usual stylistic and verbal hallmarks. It was published via Pastebin on June 7, 2011 (the day of his arrest), and also sent to me via e-mail by a source. Full essay here: http://pastebin.com/TVnGwSmG.

The details about Monsegur's internships as a teenager were sourced from a web archive of the iMentor website from August 2002, which listed Monsegur as a member of the staff and provided a short biography that mentioned his stints at the NPowerNY Technology Service Corp and the Low-Income Networking and Communications Project (LINC) at the Welfare Law Center.

Text for *The Hacker Manifesto* by the Mentor can be found here: http://www.mithral.com/~beberg/manifesto.html. I have exchanged e-mails with Lloyd "the Mentor" Blankenship to corroborate details about his writing of the 1986 essay.

Sabu/Monsegur provided me with links that still showed the deface message he published on the Puerto Rican government websites. Further details on the

U.S.-China cyber war that Sabu involved himself in were corroborated by news reports such as *Wired*'s "It's (Cyber) War: China vs. U.S.," published in April of 2001, and CNN's "China-U.S. Cyber War Escalates," published on May 1, 2001. Further details about Monsegur and his attempts to start a group for local programmers in 2002 also come from a "dox" file posted by a security researcher nicknamed Le Researcher, who pasted a variety of screenshots of e-mails, deface messages, and forum posts on http://ceaxx.wordpress.com/uncovered/. Sabu's message on AnonOps, in which he asks how to find *Wired*'s John Abell, came from the online database http://blyon.com/Irc/.

Details about the anticorruption protests in Tunisia were widely reported in late December of 2010 and early January of 2011, and details of the government's phishing campaign, aimed at spying on potential dissenters, were published by Al Jazeera and Ars Technica. Censored sites would typically say "Error 404: page not found." An officially blocked site will usually say "Error 403," so the use of 404 suggested unofficial censorship. One journalist and blogger, Sofiene Chourabi, had reportedly been blocked from accessing his Facebook account; his 4,200 friends were also hacked. Other journalists claimed that their entire blogs were deleted of content, and suspected the Tunisian Internet Agency was behind it. Many Tunisians also claimed they were unable to change their Facebook passwords. The phishing operation was sophisticated, hitting several high-profile targets in a single day, and was carried out by a malware code, according to Al Jazeera, which cited "several sources." The TechHerald's Steve Ragan reported seeing examples of the embedded script and new source code injected in Gmail, Yahoo, and Facebook, confirming with four different experts that the embedded code was "siphoning off login credentials" and that "code planting of this scale could only originate from an ISP (Internet Service Provider)."

Details of the antiphishing script developed by Tflow are available on the script-sharing website http://userscripts.org, under the user name "internetfeds." Sabu, Topiary, and one other senior figure in Anonymous said that Tflow originally wrote the script. Tflow had written a browser JavaScript plug-in that effectively stripped the government's added Java code and redirected Tunisian Internet users away from its phishing servers (essentially fake Gmail, Yahoo, and Facebook sites) and back to the original, true hosts. Tunisian Internet users first had to install the Greasemonkey add-on for Firefox. Then it was just a matter of opening Firefox and going to Tools, then to Greasemonkey and New User Script, to paste in the code. Having clicked "Okay,"

Tunisians could within a minute or two access Facebook, Twitter, Blogger, Gmail, and Yahoo without exposing their login details.

I have sourced the story about Sabu remotely controlling a Tunisian man's computer to deface the website of the country's prime minister from interviews with Sabu himself, conducted in April of 2011. It's still not clear exactly how Sabu hit the Tunisian DNS, but one expert who knew him suggests he may have used a so-called smurf attack to bring down the domain servers of the Tunisian government. This refers to a unique type of denial of service (DoS, without the *d* for "distributed") attack that can be carried out from a single computer. Instead of using a botnet, it uses servers with significant space and speed to transfer the junk data. A smurf attack, specifically, needs broadcast servers. It sends a ping request to one or more of the servers, communicating (falsely) that the return IP address is the target. In hackerspeak, they are sending "spoof packets." The broadcast server then tells its entire network to respond to the target machine. One computer by itself can send perhaps 500 megabytes worth of packets at most, but a smurf attack allowed Sabu to amplify 40 gigabytes worth. A screenshot of the deface message that was uploaded to Prime Minister Ghannouchi's site is available online.

Chapter 10: Meeting the Ninja

Opening paragraphs of this chapter are sourced from online interviews with Topiary. His deface message on the government of Tunisia is still viewable here: http://pastehtml.com/view/1cw69sc.html. The point about cyber attacks on the governments of Libya, Egypt, Zimbabwe, Jordan, and Bahrain came from testimony by Topiary and was corroborated with various online news reports. I saw the deface of the Fine Gael website myself and confirmed it on the phone with a press spokesman for the Irish political party.

The description of Kayla's style of writing, which includes "lol"s and smiley faces, is based on my own observations as well as those of Anonymous members. Her view of hacking as an addiction comes from a later, online interview.

The online poll by Johnny Anonymous was described to me in a Skype interview with Johnny Anonymous himself, conducted on March 7, 2011.

Descriptions of Kayla's obsessive attempts to keep her identity hidden are sourced from interviews with Kayla, conducted largely by e-mail, in March of 2011. I was first introduced to Kayla (and Sabu, Tflow, and the others who would later make up LulzSec) by Topiary. Details of Kayla's life experiences and getting hacked by a man who "screamed" down the phone at her came from interviews also conducted in March of 2011. Kayla's involvement in the Gawker hack, which has been reported by Gawker itself, was mentioned in an Internet Relay Chat interview with the hacker on May 23, 2011, in which she described in detail how she and a group of online friends in the IRC channel #gnosis carried out their hack over the course of several months. Confirmation of the existence of Kayla's "tr0ll" IRC network came from archived web pages and Pastebin posts that mention the network, and a source who did not wish to be named. In addition to telling me about the "vulnerability in the servers hosting Gawker.com," Kayla explained that she and the other hackers managed to obtain user and password details for the site's root, MySQL. These are key features that gave them almost unfettered access to the website's database.

The vulnerability that Kayla found in the United Nations website was shown to me in an IRC chat with Kayla in the summer of 2011.

Dialogue from #InternetFeds came from screenshots of the private IRC channel e-mailed to me by Matthew Keys.

Regarding the WikiLeaks IRC network, where Kayla first met q, anyone could access it via a browser at chat.wikileaks.org. Several sources close to Wiki-Leaks confirm q (real name known but not disclosed here) had habitually lied to supporters, and that he and Assange were close, like a "stepson to Assange," according to one.

Chapter 11: The Aftermath

The opening paragraphs of this chapter are sourced primarily from phone interviews with Aaron Barr. I have seen the comment about Barr's children that prompted him and his wife to temporarily flee their home on Reddit.

Details about HBGary Inc.'s hiring of law firm Zwillinger & Genetski are sourced from phone interviews with lawyers Marc Zwillinger and Jennifer Granick. The detail about Ted Vera's and Greg Hoglund's passwords came from interviews with Topiary.

The subsequent quotes from Aaron Barr are sourced from a phone interview with Barr that took place early that Monday morning, just hours after the Super Bowl Sunday attack. HBGary's open letter is still viewable here: http://www.hbgary.com/open-letter-from-hbgary.

The hackers stored the social security numbers of HBGary employees and other data on a private Web text application called Pirate Pad, which anyone from the group could edit. The online document was later deleted. Stolen data like this often wound up gathering dust somewhere in the cloud, or on someone's computer—forgotten until an arrest turned it into evidence.

The account of Kayla informing Laurelai Bailey of the HBGary attack and then inviting her into the private IRC channel for the company's attackers, #HQ, is sourced from interviews with Bailey. Those interviews were also the source for details about Barr's controversial proposals to Hunton & Williams. In order to stumble upon Barr's all-important WikiLeaks connection, Laurelai had to first port Barr's published e-mails onto an e-mail client called Thunderbird, then transfer them to Gmail. This allowed her to search through the e-mails using key words like "WikiLeaks."

The notion that Topiary, Sabu, and Kayla didn't know about the anti-WikiLeaks proposals in the days immediately after the attack were conveyed to me by Topiary, who I was interviewing at the time. I had also been following developments after the attack and noticing that his small group was trawling through Barr's e-mails, looking for something controversial, before Laurelai spotted the motherlode.

Dialogue between the group in the #HQ room comes from logs that were eventually leaked by Laurelai to Jennifer Emick (see chapter 14). Details about the publication of the HBGary e-mails and snippets of content were sourced from the HBGary viewer itself, http://hbgary.anonleaks.ru (now offline).

Details about the investigation into HBGary, its partners, and their military contracts by U.S. congressman Hank Johnson were confirmed in a phone interview with Johnson on March 23, 2011. I first heard about the investigation on March 17, when, late that evening, Topiary saw a *Wired* story saying that Congressman Johnson had started investigating the U.S. military's contracts with HBGary Federal, Palantir Technologies, and Berico Technologies. Soon after, at least ten Democrats from the House of Representatives had signed a petition to launch an investigation into Hunton & Williams and the three security firms.

The "growing sense of unease" among the hackers comes from observations of their sometimes paranoid conversations in #HQ as well as from testimony by Topiary, who was also the source for the information about the regular phone calls with Sabu and the coded greeting "This is David Davidson." Sabu's mistrust of Laurelai is clear from his comments in #HQ, but was also corroborated by testimony from Topiary.

Jennifer Emick has confirmed that she was behind the Twitter handle @FakeGreggHoush; this has been an open secret in Anonymous since Backtrace was doxed in the early summer of 2011. I relied on interviews with both Emick and Bailey to piece together how and why Bailey ended up passing her the #HQ logs.

Part 2
Chapter 12: Finding a Voice

The opening paragraph, describing Topiary's popularity on AnonOps, including details such as the number of private messages he was regularly receiving, are sourced from interviews with Topiary as well as from observations of chat logs, IRC conversations, and statistics showing the number of times people were reaching out to him through Twitter. The detail about requests to hit various targets, such as Facebook, also comes from those interviews. According to Topiary, people sometimes directly e-mailed supporters in AnonOps or sent messages to certain representative blogs. It was difficult to track the way Anonymous chose its targets, since it was often done chaotically, spontaneously, and behind the scenes. However, for the most part, target requests that came from outside Anonymous were rarely pursued.

Details about Westboro Baptist Church are sourced from various news reports as well as from Louis Theroux's engrossing BBC documentary *The Most Hated Family in America*, first aired in 2007. The detail that Nate Phelps had accused his father, Fred, of abuse is sourced from a number of press reports including Nate Phelps's official website, which in its "Bio" page refers to his father's "extreme version of Calvinism" and "extreme physical punishments and abuse."

The February 18 press release announcing that Anonymous was going to hit Westboro—the first such announcement—appeared on AnonNews.org. The detail about an IRC operator running a search of the network's chat channels to find the organizers was sourced from interviews with Topiary. IRC operators, both within AnonOps and in other networks, regularly ran searches to keep an abreast of any odd operations that no one knew about, such as conspiracies to take down the network or improper discussions about child porn. Sometimes trolls would create a child porn channel to try to make AnonOps look illegal. This was the only topic of discussion that was banned on AnonOps IRC; everything else was fair game. Similarly, talk of hacking was banned on other networks, which was why Tflow and the other support-ers of Operation Payback migrated from networks like EFnet, Freenode, and Quakenode in late 2010—these IRC operators did not like the heat.

The follow-up press release about attacking Westboro, written by five writers in #philosoraptors, originated when one person started writing it on his com-puter and then uploaded it to Pirate Pad so others could edit it. "Dear Phred Phelps and WBC Phriends," it began. This release was much more in line with the irreverent, clownish tone of Anonymous. It went on to say, "Stay tuned, and we'll come back to play another day. We promise," and added a reprimand: "To the Media: Just because it's posted on AnonNews doesn't mean every single Anon is in agreement."

Details about *The David Pakman Show,* Pakman himself, and the live Westboro hack are sourced from a phone interview with Pakman that took place on November 18, 2011, as well as from interviews with Topiary. Comments made by Shirley Phelps-Roper on Pakman's show are sourced from YouTube videos. All dialogue from the show regarding the live Westboro hack was sourced from the main YouTube video of the program. Pakman's and Topi-ary's accounts differ about how much Pakman knew of what was going to happen to Westboro's website during the show. Pakman denied ever know-ing that Topiary or anyone else from Anonymous was going to hit the West-boro site in the middle of his show. "No. Absolutely no," Pakman said in the phone interview, conducted about eight months after the event. "They basi-cally said, 'We'll come on your show to talk about this.' It was very vague. I said, 'I'm interested. Would you be able to come on with Shirley?' and they said yes. I reached out to Westboro.... They both said yes. The timing worked out." Today the number of hits on the video of the live Westboro hack has approached the two million mark and it is the most popular video ever posted for *The David Pakman Show*.

Regarding Topiary's deface messages: he wrote all of them in a very simple text-editing program called Notepad++. Every PC has Notepad in its Accessories folder, but Notepad++ is a free program that one-upped the original Notepad by allowing users to organize their documents in tabs, enabling them to have mul-tiple open files. Topiary only had to hit the left arrow key on his laptop to get different text formats, a list of links to vulnerable websites, or other Anonymous press releases he hadn't read yet. He would make all his deface messages com-patible with the Web language HTML by converting them at a website called Pastehtml.com. If Topiary copied and pasted a two-hundred-word message directly from Microsoft Word, it would likely show up in Pastehtml.com with the Anonymous logo too far to the left, or with odd spaces within the text, which he'd have to then tinker with in the so-called source code, the complicated programming commands behind the text. Writing it in Notepad++, on the other hand, meant it was automatically "cleaned up," so that when it was converted into an HTML file it looked exactly the same online as it did offline on his computer. No tweaking required. In total, Topiary produced approximately ten deface messages using this method for Anonymous, and helped others to produce an additional ten. The use of a simple program, combined with Topiary's basic knowledge of HTML, are the reasons that all his messages, which made up the majority of defacements reported by the news media in the spring of 2011, appeared as plain text on a white background.

Chapter 13: Conspiracy (Drives Us Together)

The opening paragraphs of this chapter are sourced from interviews at the time (and then months afterward for hindsight) with Topiary. Sabu and Kayla had moved on from the HBGary attack and were not involved in reading through Barr's e-mails. Both also claimed to have busy lives outside of Anonymous and the Internet. In my phone interviews with Sabu, for instance, he was often being interrupted by people in his household and by other phone calls.

Details about Barrett Brown's experience delving through the HBGary e-mails, forming a team of researchers, and his personal life are derived from my phone interview with Brown, conducted on November 24, 2011. Further details about his dealings with Topiary and other Anons have come from interviews with Topiary. I also sourced an audio recording of Brown's phone interview with William Wansley, which he uploaded to the media-sharing site MediaFire.com. I had been alerted in advance to the Radio Payback appearance of Brown, Topiary, and WhiteKidney and was taking notes as it happened, before I downloaded the audio file itself. The description of the *NBC Nightly News* broadcast with Michael Isikoff was taken from my viewing of the video online. The note that Brown's "bones ached" because of withdrawal from Suboxone, along with the point about his relapse in New York in April of 2011, were sourced from my phone interview with Brown. Some extra details about Operation Metal Gear and its research were sourced partly from Brown's Project PM wiki, http://wiki.echelon2.org/; partly from the Metal Gear website, http://opmetalgear.zxq.net/, before it became dis-used; and partly from the Booz Allen Hamilton website.

Descriptions of the general opinion among Anons toward Brown were sourced from discussions with a handful of Anons, including William, as well as from my observation of relevant comments on AnonOps IRC. Brown thought he saw a connection to HBGary's interest in bidding for a contract to sell the U.S. military personnel management software, a technology that essentially allowed the user to spy on others over the Internet and social media.

Details about the young man nicknamed OpLeakS and his offer of apparently ex-plosive information from Bank of America were sourced from interviews with Brown and Topiary, with further details coming from the bankofamericas-uck.com website, OpLeakS's Twitter feed, and a variety of news reports. E-mails posted on OpLeakS's website clearly showed the name of the disgruntled Bank of America employee who was "leaking" information, Brian Penny.

When he used the term "nerdy hacker group," Topiary was referring to the hacker groups of the eighties and nineties, some of which used skull-and-crossbones imagery and generally took themselves too seriously.

It was not unusual in Anonymous to hop from one operation to another, reflecting the sometimes limited attention spans of its groups and supporters. Along with Operation Metal Gear, there was Operation Wisconsin, Operation Eter-nal Ruin, and operations focused on Libya and Italy, each of which had anywhere from two to a dozen people involved. In early 2011, the original version of Operation Payback, launched against copyright companies, came back for round two by targeting more copyright-related websites. Topiary observed, however, that its proponents kept switching targets—for instance, they called agcom.it a target, causing a few people to be fired but failing to generate enough momentum to take the site down—providing others with a reason to move on to something else. Frequently switching targets is one of the crucial reasons why Operation Payback had dwindled to around fifty people in October of 2010 and nearly died out—until WikiLeaks came along by chance, and thousands of people suddenly jumped in.

Chapter 14: Backtrace Strikes

The opening paragraphs of this chapter are sourced from interviews with Jennifer Emick, with some added details—including the name of her Skype group, the Treehouse—coming from Anonymous-related blogs.

Details about the arrests in the Netherlands and Britain are sourced from various mainstream news reports. The U.K.'s Metropolitan Police announced on January 27 that they had arrested five people in morning raids across the country. According to a report in The TechHerald at the time, they were allegedly tracked with "little more than server logs and confirmation from their ISP."

Descriptions of what Emick was finding on DigitalGangsters.com were originally sourced from Emick and corroborated by my own observations of the website, especially its "About" page. I also interviewed a member of the forum site nicknamed Jess, who was a close friend of the twenty-three-year-old Seattle woman on the site who went by the name Kayla and whose real name is Kayla Anderson. Jess confirmed that the woman is not the same Kayla of LulzSec, though she and her friend considered the hacker known as Xyrix as an acquaintance. It was most likely a coincidence, she added, that Xyrix was being connected to both a Kayla from DigitalGangsters.com and the Kayla of LulzSec. Emick doubted this account when I put it to her in November of 2011 and believed that there was a connection between the two Kaylas.

Incidentally, Corey "Xyrix" Barnhill has denied being Kayla, both by leaving comments on online news reports about Kayla and by e-mailing me directly. The AnonOps Kayla also told me and certain members of Anonymous that she went along with rumors that she was Xyrix because it helped obfuscate her real identity.

The descriptions of YTCracker and the story about the hack on DigitalGangsters.com were sourced from phone interviews with Bryce "YTCracker" Case himself, as well as from my observations of the deface message that was posted on his site when Corey "Xyrix" Barnhill, Mike "Virus" Nieves, and Justin "Null" Perras had, according to Case, switched the DigitalGangster.com domains to point at their own servers.

My own observation of DigitalGangsters.com showed posts advertising jobs that required hacking into websites via SQL injection, stealing databases of names and e-mail addresses, or just stealing addresses and sending them to spammers. A database with passwords was worth more, since spammers could then send spam from legitimate addresses. Occasionally a thread would start with a post seeking "freelancers" who could program in C, Objective-C, C#, VB, Java, and JavaScript. One post from June of 2010 had the title "DGs [Digital Gangsters] in Washington? Be my mail man in the middle," followed by: "Heres how it works. A delivery gets shipped to your address, You open the package remove item, Reship the item to me in a new container with a false return address. when item arrives you get paid. interested?"

The description of Jin-Soo Byun was sourced from interviews with Jennifer Emick and Laurelai Bailey; the note that Aaron Barr was helping her investigation was sourced from an interview with Barr. The details about Emick setting up the initial Backtrace investigation into Anonymous, and then tracking down "Hector Montsegur" [*sic*], are sourced from interviews with Emick. Descriptions of some of Sabu's defaces come from screenshots provided by Sabu himself as well as from a blog post by Le Researcher, an anti-Anonymous campaigner who works with Emick. Another group that includes longtime EFnet user Kelley Hallissey claims it doxed Sabu in December 2010 and passed his details to Backtrace in February 2011. Emick denies this.

Sabu's statement that he was "going to drive over to [Laurelai's] house and mess him up" was sourced from Topiary's testimony.

The origins of the word *backtrace* point to one of the most notorious 4chan and Anonymous operations ever conducted. It started in July of 2010, when 4chan's /b/ users began trolling an eleven-year-old girl named Jessica Leonhardt. Online, she was known as Jessi Slaughter, and was a minor e-celebrity after uploading videos of herself onto a site called StickyDrama. When other StickyDrama users started bullying Slaughter, she filmed a series of tearful ripostes, including one in which her mustached father could be seen over her shoulder jabbing his finger at the webcam and shouting, "You bunch of lying, no-good punks! And I know who it's comin' from! Because I BACKTRACED it!" The broadside spawned a number of Internet catchphrases and memes, including "backtrace," "Ya done goofed," and "Consequences will never be the same!" By February of 2011, Jessi Slaughter had been placed under police protection and admitted to a mental institution. The following August, her father died of a heart attack at the age of fifty-three.

The dialogue among Topiary, Kayla, Tflow, and AVunit, starting with the quote "They all think i'm Xyrix!" was sourced from their March 21, 2011, discussion on a private IRC channel called Seduce. By this point, Topiary had introduced me to Kayla (with whom I had been communicating by e-mail) and it was in this room that I first spoke to AVunit, Tflow, and Sabu. From there I organized separate interviews with each of them. The group was already communicating with each other in their own separate channel, and #seduce was set up for the purpose of speaking with me and providing testimony for this book. The name Seduce came from the late-February revelation in the #HQ chat log that Kayla would be talking to me; she quipped that "She wrote good stuff about us so far...she talked with Topiary. he has her seduced I guess." Later, when the group would switch to a different IRC server, they would create another channel, named #charmy, also for talking exclusively with me. I was later told that Sabu was extremely wary of talking to me in the #seduce channel in March, and I observed that he was rarely in the room or would make excuses to leave. On April 13, 2011, however, we held our first real interview on IRC and he became more forthcoming.

It is unclear if "Christopher Ellison," the name associated with AVunit in Backtrace's final document, was correct or not. There have been no press reports or police announcements related to the arrest of someone connected to the nickname, and no information about the whereabouts of the real AVunit as of mid-April 2012.

The study by Francois Paget was published on October 21, 2011, in a McAfee blog post entitled "The Rise and Fall of Anonymous."

The detail about the FBI contacting Jennifer Emick comes from conversations with Emick. The additional point that the FBI needed to wait to corroborate Sabu's identity and gather enough evidence to threaten him with a long sentence was sourced from the FoxNews.com report "Infamous International Hacking Group LulzSec Brought Down by Own Leader," published on March 6, 2012.

Laurelai Bailey hadn't been the only log leaker. Less damaging, though still embarrassing, was a leak from freelance television and Web journalist Matthew Keys, who had been given access to #InternetFeds from December of 2010 to January 6, 2011, when he was banned after the channel's members suspected him of leaking information to the *Guardian*. Sabu later claimed that Keys had given away administrator access to the online publishing system of Tribune, his former employer, in return for the chance to "hang out in our channel." Keys denies this.

A note on making IRC channels: generally, the person who comes up with the idea for a channel is the person who creates the channel. Creators can make channels more secure by adding commands like +isPu and +k to gain more control of who comes in. But sometimes the best way to make a channel secure is to make it completely open, with no invite policy at all, and to keep switching between different channels every day or two. Making a channel "invite only" is "like holding a red flag in front of a bull," according to AVunit, who added that this was why he and his the team avoided invite-only policies. To find each other, team members would use normal IRC queries, check which channel was active, or just type in the relevant channel in IRC and rejoin the discussion.

It's worth noting that Backtrace itself was the subject of numerous doxing episodes. From at least the spring of 2011, a number of Anonymous supporters unveiled its members as Jennifer Emick, Jin-Soo Byun, and John Rubenstein, publishing their home addresses, telephone numbers, some family details, and other online profiles on the web tool Pastebin.

Chapter 15: Breaking Away

The descriptions of "three ways to respond to a dox" were derived from my conversations with Topiary and my observations of the way Anonymous supporters, such as Ryan Cleary, reacted to having their true identities unveiled. Further details about "drama" in Anonymous and the culture bred through the morass of channels on IRC were sourced from my conversations with adherents of Anonymous and my own observations. The detail about Aaron Barr's idea for getting into private coding channels, as well as the description in this chapter of "No," come from Topiary's testimony. The details of Renee Haefer's FBI raid were sourced from an interview that Haefer gave to Gawker for an online story entitled "An Interview with a Target of the FBI's Anonymous Probe," published on February 11, 2011. Details on the five Britons arrested on January 27 are sourced from a Metropolitan Police announcement and from news reports.

The paragraphs detailing Topiary's elaborate getaway were sourced from interviews with Topiary himself. I have edited the faked log substantially for brevity; the log had mentioned that Topiary's wireless router had been left on. This was meant to cause further confusion among the hundreds of regular users on AnonOps, because routers were the number one item that was looked for in a raid. The ruse almost got too elaborate. One online female friend was already freaking out so much that she had tried contacting Topiary's then-girlfriend, a Canadian girl he had met online about three years prior. Problematically, this friend then let slip to others that Topiary's girlfriend existed. Until then, he had been trying to insulate his girlfriend from his activities with Anonymous, so that she would not be roped in as a co-conspirator if he were ever arrested. To fix this problem, he wrote up another faked message, this time from his girlfriend, hinting that she was suddenly jealous of the worried female friend. The suggestion distracted the girl enough from suspecting the truth: that Topiary had not been arrested but had broken away from Anonymous.

Quotes from the Anonymous press release directed at Sony were sourced from the press release itself, which is still available on AnonNews.org. Details of William's involvement in OpSony come from interviews with him. William also e-mailed me a link to some of the handiwork of SonyRecon, including Sony CEO Howard Stringer's old and current home addresses in New York, his wife's name, the names of his children, and the name of his son's old school. The post is still online at JustPaste.

The details about Sony's lawsuit against George Hotz come from various mainstream news reports.

"Angering millions of gamers around the world" is my interpretation of myriad angry comments on forums for gamers as well as on the official PlayStation Network website, which contains statements showing that the PSN is used by tens of millions of people.

Sony's eight-page letter to the U.S. House of Representatives dated May 3, 2011, is viewable on Flickr.

The publication of 653 nicknames and IP addresses on AnonOps was pasted in a public document online, which I have seen and which was brought to light by various news reporters, including by *Forbes*'s Andy Greenberg. His story "Mutiny Within Anonymous May Have Exposed Hackers' IP Addresses" was published on May 9, 2011. I made the point that "AnonOps IRC became a ghost town" as a result of my own and Topiary's observations of the network. The statement by various AnonOps operators that they were "profoundly sorry for this drama" was posted and reposted on various blogs. The original post also mentioned that AnonOps would "stage a comeback and return to full strength eventually." Ryan Cleary, who was behind the IP leak, gave an interview to the tech blog thinq_, saying that the operators behind AnonOps were "publicity hungry" and had "begun engaging in operations simply to grab headlines" and "feed their own egos." "They just like seeing things destroyed," thinq_ quoted Ryan as saying.

I saw the dox file about Ryan when it was first posted online. It included his real address in Wickford, Essex, his cell phone number, and the names and ages of his parents. The dox page said that Ryan had been "owned" by Evo, adding

"Who's the 'pet' now, bitch?" The document also gave "shouts," or acknowl-
edgments, to Sabu, Kayla, Owen, #krack, and all of AnonOps.

The assertion that Anonymous was "starting to look like a joke" comes from my
own observations as well as discussions with supporters.

Chapter 16: Talking About a Revolution

Most of the details and descriptions from this chapter were derived from interviews
with Topiary and Sabu over the course of several months, including Internet Relay Chat interviews, discussions by phone, and face-to-face meetings.

The point about New York mayor Rudy Giuliani increasing the city's police force
to 40,000 was corroborated by the April 11, 2000, Congressional Record for
the House of Representatives and by press reports.

The details about COINTELPRO were corroborated by information on the FBI's
own website, which states that the project was "rightly criticized by Congress
and the American people for abridging first amendment rights and for other
reasons." See http://vault.fbi.gov/cointel-pro

The point that Kayla, Tflow, and AVunit had been on "breaks" before the for-
mation of LulzSec was corroborated by Sabu and at least one other LulzSec
supporter.

The quote "Most professional and high-level hacks are never detected" comes
from an interview with a hacker supporting Anonymous who did not wish
to be named.

Chapter 17: Lulz Security

The majority of details in this chapter were sourced from interviews with Topiary,
Sabu, and Kayla. Additional details, including dialogue from Pwnsauce, was
derived from my observation of discussions among Topiary, Kayla, Tflow,
AVunit, and Pwnsauce in the IRC channel #charmy, which was set up for
discussions that I could repeat in this book. I also held interviews with some
in the group, such as Pwnsauce, in this channel.

The assertion that it "took a week for Fox's IT administrators to notice the
breach" was derived from interviews in #charmy.

Regarding the original Twitter feed for LulzSec, @LulzLeaks: the original account that contains that first tweet is still online.

I corroborated that LulzSec had indeed posted a database of potential contestants for *The X Factor* by speaking to a spokesman from Fox about twenty-four hours after the hack was first announced. I also saw the published database on Pastebin.

Chapter 18: The Resurrection of Topiary and Tupac

Details about the PBS hack were sourced from interviews with the hackers involved, as well as from a post that Topiary had put on Pastebin that gave details about what sort of tools, such as Havij, the group had used. According to a March 2012 article on darkreading.com, the tool "favored by hacktivists" was created by Iranian hackers, and its name is derived from the Persian word for "carrot," also a nickname for the male sexual organ.

The statement that "people in the #anonleaks chat room on AnonOps IRC went into a frenzy" when Topiary posted something on Twitter from his personal account was sourced from interviews with Topiary after he visited the chat network.

Chapter 19: Hacker War

Regarding Pastebin's boost in traffic, the website's controllers would later show their appreciation for LulzSec by retweeting @LulzSec's July 13, 2011, announcement that "If @pastebin reaches 75,000 followers we'll engage in a mystery operation that will cause mayhem." (This was one of the rare tweets from @LulzSec after the group officially disbanded.) Hours later, @Pastebin tweeted, "The # of followers @pastebin is growing very rapidly since @lulzsec is sending their love," followed by "The twitter madness continues thanks to @lulzsec." That same day, Topiary exchanged e-mails with Pastebin owner Jeroen Vader, a twenty-eight-year-old Dutch entrepreneur, in which Topiary requested a "unique green crown" icon next to his personal "Topiary" account on Pastebin, which, when highlighted, would also say "CEO of consuming pie." Vader agreed, saying, "I'll be sure to fix you up with a very special crown. Many thanks for trusting Pastebin with your 'special' releases." Pastebin statements from LulzSec and Anonymous rank among the top-trafficked posts on Pastebin, along with LulzSec's final "50 Days of Lulz" release on June 25, 2011, which clocked 411,354 page views as of April 3, 2012. (Pastebin hosts ads on its site, so the extra traffic will have aided its bottom line.) Ironically, Vader said in early April of 2012 that he would hire more staff to help police "sensitive information" that got posted onto the site, according to BBC News.

Details about The Jester's hangout on 2600 and the other people who frequented it were sourced from LulzSec's leaked #pure-elite chat logs, from interviews with Topiary, and from my own observations of the 2600 IRC network. The points about the origins of *2600: The Hacker Quarterly* were sourced from various Web articles, including the *PCWorld* feature story "Hacking's History," published on April 10, 2001.

The information about the creation of a secondary ring of LulzSec supporters was sourced from conversations with Topiary and Sabu. The detail about Antisec and its original adherents comprising "a few hundred skilled hackers" was sourced from my conversations with Andrew "weev" Auernheimer, who was a hacker during the early days of the Antisec movement, and from various Web articles, including the 2002 *Wired* story "White-Hat Hate Crimes on the Rise."

The nicknames of "secondary crew members" of LulzSec, such as Neuron and M_nerva, were sourced from the #pure-elite chat logs that were first leaked online by Pastebin on June 5, 2011, in a post entitled "LulzSec Private Log." The logs were republished by The *Guardian* three weeks later, on June 25, which garnered more mainstream media attention. Further descriptions about the room and its members, and the context of their discussions, were sourced from interviews with Topiary and with one other hacker, who did not wish to be named.

The detail that Adrian Lamo was diagnosed with Asperger's is sourced from the *Wired* article, "Ex-Hacker Adrian Lamo Institutionalized, Diagnosed with Asperger's," published May 20, 2010.

Chapter 20: More Sony, More Hackers

Regarding LulzSec and Sony: a couple of days before the PBS attack, LulzSec had already published two databases of internal information from the website of Sony Japan. It failed to cause a stir, since Topiary had simply pasted specific Web addresses that were vulnerable to a hack by simple SQL injection. One of them, for example, looked like this: http://www.sonymusic.co.jp/bv/cro-magnons/track.php?item=7419. Topiary announced the finds with a press release, telling other hackers, "Two other databases hosted on this boxxy box. Go for them if you want." He added that the "innards" were "tasty, but not very exciting." Details about the way LulzSec's core and secondary members gathered and explored website vulnerabilities within the network of Sony and elsewhere were sourced from discussions with Topiary, as well as with Sabu and Kayla. Dialogue among the hackers was also sourced from interviews with the trio. Most of the data that LulzSec stole from Sony came from the websites SonyPictures.com, SonyBMG.nl, and SonyBMG.bg—but 95 percent of the hoard came from SonyPictures.

Descriptions of Topiary's style of writing are based on my own observations of the press releases he wrote and the Twitter feed he manned.

Context on the extent of the cyber attacks on Sony was sourced from the cyber security website attrition.org and its article "Absolute Sownage: A Concise History of Recent Sony Attacks." It includes what is probably the most comprehensive table of cyber attacks on the company that took place between the months of April and July 2011.

The rumors about the PlayStation Network hack involving a disgruntled employee and the sale of a database for $200,000 come from press reports and from one source within Anonymous who does not wish to be named. It was unclear if the PSN hackers had sold it all on a carders' market or in chunks. But in certain online markets it was possible to make $1,000 selling a six-year-old database containing the names of 300,000 users—the price in the market at large depended on the age of the database, according to people familiar with the matter. This meant that more than 100 million fresh logins from Sony would easily have been worth tens of thousands of dollars. A June 23, 2011, Reuters article cited a lawsuit against Sony that claimed that the company had laid off employees in the unit responsible for network security two weeks before the data breach occurred, and that while the company "spent lavishly" on security to protect its own corporate data it failed to do the same for its customer data. The lawsuit, filed in a U.S. District Court, cited a "confidential witness."

Details about the way LulzSec attacked Karim Hijazi come from interviews with Topiary and Kayla, as well as from chat logs released by both LulzSec and Hijazi. Further details come from telephone interviews with Hijazi in the days after his attack was announced and from interviews with his press spokesman.

Details about the ~el8 hacking group were sourced from their four e-zines, which are still available online, and from the 2002 *Wired* article "White-Hat Hate Crimes on the Rise."

Details about Andrew "weev" Auernheimer's disclosure of a security flaw for iPad users on AT&T's website were sourced from interviews with Auernheimer, from the Gawker story "Apple's Worst Security Breach: 114,000 iPad Owners Exposed," dated June 9, 2010, and from the CNET article "AT&T-iPad Site Hacker to Fight on in Court," published on September 12, 2011. In July 2011, a federal grand jury in Newark, New Jersey, indicted Auernheimer on one count of conspiracy to gain access to computers and one count of identity theft. From September 2011 and as of mid-April 2012, he was on bail, and reportedly banned from using IRC or consorting with people from his hacking group.

The statement that the AnonOps IRC was "a mess, everyone was on edge" was sourced from my own observations of the chat network and from interviews with Topiary.

The assertion that a few white hats "secretly wished they could be part of the fun" was sourced from my observations of comments made by white hat security specialists on blogs and on Twitter, which often professed admiration for LulzSec and expressed gratitude that the group had demonstrated the necessity of the Internet security profession. A good example is the article by Australian security expert Patrick Gray on his risky.biz blog entitled "Why We Secretly Love LulzSec," posted on June 8, 2011. The post quickly went viral on Twitter.

Regarding Ryan's DDoS attack on LulzSec's public IRC channel—he had been sending the same message to anyone who was an operator in the IRC channel.

Chapter 21: Stress and Betrayal

Details about Kayla's side operation were sourced from interviews with Kayla and Topiary, while dialogue in this chapter was sourced from the leaked #pure-elite logs. Further context on the InfraGard hack, #pure-elite discussions, and Bitcoin donations comes from interviews with the founding members of LulzSec. Some dialogue, such as the reaction to the $7,800 BitCoin donation, was also sourced from interviews.

NATO's draft report on Anonymous can be found on the organization's website here: http://www.nato-pa.int/default.asp?SHORTCUT=2443. It was first mentioned on tech blogs, such as thinq, in early June.

The deleting code rm -rf/* is well known among Web trolls, who at one time made a practice of telling Mac and Linux users to type the code into their copy of Terminal, the application that allows users to engage with their computers using a command-line interface. This can lead users to inadvertently wipe out their hard drives. According to KnowYourMeme.com, the trolling scheme against PC users has been around since the early 2000s, but became popular through its promulgation on 4chan around 2006. Users of /b/ would post digital flyers or start discussion threads saying, for example, that Microsoft had included a folder called system32 on all PCs and that this folder held 32 gigabytes of "worthless crap." They added that the company did this to sell more system-cleaning software, and that the way to get back at money-hungry Microsoft was to delete the file. This was, of course, completely untrue.

Here is a translation of the UNIX code rm -rf/* itself: "rm" is the command short for remove; a blank space then indicates the end of the command. The "-" begins the options, with "r" meaning "recursively delete all directories" and "f" meaning "override file permissions." "/*" means that everything after the root of the tree ("/") is to be affected. The entire command means "remove everything forcefully."

The assertion that "many news outlets bought this line"—i.e., the line that LulzSec had hacked InfraGard in response to the Pentagon announcement—was sourced from a number of news reports. Among them is the digitaltrends.com story "LulzSec Hacks FBI Affiliate, Infragard."

Details about the arrest of Sabu were sourced partly from Fox News reports, including the one entitled "Infamous International Hacking Group LulzSec Brought Down by Own Leader," and partly from an interview with an anonymous source who had knowledge of the arrest and FBI investigation. Further details about Sabu's arrest and his later appearance in a secret court hearing are laid out in chapter 26.

Details about Cisco's promotional tweet appearing on Twitter searches for LulzSec were sourced by my own observations and were corroborated by Cisco spokesman John Earnhardt, who said that LulzSec was a "term of interest" in the security industry. The day after I wrote a blog post on the promotion for *Forbes,* entitled "How Cisco Is Capitalizing on LulzSec Hackers' Popularity" and published on June 15, 2011, the promotion disappeared.

Joseph K. Black, founder of the Black & Berg IT security company, most likely faked the attack on his own website. This assertion is based on interviews with Topiary, who said that no one in the group had hit or had planned to hit

Black & Berg, and on interviews with Jennifer Emick, who spent some time investigating Black. I also base this conclusion on my opinion that Black is not a credible source. Cyber security and antivirus expert Rob Rosenberger wrote a column for SecurityCritics.org on February 15, 2011, in which he referred to Black as a "charlatan" whose activities until that point already "qualified as 'unethical behavior' done for shameless self-promotion." The cyber security site attrition.org later wrote a damning indictment of Black on February 28, 2011, in an article entitled "Joseph K. Black: Social Media Experiment Gone Horribly Wrong," which offered the prediction that Black would never obtain his professed dream job of "National Cybersecurity Advisor." It posted screenshots of his Twitter feed from January of 2011, including tweets such as "I just did my 2nd line of coke and it's only 4.15; WOW!" Another tweet, directed toward Attrition itself, said, "Your [sic] just jealous that the Feds haven't taken you off the grid yet. Sucker.Im untouchable.I got the Feds in my pocket.Im comfy." In October of 2011, Black was pursued by police in a thirty-five-minute car chase over four U.S. counties, after which he got out of his car holding a small dog and pointed his finger at the police, making shooting noises. He was promptly Tasered (source: "Omaha Man Caught after Early Morning Pursuit," the *North Platte Bulletin,* October 31, 2011). By early 2012, Black & Berg had folded and Black had posted a photo of himself on an about.me Web page, where he listed himself as "Advisor to Anonymous and #Antisec operations." In the photo, Black was standing in front of a mirror, wearing a hoodie, sunglasses, and a gold chain necklace. Black did not respond to a question e-mailed to him on the matter of his website's defacement, or to an interview request. Ironically, in spite of the overwhelming evidence that the deface on Joseph K. Black's website had been self-inflicted for publicity purposes, British prosecutors would later list an attack on Black & Berg among the charges against Jake Davis and three other young men associated with LulzSec.

Details about other copycat hacker groups, such as LulzSec Brazil and LulzRaft, were sourced from the groups' own Twitter feeds, announcements, and press reports, and from interviews with LulzSec members.

Topiary's statement "I'm starting to get quite worried some arrests might actually happen" was made in an interview with me.

Chapter 22: The Return of Ryan, the End of Reason

Details in this chapter about activities within LulzSec, dialogue about the disappearance of Sabu, and descriptions of Ryan were sourced from interviews
with LulzSec's founding members. Details about Topiary's first call with
Sabu were sourced from interviews with Topiary.

The name David Davidson comes from the widely panned 2000 comedy film
Freddy Got Fingered, starring Tom Green. It has often been used online as
a joke name, but perhaps not enough to be considered an outright Internet
meme.

Ryan first rekindled his relationship with LulzSec's members by offering to let
the group house its IRC network on his servers. This was a welcome offer,
although eventually the crew would be hopping between servers owned by
AnonOps and the public IRC networks provided by EFnet, Rizon, and 2600.

Topiary did not believe that the dox released for Ryan earlier that year by Evo
was real. He also believed that the real Ryan was relatively safe, since Ryan
claimed, for instance, to have his neighbor receive all his packages, which
were addressed to a fake name anyway, before passing them over to him, so
that he never had to give out his real address.

The Skype number 1-614-LULZSEC was off at all times and redirected to another Google number, which was also offline and redirected instantly to the
main Skype account that Topiary and Ryan were using. This account had
been registered via a fake Gmail account on a random IP address.

I have sourced the assertion that Assange was "chuckling" to himself from interviews with Topiary, who said that when he was first talking to Assange on
IRC, Assange claimed that he and others in WikiLeaks had "laughed" when
they heard about the DDoS attack on the CIA.

Details about Julian Assange's state of affairs in June of 2011, including his defense
against extradition and the wearing of an electronic tag, were sourced from
various press reports, such as "Julian Assange Awaits High Court Ruling on
Extradition," published by the *Guardian* on November 2, 2011.

Details about the IRC discussions within LulzSec (first between Topiary and
Sabu, then among other members of the team) were sourced from interviews
with Topiary and with one other hacker associated with LulzSec who does
not wish to be named. I have also seen and taken screenshots of the video of
Assange taken by q, which was temporarily uploaded to YouTube. The video
showed the IRC discussion between LulzSec and a panning shot of Assange

looking at his laptop. Dialogue from the discussion between Sabu and q is taken from the same video, which also featured text from the IRC channel they were both in at the time. Sources close to WikiLeaks confirm that q had organized meetings in the past between Assange and other third parties via IRC, and that q is from Iceland. Regarding the filename RSA 128: RSA is a cryptographic algorithm (by Rivest, Shamir, and Adleman). The 128 would refer to the key length, or the strength of encryption measured in bits.

Chapter 23: Out with a Bang

Details about 4chan's reaction to LulzSec were sourced from interviews with William and Topiary. Ironically enough, LulzSecurity.com was at one point hosted in the same data center as 4chan, according to Topiary.

Regarding the release of 62,000 e-mails and passwords, Topiary had uploaded the database a second time to the file hosting site MediaFire.com. However, before it was again taken down, random users had downloaded it almost 40,000 times.

Further details about LulzSec's instigation of a revived Antisec movement, and details about Topiary's relations with Ryan, were sourced from interviews with Topiary; context for these details was provided by interviews with Sabu.

Details about someone from SOCA e-mailing the Metropolitan Police about a DDoS attack were sourced from prosecutor notes, which were passed on to the arrested LulzSec members.

Details about the arrest of Ryan were sourced from press reports, such as the *Daily Mail* article "British Teenager Charged over Cyber Attack on CIA as Pirate Group Takes Revenge on 'Snitches Who Framed Him,'" published on June 22, 2011, and from interviews with LulzSec members. Soon after Ryan's arrest, an Anon with links to Ryan Cleary approached Topiary on IRC and told him with dead seriousness that a photographer from the *Sun* was planning to fly to Holland to try to snap a photo of the "real Topiary."

Details about the Arizona police leak, and dialogue from the discussion between LulzSec founding members about disbanding, were sourced from interviews with Topiary, with some added context provided by Sabu in later interviews.

Chapter 24: The Fate of Lulz

The analogy of "cavemen smearing buffalo blood" over rocks was drawn from a
discussion with Topiary.

Details about the Script Kiddies hacking into the Twitter feed of Fox News
were sourced from various news reports, such as "Fox News Hacker Tweets
Obama Dead," published by BBC News online on July 4, 2011. The group's
defacement of the Pfizer Facebook page was sourced from their posts on
Twitter and from my own subsequent observations of the defaced Facebook
page. Details about other hacker groups from countries such as the Philippines, Colombia, and Brazil were sourced from various stories on TheHack-
erNews.com.

The statement that there were more than six hundred people in the AnonOps
chat room #Antisec after LulzSec disbanded comes from my own observations while on the IRC network.

Sabu's statement "I'm doing the same work, more revolutionary" was sourced
from my IRC interview with Sabu.

Details about Topiary's "break" from Anonymous after LulzSec disbanded were
sourced from interviews with Topiary.

The assertion that "several mainstream press outlets' ears perked in envy" at
Sabu's claim of granting certain media outlets access to *News of the World* e-
mails was sourced from news reports such as "LulzSec Claims to Have News
International E-mails," published by the *Guardian* on July 21, 2011.

The detail about Rebekah Brooks's husband dumping her laptop in a black
garbage bag is sourced from the *Guardian* story "Police Examine Bag Found
in Bin Near Rebekah Brooks's Home," published on July 18, 2011.

The assertion that police across eight countries had arrested seventy-nine people
in connection with activities carried out under the names Anonymous and
LulzSec was sourced from various news reports about these arrests and a
tally on Pastebin. Details about the looming arrest of Topiary were sourced
from Topiary, with certain facts, including that about the hiring of a private
plane, corroborated by news reports, such as the *Daily Mail*'s "Autistic Shetland Teen Held over Global Internet Hacking Spree 'Masterminded from
His Bedroom,'" published on July 31, 2011.

Part 3
Chapter 25: The Real Topiary

Details about Topiary's arrest, including descriptions of his encounter with the police, were sourced from later interviews with Jake Davis. The details about the police's visit to Jake's mother's home in Spalding were sourced from discussions with Jennifer Davis. Descriptions of Ms. Davis walking into the Charing Cross police station are based on my own observations after visiting the station that day.

The assertion that the AnonOps chat rooms were "ablaze with rumors" are based on my own observations after visiting the IRC network; Sabu's statement that he was "pretty fucking depressed" comes from my interview with him.

The statement that the name Jake had popped up in the AnonOps chat room after an error involving his VPN connection was sourced from my observations of the December 8 AnonOps public chat log database on http://blyon.com/Irc/. The rumor about the friend from Xbox forums posting "Jake from Shetland" was sourced from Sabu's published chat log with Mike "Virus" Nieves (see chapter 26) and the Gawker story "How a Hacker Mastermind Was Brought Down by His Love of Xbox," published on August 16, 2011.

Details about VPN provider HideMyAss responding to a U.K. court order to help identify a member of LulzSec were sourced from a blog post on HideMyAss's website entitled "LulzSec Fiasco," published on September 23, 2011. HideMyAss did not respond to repeated requests for interviews and did not list a phone number on its website.

The item about the Department of Homeland Security expecting more significant attacks from Anonymous was sourced from the department's National Cybersecurity and Communications Integration Center bulletin published on August 1, 2011.

Details about and descriptions of Jake Davis's court appearance were sourced from my observations while attending the hearing, with added context provided by later interviews with Davis.

The book *Free Radicals: The Secret Anarchy of Science* got a significant boost in its Amazon rankings after Jake Davis flashed its cover to the cameras, according to an interview with the book's author, Michael Brooks.

Descriptions of the propaganda images and digital posters made of Jake Davis after his court appearance were sourced from my own observations after speaking to several Anonymous supporters on AnonOps, one of whom directed me to a growing repository of these images.

Details about Jake Davis's fan mail and his life at home were sourced from interviews with Davis, which included visits to his home in Spalding, and from my own observation of some of the letters he received.

Details about the raid executed by William and other members of /b/ against a sixteen-year-old girl on Facebook named Selena (not her real name) were sourced from interviews with William conducted via e-mail and in person.

Davis's meeting with William was arranged by me. I had thought for some time that it would be intriguing to observe what would happen if two people from Anonymous were to meet face-to-face. I had also wanted to arrange for an Anon and a victim of Anon—e.g., Jake Davis and Aaron Barr—to meet in person. Distance and time constraints made a meeting between Barr and Davis impractical, so the next best thing seemed to be a meeting between William and Topiary. I asked each of them if he was willing to meet the other, and after they agreed I set a date in February of 2011. On the appointed day, I met first with William before traveling with him by train to the meeting place with Davis. I accompanied them both to a restaurant, where we talked over lunch. As the two men discussed Anonymous, I asked questions and took notes.

Chapter 26: The Real Sabu

Details about Sabu's cooperation with police, and his criminal misdemeanors outside the world of Anonymous and LulzSec, were sourced from his criminal indictment and from a transcript of his August 5, 2011, arraignment in New York's U.S. District Court. Further context and description was provided by an interview with a source who had knowledge of the FBI investigation of Sabu, as well as interviews with Anonymous hackers who had worked with Sabu in the months after LulzSec disbanded and during his time as an FBI informant. All sources claimed not to have known categorically that Sabu was an informant, though they had varying degrees of suspicion.

The description of Hector "Sabu" Monsegur was sourced from the Fox News report "Infamous International Hacking Group LulzSec Brought Down by Own Leader," published on March 6, 2012, and from the *New York Times* story "Hacker, Informant and Party Boy of the Projects," published on March 8, 2012.

Further descriptions of Sabu were sourced from my own conversations with him online and by telephone, from my observations of his Twitter feed, and from a leaked chat log between Sabu and hacker Mike "Virus" Nieves. The chat log was published on Pastebin on August 16, 2011, and entitled "sabu vs virus aka dumb & dumber part 2."

The comprehensive dox of Sabu, which this time included a photo of Hector Monsegur, was posted by a white hat security researcher nicknamed Le Researcher, who pasted a variety of screenshots of e-mails, deface messages, and forum posts on http://ceaxx.wordpress.com/uncovered/.

The assertion that hacktivism is "extremely popular in Brazil" was sourced from a report by Imperva entitled "The Anatomy of an Anonymous Attack," published in February of 2012, as well as from my own observations of the number of press reports about cyber attacks by Anonymous in Brazil.

Descriptions of and dialogue from Sabu's interactions with sup_g, aka Jeremy Hammond, ahead of the Stratfor attack were sourced from Hector Monsegur's criminal indictment, with further context, including details about his relations with WikiLeaks, taken from interviews with other hackers who took part in the Stratfor attack.

The reference to the *New York Times* article in which the FBI denied they had "let [the Stratfor] attack happen" is sourced from the story "Inside the Stratfor Attack," published on the paper's Bits blog on March 12, 2012.

Details about Donncha "Palladium" O'Cearrbhail hacking into the Gmail account of a member of the Irish national police to listen in on a call between the FBI and the Metropolitan Police were sourced from both O'Cearrbhail's and Monsegur's indictments.

Details about Monsegur passing himself off as a federal agent to the NYPD were sourced from his criminal indictment.

Chapter 27: The Real Kayla, the Real Anonymous

Descriptions of Ryan Mark Ackroyd were sourced from my observations of Ackroyd at his first court appearance, on March 16, 2012. Details about his younger sister, Kayleigh, were sourced from a directory search on Ryan Ackroyd's name, which revealed the names of Ackroyd's parents and siblings; the physical description of Kayleigh was sourced from her public Facebook account, as were the comments she posted on her brother Keiron's Facebook wall.

Notes and Sources

The dates and basic details about the first and second arrests of Ryan Ackroyd were sourced from Metropolitan Police press releases for both incidents. Interview requests with the Metropolitan Police for further details about Ryan Ackroyd and the Met investigation into Anonymous generally were denied.

Details about the reaction in the Anonymous community to news that Sabu had been an informant for eight months were sourced from interviews with academic Gabriella Coleman, Jake Davis, and a handful of Anons, along with my observation of various Twitter feeds, blog posts, and comments on IRC channels frequented by Anonymous supporters.

Glossary

4chan: A popular online image board frequented by 22 million unique users a month. Originally billed as a place to discuss Japanese anime, it morphed into a meeting ground for the discussion of all manner of topics, including online pranks, or "raids," against other websites or individuals (see chapters 2 and 3). A key feature is the forced anonymity of its users, who are thus able to post freely, fearing neither inhibition nor accountability.

Anonymous: A name that refers to groups of people who disrupt the Internet to play pranks or as a means of protest. Derived from the forced anonymity of users of the image board 4chan, it has evolved over the last five years to become associated with high-profile cyber attacks on companies and government agencies. With no clear leadership structure or rules of membership, it exists as a fluid collective of people who follow a loose set of principles derived from the 47 Rules of the Internet. The wider collective takes on various guises, depending on whoever happens to be endorsing the name at the time—

e.g., the Chanology organizers of 2008 (see chapter 5) and the LulzSec hackers of 2011 (see chapter 17).

Antisec (Anti Security): A cyber movement started in the early 2000s in which black hat hackers campaigned to end the system of "full disclosure" among IT security professionals, often by attacking those same white hat professionals. LulzSec revived the movement in the summer of 2011, with the vague goal of attacking government agencies and figures of authority in a sometimes superficial effort to expose corruption.

/b/: The most popular board on 4chan, visited by about a third of the site's users. /b/ was originally billed as the site's "random" board by 4chan creator Christopher "moot" Poole. It ended up serving as a blank slate on which a host of creative Internet memes, such as Lolcats, were born, and is widely considered to be the birthplace of the Anonymous "hive-mind." Many Anonymous supporters say they first found Anonymous through /b/. It is infamous for its lack of moderators.

Black hat: Someone who uses knowledge of software programming for malicious means, such as defacing a website or stealing databases of personal information for the purpose of selling it to others. A black hat is also referred to as a "cracker."

Botnet: A network of so-called zombie computers that have been brought together by spreading a virus or links to bogus software updates. Botnets can be controlled by one person, who can order thousands, sometimes millions, of computers to carry out Web-based commands en masse.

Chanology: Also known as Project Chanology, this is the series of cyber attacks, protests, and pranks conducted by supporters of Anonymous throughout most of 2008 against the Church of Scientology, the name being a portmanteau of "4chan" and "Scientology."

DDoS (Distributed Denial of Service): An attack on a website or other network resource carried out by a network of computers that temporarily knocks the site offline by overwhelming it with junk traffic. The attack can be carried out by a network of volunteers behind each computer (see "LOIC") or a network whose computers have been hijacked to become part of a botnet.

Deface: When used as a noun, this term refers to the image and text that is published on a site that has been hacked, announcing that it is a target and the reason it has been attacked. When used as a verb, it means to vandalize a website.

Dox: When used as a verb, this term refers to the act of unearthing personal details, such as real names, phone numbers, and home addresses, usually through Google or social engineering. The resultant information is a person's "dox." Doxing is often thrown around as a threat in Anonymous and among hacker communities, which are inhabited by online personalities who use nicknames and almost never reveal their true identities.

Encyclopedia Dramatica: A website that chronicles much of the goings-on in Anonymous, including Internet memes, 4chan language, and online discussions among the more popular users of various blogs and IRC networks. The site is almost a parody of Wikipedia; it has the same look and is also edited by users, but its style is irreverent, profane, and occasionally nonsensical, filled with in jokes and links to other ED entries that only insiders can understand.

Hacker: A loosely defined term that, in the context of Anonymous, refers to someone who has the technical skills to break into a computer network (see "black hat" and "white hat"). Generally speaking, the term can refer to a computer programming enthusiast or hobbyist who enjoys tinkering with internal systems and creating shortcuts and new systems.

Hacktivist: A portmanteau derived from "hacker" and "activist," it refers to someone who uses digital tools to help spread a political or sociological message. Among the more illegal methods used are DDoS attacks, website defacements, and the leaking of confidential data.

Image board: An online discussion forum with loose guidelines in which users often attach images to help illustrate their comments. Also known as "chans," they are easy to create and maintain. Certain image boards are known for specific topics, e.g., 420chan is known for its discussion of drugs.

IP (Internet Protocol) address: The unique number assigned to every device that is connected to a computer network or the Internet. Each IP address consists of four sets of numbers separated by periods.

IRC (Internet Relay Chat): Perhaps the most prevalent method of communication among supporters of Anonymous, IRC networks offer the kind of real-time text conversation that image boards cannot. IRC allows users to talk to one another within chat rooms, or "channels," and have existed since the late 1980s. Each IRC network attracts communities who share a common interest, such as the AnonOps IRC, which attracts those interested in Anonymous. Network and channel "operators" moderate the discussions on these networks; such roles are seen as an indicator of high social status.

LOIC (low orbit ion cannon): Originally created as a stress-testing tool for servers, this open-source Web application has become popular among supporters of Anonymous as a digital weapon that, if used by enough people, can be used to carry out a DDoS attack on a website.

Lulz: An alteration of the abbreviation LOL (laugh out loud), this term is thought to have first appeared on an Internet Relay Chat network in 2003 in reaction to something funny. It now refers to the enjoyment felt after pursuing a prank or online disruption that leads to someone else's embarrassment.

LulzSec: A splinter group of hackers who temporarily broke away from Anonymous in the summer of 2011 to pursue a series of more focused, high-profile attacks on companies like Sony and government agencies like the FBI. Founded by hacktivists nicknamed Topiary and Sabu, it had six core members and between a dozen and two dozen second-tier supporters at any one time.

Lurk: To browse a site, IRC network, or image board such as 4chan without posting for any length of time, often with the intent of learning the site's culture so as not to stand out as a new user. Lurkers can be deemed unwelcome in certain IRC networks if they never contribute to discussions.

Meme: A catchphrase or image that has become inadvertently popular, thanks to the viral quality of the Internet, and whose meaning is typically lost on mainstream Web users. Often serving as in jokes for Anonymous supporters, many memes, such as "over 9000" or "delicious cake," are sourced from old computer games or originate from discussions on /b/. Other examples: "Rick Rolling" and "pedobear."

Moralfag: A label attached to either a 4chan user or an adherent of Anonymous who disagrees with the moral direction of a post, image, trolling method, idea, raid, or activity. Often used as a derogatory term.

Newfag: A user on 4chan's /b/ who is either new or ignorant of the customs of the community.

Oldfag: A user on /b/ who understands the customs of the community, usually after spending years on the site.

OP (original poster): Anyone who starts a discussion thread on an image board. In 4chan culture, the OP is always called "a faggot."

Pastebin: A simple but extremely popular website that allows anyone to store and publish text. The site has been increasingly used over the last two years by supporters of Anonymous as a means to publish stolen data, such as confidential e-mails and passwords from Web databases. It has also served as a platform for hackers to publish press releases, a method used by the Anonymous splinter group LulzSec during their hacking spree in the summer of 2011.

Rules of the Internet: A list of 47 "rules" that are thought to have originated from an IRC conversation in 2006, and from which the Anonymous tagline "We do not forgive, we do not forget" originates. The rules cover cultural etiquette on image boards such as 4chan and things to expect from online communities, such as an absence of women.

Script: A relatively simple computer program that is often used to automate tasks.

Script kiddie: A derogatory term used for someone who may hold ambitions to be a black hat hacker and who uses well-known and freely available Web tools, or "scripts," to attack computer networks. Script kiddies often seek to boost their social status among friends by hacking.

Server: A computer that helps process access to central resources or services for a network of other computers.

Shell: A software interface that reads and executes commands. On certain vulnerable websites, a hacker can get a shell to a server on which the site is hosted, using its admin control panel, and the shell, as the new interface, then gives that hacker control of the site.

Social engineering: The act of lying to or speaking to a person in the guise of a false identity, or under false pretenses, in order to weed out information.

SQL injection: Also known as SQLi and sometimes pronounced "sequel injection," this term refers to a method of gaining access to a vulnerable Web database by inserting special commands into that database, sometimes via the same web forms as the site's normal users. The process is a way of acquiring information from a database that should be hidden from normal users.

Troll: A person who anonymously harasses or mocks another individual or group online, often by leaving comments on website forums or, in extreme cases, by hacking into social media accounts. When used as a verb, "trolling" can also mean spinning an elaborate lie. The goal is ultimately to anger or humiliate.

VPN (virtual private network): Network technology that provides remote, secure access over the Internet through a process known as tunneling. Many organizations use VPNs to enable their staff to work from home and connect securely to a central network. Hackers and supporters of Anonymous, however, use VPNs to replace their true IP addresses, allowing them to hide from authorities and others in the community.

White hat: Someone who knows how to hack into a computer network and steal information but uses that ability to help protect websites and organizations.

Index

Index

Index

HBGary Federal career, 5–6, 158, 164; and LulzSec, 254–55, 283, 324; military career of, 5; passwords of, 13–14, 163, 248

BBC, 117, 202, 339–40, 353, 366

Berico Technologies, 162, 164, 451n

BillOReilly, 115, 116, 444n

Bitcoin, 264–65, 270, 284, 304–06

Black, Joseph K., 310, 466–67n

Black, Rebecca, 251

Black & Berg, 310, 466–67n

Blankenship, Lloyd, 135

Booz Allen Hamilton, 191–92, 198, 455n

botnets, 74–75, 77, 101–02, 103, 114, 115–20, 122, 129–30

Brazil, 394

Britain, 206, 223, 352–53, 401, 456n

Britain's Ministry of Finance, 334

broadcast servers, 143, 449n

Brooks, Rebekah, 354

Brown, Barrett: and Barr's e-mails, 191–94, 196, 198, 199, 454n; drug addiction of, 194–95, 196; involvement in Anonymous, 194, 197, 455n; nickname of, 22, 194; and Operation Metal Gear, 194, 197, 198, 199, 201–02, 204, 454–55n; theories of, 206; and Topiary, 166, 190–91, 193, 194, 197, 202, 203, 204, 259, 454n

B-Sides conference, 6, 9

Bunker, Mark, 438n

Byun, Jin Soo, 209–10, 213, 272, 457n

Cammerman, Gideon, 367, 368

Case, Bryce, 207

Chen, Adrian, 151, 213, 283, 304

Christmam, Tory "Magoo," 81

Church of Scientology (COS): Anonymous attacks on, 22, 59, 67–87, 90–91, 223; and Cruise video, 60–62, 69, 70, 133, 151, 438n; and 4chan, 62–68, 70, 82, 87

CIA (Central Intelligence Agency), 323, 324–25, 326

Civil, 113–19, 120, 121, 122, 130

Cleary, Ryan, 119–20, 229, 335–37, 366, 459n, 460–61n

Clinton, Bill, 138

Clinton, Hillary, 108

Cluley, Graham, 64, 438–39n

CNN, 50, 66, 94, 195, 202

COINTELPRO, 235, 461n

Coleman, Gabriella, 405–06, 444n

CommanderX, 15–16, 434n

Computer Fraud and Abuse Act (U.S.), 64, 226

Computer Misuse Act (U.K.), 365

Computerworld.com, 118

Conservatives4Palin, 131

Cooper, Ben, 445n

CopyrightAlliance.org, 104, 204, 443n

Correll, Sean-Paul, 111, 112, 117, 118, 128, 444n

Cross-Goldenberg, Peggy, 308

Crowdleaks, 161–63

Cruise, Tom, 60–62, 69, 70, 102, 133, 151

Daily Kos, 190–91

Daily Mail, 365

The David Pakman Show, 179, 180, 182–83, 453n

485

Index

Davis, Dot, 44, 45

Davis, Jake: amblyopia of, 45–46, 47, 369; and Anonymous, 380–86; arrest of, 359–63, 365–66, 436n; bail conditions of, 369–70, 386–87; and /b/ board on 4chan, 48, 49; court hearing of, 366–69; education of, 231–32; family background of, 43–47, 105–07, 436n; and 4chan, 48, 49–50, 370; on the Internet, 411–13; and Internet Relay Chat, 51, 437n; online friends of, 47–48, 106; pranks of, 46, 47–49, 50, 51–52, 106, 436n; synesthesia of, 44; as trusted source, 445n; and William, 370–71, 378–86, 472n. *See also* Topiary

Davis, Jennifer, 44–47, 361, 362, 367, 368–69, 436n

Davis, Josh, 361

Davis, Sam, 44, 45

DDoSs (distributed denial of service attacks): and Aiplex attacks, 102–04; Aiplex's use of, 101–02, 442n; and botnets, 74–75; and Church of Scientology attacks, 64–67, 70, 73, 74, 78, 80, 83, 86, 89, 438–39n, 440n; as form of Anonymous attacks, 9, 13, 15, 22; and Gawker attack, 151; and Internet Relay Chat, 79; and LOIC, 76–77; and PayPal attacks, 110, 113–17, 154, 161, 165, 200; and Sony attacks, 226, 227, 280; of Wiki-Leaks, 108, 267

Deep Web, 31

Denton, Nick, 61, 62, 152

Digg, 66, 72, 180

DigitalGangsters, 207, 208, 456–57n

DoS attacks (denial of service attacks), 272

doxing, 29, 56, 96, 459n

Dunbar-Hester, Christina, 100

Earnhardt, John, 466n

eBaum's World, 50, 64, 66, 69, 79

Ebner, Mark, 61, 438n

EduPro, 137

EFnet, 51, 55, 135, 228

Egeste, 291–92

Egypt, 148, 165, 204, 213

Electronic Freedom Foundation, 159

Ellison, Christopher, 215, 458n

Emick, Jennifer: and Anonymous's HBGary Federal attack, 207; and Bailey, 95, 172, 175, 205, 211, 212, 215–16, 452n; and Black & Berg, 466–67n; and Byun, 209–10; and exposure of Anonymous, 167, 169–72, 175, 190, 205, 206–17, 218, 223, 452n, 457n; and The Jester, 272; and Kayla, 207, 208–09, 211, 213, 214, 215, 411, 456n; and LulzSec, 265, 266; and Project Chanology, 90–91, 92, 93, 170, 205, 440–41n; and Sabu, 211–12, 213, 214, 286, 307, 399, 405

Encyclopedia Dramatica (ED), 34, 68, 70, 149, 208, 251, 317, 318

Enturbulation.org, 84, 92, 94, 98–99

EveryDNS.com, 108, 111

evilworks, 109, 115, 351–52

Evo, 229, 468n

Facebook: Anonymous's hacking of Barr's account, 4, 14, 18–19; Barr's

Index

Index

and The Jester, 216; leadership of, 202; and LOIC, 111, 112, 113, 114–15, 117–18, 119, 120–22, 125; and Mastercard attacks, 205; and Operation Leakspin, 161; and PayPal attacks, 117, 118, 205, 223; and Sabu, 235; targets of, 110, 455n; and Tunisia, 144–45; and Wiki-Leaks, 107, 110–12, 133, 141, 166

Operation Wisconsin, 455n

OpLeakS, 199–202, 455n

OPs (original posters), 34, 35, 36, 38

Owen, 109, 129–30, 176, 206, 229, 446n

P4ntera, 138

Paget, Francois, 216

Pakman, David, 179–80, 182–86, 188, 453n

Palantir, 162, 164, 451n

Palin, Sarah, 108, 131, 446n

Palladium, 247, 400–401, 402

Panda Security, 111, 117, 128, 408

Partyvan, 57, 69, 71, 73, 79, 80, 93, 208, 440n

Pastebin, 266, 317, 364, 462–63n

Pastore, James, 389–90

PayPal: Anonymous attacks on, 6, 7, 11, 110, 112, 113, 114–17, 118, 119, 121–22, 124, 126, 129–30, 131, 140, 153, 154, 205, 223, 446n; and Wiki-Leaks, 108–09

PBS attack, 258, 259–64, 265, 266, 267, 269, 270, 279, 280, 462n

Pentagon, on cyber attacks, 296–97, 298

Phelps, Fred, 177, 179, 452n

Phelps, Nate, 179, 452n

Phelps-Roper, Megan, 177

Phelps-Roper, Shirley, 179–87, 453n

Pieniadz, Patty, 61, 438n

The Pirate Bay, 15, 24, 101–02, 103, 104, 250

Pirate Pad, 182, 450–51n, 453n

PlayStation Network, 226, 227, 228, 281, 283, 464n

Police and Justice Act (U.K.), 64

Poole, Christopher, 26–27, 109, 436n

PostFinance.ch, 111, 112

Poulsen, Karen, 253

Poulsen, Kevin, 159

Praetox, 76

Primer (film), 11

Project Chanology: and Bailey, 92–96, 170; and botnets, 74–75; and Cruise video, 133, 151; and Emick, 90–91, 92, 93, 170, 205, 440–41n; and 4chan, 62–68, 70, 82, 87, 92; and Housh, 71, 72–73, 78, 80–81, 83–85, 94, 439n; initiation of, 68–69; and Kayla, 99, 274, 437n; leadership of, 85, 202; and LOIC, 74, 75–80, 86, 125, 440n; and Mettenbrink, 77–79, 86–89, 102, 440n; planning of, 141, 436n; timeline of, 439n

Prolexic Technologies, 80, 89

Pwnsauce: arrest of, 406; and Gawker, 153; identity of, 402; involvement in Anonymous, 246; and LulzSec, 245–46, 264, 269, 279, 303, 306, 343

Python, 139

Q (Anonymous), 22, 142, 149, 220, 232, 346. *See also* Marduk

Index

Index

About the Author

Parmy Olson is the London bureau chief for *Forbes* magazine. She lives in London.